MARY WOLLSTONECRAFT AND THE FEMINIST IMAGINATION

In the two centuries since Mary Wollstonecraft published *A Vindication of the Rights of Woman* (1792), she has become an icon of modern feminism: a stature that has paradoxically obscured her real historic significance. In the most in-depth study to date of Wollstonecraft's thought, Barbara Taylor develops an alternative reading of her as a writer steeped in the utopianism of Britain's radical Enlightenment. Wollstonecraft's feminist aspirations, Taylor shows, were part of a revolutionary programme for universal equality and moral perfection that reached its zenith during the political upheavals of the 1790s but had its roots in the radical-Protestant Enlightenment. Drawing on all Wollstonecraft's works, and locating them in a vividly detailed account of her intellectual world and troubled personal history, Taylor provides a compelling portrait of this fascinating and profoundly influential thinker.

BARBARA TAYLOR is Reader in History in the Department of Cultural Studies at the University of East London. She is a leading intellectual and cultural historian, specialising in the history of feminism, and the author of *Eve and the New Jerusalem: Socialism and Feminism in the Nineteenth Century* and numerous articles on Mary Wollstonecraft.

CAMBRIDGE STUDIES IN ROMANTICISM 56

MARY WOLLSTONECRAFT AND THE FEMINIST IMAGINATION

CAMBRIDGE STUDIES IN ROMANTICISM

This series aims to foster the best new work in one of the most challenging fields within English literary studies. From the early 1780s to the early 1830s a formidable array of talented men and women took to literary composition, not just in poetry, which some of them famously transformed, but in many modes of writing. The expansion of publishing created new opportunities for writers, and the political stakes of what they wrote were raised again by what Wordsworth called those 'great national events' that were 'almost daily taking place': the French Revolution, the Napoleonic and American wars, urbanization, industrialization, religious revival, an expanded empire abroad and the reform movement at home. This was an enormous ambition, even when it pretended otherwise. The relations between science, philosophy, religion and literature were reworked in texts such as *Frankenstein* and *Biographia Literaria*; gender relations in *A Vindication of the Rights of Woman* and *Don Juan*; journalism by Cobbett and Hazlitt; poetic form, content and style by the Lake School and the Cockney School. Outside Shakespeare studies, probably no body of writing has produced such a wealth of response or done so much to shape the responses of modern criticism. This indeed is the period that saw the emergence of those notions of 'literature' and of literary history, especially national literary history, on which modern scholarship in English has been founded.

The categories produced by Romanticism have also been challenged by recent historicist arguments. The task of the series is to engage both with a challenging corpus of Romantic writings and with the changing field of criticism they have helped to shape. As with other literary series published by Cambridge, this one will represent the work of both younger and more established scholars, on either side of the Atlantic and elsewhere.

For a complete list of titles published see end of book

MARY WOLLSTONECRAFT AND THE FEMINIST IMAGINATION

BARBARA TAYLOR

CAMBRIDGE
UNIVERSITY PRESS

CAMBRIDGE UNIVERSITY PRESS
Cambridge, New York, Melbourne, Madrid, Cape Town,
Singapore, São Paulo, Delhi, Mexico City

Cambridge University Press
The Edinburgh Building, Cambridge CB2 8RU, UK

Published in the United States of America by Cambridge University Press, New York

www.cambridge.org
Information on this title: www.cambridge.org/9780521004176

First published 2003
Third printing 2004

A catalogue record for this publication is available from the British Library

ISBN 978-0-521-66144-7 Hardback
ISBN 978-0-521-00417-6 Paperback

For Michael Pokorny

Contents

Illustrations

Acknowledgements

This book was originally commissioned by Ursula Owen in 1982 for a series of short books about pioneering women intellectuals. In the two decades since, I have accumulated a very long list of debts to individuals and grant-giving agencies. To begin with the latter: my grateful thanks to the Nuffield Foundation (for a Postdoctoral Fellowship in 1983/4); to the Social Science and Humanities Council of Canada (for a Postdoctoral Fellowship in 1984/5 and 1985/6); to Clare Hall, Cambridge (for a Visiting Fellowship, in 1984/5); to the Leverhulme Trust (for a Research Fellowship, in 1996/7); to the British Academy (for a Research Leave Grant in 1997); and to the John Simon Guggenheim Memorial Foundation (for a Research Fellowship in 1998). I am also grateful to the Leverhulme Trust for its award of an Institutional Fellowship (1998–2001) which, among other things, permitted me to finish the book.

My colleagues in the Department of Cultural Studies at the University of East London have been generous and supportive, particularly Alan O'Shea. The History Department at Royal Holloway gave me an intellectual perch when I needed one, and later housed my 'Feminism and Enlightenment' research project – for which my thanks.

Every writer needs help from friends, but some much more than others. To the many good friends who helped to ensure this book's completion, my heartfelt gratitude: Sally Alexander, Sarah Benton, Michèle Barrett, Veronica Beechey, Lesley Caldwell, Judi Coburn, Rosalind Coward, Jane Caplan, Anna Davin, Rosalind Delmar, Rosemary Donegan, Catherine Hall, Cora Kaplan, Alison Light, Mandy Merck, Keith McClelland, Ruthie Petrie, Lyndal Roper, Chris Robinson, Denise Riley, Jacqueline Rose, Ann Scott, Lynne Segal, Gareth Stedman Jones, Sophie Watson, Judy Walkowitz, and Annie Whitehead.

Draft chapters were read by Christine Battersby, Monica Bolufer, Catherine Hall, John Hope-Mason, Robin Howells, Sarah Hutton, Gareth Stedman Jones, Cora Kaplan, Sarah Knott, Alison Light, Phyllis Mack,

Jenny Mander, Karen O'Brien, Mary Poovey, Jane Rendall, Jacqueline Rose, Lynne Segal, Kate Soper, David Wootton, and Eileen Yeo, and I thank them for their perceptive comments and advice (which I didn't always heed). Mark Philp, whose knowledge of 1790s radicalism is unrivalled, read the 'Feminism and revolution' chapters and made excellent suggestions. My sister, Lise Henderson, brought an ideal reader's eye to the book, and I appreciate her generous handling of it. Matthew Beaumont corrected my citations very efficiently.

The manuscript was read in its entirety by Vivien Jones, Sally Alexander and Norma Clarke. Three wiser commentators on feminist literary and political traditions would be hard to imagine, and whatever failings the final text retains are certainly not down to them.

Leslie Adamson, Maurice Hatton, Tim Mason and Raphael Samuel died while I was writing the book, and I hate not being able to show it off to them. My fellow editors on *History Workshop Journal* kept me in touch with the joys of history-writing when the agonies felt uppermost. My erstwhile flatmate, Blue, bickered over interpretations as over nearly everything else, and is fondly remembered. Joy Dalton, who understood how much history mattered to me, gave me much-needed assistance at a critical moment and I thank her for it. My fellow researchers on the 'Feminism and Enlightenment' project, with whom I'd begun working while completing the book, taught me more than I sometimes wished to know at that eleventh hour – and I am grateful to them for the insights and stimulus, especially Sarah Knott.

My agent, Rachel Calder, has been warmly supportive, and my editor at Cambridge University Press, Linda Bree, has been everything one could ask and more. Marilyn Butler, editor of the Studies in Romanticism series, encouraged me in the writing of the book and gave me helpful comments on the manuscript.

Norma Clarke, Nick Tosh and William Tosh lit up my life during the last phase of the book's production. Finally, without Michael Pokorny's wisdom, determination, and kindness there would have been no book – and so it is dedicated to him.

Earlier versions of chapter 3 appeared in 'For the Love of God: Religion and the Erotic Imagination in Wollstonecraft's Feminism' in E. Yeo (ed.) *Mary Wollstonecraft and 200 Years of Feminisms* (London, Rivers Oram, 1997), and 'The Religious Foundations of Wollstonecraft's Feminism', in Claudia Johnson, ed., *Cambridge Companion to Mary Wollstonecraft* (Cambridge

University Press, 2002). Passages from the introduction and chapter 1 will appear in 'Mary Wollstonecraft', *The New Dictionary of National Biography* (Oxford, Basil Blackwell, 2004). The discussion of Wollstonecraft's 'misogyny' in the introduction was rehearsed in 'Feminism and Misogyny: the Case of Mary Wollstonecraft', *Constellations: an International Journal of Critical and Democratic Theory*, 6:4, 1999 (reprinted in C. Jones and D. Wahrman, eds., *The Age of Cultural Revolutions: Britain and France, 1750–1830*, University of California Press, 2002).

Chronology

1759 (27 April)	MW's birth in Spitalfields, London.
1763	Wollstonecraft family moves to Epping Forest.
1765	MW's family moves to Barking. Paternal grandfather dies, leaving his fortune to MW's father and eldest brother.
1768	MW's family moves to Beverley, Yorkshire. MW meets Jane Arden whose father, John Arden, is the first intellectual influence on MW.
1774	MW's family moves to Hoxton, north of London.
1775	MW meets Fanny Blood, the woman who (according to Godwin) became the 'ruling passion of her mind'.
1776	MW's family moves to Laugharne, in south-east Wales.
1777	MW's family moves to the London suburb of Walworth, near the Bloods' home in Newington Butts.
1778	MW becomes paid companion to Mrs Dawson of Bath, the widow of a wealthy merchant. Her summers are spent in Southampton and Windsor.
1780	MW's parents and younger siblings move to Enfield, north London.
1781	MW returns home to nurse her dying mother.
1782	Mrs Wollstonecraft dies. MW's sister Eliza marries Meredith Bishop. Mr Wollstonecraft remarries and returns to Wales. MW goes to live with the Blood family.
1783	MW engineers Eliza's separation from her husband after her sister suffers a post-partum breakdown.
1784	MW, her sisters Eliza and Everina, and Fanny Blood open a school for girls in Newington Green. MW meets Richard Price and other radical Dissenters.

1785   Fanny Blood marries Hugh Skeys in Lisbon, becomes pregnant and sends for MW. Fanny goes into premature labour and dies in MW's arms.

1786   MW closes her school, which has got into financial trouble. She writes *Thoughts on the Education of Daughters* and meets Joseph Johnson, who agrees to publish it. She becomes governess to the daughters of Viscount Kingsborough of Mitchelstown, County Cork, Ireland.

1787   MW is dismissed by the Kingsboroughs and returns to London, where she stays for a time with Joseph Johnson and writes *Mary, a Fiction* and *Original Stories*.

1788   *Mary, a Fiction* and *Original Stories* are published by Johnson, along with MW's translation of Jacques Necker's *The Importance of Religious Opinions*. MW begins writing for Johnson's *Analytical Review*, and meets other radical writers in Johnson's stable, including Fuseli and Holcroft.

1789   Johnson publishes MW's *Female Reader*. She becomes romantically involved with Fuseli.

1790   MW's *A Vindication of the Rights of Men* is published anonymously by Johnson, along with her translations of Christian Salzmann's *Elements of Morality* and Maria Geertruida van de Werken de Cambon's *Young Grandison*.

1791   MW meets William Godwin. The second edition of *A Vindication of the Rights of Men* is published with her name on the title-page.

1792   *A Vindication of the Rights of Woman* is published. MW's involvement with Fuseli ends; she leaves for Paris in December.

1793   MW meets Gilbert Imlay in Paris, and they become lovers. Imlay registers her as his wife so as to afford her the protection of American citizenship.

1794   MW, pregnant, joins Imlay in Le Havre, where their daughter Fanny is born. Her *Historical and Moral View of the Origin and Progress of the French Revolution* is published.

Introduction: Mary Wollstonecraft and the paradoxes of feminism

A wild wish has just flown from my heart to my head, and I will not stifle it, though it may excite a horse-laugh. I do earnestly wish to see the distinction of sex confounded in society, unless where love animates the behaviour.

(Mary Wollstonecraft, *A Vindication of the Rights of Woman*, 1792)[1]

A mind vigorous in imagining is also vigorous in judging.

(Thomas Beddoes, *Alexander's Expedition*, 1792)[2]

... fantasy's supreme characteristic is that of running ahead of itself.

(Jacqueline Rose, *States of Fantasy*, 1998)[3]

As a young woman, Mary Wollstonecraft regarded herself as an inveterate fantasist, a compulsive manufacturer of 'Utopian dreams'.[4] In some moods this was cause for self-criticism. 'I too frequently... forget the convictions of reason, and give way to chimerical hopes which are as illusive [*sic*] as they are pleasant,' she wrote to her sister Everina in 1787 from Ireland, where she was employed as a governess by the aristocratic Kingsborough family.[5] 'I commune with my own spirit – and am detached from the world...' Twenty-eight at the time, confused and unhappy among the Irish *bon ton* ('a poor solitary individual in a strange land'[6]) she spent her free hours alone in her room reading and 'moulding shapes in the fire'. 'I think, and think,' she sighed to Everina, 'and these reveries do not tend to fit me for enjoying the *common* pleasures of this world...'[7]

The melancholy fantasist was a fashionable image in the late eighteenth century, one particularly attractive to a young intellectual just starting out in the world, keen to distinguish herself from the common run of humankind. Writing to another correspondent in 1787, Wollstonecraft lamented the 'too great refinement of mind' which made her unsuitable for the society of the 'silly females' of the Kingsborough set. '[R]efinement genius – and those charming talents which my soul instinctively loves' drew her away from the vulgar concerns of ordinary mortals onto mental terrain where only

I

those of peculiar ability dared to tread.[8] '[S]ensibility renders the path of duty more intricate – and the warfare much more severe...' she told her friend Reverend Henry Gabell with a touch of complacency, so that at times indeed 'my reason has been too far stretched, and tottered almost on the brink of madness...'[9] But despite these hazards the attractions of the inner life remained irresistible. 'Why have we implanted in us an irresistible desire to think – if thinking is not... necessary to make us wise onto salvation....' she quizzed Gabell: 'these flights into an obscure region open the faculties of the soul.'[10]

Over the years this note of naive grandiosity gave way to more sophisticated modes of self-representation. But the sense of herself as one 'too much under the influence of an ardent imagination to adhere to common rules' persisted throughout Wollstonecraft's life.[11] The imagination was a controversial faculty in the eighteenth century. Increasingly celebrated for its Promethean creativity – the 'true fire' of original genius, as Wollstonecraft eulogised it – the imagination was also seen as a dangerously maverick influence, particularly in political life.[12] Critics of Wollstonecraft regularly described her ideas as over-imaginative: 'fanciful', 'delusory', 'fantastical', or, to use her own word, 'wild'. In the fierce debate over French revolutionary principles that raged in Britain in the early 1790s, the revolutionary imagination was repeatedly condemned for its delusory excesses. 'What, O countrymen, are you about to do?' one anxious loyalist demanded of English radicals in 1793, 'What are these chimeras of which you are in pursuit? What these boasted Rights of Man? This Liberty? This Equality? O, shame, shame, return back, I beseech you, to reason; and learn, that you are pursuing a phantom which exists but in the imagination.'[13]

To conservative Britons, even the most modest democratising ambitions appeared chimerical. But the reforms advocated by 1790s radicals were regarded as particularly fantastical because they were seen as stepping-stones to a radical-democrat utopia. Like their seventeenth-century 'levelling' predecessors, British jacobins were accused of hankering after a libertarian Eden: a 'promised land', as Burke wrote derisively in his *Reflections on the Revolution in France* (1790), based on 'the wildest democratic ideas of freedom'.[14] The charge was untrue of most 1790s radicals, whose political ambitions were limited and pragmatic; but it *did* apply to a small band of ultra-radical intellectuals of whom Wollstonecraft was one. Wollstonecraft is not usually described as a utopian thinker, but the visionary, world-transformative tenor of her thought is plain. Like her fellow radical and mentor, Richard Price (one of Burke's main targets), and others of her close associates, Wollstonecraft regarded the political revolutions of the 1770s and

90s as harbingers of that 'glorious future' of universal freedom and happiness foretold in scripture and realised through the liberating force of enlightened reason: 'A new spirit has gone forth, to organise the body-politic,' she wrote from Paris in 1793. 'Reason has, at last, shown her captivating face, beaming with benevolence; and it will be impossible for the dark hand of despotism again to obscure it's [sic] radiance...'[15]

The wildest element in this political vision, as far as opponents were concerned, was its uncompromising egalitarianism ('miserable phantoms of metaphysical equality', critics sneered[16]), which in Wollstonecraft's writings became a passionate call for an end to gender hierarchy, a 'wild wish... to see the distinction of sex confounded' as she put it. The use of the word 'distinction', with its dual meaning of ranking and difference, alarmed some readers who interpreted it as implying not just an equalisation of women's status relative to men – a startling enough ambition in itself – but the complete eradication of sexual difference: truly the *ne plus ultra* of democratic levelling. Some two centuries after the first publication of *A Vindication of the Rights of Woman* (1792), it takes some effort of the historic imagination to feel the seditious force of Wollstonecraft's text, with its scandalous rejection of masculine authority and its deliberate linking of women's liberation to the elimination of *all* hierarchical divisions ('artificial distinctions' in Wollstonecraft's lexicon) of rank, sex, age, race, and wealth. To a modern reader Wollstonecraft's brand of feminism can seem unadventurous; her political prescriptions too familiar to excite. But here, as so often, hindsight is deceptive. Most nineteenth- and early twentieth-century feminists, it is important to recall, were not root and branch egalitarians in Wollstonecraft's mould, tending instead to combine opposition to sex-based subordination with firm class and racial loyalties. As a radical who, if not quite the 'equalising' extremist her enemies declared her to be, was hostile to hierarchy and injustice of every kind, Wollstonecraft stands well to the left of the feminist spectrum, and it is only by scrutinising her ambitions for women in this light that their nature and scope become apparent.

This is not, for me, a new argument. Writing about Wollstonecraft some twenty years ago, I described her as a forerunner to the Owenite-socialist feminists of the 1830s and forties who, like her, regarded the liberation of their sex not as an isolated goal but as part of a historic movement toward a 'new age... of perfect harmony between the aspirations of the individual and the collective needs of humanity as a whole'.[17] Subsequent research has confirmed this judgement but also complicated it, principally by revealing the central part played by religion in Wollstonecraft's thought. The religious basis of Wollstonecraft's radicalism is its least-explored aspect, yet it is impossible to understand her political hopes, including her hopes for women, outside a theistic framework. Her contemporaries knew this – they probably took it for granted – but today it is overlooked by most commentators who, if they acknowledge her piety at all, tend to hurry past it to less archaic, more obviously political themes. Most interpretations of the *Rights of Woman* simply obliterate its religious underpinnings. But to secularise Wollstonecraft's radical vision is not only to tear it from its eighteenth-century context but also to lose its utopian thrust: that unwavering faith in divine purpose that, suffusing her radicalism, turned anticipations of 'world perfected' into a confident political stance.[18]

This book is a study of Mary Wollstonecraft's radical imagination, particularly her feminist imaginings. I say 'imagination' rather than 'thought' partly because the imagination was such a key concept in late eighteenth-century moral and political discourses, especially in discourses centring on women, but also because I want to exploit the word's ambiguity: its dual reference to conscious, reasoned creativity – the sort of mental inventiveness that, in the political arena, gives rise to revisionary theories, reformist strategies, utopian projections – and to the implicit, often unconscious fantasies and wishes that underlie intellectual innovation. So while this is in many respects a conventional intellectual history, it is also an investigation into the inner sources of Wollstonecraft's radicalism. Wollstonecraft's career as a public intellectual spanned a variety of late eighteenth-century contexts: 'rational' Protestant nonconformity (that quintessentially English version of Enlightenment); the revolutionary intelligentsia of the 1790s; the feisty commercial world of the professional literary woman. To all these she brought a gritty unfeminine iconoclasm, a manner that friends and enemies alike described as 'Amazonian'. Convinced that 'mind has no sex', she handled herself accordingly. But sex was not to be so easily discarded, even in her avant-garde circles. Reminded at every turn of her femaleness – sometimes very cruelly – Wollstonecraft found that she was not just another radical *philosophe* but a woman (in E. P. Thompson's sensitive formulation) 'exceptionally exposed within a feminine predicament'.[19] Her political aspirations and her individual situation were inseparable, nor do I try to separate them here. So while this not a biography – anyone looking for new revelations about her private life will be disappointed – it does seek to uncover the pressures her life and times exerted on her thought, and her imaginative responses to these. The decade between Wollstonecraft's first appearance in print and her death in 1797 witnessed an explosion of imaginative political energies greater than any before it, and it was immersion in this fervidly creative atmosphere that transformed a young woman's bitter sense of feminine grievance, and fierce, unfeminine aspirations, into a critical philosophy and a visionary political programme.

The powers of imagination, utopian or otherwise, are generally neglected by intellectual historians, partly because their traces can be hard to identify, but also because the imaginative life of a thinker is generally assumed to play no part in his or her theoretical cogitations. Systematic, consistent reasonings – not the dreamlike, equivocal conjurings of fantasy – are seen as the hallmark of the philosophical mind. Yet when Wollstonecraft herself examined the relationship between reason and imagination, as she did in her writings on Burke and Rousseau, what she found were paradoxes. Wollstonecraft liked paradoxes (especially Rousseau's): she enjoyed picking away at them, and was intrigued by what they revealed of a writer's inner life. Her critique of Rousseau's sexual philosophy turned, in places, on the paradoxical relationship between his personal fantasies and his published views on women. Wollstonecraft herself displayed plenty of similar paradoxes in her attitudes toward women, whom she criticised so savagely in her *A Vindication of the Rights of Woman* that the work has sometimes been described as misogynistic.[20] Exploring this disconcerting element in her feminism takes us into a study of anti-woman sentiments in eighteenth-century Britain, but also onto the more elusive terrain of her familial and emotional history. Why would a woman who, at one stage in her life at least, found the generality of her sex stupid, frivolous, and morally vicious, make female emancipation her political priority? Paradoxical indeed.

* * *

Mary Wollstonecraft was born in Spitalfields, London on 27 April 1759. The family she entered was modestly prosperous: her paternal grandfather owned a successful Spitalfields silkweaving business; her mother's father was a wine merchant in Ireland. In 1765 her paternal grandfather died, and her father inherited the family business. Unlike his father, however, Edward Wollstonecraft had little taste for the commercial life, opting instead to become a gentleman farmer. In the early 1760s he took his young family to live on a farm in Epping: the first of six moves in Wollstonecraft's childhood, each of which saw a marked decline in the family's financial fortunes. Edward, it seems, had no talent for farming, nor for anything else. According to his daughter, he was a childish bully, given to abusing his wife and children after heavy drinking sessions. Mary, who often intervened to protect her mother from his drunken violence, later told Godwin how much she had despised her father. '[Mary] was not formed to be the contented and unresisting subject of a despot,' Godwin commented in his posthumous *Memoirs* of his wife.[21]

Wollstonecraft's mother, on the other hand, apparently submitted to her husband's behaviour without protest. To her oldest daughter at least, Elizabeth Wollstonecraft seems to have been an uncaring mother. She idolised her eldest son, Edward or Ned, to the point where 'in comparison with her affection for him, she might be said not to love the rest of her children'.[22] Ned, who was heir to one-third of his grandfather's fortune, enjoyed prospects and prestige much greater than the rest of his six siblings, including his clever oldest sister whose acuity and forcefulness, so unconventional in a girl, did not improve her standing in the family. 'Such indeed is the force of prejudice,' Wollstonecraft later wrote bitterly, 'that what was called spirit and wit in him, was cruelly repressed as forwardness in me.'[23]

By the end of the 1770s the Wollstonecraft family resources had sunk to a low ebb. As the Wollstonecraft children looked about them, prospects for the future must have seemed very gloomy, particularly for the girls. Poverty seriously undermined a woman's opportunities in the marriage market, while remaining unwed reduced status and life-chances even further. Throughout the eighteenth century, employment opportunities for such women were thin on the ground. Teaching, governessing, needlework, 'lady's companion': these were some of the few jobs open to genteel women of small means, and by the late 1780s Wollstonecraft had done – and hated – them all. Literary work, however, was also open to women with the confidence, or the desperation, to attempt it; and in 1786, while running a failing girls' school in London, Wollstonecraft decided to try her hand. Her first book, a sternly didactic tract on female manners titled *Thoughts on the Education of Daughters*, earned her ten pounds. Wollstonecraft was delighted. 'I *hope* you have not forgot that I am an Author,' she boasted grandly to her sister Eliza a year later.[24]

For a woman to take up her pen in this way was, as we shall see, much more common in the eighteenth century than is often realised. Indeed at least one sector of the literary marketplace – the rapidly expanding world of popular fiction – was said to be nearly monopolised by women authors. Nevertheless, as a career move it was sufficiently unusual to require a fair degree of hubris on a woman's part: something in which Wollstonecraft was never deficient. In her case, however, the turn toward professional writing was also facilitated by a new circle of acquaintances. These were the Rational Dissenters (later known as Unitarians) living around Newington Green in north London, where Wollstonecraft and her sisters opened a school for girls in 1784. Rational Dissent was a very reform-minded creed, and under its influence – particularly that of Richard Price, philosopher and minister at Newington Green – Wollstonecraft's theological and political opinions began to move rapidly leftward.

In 1786 Wollstonecraft met the official publisher of Rational Dissent, Joseph Johnson. Johnson, a large-minded man with an appreciation of ability regardless of sex, soon agreed to publish her *Thoughts on the Education of Daughters* and then, after she was sacked from her last teaching post (as governess to the Kingsboroughs in Ireland), employed her to write on a regular basis for his new literary review, the *Analytical Review*. In 1788 he published her first novel, *Mary, A Fiction*, and her *Original Stories* for children; the following year he brought out a *Female Reader* compiled by her under a male pseudonym. Wollstonecraft also produced some translations for him – of Jacques Necker's *Of the Importance of Religious Opinions* (1788); of Christian Salzmann's *Elements of Morality* (1790); of Lavater's *Physiognomy* (which was never published) – and 'remodelled' a didactic work by a Dutchwoman, Mme de Cambon, *Young Grandison* (1790).

Hack labours of this sort were the staple of professional authorship, and there was little in Wollstonecraft's career in the 1780s to set it apart from other literary women of her day. But in 1789 all that changed. 'The French revolution,' Godwin later wrote, 'while it gave a fundamental shock to the human intellect through every region of the globe, did not fail to produce a conspicuous effect in the progress of Mary's reflections.'[25] The impact was apparent almost immediately. In 1790 Edmund Burke, to the disgust of his liberal-Whig associates, published his famous attack on French revolutionary principles, *Reflections on the Revolution in France*. Wollstonecraft, with Johnson's encouragement, decided to reply, and rapidly produced *A Vindication of the Rights of Men*, the first in a general radical onslaught on Burke. It was well received and she began to get a reputation; two years later she followed it up with *A Vindication of the Rights of Woman*, which brought her much greater fame. Her name was bracketed with Tom Paine's, whose own *Rights of Man* appeared in 1791; she was commended in France and America, and fêted by fellow radicals in England. Conservatives blustered; professional wits sneered; one of her sisters even reported threats to burn her in effigy. It was a marvellous time for a feminist polemicist, and Wollstonecraft revelled in it.

Personal affairs, however, were another matter. In close relationships Wollstonecraft seems always to have been deeply insecure and, as a result, very demanding. Her first passion, in her early twenties, was for a young female friend, Fanny Blood, who died, attended by Wollstonecraft, in childbirth. Romantic friendships between women, with no implication of a sexual bond, were common in Wollstonecraft's day; nonetheless, the fervency of Wollstonecraft's feelings for Fanny (so powerful, according to Godwin, as 'for years to have constituted the ruling passion of her mind'[26]) at least raises the possibility of a homosexual attachment; nor was her next passion any more conventional. This was for the painter, Henry Fuseli, a married bisexual with whom she had a torrid but apparently unconsummated romance between 1789 and 1792. The *affaire* ended miserably, with Wollstonecraft rejected and humiliated. But a trip to France that she and Fuseli had planned still appealed; so at the end of 1792 she travelled to Paris alone, to nurse her wounds and witness the revolution at first-hand.

Paris on the brink of the Terror was frightening, and Wollstonecraft – despite immediate plunging into political activity – was nervous and lonely. Then in the spring of 1793 she met Gilbert Imlay, an American army captain and commercial adventurer. Imlay introduced her to sex, fathered her first daughter, Fanny, and – after two years of increasingly panic-stricken clinging on Wollstonecraft's part and growing waywardness on his – left her, precipitating two suicide attempts. After the first of these attempts, Imlay persuaded her to take a business trip on his behalf to Scandinavia: an extraordinary undertaking that resulted in another book, probably Wollstonecraft's literary best, *A Short Residence in Sweden* (1796). But on returning to London, where Imlay was now living, Wollstonecraft found him ensconced with a new mistress, and again attempted to take her life. 'I shall make no comments on your conduct, or any appeal to the world,' she wrote to him just before throwing herself into the Thames, 'Let my wrongs sleep with me! Soon... shall I be at peace.'[27]

Rescued and grudgingly restored to life, Wollstonecraft's energies gradually revived, and in the spring of 1796 she took tea with William Godwin, by then Britain's foremost radical philosophe. They had met several times before and grated on each other, but this time things went very much better. Soon they were lovers, and by the winter Wollstonecraft was pregnant. They married, and on 30th August 1797 Wollstonecraft's second daughter, the future Mary Shelley, was born. The birth itself was straightforward, but the placenta failed to deliver spontaneously and was extracted manually, which led to haemorrhaging and infection. Wollstonecraft died of puerperal fever ten days later. 'I have not the least expectation that I can now ever know happiness again,' Godwin wrote to a friend.[28] Out of respect for her piety, and despite his own aversion to religious ceremonies, he gave her a Christian funeral. She was buried in St Pancras churchyard on 15 September; in 1851 her remains, along with Godwin's, were moved to St Peter's churchyard in Bournemouth.

* * *

Wollstonecraft died a celebrity, the best-known female political writer of her day. Less than five months after her death, however, fame turned to notoriety when Godwin published his *Memoirs of the Author of a Vindication of the Rights of Woman* where, amidst panegyrics to his wife's courage and creativity, he revealed her sexual history. A fog of censure descended on her reputation that was not to disperse for almost a century. Many former friends repudiated her, and only the most radically minded – Owenite socialists, Chartists, a few radical Unitarians – continued to publicise her ideas. But the rise of organised feminism in the mid nineteenth century brought her new admirers, and by the first anniversary of the *Rights of Woman*, at the height of the women's suffrage movement, she was edging to the front of the feminist pantheon. A century-plus further on and she has become western feminism's leading heroine. The *Rights of Woman* – whose 1790s readership, respectably large for its day, was small by twenty-first century standards[29] – has since appeared in scores, possibly hundreds, of editions, including translations into most major languages. Her novels, unavailable since the 1790s, have been regularly re-printed since the 1970s; in 1989 a definitive edition of her entire *corpus* was published.[30] Meanwhile, biographical and critical studies have proliferated: in 1976 Janet Todd published a 116-page bibliography of such works; today a similar inventory would probably run to at least twice that length.[31] Students in schools and colleges around the world study her writings, while innumerable scholarly conferences debate her ideas, her life, her political legacies. And in recent years she has even found her way into a few general surveys of eighteenth-century thought: an unprecedented ascent into academic respectability for a not-so-respectable feminist polemicist.[32]

Posthumous celebrity on this scale poses a considerable challenge to interpreters, particularly when it is politically invested. Perched on her pedestal, Wollstonecraft has acquired a mythic patina that blurs and distorts her historical contours. Every feminist generation reinvents her: to late nineteenth-century women's rights activists, struggling in the suffocating embrace of the 'angel in the house', she appeared a classic Victorian individualist, laying claim to those qualities – independence, self-regulation, self-reliance – valued in Victorian men but denied to their womenfolk. To *fin-de-siècle* New Women she personified romantic bohemianism, while to leftwing women like Eleanor Marx and Emma Goldman she was the embodiment of the democratic spirit, an 'indomitable' champion of 'the disinherited of the earth'.[33] Women's Liberationists of the 1960s and 70s, caught up in a complex feud with western liberal-democratic traditions, praised her personal unorthodoxy while criticising her, mistakenly, as a bourgeois liberal.[34] The personae were as diverse as the political agendas prompting them, yet with one feature in common: an imaginary modernity. Whichever face she turned to her interpreters, Wollstonecraft appeared strikingly up-to-date; a figure who seemed 'to leap straight from the eighteenth century' into the present[35]; a woman – the catch-phrase remains ubiquitous – 'ahead of her time'.[36] A raft of historically based studies of Wollstonecraft have appeared in recent years, yet still this presentism persists. 'Wollstonecraft was ahead of her time,' the feminist critic Elaine Showalter writes, 'as "incomprehensible to the eighteenth century as the fourth dimension to a class in fractions"'.[37] *Then* vanishes into *now* in an appropriative gesture that strips both life and ideas of historic meaning, the life becoming emblematic of the dilemmas of contemporary womanhood, the ideas evaluated as if they were present-day precepts. Is this how a feminist ought to live, and do her arguments persuade us? The questions, impervious to time's changes, are designed to elicit partisan responses and regularly do so, with each new version of Wollstonecraft acting as a lightning-rod for competing feminist visions.[38]

If all history is contemporary history, as many now claim, then my own book, with its typically post-1980s fascination with the unacknowledged, equivocal elements of a political credo, is no exception. Nor am I wanting to suggest that Wollstonecraft – a very future-oriented thinker, after all – has nothing of relevance to say to present-day audiences. But ripping her from her own intellectual world to claim her for ours has had the paradoxical effect of reducing her real intellectual significance. I am far from the first to complain about this. As far back as 1885, a writer for the London *Athenaeum*, reviewing a new biography of Wollstonecraft by the American writer Elizabeth Pennell, objected strongly to Pennell's representation of Wollstonecraft as a lone, tragic rebel. Wollstonecraft, the reviewer insisted, had been no 'isolated thinker' but a woman who 'felt keenly the influence of her time': 'she is a distinctly historical figure, and should have been treated as such'.[39] Nearly a century later a similar point was made by E. P. Thompson who, in a review of Claire Tomalin's *The Life and Death of Mary Wollstonecraft*, accused Tomalin and other biographers and critics of focusing on Wollstonecraft's intimate history at the expense of her intellectual achievements: 'She is seen less as a significant intellectual . . . than as an Extraordinary Woman. And the moral confusions, or personal crises, of a woman are always somehow more interesting than those of a man:

they engross all other aspects of the subject.'[40] It was time, Thompson insisted, to abandon the mythologised, scandalous Wollstonecraft in favour of Wollstonecraft the jacobin philosophe, 'one of the five or six truly significant ultra-radicals in England of the 1790s': advice that I, a graduate student at the time, took very seriously. Why should Wollstonecraft's ideas merit any less serious attention than, say, Tom Paine's or William Wordsworth's? (To mention two other revolutionists of the 1790s with unconventional private lives.) Again, the question, coming as it did at the beginning of a new wave of feminist scholarship, reflected a sea-change in writings on women, and soon a host of new historical-critical studies were appearing which, by the time I was beginning my own research, were resulting in a much clearer picture of Wollstonecraft the eighteenth-century theorist and politician.[41] (My debt to this scholarship, as my endnotes make evident, is enormous.) Yet still the iconic woman pursues the original, leaving a trail of adulation and opprobrium — the twin children of idolatry — in her wake.

Wollstonecraft, it should be said, liked imagining herself an intellectual Prometheus, a woman 'bold enough to advance before the age'.[42] What the boast signalled, however, was not a Women's Liberationist *avant la lettre* but a writer immersed in the boldest of ages. Well versed in avant-garde theory (the works cited in her writings add up to a pretty full bibliography of what she described, significantly, as 'the enlightened sentiments of a masculine and improved philosophy'[43]) and embroiled in the greatest political experiment the world had yet witnessed, Wollstonecraft's self-image as a pathbreaker was emphatically of her times. Likewise her feminism which, while certainly at odds with traditionalist sexual opinion, was steeped in the eighteenth century spirit of 'innovation'. The century prior to the *Rights of Woman* had seen a steady flow of writings by enlightened *literati* of both sexes arguing for a higher valuation of women's character and an enhancement of female intellectual and social status. The claims were urged through a variety of genres: theological works, literary biographies, plays, novels, educational reform literature, and political tracts, including at least one previous vindication of female rights.[44] The issues were sufficiently well rehearsed that readers of the *Rights of Woman* initially thought themselves on well-trodden ground, although the book's 'de-sexing' tendencies and strong endorsement of revolutionary principles provoked some disquiet. Soon, as the wave of popular radicalism that swept Britain in the wake of the French Revolution reached its zenith, it became apparent that enlightened championship of women had mutated into a much more subversive phenomenon; its spokeswoman not just another stock defender of her sex but 'the first female combatant in the new field of the

Rights of Woman'.[45] A new pro-woman creed, the 'Wollstonecraft school' as supporters and opponents alike dubbed it, had entered the political scene.

Describing this creed as feminist is problematic, and I do it only after much consideration. The label is of course anachronistic, having first come into use in the early twentieth century; but its real disadvantage lies in its implicit assimilation of Wollstonecraft's ideas to those of her successors. Treating Wollstonecraft's thought as an anticipation of nineteenth and twentieth-century feminist arguments has meant sacrificing or distorting some of its key elements. Leading examples of this, already mentioned, have been the widespread neglect of her religious beliefs, and the misrepresentation of her as a bourgeois liberal, which together have resulted in the displacement of a religiously inspired utopian radicalism by a secular, class-partisan reformism as alien to Wollstonecraft's political project as her dream of a divinely promised age of universal happiness is to our own. Even more important however has been the imposition on Wollstonecraft of a heroic-individualist brand of politics utterly at odds with her own ethically driven case for women's emancipation.

Wollstonecraft's leading ambition for women was that they should attain virtue, and it was to this end that she sought their liberation: 'for how can woman be... virtuous... unless freedom strengthen her reason till she comprehend her duty, and see in what manner it is connected with her real good?'[46]. This freedom, as she imagined it, was not the ability to do what one pleased – which she would have called licence – but to act rightly, according to God's design:[47] a right-doing that, to her mind, bore no resemblance to the self-immolating docility demanded of women by male supremacists, but was rather an active, self-enlarging virtue that, rooted in liberated reason, would fulfil women's natural potential, without regard to their gender. All God's children are inherently perfectible, Wollstonecraft insisted, and it is only human malfeasance that mars His human creation. In a free world, women would be as good as God intended them to be: '[l]et women share the rights, and she will emulate the virtues of man; for she must grow more perfect when emancipated...'[48] In their present slavish state, however, women are very bad indeed. The assessment – so startling to a modern readership – is at the heart of her argument. The *Rights of Woman* castigates its female readers in the harshest terms for classic feminine follies: vanity, irrationalism, intolerance, frivolity, ignorance, cunning, fickleness, indolence, narcissism, infantilism, impiety and, above all, sexual ambition. '[B]rimful of sensibility, and teeming with capricious fantasies' women's giddy minds have one fixed preoccupation:

the desire of establishing themselves ... by marriage. And this desire making mere animals of them, when they marry they act as such children may be expected to act – they dress, they paint, and nickname God's creatures. Surely these weak beings are only fit for a seraglio![49]

The savagery of the denunciation is shocking. And while the feminist point behind it – the point to which the whole book tends – is that women are coerced into this debilitated condition by a male-dominated society, the rhetorical weight of Wollstonecraft's attack falls so heavily on her own sex as to make a reader begin to wonder whether the aim is less to free women than to abolish them – an aspiration strongly implied at various points in the text. It is the 'desire of being always women' which is the 'very consciousness which degrades the sex' Wollstonecraft writes, while again, 'Men are not always men in the company of women; nor would women always remember that they are women, if they were allowed to acquire more understanding'.[50] The woman of wisdom and virtue, she tells her readers, is one who can 'forget her sex' even at that time of life when sexual consciousness is most insistent, promoting in herself instead those capacities common to all humanity, 'regardless of the distinction of sex'.[51]

Within these strictures, the vice that attracts Wollstonecraft's harshest censure is erotic guile, which she condemns with a fierceness that has led many critics to describe her as a sexual puritan. Deprecation of coquetry was near-universal among enlightened intellectuals, and in exploiting the theme Wollstonecraft stresses that it is men themselves, whose 'passions ... have placed women on thrones',[52] who are ultimately responsible for female sexual machiavellianism. But the exculpatory point almost disappears amidst the horde of vamps and jezebels 'render[ing] both men and themselves vicious to obtain illicit privileges'.[53] In her final writings, particularly her posthumous novel *The Wrongs of Woman, or Maria*, Wollstonecraft was uncompromising in her indictment of men's victimisation of women. But in the *Rights of Woman* it is the eternal Eve who predominates, joined in iniquity by a feminised Satan who 'with serpentine wrigglings of cunning ... mount[s] the tree of knowledge ... only [to] acquire sufficient to lead men astray'.[54] The phobic, phallicised image could as easily have been penned by Rousseau, Wollstonecraft's chief polemical target, whose insistence that such power-mongering is innate to women, rather than a symptom of their degradation, is a pivotal *casus belli* in her quarrel with him. ' "Educate women like men", says Rousseau' – Wollstonecraft quotes him – ' "and the more they resemble our sex the less power they will have over us." This is the very point I am at. I do not wish them to have power over

men but over themselves.'[55] It is 'not empire, – but equality, that [women]
should contend for'.[56] The libertarian conclusion comes as a relief amidst
the misogynist caricatures, but leaves intact both the defamatory images
and their implicit agenda: not just to re-form femininity but to eradicate
it. How can we explain this element in Wollstonecraft's thought, surely its
most disquieting and paradoxical?

* * *

... from every quarter have I heard exclamations against masculine women; but
where are they to be found? If by this appellation men mean to inveigh against
their ardour in hunting, shooting, and gaming, I shall most cordially join in the
cry; but if it be against the attainment of those talents and virtues, the exercise
of which ennobles the human character, and which raise females in the scale of
animal being, when they are comprehensively termed mankind; – all those who
view [women] with a philosophic eye must, I should think, wish with me, that
they may every day grow more and more masculine.[57]

Open displays of misogyny, acceptable in the decades of Swift and Pope,
were no longer fashionable in the polite society of Wollstonecraft's day,
where they were giving way to romanticised images of women of the kind
that were eventually to dominate mid-Victorian Britain. Rousseau's ambiguous celebrations of female sensibility and influence in his two great
novels, *Emile* and *La Nouvelle Héloïse*, were an important influence here,
as too were a host of didactic works by British moralists praising feminine
merit and manners. 'Gallantry', as Wollstonecraft (and many other critics)
labelled this updated version of medieval chivalry, was a highly aspirational
discourse, encouraging middle-class women to emulate aristocratic canons
of politeness. But it was also an extremely inhibitory code, locking women
into feminine protocols that left little room for individual idiosyncrasies or
unorthodox initiatives. This coercive element was particularly evident in
middle-class advice literature, including two hugely influential texts by the
Scottish Enlightenment writers James Fordyce and John Gregory.[58] In the
Rights of Woman Wollstonecraft singled out Fordyce and Gregory's texts
for censure, denouncing their 'lover-like phrases' of praise for women as
covertly degrading: 'Why are girls to be told that they resemble angels; but
to sink them below women? ... Idle empty words! What can such delusive
flattery lead to, but vanity and folly?' And 'why must [women] be cajoled
into virtue by artful flattery and sexual compliments? Speak to them the
language of truth and soberness, and away with the lullaby strains of condescending endearment!'[59]

Wollstonecraft's slating of gallantry as inimical to women's interests was
certainly prescient. But it also marked a watershed in her relationship to

male opinion, placing her at odds not just with women's traditional detractors – misogynist satirists, Pauline churchmen, backwoods bigots – but
also with leading representatives of the male avant-garde. One of the most
revealing ways of reading the *Rights of Woman* is as part of an in-house quarrel among Enlightenment thinkers about the role and status of women in
modern civilisation.[60] Progressive intellectuals in the eighteenth century
regarded women with marked ambivalence, simultaneously viewing them
as a modernising force – a carrier and beneficiary of civilised values – but
also, in their more invidious incarnations, as an obstacle to modernity,
their ignorance, superstition and sensual egoism acting as a major barrier
to civilised progress. Many enlightened works displayed both attitudes, but
in general the positive assessment was most pronounced in educational
theory and moral philosophy while the negative held sway in the political
realm, particularly in oppositional political discourses where women and
womanliness were deprecated in themselves and as symbols of elite moral
pusillanimity and degeneracy.[61] British radicalism pre-1789 made generous
use of such anti-feminine rhetoric, which was then reinforced by French
republican propaganda. As the ideological impact of events in France re-
verberated across British radicalism, Enlightenment hostility to women as
agents of moral darkness became welded to feminised images of elite power
and corruption: a potent ideological brew.

It is this enlightened-radical animus against Woman that is audible
throughout the *Rights of Woman*. Rejecting gallantry's 'specious homage',[62]
Wollstonecraft turns instead to anti-elite misogyny, churning out philip-
pics against feminine frivolity and vice which, despite their generalising
tone, are aimed not at her sex *tout court* but at what she scornfully dubs
'ladies', meaning women of the landed aristocracy and their *nouveau riche*
imitators. Addressing women and men of the middle class, the *Rights of
Woman* represents women of higher ranks, 'ladies of fashion', as demonised
not only in male anti-elite writings but also in works by other 1790s radical feminists like the republican historian Catherine Macaulay[63] and the
jacobin novelist Mary Hays. '[S]poiled by prosperity and goaded on by
temptation and the allurements of pleasure, [women of fashion] give a
loose rein to their passions, and plunge headlong into folly and dissipation... to the utter extinction of thought, moderation, or strict morality'
Hays wrote sternly in 1798, adding that '[i]f this sentence, which I presume to pronounce on a considerable portion of my own sex, be deemed
severe; let me be permitted to appeal to the votaries of fashion themselves; and let their own hearts tell, whether or not I judge harshly of their
conduct.'[64]

This anti-elite excoriation of Woman was to prove a real intellectual albatross for Wollstonecraft. Yet her aim in reiterating it is plain enough. For if women are so malign – selfish, vain, sexually manipulative – who is it, the *Rights of Woman* demands, who has made them so? Wollstonecraft's genius is to make the question, and her reply, seem almost inevitable. Cramming her text with rich flirts and sluts, she offers them as stock emblems of aristocratic decadence but also – the crucial also, the plus in the argument that equals feminism – the debilitated products of male tyranny. Wicked women, and their invidious effects, are men's handiwork. The argument moves back and forth, mobilising the radical critique of absolute power to expose women's debasement at the hands of men, and then returning to 'artificial distinctions' of rank and power to depict them in gendered terms, with women equated not to the lower orders, as in late twentieth-century feminist polemic, but to the corrupted upper ranks, the 'great'. 'Perhaps the seeds of false refinement, immorality and vanity have ever been shed by the great,' Wollstonecraft writes, in a passage whose class and gender referents are virtually indistinguishable:

Weak, artificial beings, raised above the common wants and affections of their race, in a premature unnatural manner, undermine the very foundation of virtue, and spread corruption through the whole mass of society! As a class of mankind, they have the strongest claim to pity...[65]

Much of the persuasive force of the *Rights of Woman*, for eighteenth-century readers, would have been due to its rhetorical positioning on this familiar ethical landscape. Educated women and men in Hanoverian Britain were profoundly concerned about the relationship between wealth, morals and manners. The spread of 'false refinement' from the aristocracy to the newly affluent commercial middle class was constantly bemoaned. Placing herself firmly within this tradition, Wollstonecraft denounces *arriviste* women who, aping the leisured lifestyle of the rich, waste their days in gossip, flirtation, and 'bargain-hunting' when they could be managing a shop or running a little business.[66] The *Rights of Woman* is redolent with nostalgia for an idealised *petit bourgeois* world of craft manufactories, shops, and other small independent enterprises in which women could fully participate both as workers and wives, rather than frittering their lives away as 'voluptuous parasites'. The reality behind this ideal was more complex than Wollstonecraft's rhetoric allowed, but the impact of commercialism and consumerism on the lives of Englishwomen are very evident in her views, as are attendant changes in women's position in a highly competitive marriage market.[67] Women's increased dependence on marriage, and the miserable fate of those without male support – spinsters, widows, abandoned wives – was a major stimulus behind Wollstonecraft's feminism, as it was central to her own life experience. With the exception of Wollstonecraft herself, this book does not attempt any detailed investigation into the changing material and social circumstances of eighteenth-century British women; the conditions that encouraged the growth of a feminist mentality are discussed in terms of her life only. But watching Wollstonecraft struggle for economic survival, first as a lady's companion and teacher and then as a literary professional, it is important to recognise the ordinariness of her predicament, even if her solutions were less commonplace. The *Rights of Woman* was, after all, first and foremost a potboiler – written to satisfy Wollstonecraft's commitments to her publisher, and to keep the wolf from her family's door.

Do these difficult personal circumstances serve to explain Wollstonecraft's anti-womanism? Wollstonecraft's resentment of women whose lives were easier and happier than her own is very evident from her writings and correspondence, particularly during her years as a companion and governess. Humiliated by dancing attendance on wealthy women, and envious of silly, fashionable girls with plenty of idle pleasures and beaux while she – the poor clever girl – had neither, the young Wollstonecraft robed herself in a sense of superiority to the feminine 'herd' that never left her.[68] Carrying this into her literary career, she imagined herself a renegade to her sex, one of those 'few extraordinary women' who 'rush[ing] in eccentrical directions out of the orbit prescribed to their sex' are perhaps '*male* spirits, confined by mistake in female frames'.[69] Deprecating other women writers of her day as incompetent ninnies, she sought to consolidate her self-image as a 'peculiar' genius, an 'exception to general rules', while at the same time repudiating the idea of the exceptional woman as injurious to womankind in general.[70] Attacking the 'factitious' femininity foisted on women, she tried to see herself as a woman *sans* Woman, a self undivided by sexual distinctions, a genderless soul forged in God's image. But denigrated femininity returned to haunt her, fuelled by erotic insecurity and a crippling personal dislike rooted in her miserable early history. Contempt for weak, egoistical womanhood reappeared as bitter self-disdain, scarring even her most affectionate relationships. 'There is certainly a great defect in my mind – my wayward heart creates its own misery,' she wrote wretchedly to Joseph Johnson in the winter of 1792, after the collapse of her first romance, '... surely I am a fool –'[71] So foolish and defective that personal happiness seemed merely a dream, she later told Imlay, despite her passionate cravings for it.[72]

Should the negative image of women in the *Rights of Woman* be construed then not just as a feminist version of anti-elite misogyny but also as

a self-portrait, a 'debased... kind of "anti-narcissism"', as the literary critic
Susan Gubar has suggested?[73] The answer must surely be yes, at least in
part. Born into a family where she was alternately neglected, abused and
envied, Wollstonecraft performed the unhappy child's usual trick of imagining herself the deserving object of such treatment. A restless, histrionic
girl, she later described with resentment how the 'arduous struggles of her
youth' had left her with no expectation of 'simple affection' but only the
'most melancholy views of life'.[74] To intimates, she presented herself as
pitiable but also rather peevish, full of 'childish complaints and the reverses
of a disordered imagination'.[75] To Godwin she confided how her father's
cruelty had filled her with an 'agony' of abhorrence while her mother, un-
aware of or indifferent to her eldest daughter's misery, left her aching for
love. The coldly egoistical mothers that stalk the *Rights of Woman* probably
owe much to Elizabeth Wollstonecraft, as too the hapless female victims
of male brutishness in *Maria*. All her life Wollstonecraft was to display
strongly ambivalent attitudes toward women: falling in love with Fanny
Blood, she treated her to an awkward blend of idealising ardour and domineering condescension, and then went on to portray her as a sweet-natured
featherbrain in her first novel. Women whom she might have been expected to regard as kindred spirits, that is other writers and intellectuals,
elicited scorn or, at best, grudging respect (with the exception of Catherine
Macaulay whom she revered but never actually met). Friends pronounced
her a 'rigid' critic, 'severe and imperious in her resentments'[76] – a draconi-
anism that, targeting others, was unpleasant but focused on herself became,
at times, literally murderous. 'Mary', Godwin recalled after her death, with
mixed regret and admiration, 'was what Dr Johnson would have called a
"very good hater"'[77]: a hate that directed outward made her a brave enemy
of injustice, but turned inward became a violent and grievous burden.[78]

If we speculate, as seems fair, that Wollstonecraft's diatribes against
women were fuelled by this self-animus, does this invalidate her feminism?
Explaining a thinker's ideas in terms of their personal psychology is generally regarded as trivialising or pathologising, which in the case of feminism –
already regarded by many as neurotic belly-aching dressed up as political
protest – might seem one trivialisation too many. For a feminist's viewpoint
to be taken seriously, at least in academic circles, it must be grounded on abstract political principles, expunged of merely personal grievances and prejudices. This split between public-political thought and the private self is an
orthodoxy seldom questioned by intellectual historians; to Wollstonecraft
and her contemporaries, however, it would have seemed nonsensical. To the
eighteenth-century mind, reason and imagination, public professions and

private emotions were inseparably (if often problematically) conjoined. 'We reason deeply, when we forcibly feel,' Wollstonecraft wrote of her feminism in 1795 – a truism to her readership, however outré it may seem to present-day scholars.[79]

The notion of a politics purged of feeling and fantasy is a chimera, a modern myth. There is, as the critic Jacqueline Rose has argued, no political commitment that can 'divest itself of its affective colours', no method 'of understanding political identities and destinies without letting fantasy into the frame.'[80] And what is true of politics in general is emphatically true of feminism, where subjectivity itself is a primary focus of political energies. The feminist critical gaze, as the historian Sally Alexander has observed, is dual-focused, simultaneously looking outward to women's social condition, and inward, to womanliness as a psychic landscape, a self-envisaging that to most feminists – as indeed to most women – appears simultaneously natural and profoundly alien.[81] Psychological femininity, as Alexander argues and the history of feminism shows, is an imaginary condition ('factitious' in Wollstonecraft's terminology) with very mixed political consequences. Far from unique to Wollstonecraft, the repudiation of Woman has been a key element of feminism from its inception. Flirts, tarts, bimbos, and, above all, bad mothers loom large in feminist demonology. 'If you look for the provenance of the feminist writer,' the critic Lorna Sage has written, 'mother is the key ... you aim your feminism less at men than at the picture of the woman you don't want to be, the enemy within.'[82] This hostility to mothers and their legacies may be one important reason why Wollstonecraft – rebel daughter *par excellence* – has been the icon of choice for so many feminist intellectuals: like the American anthropologist Ruth Benedict who, hating her mother and thinking it 'a terrible thing to be a woman', on a visit to the National Portrait Gallery in London in 1914 took courage from Wollstonecraft's visage:

I remember the child I was when I saw it first, haunted by the terror of youth before experience. I wanted so desperately to know how other women had saved their souls alive. And the woman in the little frame arrested me, this woman with the auburn hair, and the sad, steady, light-brown eyes, and the gallant poise of the head. She had saved her soul alive; it looked out from her steady eyes unafraid. The price, too, that life had demanded of her was written ineradicably there. But to me, then, standing before her picture, even that costly payment was a guarantee, a promise. For I knew that in those days when she sat for that picture, she was content. And in the light of that content, I still spell out her life.[83]

A moving image: the adolescent girl, 'haunted by the terror of youth', searching in the face of Mary Wollstonecraft for the secret of growing up unafraid, of becoming a woman who could 'save her soul alive'. All political movements invent heroes for themselves, but few project into their idols such elemental conflicts, such fierce battles with inner foes, as feminism does. 'It is not against man we have to fight,' Olive Schreiner (another mother-hater) told a feminist friend, 'but against *ourselves* within ourselves'.[84]

As a politics with Woman as both its object and its agent, feminism has always been beset by paradoxes like these. 'Why would anyone who likes being a woman *need* to be a feminist?' one 1970s activist recalls demanding of another, and the question has lost none of its saliency.[85] To strive for equality as a woman; or to renounce womanhood *tout court*, to 'see the distinction of sex confounded in society' and women and men both freed from the prison of gender? The pressures toward both, so audible in the *Rights of Woman*, have saddled feminists with a contradiction that many believe can be resolved by concrete reforms, but which others, including myself, suspect of being more recalcitrant.[86] 'Only the concept of a subjectivity at odds with itself,' Jacqueline Rose writes, 'gives back to women the right to an impasse at the point of sexual identity' – an impasse which can be heard throughout the feminist tradition.[87]

Explaining how this impasse arises, psychoanalytic feminists like Rose and Sally Alexander look also to the imagination, but now to its unconscious operations. Interpreting oneself as female, they propose, is an imaginative act founded on unconscious fantasies of masculinity and femininity – derived in the first instance from parental figures – whose outcome is never Woman in some absolute sense but a sexual identity that is always partial, defensive, wishful. We feel ourselves to be female because of our fantasies about what it would feel like to be male: imaginings that pull us to and fro along the gender axis.

Does viewing feminist 'misogyny' in this light offer new insights? I believe that it does, that the unsettled relationship women have to our womanhood has infused feminist politics with unconscious conflicts and imaginings – wild wishes in Wollstonecraft's formulation – which are neither pathological nor counter-feminist, but an inevitable feature of a gender-based politics. In Wollstonecraft's case, we can only speculate about the fantasies motivating her political ideals and aspirations. Yet reading her decrials of women in the light of her painful emotional history, it seems proper to probe these for deeper significance. Historians and critics tend to put a high premium on intellectual consistency, as if any failure in this respect were a mark of mental infirmity. But if we adopt a less donnish, more psychologically generous view of intellectual creativity, then paradox and contradiction are no longer embarrassments to be brushed aside, but keys to a realm of hidden meanings.

Denouncing modern women as vicious and corrupt, what alternative did Wollstonecraft imagine for her sex, what revolution of inner being that would transform Woman from a degraded object of male tyranny into a worthy object of God's love? The answer, as we shall see, was a female self redeemed by transcendent fantasy, a Christian-platonic ideal of a feminine imagination 'shaping itself to ideal excellence, and panting after good unalloyed'.[88] And it is in the realm of fantasy, I suggest below, that the impulse behind this vision can be discerned, in the amorous identification with a sacralised parental figure that moulded Wollstonecraft's piety. The argument, in chapter 3, is the most explicitly psychoanalytic in the book, although an emphasis on the wishful, fantastic elements in her thinking is present throughout. The application of psychoanalytic concepts to past mental states is controversial; but used, as here, to explore the interplay between unconscious imaginings and utopian aspirations the approach does, I believe, prove illuminating.[89] To Wollstonecraft, the imagination was a sacred faculty, linking the fantasising mind to its Maker. Psychic life was the realm not of an isolated 'I' but of a yearning soul reaching toward its God.[90] All Wollstonecraft's struggles for a larger life were framed by this credo, although at times of acute emotional conflict even the divine light occasionally dimmed and she was left floundering in darkness, bewildered and forlorn. 'What a long time it requires to know ourselves,' she sighed during a period of melancholy introspection following her first suicide attempt, 'and yet almost every one has more of this knowledge than he is willing to own, even to himself'[91] – an observation which should serve to remind us that hidden or disowned parts of the self are hardly a modern invention.

* * *

The book is divided into two parts, both of them drawing on Wollstonecraft's entire *corpus*. Part I, 'Imagining women', begins with a scene-setting discussion of Wollstonecraft's career as a literary professional and radical philosopher, and then goes on to explore her views on the imagination and sexual difference, via a discussion of her quarrels with Burke and Rousseau. The final chapter in this section is an extended exploration of her religious beliefs, and their influence on her sexual attitudes. Part II, 'Feminism and revolution', examines her case for women's emancipation in the context of her utopian radicalism. After an opening discussion of British Jacobinism, this section goes on to explore the intellectual and political background to 1790s feminism, giving particular attention to the symbolic importance of Woman in Enlightenment philosophy and Franco-British radicalisms. Wollstonecraft's career as a revolutionary propagandist is investigated and compared to those of other radical intellectuals of her day, and her arguments for women's rights and female independence examined in detail. The section concludes with a chapter discussing her unfinished posthumous novel, *The Wrongs of Woman, or Maria*, as a representation of future feminist possibilities. An epilogue traces Wollstonecraft's posthumous career as a feminist heroine from 1798 to the present.

PART I

Imagining women

The female philosopher

The narrow path of truth and virtue inclines neither to the right nor left – it is a straightforward business, and they who are earnestly pursuing their road, may bound over many decorous prejudices, without leaving modesty behind.

(Wollstonecraft, *Rights of Woman*)[1]

On 3 January 1792, Wollstonecraft sat down to reply to a letter she had received some weeks earlier from her friend, the Liverpool radical, William Roscoe. 'I should have written to you sooner,' she apologised,

had I not been very much engrossed by writing and printing my vindication of the Rights of Woman ... I shall give the last sheet to the printer today; and, I am dissatisfied with myself for not having done justice to the subject. – Do not suspect me of false modesty – I mean to say, that had I allowed myself more time I could have written a better book...[2]

In fact she had allowed herself about three months to produce over three hundred pages, and whatever her own doubts about it, *A Vindication of the Rights of Woman* was an immediate success. Booksellers hurried to supply impatient customers while subscribers to circulating libraries complained that the book was so much in demand that 'there is no keeping it long enough to read it leisurely'.[3] Within the year a second English edition, two American editions, and a French translation had been published, with a German translation soon to follow. Reviews appeared in all the major magazines while across the country men and women of influence absorbed and discussed the book's message. 'Have you read that wonderful book, *The Rights of Woman*?' the poet and critic Anna Seward enquired of a friend,

It has by turns, pleased and displeased, startled and half-convinced me that its author is oftener right than wrong. Though the ideas of absolute equality in the sexes are carried too far, and though they certainly militate against St Paul's maxims concerning that important compact, yet do they expose a train of mischievous

1 Mary Wollstonecraft by an unknown artist, *c.* 1791–2.

mistakes in the education of females; – and on that momentous theme this work affords much better rules than can be found in the sophist Rousseau, or in the plausible Gregory. It applies the spear of Ithuriel to their systems. [4]

Asked to classify Wollstonecraft's book, most of these readers would have described it as a work of philosophy. The dramatist Hannah Cowley, who encountered in the work a 'body of mind as I hardly ever met with', regarded its arguments as 'politics', and thankfully beyond the ordinary woman's intellectual remit. '[W]ill Miss Wolstonecraft [sic] forgive me... if I say that politics are *unfeminine*? I never in my life could attend to their discussion.'[5] Listing the book along with other publications reviewed in 1792, the *Analytical Review* categorised it as 'political economy'; its reviewer, however, described it as 'an elaborate treatise of female education', and it was in this light that it was viewed by many liberal-minded commentators, like Anna Seward, who identified it as a contribution to the well-established tradition of educational reform.[6] But the most widespread perception of Wollstonecraft's book, among admirers and critics alike, was as a philosophical text, in the peculiarly eighteenth-century meaning of the term. It was as a 'philosopher' and a 'moralist' that Wollstonecraft addressed her readers, and it was in this spirit that her *magnum opus* was generally received.[7] Early readers of the *Rights of Woman* noted its 'philosophical air of dignity and gravity', its 'strong and impressive' style of argument.[8] 'In the class of philosophers, the *author* of this treatise – whom we will not offend by styling authoress – has a right to a distinguished place,' the Dissenting minister William Enfield wrote in the radical *Monthly Review*, adding that in this Wollstonecraft had given 'indubitable proofs' that 'the women are no less capable of instructing than of pleasing', and that 'mind is of no sex'.[9]

The approbatory note struck by Enfield and others at the time of the book's publication was audible, to a greater or lesser degree, throughout the educated world to which the majority of Wollstonecraft's readers belonged.[10] Of the male critics reviewing the *Rights of Woman* for the periodical press, only one (writing for that 'timid, mean production', the *Critical Review*) dismissed it out of hand.[11] Notices in the radical press, unsurprisingly, were the most enthusiastic, but even some journals of a more Establishment bent commented favourably on Wollstonecraft's philosophical reflections on female manners and moral improvement, while managing to ignore or understate her challenge to male authority. By the end of the century, however, this welcoming attitude had evaporated. The intellectual hubris which had given birth to Wollstonecraft's book was almost wholly discredited, and text and author both fiercely condemned. The chief factors behind this reversal – the conservatising impact of the French Revolution on English intellectual life, combined with Godwin's revelations about his wife's sexual history – are explored further on, but it's worth pausing here to note the scale of the change. For if to describe oneself as a philosopher in 1792 was to be perceived as part of a broad intellectual movement toward a more humane, thoughtful and culturally open society – that distinctively English version of a philosophical Enlightenment – by 1798 'philosophy' had become a synonym for revolutionary zealotry, with 'philosopher' and 'jacobin' serving as virtually interchangeable terms. 'Modern philosophers of the French system', as one typical critic put it, were 'monstrous', 'savage' infidels who 'should be driven from our fellowship with contempt'.[12] Women promulgating such ideals were an unchristian 'Amazonian band'.[13] Reviewing Godwin's *Memoirs* of Wollstonecraft, the *European Magazine* derided her as a 'philosophical wanton' whose immoralism enacted jacobin principles.[14] The decade after her death saw the publication of dozens of works – some authored by women, including erstwhile admirers and associates – satirising her as an addlebrained fanatic addicted to utopian system-mongering while abusing or neglecting everyone around her.[15] Other writers continued to defend her, but the tide of opinion flowed so strongly against philosophical radicalism that supportive voices were soon drowned in the hostile clamour.

In one sense of course, none of this controversy was new. From Plato's Diotama onward, the figure of the woman intellectual – the learned lady, female pedant, *femme savante*, *precieuse*, *femme philosophe* (English writers often retained the French labels to underline the exoticism of the phenomenon) – had hovered on the margins of western intellectual life. With the epistemological revolutions of the seventeenth century she had edged closer to centre-stage, as first Cartesian rationalism and then Lockean empiricism wrenched the philosophical enterprise open to all possessed of natural intelligence. Materialist-atomist epistemology did not recognise gender distinctions: as all minds received sensory impressions, so all were capable of reasoned reflection on experiential data. The brains of women, the feminist pamphleteer 'Sophia' insisted in 1739, 'receive the impressions of sense as [men's] do, we martial and preserve ideas for imagination and memory as they do, and we have all the organs they have, and apply them to the same purpose as they do'.[16] Thus 'we might without vanity aspire to being as able *philosophers* or *divines* as the Men, perhaps better...'[17]

The spread of Enlightenment gave further stimulus to female claims. Unfettered thought – untouched by scholarly dogma, avid for truth – was the agent of illumination, and here women's untutored intellects readily qualified. In 1712 *The Spectator* famously announced its intention to bring philosophy 'out of Closets and Libraries' into the social venues of the urban middle class, including the 'Tea-Table' society of women.[18] During succeeding decades booksellers took note of a growing middle-class appetite for that wide range of genres deemed philosophical, including not

2 Joseph Johnson by W. Sharpe after Moses Haughton, no date.

only metaphysical and moral treatises but also published sermons, theological pamphlets, essays in aesthetics, conjectural history, educational theory, politics. Philosophy, in this eagerly self-improving world, encompassed reasoned arguments of all sorts, and its practitioners tended to be just as miscellaneous: freelance intellectuals; erudite preachers; bluestocking literatae, and, at its more scholarly end, Dissenting academicians and Scottish university professors – but even these were far from ivory-tower figures.[19] Crafting their works for a wide public, these men and women were not interested in abstruse scholarship or the edification of a few select minds, seeing their task rather (in the words of the Scottish philosophe Dugald

Stewart) 'to diffuse, as widely as possible, that degree of cultivation which may enable the bulk of a people to possess all the moral and intellectual improvement of which their nature is susceptible'.[20] In a broad pedagogic culture, philosophy and personal betterment went hand in hand.

This demotic intellectual stance, a cause for much self-congratulation at the time, could all too easily spill over into a John Bullish philistinism, as the sturdy empiricism and commonsensical pragmatism of British thinkers were contrasted to the philosophic excesses of continental metaphysicians.[21] But the style of thought and debate it encouraged – open, dynamic, undogmatic – was not only in tune with the enterprising attitudes of a burgeoning industrial society, but also much more accessible to women than antecedent intellectual modes. In 1795 the novelist and educationalist Maria Edgeworth, surveying European intellectual progress, noted how abstruse ideas and 'unintelligible jargon' had once kept 'the fair sex . . . in Turkish ignorance':

but now writers must offer their discoveries to the public in distinct terms, which every body may understand . . . and the art of teaching has been carried to such perfection, that a degree of knowledge may now with ease be acquired in the course of a few years, which formerly it was the business of a life to attain.[22]

'All this,' Edgeworth concluded, 'is much in favour of female literature' – and in fact from the mid seventeenth century on Europe had experienced such a dramatic increase in the number of women engaged in learned pursuits that it has led one historian to postulate the rise of a 'learned feminist wave' over this period.[23] This is probably too enthusiastic an assessment, but certainly it is true that seventeenth-century *savantes* had been a significant cultural presence, with some of the most preeminent – Anna Maria van Schurman in Holland, Marie de Gournay in France, Margaret Cavendish and Mary Astell in England – prepared to publicly argue for female intellectual equality. Eighteenth-century women intellectuals, prior to the 1790s, were less inclined to see themselves as spokeswomen for their sex, but they too often enjoyed a high degree of cultural prestige.[24] Lettered Georgian society, particularly the liberal urban *literati*, liked to pride itself on its positive attitude toward clever women.

However, this optimistic account is only half the story. In England, as elsewhere in Europe, admiration for women intellectuals had always been shadowed by hostile denigration. Molière's early eighteenth-century caricatures of Parisian *precieuses* had found plenty of echoes across the Channel where, according to Lady Mary Wortley Montagu, there was 'hardly a character more Despicable or more liable to universal ridicule than that of the Learned Woman'.[25] Over the course of the century such attitudes had been strongly challenged, but also sharply reinforced by fears about the subversive impact of female intellectualism. The emergence of the professional woman writer within the distinctly unlearned but very dynamic world of popular writing heightened public awareness of the female mind while simultaneously intensifying the anxieties surrounding it. Thus by the time Wollstonecraft picked up her pen the lady author – whether scholarly pedant or mass-market scribbler – was both a very familiar and chronically controversial figure. A facetious mid century warning issued by Dr Johnson against the 'Amazons of the pen' who bestrode the literary field, openly challenging the 'usurpations of virility', by the 1780s seemed less diverting than uncomfortably prophetic.[26]

* * *

Biographers tend to present Wollstonecraft as an exceptional figure, a heroic pioneer, and that was how she generally liked to be viewed. 'You know I am not born to tread in the beaten track' – she told her sister Everina on entering Joseph Johnson's employ, 'the peculiar bent of my nature pushes me on.'[27] As a professional woman writer she was, she boasted to Everina, the 'first of a new genus'.[28] In fact she was nothing of the sort, but the delicious sense of avant-gardism – of moving toward a unique and extraordinary destiny – was more than just grandiose fantasy.

In the best piece of biographical writing on Wollstonecraft to date, Margaret Walters has pointed to the strength of Wollstonecraft's impulse toward self-creation, her insistent testing out of attitudes and roles suited to her 'peculiar' character. Like the heroine of her first novel, *Mary, a Fiction*, who rejects both her parents, Wollstonecraft had 'no models, no one to identify with, so she ha[d], literally, to invent herself' while at the same time struggling with obstacles encountered by all self-made women.[29] It is this incessant, painful quest for a subjectivity to inhabit which, Walters suggests, gives Wollstonecraft's story its peculiarly contemporary flavour, and makes it so easy for women to identify with her centuries later.[30]

This experimental drive was never more evident than in Wollstonecraft's diverse, often highly dramatised self-presentations as a writer. Over the years she ran through an extraordinary range of literary *personae*, from the prissy moralist of her earliest *Thoughts on the Education of Daughters* (1787), to the bluntspoken philosophic radical of the two *Vindications* (1790, 1792), to the lyrical romantic of her letters from Sweden (1796), with many other postures – satirist, teacher, melancholy *solitaire* – tried out along the way. Still in her late twenties, with a failed career as a schoolteacher behind her and only the bleak prospect of governessing ahead, she doffed the pedant's cap to lecture her readers in tones which 'will, by some, be thought too grave': 'I am sorry to observe,' *Thoughts on the Education of Daughters* begins, 'that reason and duty have not so powerful an influence over human conduct, as instinct has in the brute creation', hence it is her task to instruct her readers in the cultivation of reason and governance of impulses which if left uncontrolled 'will run wild'.[31] Severe advice follows on everything from how to treat servants (who 'are, in general, ignorant and cunning' and thus require a very firm hand) to the perils of card-playing and the moral dangers of the theatre.[32] This repressively didactic note persisted throughout the late 1780s, in her 1789 anthology, *A Female Reader* and her *Original Stories* for children, published the previous year. But it was in these years too, as she later told Henry Fuseli, that she was testing out a very different self-image: that of an impoverished bohemian forsaking the temptations of the world for the higher claims of mind and spirit. She denied herself meat and most of the other 'necessaries of life', she told Fuseli, in order that she 'might be able to pursue some romantic schemes of benevolence'.[33] Dressed in a coarse cloth garment and black worsted stockings like those worn by milkmaids, with her hair hanging down around her shoulders rather than pinned up like a lady, she looked – according to one unfriendly account – like a 'philosophical sloven'.[34] And although her appearance became more conventional in the 1790s, this romantic bohemianism was to remain part of Wollstonecraft's self-identity throughout her life.

The common thread linking all these writerly personae was Wollstonecraft's deep, at times obsessive, preoccupation with personal authenticity. To possess and express one's true self, she insistently emphasised, was the foundation of all genuinely creative authorship. 'Those compositions only have power to delight... where the soul of the author is exhibited,' the Advertisment to *Mary, a Fiction* explained, for it is only such writings that 'animate the hidden springs' of those 'who do not measure their steps in a beaten track'.[35] It is texts expressive of the evolving inner life of the writer that offer to their readers the 'subtile spirit' of literary truth.[36] A letter to Godwin written in 1796 explained that she wished him to 'see my heart and mind just as it appears to myself, without any veil of affected humility over it':

> ... I am compelled to think that there is some thing in my writings more valuable, than in the productions of some people on whom you bestow warm elogiums [sic] – I mean more mind – denominate as you will – more of the observations of my own senses, more of the combining of my own imagination – the effusions of my own feelings and passions than the cold workings of the brain on the materials procured by the senses and imagination of other writers –[37]

This emphasis on authentic self-expression may now seem ordinary enough, but in Wollstonecraft's day it could still strike a sharply dissident note, particularly when sounded by a woman. Women, after all, were not meant to have a true self to discover or express. Like a pretty dress, a properly feminine self was one designed for masculine tastes. So Wollstonecraft's persistent concern that her writings should stem from the 'original source' of her being, rather than 'the prescribed rules of art', signalled not only her literary modernism but also her commitment to a personal authenticity sharply at odds with the masquerades of femininity.[38] *A Vindication of the Rights of Woman* denounced the 'system of dissimulation' by which women were 'always to *seem* to be this and that', 'levelled, by meekness and docility, into one character of yielding softness and gentle compliance'.[39] Wollstonecraft's refusal to be flattened by conventional womanliness in this fashion was a principal determinant of her life choices, and a key source of her feminism.

Nonetheless, up to 1789 there was little in Wollstonecraft's professional life to distinguish her from any other member of the small army of women working at the lower end of the eighteenth-century literary scene. Ploughing through book after book for Joseph Johnson's *Analytical Review*; struggling with foreign languages until she was sufficiently proficient to do translations; producing stories and anthologies for a popular readership: all were typical hack labours, undertaken as Godwin (who was all too familiar with such employment) later wrote, 'to . . . answer the mere mercantile purpose of the day', and thus hardly likely to elicit those 'daring flights' of intellect which he later attributed to her.[40] Nor did the young Wollstonecraft seem inclined to try for greater things. The preface to her *Female Reader* primly warned that for a woman 'to obtrude her person or talents on the public when necessity does not justify and spur her on' was a deplorable 'breach of modesty'.[41] The statement might have been a sop to critics, but Godwin tells us that at the time she had a 'vehement aversion' to being known as a writer, even employing 'some precautions to prevent its occurrence'.[42] Exactly what is meant by this is unclear since, with the exception of her book reviews and *The Female Reader*, which was published under a male pseudonym, all of Wollstonecraft's writings prior to 1790 appeared under her own name.[43] But if – like many women – she *was* diffident about publicising her authorial achievements, this was much of a piece with the overall conventionalism of her youthful literary stance.

The genres to which Wollstonecraft first contributed – conductbooks, children's stories, ladies' anthologies – were all ones that late eighteenth-century cultural arbiters approved as properly feminine. Modern feminist critics have been keen to identify proto-feminist elements in these works, and there are hints of these.[44] *Thoughts on the Education of Daughters* and *Original Stories* for children offer exceptionally strong versions of the Protestant defence of female moral dignity and rational seriousness. A woman, even if she is a 'weaker vessel' than a man, must nonetheless not allow her reasoning capacities to 'lie dormant', *Thoughts* insists, since it is only persons of 'cultivated mind' who possess true virtue and happiness.[45] *Original Stories* is likewise centrally preoccupied with issues of female intellectual authority.[46] But the authoritative voices in the *Stories*, as in the earlier *Thoughts*, all belong to women fulfilling traditional female educational obligations: mothers, governesses, teachers. It is only as pedagogues instructing their inferiors – children, servants or less rational women – that the young Wollstonecraft permitted women intellectuals to speak.

   Original Stories from Real Life; with Conversations Calculated to Regulate the Affections, and Form the Mind to Truth and Goodness, published in 1788, tells the tale of two little girls whose mother has died and who are now in the care of one Mrs Mason, a 'woman of tenderness and discernment' determined to replace habits of fashionable frivolity acquired from their mother with virtuous thought and behaviour. Mrs Mason, a pious woman of formidable self-assurance and severe (some might say sadistic) pedagogic style, takes her charges through a variety of edifying experiences which together serve to dramatise the moral lessons of the conductbook, while at the same time offering a vision of exemplary womanhood. What sets Mrs Mason apart from many teachers and most mothers is that she wants her pupils not just to behave well but 'to be taught to think' – something in which girls seldom received any training.[47] As a paragon of intellectual rigour, she was deliberately drawn by Wollstonecraft as a counterexample to the vast majority of ordinary women whose trivial impulses and foolish conduct, particularly as parents, demanded correction. As Wollstonecraft wrote to Johnson, 'If parents attended to their children, I would not have written the stories'; but since most mothers were unenlightened, it took a professional pedagogue to set them straight.[48] The same theme appeared again in her later 'Letters on the Management of Infants' and 'Lessons' for children, which were both intended for 'mothers in the middle class' to persuade them to exercise sound reason in place of fashionable custom in their child-rearing practices.[49]

   Godwin claimed that Wollstonecraft was a wonderful teacher and mother, and perhaps this was so, although to a twenty-first-century ear the coercive tone of *Original Stories* is chilling.[50] But to be a successful female pedagogue didn't require maternal experience (in 1788 Wollstonecraft was childless), but the possession of a cultivated mind and a mature grasp of moral principles. As a teacher, in other words, a woman must project an image of proper grown-upness, in contrast to the generality of her sex who remained locked in what Mary Hays described as 'PERPETUAL BABYISM'.[51] Nonetheless, the model of adult authority offered by *Original Stories*, in common with other texts in the genre, remained specifically and narrowly feminine. Mrs Mason might be a paragon of rational virtue, but she offers no challenge to male intellectual regimes and she is certainly no philosopher.

In the same year that she published *Original Stories*, however, Wollstonecraft created another, very different sort of intellectual heroine. The Advertisement to her first novel, *Mary, A Fiction*, announced it as a tale of female genius:

In an artless tale, without episodes, the mind of a woman, who has thinking powers is displayed. The female organs have been thought too weak for this arduous employment; and experience seems to justify the assertion. Without arguing physically about *possibilities* – in a fiction, such a being may be allowed to exist; whose grandeur is derived from the operations of its own faculties, not subjugated to opinion; but drawn by the individual from the original source.[52]

The novel opens with Mary, a disregarded child, struggling to acquire an education. Her wealthy parents cannot be bothered to find a governess for her, so the household servants teach her to read. Soon Mary is devouring 'with avidity every book that came in her way'.[53] Left thus 'to the operations of her own mind', and thereby avoiding the usual constraints placed on female mental processes, she finds herself reflecting freely on 'everything that [comes] under her inspection' and so learns 'to think'.[54] And since she possesses a naturally philosophic mind – a 'wonderful quickness in discerning distinctions and combining ideas' – Mary's thoughts take her deep into theology and metaphysics, and even (in order to try and alleviate the tubercular symptoms of her bosom friend, Ann) into the study of medicine.[55] They also form her sexual tastes, since as a young adult she quickly discovers that she is only attracted to 'men past the meridian of life, and of a philosophic turn', and promptly falls in love with a man of this sort.[56]

Mary is a true original, a woman who obeys convention only when reason and virtue dictate that she should. Unlike the ordinary women around her, she possesses deep emotional sensibilities (in fact her emotional responses are so highly pitched that they verge on the chronically hysterical), is indifferent to fashion in both dress and morals, and has intellectual tastes far loftier than those of her beloved Ann.[57] Her religious commitment, like that of her author, is not a mere matter of form but a product of rigorous study and an object of constant, passionate reflection. Female society, with its petty gossip and mindless preoccupations, offers no sympathetic response to Mary's genius, so for this she turns instead to a male thinker conveniently to hand. He is a sweetnatured chap named Henry, an invalid 'with a face rather ugly, [with] strong lines of genius', who although 'a man of learning' has 'also studied mankind, and knew many of the intricacies of the human heart, from having felt the infirmities of his own'.[58] Henry's genius, in other words, is as much emotional as aesthetic and cerebral, and in this way he serves as an ideal mentor-cum-partner to the reflective, hyper-sensitive Mary.

Wollstonecraft later described *Mary, A Fiction* as a 'crude production', and the assessment seems about right.[59] But the book was also highly innovative in many respects, not least in its use of fiction to explore female intellectual 'possibilities'. Mary is a philosopher in the making, and in this sense she represents a radical break with conventional feminine ideals. She is also a writer, who over the course of the novel increasingly turns to her journal – often her 'only confident' – to ruminate on the larger implications of her experiences. (The heroine of Wollstonecraft's final novel, *The Wrongs of Woman, or Maria*, likewise keeps a journal, and much of her story is told through its entries.) The solitary reflections Mary pens, mostly on moral and religious themes, serve not only to underline the creativity of her intellect but also to demonstrate the proper functions of writing itself. Mary writes not to entertain herself, or even to console, but to *understand*, and in this she is also – Wollstonecraft implies – very unlike other lady authors of her day.

* * *

By the end of 1788, with three books and seven months of professional reviewing under her belt, Wollstonecraft had gained some minor recognition as a woman writer. The world of 'reading and writing ladies' – as the bluestocking Hester Chapone described the late eighteenth-century female literary scene – was becoming her own.[60] This was not cause for self-congratulation. Throughout her career, Wollstonecraft sought to distance herself from the generality of women writers, whom she regarded as inveterately second-rate. Female novelists in particular came in for strong censure for their artificial style and 'gross' sentiments. Almost from the moment she began writing for the *Analytical Review*, Wollstonecraft took female-authored novels as a chief polemical target. 'It has been sarcastically said, by a snarling poet [Pope], that most women have no character at all: we shall apply it to their production. – Novels', a 1789 review of a novel titled *The Fair Hibernian* began, while another book, *The Child of Woe*, was dismissed with 'having no marked features to characterize it, we can only term it a truly feminine novel'.[61] 'More minute criticism on this novel would be absurd,' another review (of *Juliet*, by 'A Lady') concluded, 'as it sinks before discriminate censure.'[62]

Reviewing celebrated writers like Fanny Burney, Charlotte Smith, and Charlotte Lennox, Wollstonecraft's tone became more respectful; but these were exceptions to the general 'herd' of lady authors who 'like timid sheep... jump over the hedge one after the other', producing works of such artificial 'double-refined sensibility' and so many 'unnatural characters [and] improbable incidents', that the only intelligent response to them was derision.[63] The corrupting effects of such novels on female readers – an *idée fixe* of the age – worried her too, but the keynote sounded in her reviews was less the outrage of a moral censor than the exasperation of a writer forced to share her professional turf with 'this kind of trash'.[64] 'Without a knowledge of life, or the human heart, why will young misses presume to write? They would not attempt to play in company on an instrument whose principles they know nothing of: – how then can they have the assurance to publish their foolish fancies?'[65] It is only the vicious public appetite for such mindless fiction, particularly the depraved taste of women readers, that permitted such worthless amateurism to flourish.

Diatribes of this sort were common among women novelists of the period. In an intensely competitive literary market, to elevate oneself above the motley generality was essential. Professional rivalries were vigorous, with little in the way of female solidarity to offset them. There were some important exceptions to this, particularly in the bluestocking circle – that loose grouping of literary ladies presided over by the powerful businesswoman Elizabeth Montagu – whose members applauded, mentored and sometimes even financed each other.[66] But overall, women writers displayed little sense of feminine fellowship. Asked, at the end of the century, to write for a journal produced by and for women, the poet and essayist Anna Barbauld refused, saying that 'different sentiments and different connections separate them [literary women] much more than the joint interest of their sex would unite them': a salutary reminder not only of how suffocating the category of 'woman writer' could be, but also of the diversity of the female republic of letters.[67] The world of female authorship that Wollstonecraft regarded with such contempt – and which, for its part, tended to view her with mingled respect, anxiety and censure – was as heterogeneous in its experience and attitudes as the rest of educated British society.

* * *

The professional woman writer had appeared in Britain at the point when the category of the intellectual – so long confined, as Dr Johnson put it, to 'those, who by study, or appearance of study, were supposed to have gained knowledge unattainable by the busy part of mankind' – was becoming accessible to new cultural constituencies.[68] Authors who in previous centuries had survived by private means, church livings or aristocratic patronage, over the course of the eighteenth century had found themselves operating in an increasingly commercial milieu, dominated by publishers (or booksellers, as they were still known) who blended patronage with sharp business sense. Many writers deplored this development – Goldsmith, for example, describing it as 'that fatal revolution whereby writing is converted to a mechanic trade; and booksellers, instead of the great, become the patrons and paymasters of men of genius' – but its overall effect had been to open up the world of letters.[69] A steady rise in literacy levels, particularly in the middle class, combined with a growing taste for leisure reading, meant that by the final quarter of the century the press was 'teeming' with new publications, with the result – according to Johnson again – that 'we have now more knowledge generally diffused; all our ladies read now, which is a great extension'.[70] The most widely purchased works were still devotional, but with growing competition from history, biography, poetry, bellettrist writings of all sorts, and didactic literature such as conductbooks, as well as from philosophy and that dubious new phenomenon – the popular novel. The appearance of the novel on the early eighteenth-century literary scene, and its rapid ascendancy thereafter, were seen by many observers as chiefly responsible for that 'general desire for READING, now so prevalent among the inferior orders of society', and particularly for the rise of the woman reader, whose passion for the more sensationalist varieties of popular fiction was taken as an index of the corruption as well as the democratisation of the literary world.[71] Even female domestic servants 'of the better sort', it was noted, read novels – truly an alarming sign of the levelling potential of popular print.[72]

Witnessing this explosion of opportunity, aspirant women writers across Britain had grabbed their pens. Novel-writing in particular attracted so many new female recruits that by 1773, according to the *Monthly Review*, 'this branch of the literary trade' was 'almost entirely engrossed by the Ladies'.[73] By 1798 authorship was sufficiently well established as a 'respectable and pleasing [ladies'] employment' for at least one conductbook writer to feel justified in recommending it, particularly to women in straitened circumstances.[74] During the first half of the century a woman profiting financially by her writing had tended to raise disapproving eyebrows. But by Wollstonecraft's day large numbers were scribbling for a living, albeit a modest and precarious one. The 'pot-boiler' was for many women literally that, as they struggled to feed themselves and their families on literary receipts. 'I have printed this Manuscript... with a View of settling my self in a Way of Trade,' as one woman novelist wrote, '[and] That I may be capable of providing for my ancient... Mother.'[75]

If all these labours weren't exactly Grub Street pen-pushing, they weren't particularly decorous either. Thrust into a cut-throat commercial world, women writers found themselves quarrelling with publishers over fees, fretting over poor reviews, and pandering to popular liking for the sentimental and sensational.[76] Like their male counterparts, such women also sought patronage. Often this was to be had through subscriptions: small sums collected by writers toward the publication of a work, with long lists of subscribers taking the place of the traditional dedication. But commercial patrons, usually booksellers, were not uncommon. Such patrons, unlike their noble predecessors, supported writers not because their works flattered aristocratic pretensions (or propagandised for a particular political viewpoint, as Whig and Tory nobility had employed writers to do) but because books were profitable commodities – and those who produced them intellectual workers worthy of their hire. In the winter of 1792 Mary Hays sent the manuscript of her *Letters and Essays* to Wollstonecraft for comment. With it she included a draft preface apologising for her intellectual deficiencies and thanking various eminent men who had praised her previous literary efforts. Wollstonecraft found all this 'vain humility' very irritating. 'The *honour* of publishing, the phrase on which you have laid a stress, is the cant of both trade and sex', she scolded Hays:

for if really equality should ever take place in society the man who is employed and gives a just equivalent for the money he receives will not behave with the obsequiousness of a servant.[77]

Hays should recall, Wollstonecraft went on, that if her essays 'have merit they will stand alone, if not the *shouldering up* of Dr this or that will not long keep them from falling to the ground'. More than enough bad books existed already, so if Hays thought she lacked the strength of mind 'to overcome the common difficulties' which lie in a writer's path, she should 'leave the task of instructing others to those who can'. In fact all this extravagant modesty, Wollstonecraft concluded, was really no more than authorial self-display, but 'till a work strongly interests the public true modesty should keep the author in the background – for it is only about the character and life of a *good* author that anxiety is active – A blossom is but a blossom.'[78]

The sharp professional tone, the evocation of public taste, the depiction of the writer as waged worker: here Wollstonecraft's modernity is striking.

No such obsequies for her: dedicating the *Rights of Woman* to the French revolutionary leader Talleyrand (the only dedication she ever wrote), she informed Talleyrand that she had done this so that he would not 'throw my book aside' but absorb its message and give up his opposition to female political rights.[79] As dedications went this was exceptionally heterodox, yet Wollstonecraft was by no means the first woman writer to flout sycophantic conventions. Writing in the mid century, Charlotte Charke had declared herself the 'Properest Patroness' for her *A Narrative of the Life* (1755), on the grounds that she was 'most likely to be tenderly partial to my poetical Errors', while Frances Burney, whose novel *Camilla* (1796) earned her the staggering sum of £2,000, in 1778 dedicated her first, anonymously published novel *Evelina* not to any titled patron but, cheekily, to the 'Authors of the Monthly and Critical Reviews' who serve as 'Censors for the Public'.[80] The day of the bootlicking author was effectively over: in every genre, at every level of learning or talent, the man or woman of letters was becoming, to use Dugald Stewart's phrase, a 'literary artisan'.

* * *

When Wollstonecraft was sacked from her post as governess to the Kingsborough family in the summer of 1787 she went straight to Joseph Johnson's shop in St Paul's Churchyard. He not only gave her work on his new *Analytical Review* but also lent her money, found her a home, took an active interest in the rest of her troublesome family – in short, displayed 'an uncommon interest', as Wollstonecraft told her sister Everina, which 'saved me from despair and vexations I shrink back from'.[81] This generous encouragement proved decisive in determining her to become a professional writer: 'Mr Johnson assures me that if I exert my talents in writing I may support myself in a comfortable way,' she told Everina complacently.[82]

   Wollstonecraft's relationship to Johnson gives a fascinating glimpse into the writer–publisher partnership in transition. Johnson, from what we know of him, seems to have been an admirable man: principled, good-natured, radical in his political views while careful and astute in his business dealings. As the publisher of most of the progressive thinkers of the day, as well as the official distributor of Unitarian literature, by the 1780s Johnson was an important figure in the London intelligentsia, with his 'hospitable mansion' (as Wollstonecraft referred to his combined shop and home) serving as a principal venue for the literary avant garde. In 1788 Wollstonecraft stayed for a few weeks above Johnson's shop, while many other writers and artists gathered regularly around his dinner table. Godwin's diary from the 1780s and 90s contains dozens of mentions of evenings spent discussing politics and philosophy at Johnson's, while Anna Barbauld, recalling her own visits there in the mid 1780s, remembered them as 'so truly social and lively, that we protracted them sometimes till – but I am not telling tales...'[83] 'Whenever I am tired of solitude,' Wollstonecraft wrote to Everina in November 1787, 'I go to Mr Johnson's, and there I meet the kind of company *I* find most pleasure in...'[84]

Wollstonecraft frequently described Johnson's behaviour toward her as that of a 'father and brother', and Johnson himself made no secret of his affection for his bright, prickly young protegée.[85] Since there is no evidence of sexual attraction on either side (with the possible exception of one kittenish reference by Wollstonecraft in 1792 to some gossip which had 'married' her to Johnson) this has led one biographer to suggest that their relationship gratified a mutual need to 'play at fathers and daughters'.[86] While there is probably some emotional truth to this (at least on Wollstonecraft's side), it misses the historical point. Throughout the eighteenth century women writers turned to men with clout in the publishing trade – publishers, editors, other writers – for just the sort of 'humane and *delicate* assistance' that Wollstonecraft received from Johnson.[87] Samuel Johnson, for example, despite his occasional rudeness about literary ladies, devoted a great deal of time and effort to promoting the fortunes of those he admired, while Samuel Richardson's support for the literatae was so well known that it earned him public praise.[88] 'I never was a writing lady till you made me one,' the young Hester Chapone told Richardson.[89] As well as giving advice and encouragement, men like Johnson and Richardson introduced women to publishers, wrote dedications for them, found subscribers for their books, and smoothed their path with publishers; other men, like Edward Cave of *The Gentleman's Magazine*, not only provided women with important publishing outlets in the pages of their journals but also supplied fees, introductions and a general *entrée* to the literary scene.[90] Women's reliance on such patrons, particularly women without effective male support of other kinds, clearly evoked a paternalist model of male/female relations. Yet at the same time it drew that model into a context where, given sufficient market success, a dependant could become an equal, patronage become collegiality – as happened between Wollstonecraft and Johnson.

Wollstonecraft seems always, despite her best efforts, to have owed Johnson money.[91] But her sense of general indebtedness to him was qualified by what she described as her 'independence', meaning her ability to function as an equal with others, even where some obligation existed. 'I have not that kind of pride, which makes some dislike to be obliged to those they respect,' she told Johnson in a letter written in 1788 reminding him to let her know what she owed him, while an earlier letter on the same theme adopted a tone typical of her dealings with him.[92]

My dear sir,
Remember you are to settle my account, as I want to know how much I am in your debt – but do not suppose that I feel any uneasiness on that score. The generality of people in trade would not be much obliged to me for a like ci-vility, *but you were a man* before you were a bookseller – so I am your sincere friend,

Mary[93]

The year before, while Johnson was still househunting for her, Mary went to see her sister in Henley, from where she wrote to him. 'Have you yet heard of an habitation for me?' and then a little further on: 'I long for a little peace and *independence*. Every obligation we receive from our fellow-creatures is a new shackle, takes from our native freedom, and debases the mind, makes us mere earthworms – I am not fond of grovelling!'[94] This letter, a particularly exuberant one, celebrates the new 'plan of life' which Johnson has opened to her: a life free from governessing and other 'grovelling' occupations, in the employ of a man to whom she would never kowtow, and who was frequently to find himself at the sharp end of her bossy, passionate nature. 'If you wish me to look over any more trash this month,' she wrote to him after some months of intensive book-reviewing, 'you must send it directly...If you do not like the manner in which I reviewed Dr Johnson's sermon on his wife, be it known unto you – I *will* not do it any other way...'[95] Mary, Johnson fondly recalled some years later, was a woman so incapable of disguise that the moment she entered his room he guessed her mood, and readied himself for what was to follow. 'You are my only friend – the only person I am *intimate* with,' she wrote to him after a display of ill-humour on her part. 'I never had a father, or a brother – you have been both to me, ever since I knew you...'[96]

A very personal partnership, then, but also a highly commercial one, with real financial advantage to both sides. 'I must reckon on doing some good, and getting the money I want, by my writings, or go to sleep forever,' Wollstonecraft told Godwin in 1796, adding, 'By what I have already written Johnson, I am sure, has been a gainer.'[97] On her side, writing for Johnson was so lucrative that it allowed her not only to support herself but also to give a good deal of assistance to others – her own relations, but also Fanny Blood's family – up to her death. In May 1786 Johnson handed over her first authorial fee: ten pounds for *Thoughts on the Education of Daughters*, which she immediately passed on to Fanny's parents, to pay their fares to Ireland; two years later, in May 1788, she was able to boast to Fanny's brother, George (to whom she also loaned money regularly) that she was succeeding 'beyond her most sanguine hopes' and expected to earn two hundred pounds – a very respectable sum for a working woman – that year.[98] With the publication of her political works, and particularly the *Rights of Woman*, her earnings may well have been considerably higher. For his part, Johnson, who in 1787 had hired a bright young unknown to do hack work and reviewing, by the mid 1790s found himself with one of the most widely read women authors in British history. Small wonder he had no hesitation, as he later told her brother Charles, in advancing her sums on her books before they began earning profits. '[B]esides you know that she deserves more than most women,' he confided to Charles, '& cannot live upon a trifle...'[99]

Working for Johnson made Wollstonecraft a full citizen of the republic of letters. It also educated her. '[L]ike the majority of her sex,' Mary Hays later wrote of Wollstonecraft, 'her [childhood] studies were desultory and her attainments casual, pursued with little method'.[100] A brief stint in a Yorkshire dayschool between the ages of ten and fourteen, when the family was living in Beverley, seems to have left her with little more than the rudiments of reading and writing. A letter sent to her friend Jane Arden when she was fourteen was so 'ill written' that she feared its final page was unintelligible. '[Y]ou know, my dear,' she complained to Jane wistfully, 'I have not the advantage of a Master as you have, and it is with great difficulty to get my brother to mend my pens [sic]...'[101] But a friendship with a clerical neighbour, John Clare, who supplied books and scholarly conversation, gave an important fillip to her intellectual development, and she soon became a voracious reader. Like most autodidacts, she approached this reading in a spirit of dedicated self-improvement, allowing herself no books (she later told Fuseli) 'for mere amusement, not even poetry' but only 'those works... which are addressed to the understanding'.[102] Her association with the Rational Dissenters while she was schoolteaching in Stoke Newington further fuelled this intellectual appetite, for which the Kingsboroughs' library in Ireland then proved an excellent resource. But it was her work on the *Analytical Review* from 1788 on which gave Wollstonecraft continuous access to the world of letters, so that by the time she wrote the *Rights of Woman* she was well-read in English theology, moral philosophy and *belles lettres* and had familiarised herself with the major continental philosophes, particularly Rousseau.[103] Meanwhile her letters recorded her struggles to acquire foreign languages: first French, essential for her teaching and translating as well as the broadening of her philosophical education, and then

German and Italian.[104] 'I really want a German grammar, as I intend to learn that language' she wrote to Johnson at the end of 1789, 'and I will tell you the reason why –'

While I live, I am persuaded, I must exert my understanding to procure an independence, and render myself useful. To make the task easier, I ought to store my mind with knowledge – The seed-time is passing away. I see the necessity of labouring now – and of that necessity I do not complain; on the contrary, I am thankful that I have more than common incentives to pursue knowledge, and draw my pleasures from the employments that are within my reach.[105]

The tone of high-minded resolve was characteristic of middle-class literary women, most of whom had received very little, or very inadequate, formal schooling. Eighteenth-century Britain educated its girl children very badly. Private schools catering to middle-class girls had proliferated after 1750, but these were usually devoted to grooming girlish manners for a fiercely competitive marriage market rather than promoting academic achievement. 'The cultivation of the understanding [in such schools] is always subordinate to the acquirement of some corporeal accomplishment,' Wollstonecraft (and a chorus of other critics) complained, with 'accomplishment' referring to such ornamental social graces as dancing, singing, French conversation, a little piano-playing.[106] Girls whose families could not or would not pay for such embellishments were taught at home, generally by mothers or sisters or, if they were from more affluent backgrounds, by governesses. Some few were tutored by sympathetic, well-educated fathers, but these were never more than a fortunate minority.

No institutions of higher education admitted women, although sometimes the liberal-minded Dissenting Academies allowed them to attend lectures on an informal basis. Mary Hays, who grew up with her widowed mother in Southwark, attended classes at the Dissenting Academy in Hackney in the 1780s. Even so, Hays retained a sense of mental inferiority that no amount of literary success could overcome. A highly praised pamphlet on public worship, published by her in 1792, opened with an apology that 'a woman, young, unlearned, unacquainted with any language but her own' should have presumed to author such a text; four years later she confided to her close friend and mentor, William Godwin, how after meetings with him she would often find herself miserably blushing

from the recollection of the many follies and weaknesses I have betrayed; among which, feminine foibles make no inconsiderable share: I mean, by feminine foibles, those errors which result from the present absurd systems of female education. There is a tenacity in some parts of my character, a proneness to habit, which makes reformation of my mistakes at a great distance from their direction: this perhaps, proceeds from the small number of my impressions, their consequent force and distinctness.[107]

Enlightened opinion in the late eighteenth century was unanimous about the need to remedy this debilitating situation. In the march of intellectual progress, women must not be left by the wayside, immured in ignorance and folly. 'That learning belongs not to the female character, and that the female mind is not capable of a degree of improvement equal to that of the other sex, are narrow and unphilosophical prejudices,' the educational re-former Vicesimus Knox typically declared in 1779.[108] Deciding what types of learning *did* belong to the female character, however, was another matter. Nearly all reformers remained convinced of women's lesser capacity for abstract thought, and insistent that they must avoid 'a pedantic manner of conversation'.[109] The most advanced female curriculum proposed by pedagogic theorists included history, literature, geography, languages (particularly French and Italian) and some 'superficial knowledge' of natural philosophy and mathematics, but seldom anything smacking of real erudition.[110] Some moralists were prepared to countenance the study of specific philosophers, notably Locke; but since a woman studied, as the Evangelical bluestocking Hannah More put it, 'not that she may qualify herself to become an orator or a pleader; nor that she may learn to debate, but to act', she was not to be encouraged in any studies which might lead her to 'despise the duties of ordinary life' in favour of the 'pretensions of literary vanity'.[111] The world, as More warned at the end of the century (in a text explicitly directed against Wollstonecraft's feminism) had already known too many '*precieuses ridicules*' who behaved as if their superior learning exempted them from the 'sober cares' and 'humble offices' which were women's proper province.[112]

Women should be better educated, then, not to elevate them above Female Duty but to better equip them for it. 'A woman of improved understanding and real sense is more likely to submit to her condition... and to take an active part in household management,' Vicesimus Knox explained.[113] This limited, instrumentalist case for improved provision was the most popular of the period;[114] yet alongside it ran a more expansive view of female intellectual attainments. Conservative moralists may have fulminated against learned women, but across educated society as a whole attitudes were more open and flexible. For every voice railing against the evils of feminine pedantry, another could be heard extolling female genius, particularly literary genius. Patriotic celebrations of national literary talent – a genre increasingly common after the mid century – proudly compared the achievements of British 'female muses' to the lesser feats of women of other nations, especially France. 'There never was perhaps an age wherein the fair sex made so conspicuous a figure with regard to literary accomplishments as in our own,' one enthusiast crowed in 1762, adding however with a touch of satirical unease that '[l]earning is now grown so fashionable amongst the ladies, that it becomes every gentleman to carry his Latin and Greek with him whenever he ventures into female company.'[115]

As the century advanced, and the flow of women into print accelerated ever more rapidly, this anxious note intensified. Finding their dominant position in the literary marketplace threatened, men of letters began to sound the alarm.[116] Moralists thundered against the de-sexing tendencies of the times, and issued jeremiads against the baneful effects on women of mental exertions, with particular warnings about that 'neglect of dress and of accurate cleanliness' to which learned ladies were famously inclined. Attitudes seesawed back and forth, expressing themselves in set-piece oppositions: the literary lady versus the female pedant, the sentimental authoresses versus the 'stern' philosophess, the modest muse of 'sweet and gentle voice' versus the Amazonian harridan who 'contests pertinaciously, and instead of yielding, challenges submission'. 'How forbidding an object!' James Fordyce exclaimed of such literary viragos: 'Feminality is gone: Nature is transformed... [into] a clamorous, obstinate, contentious being... fit only to be chased from haunts of society'.[117]

Caught up in this anxious wrangling, most women writers rushed to defend their feminine credentials. A futile quest for an unambiguously female position from which to wield their pens led even well-known authors to publicly condemn learned women. 'The danger of pedantry and presumption in a woman – of... exchanging the graces of imagination for the severity and preciseness of a scholar, would' Hester Chapone owned, 'be... sufficient to frighten me from the ambition of seeing my girl remarkable for learning.'[118] Likewise Anna Barbauld who, asked to assist in the creation of a college for women in 1774, denounced all such initiatives as inherently wrongheaded: 'young ladies... ought only to have such a general tincture of knowledge as to make them agreeable companions to a man of sense'.[119] Other women chorused their agreement or, if they held more advanced views, hastened to qualify them by advising female readers to avoid abstract philosophy and similarly abstruse subjects. All would have agreed with the writer who in 1787 insisted that it was wholly wrong for any 'employment of the mind' to be regarded by a women as 'sufficient excuse for neglecting domestic duties', although she went on to add that in her opinion a woman could acquire enough learning to 'fit herself to be the companion and friend of a man of sense, and yet know how to take care of his family'.[120] The authoritative voice was that of the young Wollstonecraft, offering the world her *Thoughts on the Education of Daughters*.

As Wollstonecraft's own intellectual *persona* mutated from lady-author to feminist philosophe, the issue of female erudition posed itself to her differently. Women's 'neglected education' is the 'grand source' of their oppression, the *Rights of Woman* claimed, and equal instruction the *sina qua non* of female emancipation.[121] The standard instrumentalist case for educated home-makers was here joined by a much more radical defence of women's intellectual entitlements 'regardless of the distinction of sex'. The instrumentalist argument remained the most fully articulated. Women 'will not fulfil family duties,' Wollstonecraft reminded her readers, in classic conductbook mode, 'unless their minds take a wider range.'[122] Ignorant women mistreat their babies, alienate their servants, ruin family finances. Only well-instructed women make good wives and mothers.[123] The most effective way of providing such instruction, the *Rights of Woman* proposed, would be a national network of state-sponsored, co-educational dayschools, where boys and girls of all backgrounds would be educated identically to the age of nine, at which point children destined for 'domestic employments or mechanical trades' would be siphoned off into training institutions, while those 'of superior abilities, or fortune' would continue an academic education. 'Girls and boys still together? I hear some readers ask: yes...[for] these would be schools of morality', Wollstonecraft wrote soothingly, where 'happiness...[would] flow from the pure springs of duty and affection' and where girls in particular would benefit from 'that mental activity so necessary in the maternal character'.[124] All society would gain from such elevation of the female mind, just as all society now suffered from the effects of maternal ignorance and mismanagement.

Framed thus, the arguments were sufficiently in tune with advanced opinion to meet with general approbation. But accompanying them was a second message: '[L]et the practice of every duty be subordinate to the grand one of improving our minds,' Wollstonecraft tells her female readers, for if women, like men, are rational beings with immortal souls then their education must be a 'first step [toward forming] a being advancing gradually towards perfection', rather than merely 'a preparation for life'.[125] Why should women's mental reach be artificially curtailed, when their capacities are naturally equal to those of men? And, even more daringly, why should women's minds be given over to domestic affairs when higher intellectual concerns beckon? The idea surfaces repeatedly in the *Rights of Woman*, only to be undermined by Wollstonecraft's insistence that it pertains only to an outstanding minority, who are not her political concern: 'treating of education, minds of a superior class... are not to considered; they can be left to chance...'[126] In a book devoted to the advancement of Every-woman, women of 'rare abilities' can be left to fend for themselves. One of the leading genres of eighteenth-century pro-woman writings was the collective biography of celebrated *savantes*, but Wollstonecraft had no use for these:

I shall not lay any great stress on the example of a few women who, from having received a masculine education, have acquired courage and resolution... Sappho, Eloisa, Mrs Macaulay, the Empress of Russia, Mme d'Eon etc. These, and many more, may be reckoned exceptions; and, are not all heroes, as well as heroines, exceptions to general rules? I wish to see women neither heroines nor brutes; but reasonable creatures.[127]

Panegyrics to great women were a stock feature of eighteenth-century gal-lantry, so it is unsurprising to find Wollstonecraft dismissing such eulogies out of hand. Nonetheless the offhanded brevity of her list is disconcerting, particularly with only one Englishwoman, Catharine Macaulay (1731–91) – 'the woman of the greatest abilities, undoubtedly, that this country has ever produced'[128] – appearing in it. The lonely glow with which Wollstonecraft surrounds Macaulay, amid the satirical rubble to which she reduces female authorship in general, is very striking. Yet as the leading radical woman writer of the previous generation, Macaulay was clearly an apposite role model. The first Englishwoman to author a major historical work – her eight-volume *History of England* – in the 1760s and seventies Macaulay had published a series of political pamphlets that had brought her to the forefront of the government's radical-Whig opposition. Moving between radical circles in France (where she befriended Turgot and Brissot), America (where her *History* was required reading for revolutionaries, and she advised George Washington on the drafting of the new Republic's constitution[129]), and Britain (where she lent her support to John Wilkes' electoral cam-paign), by the 1780s Macaulay was an international celebrity. In 1790 she published her sole feminist work, *Letters on Education*; but by then she was very ill, although still managing to rejoice in the French Revolution.[130] Burke's *Reflections* roused her to a final effort and she published a rebuttal, six months before her death, that Burke himself judged the best from a radical pen. '[T]he Amazon', he wrote (he also dubbed her 'our republican Virago') was the 'greatest champion' of the reform set.[131]

Macaulay's death in 1791, shortly after Wollstonecraft presented her with a copy of her own reply to Burke, terminated what could have been an important intellectual alliance. In November 1790 Wollstonecraft had written a laudatory review of Macaulay's *Letters on Education* in which she drew particular attention to Macaulay's feminist arguments, which 'might have been carried much farther' had the work not been primarily an educational treatise.[132] The following month she sent Macaulay *A Vindication of the Rights of Men* accompanied by a short note: 'You are the only female writer who I coincide in opinion with respecting the rank our sex ought to endeavour to attain in the world'.[133] Macaulay replied with equal warmth, conveying her pleasure that a

publication which I have so greatly admired from its pathos & sentiment should have been written by a woman and thus to see my opinion of the powers and talents of the sex in your pen so early verified

– and expressing her hope that the two woman might soon meet.[134] Time passed until Wollstonecraft, planning a second, feminist, *Vindication*, thought with pleasure of how Macaulay would approve the project – only to discover 'with the sickly qualm of disappointed hope' that her mentor was gone, 'suffered to die without sufficient respect being paid to her memory'.[135] In fact at the time of her death Macaulay was still highly regarded by her fellow radicals, although her reputation had taken a battering in conventional circles. A marriage to a man twenty-six years her junior, combined with her republican propagandising, prompted charges that she was 'encroach[ing] on the province of man'.[136] She was a woman of 'Masculine opinions and masculine manners' it was said: a not entirely unfriendly description, however, at least when applied to a woman's intellect. Macaulay took the accusation very coolly: '[W]hen we compliment the appearance of a more than ordinary energy in the female mind, we call it masculine', she pointed out.[137] Macaulay was a 'masculine and fervid writer', Wollstonecraft wrote in the *Analytical Review* in 1790, with powers equal to the 'argumentative talents of ancient philosophers': soon Wollstonecraft herself was being eulogised in almost identical terms.[138] 'She is a Lady of masculine masterly understanding', John Adams, the future American president, declared on reading Wollstonecraft's history of the French Revolution.[139] Manliness was intrinsic to the serious mind, it seemed, whatever the sex of its possessor.

Of all manly intellectual pursuits, political controversy was the most virile, demanding a rhetorical mode that was – as the *Monthly Review* described Macaulay's *History* – 'so correct, bold, and nervous, that we can discover no traces of a female pen...'[140] Here too was a further source of Macaulay's importance to Wollstonecraft as the younger woman – launching herself into the French revolution controversy and striving for an authoritative political voice – allowed the clear, if at times uneasy, feminine intonation of her pre-1790 works to give way to what the *English Review* praised as the 'bold and pointed' style of *A Vindication of the Rights of Men*, 'free from all female *prettinesses*'.[141] Writing anonymously in defence of French revolutionary principles, Wollstonecraft adopted the stance of a tough-talking ciceronian philosopher:[142] 'I contend for the "rights of men" and the liberty of reason,' she wrote magisterially, 'You see I do not condescend to cull my words to avoid the invidious phrase, nor shall I be prevented from giving a manly definition of it....'[143] Taking up cudgels against Edmund Burke's sentimental defence of the ancien regime, Wollstonecraft offered in its stead the plainspeak of one who, inspired by 'a manly spirit of independence', placed herself at the service of universal truth and natural justice: a truly virile stance.[144]

The publication of the *Rights of Men* took Wollstonecraft well beyond the limits of female literary decorum. Philosophy of the most undecorous, heterodox kind was now definitively her *metier*. France had shown the world what enlightenment could achieve, and it was now incumbent on every right-minded person to further the 'glorious principles' on which revolutionary government was founded. In his *Reflections*, Burke attacked the 'literary caballers and intriguing philosophers' whose theories were wreaking havoc on French society, and threatening to do the same to Britain. 'Nothing in heaven or upon earth can serve as a control' upon these 'metaphysicians', he warned, for 'finding their schemes of politics not adapted to the state of the world in which they live' such men and women 'come to think lightly of all public principle' and end up advocating 'the wildest democratic ideas of freedom'.[145] Now Wollstonecraft took it upon herself to defend these visionary ideals, and in so doing abandoned the last vestiges of feminine conformism. She also – a move that took a little longer – defied restrictions on female expression, drawing on radical philosophy as a universal language of human aspiration. Having previously praised Catharine Macaulay's philosophical mind as masculine, in the *Rights of Woman* she deliberately amended this description:

Catharine Macaulay was an example of intellectual acquirements supposed to be incompatible with the weakness of her sex. In her style of writing, indeed, no sex appears, for it is like the sense it conveys, strong and clear.

I will not call hers a masculine understanding, because I admit not of such an arrogant assumption of reason; but I contend that it was a sound one, and that her judgement ... was a proof that a woman can acquire judgement, in the full extent of the word.[146]

Philosophy was not inherently virile, nor did its female practitioners desex themselves every time they raised their pens. Strength and clarity of thought were not exclusively masculine attributes, and if the exercise of intellectual authority was unusual in a woman, her sex by no means precluded it. These were hardly new insights: Mary Astell, for example, had made the same points very forcibly almost a century earlier. But for a woman writer of the 1790s to affirm this egalitarian perspective, given the intensifying anxieties surrounding female intellectualism, demanded a high level of gender awareness and a deliberate defiance of hardening feminine conventions. Intellectual self-assertion, in other words, had become a dissident female posture: a fact that became very evident in 1792, with the writing and publication of *A Vindication of the Rights of Woman*.

* * *

Modern interpreters of the *Rights of Woman* often remark on its organisational incoherence, how its arguments appear to shunt along associative tracks that begin and end at random, or connect only through first-person interjections: 'I carry this sentiment still further...', '[t]o return from this apparent digression...', '[t]his train of reasoning brings me back to a subject...', and so on.[147] The tone is urgent and exhortatory rather than leisured; yet to a modern academic mind it all seems wonderfully unsystematic. There are some generous commentators who interpret this disorderliness in a positive light, as a sign of creative restlessness or even as a feminist protest against a phallocentric linguistic order. But in fact the messiness was mostly due to the very tight production schedule Wollstonecraft had arranged with Johnson's printer, which left her frantically scribbling with the 'Devil' (the printer's assistant) at her elbow, 'coming for the conclusion of a sheet before it is written'.[148] The result, as she wrote grumpily to her friend William Roscoe, was 'a blur' that galled and dispirited her, since systematic philosophic analysis had been her guiding aim.[149] The ambition is spelled out early on. If 'the power of generalising ideas, of drawing comprehensive conclusions from individual observations' is, as Wollstonecraft insists, 'the only acquirement, for an immortal being, that really deserves the name of knowledge', then readers are to be given a thorough-going display of such inductive rigour.[150] 'In the present state of society,' chapter 1 announces, 'it appears necessary to go back to first principles in search of the most simple truths, and to dispute with some prevailing prejudice every inch of ground'.[151] 'Plain questions' must be asked to which answers 'as unequivocal as... axioms' will be given, until the 'rights and duties of women' are so clearly demonstrated that all rational minds must acknowledge them.[152]

Indeed, so self-evident are these arguments that 'it seems almost impertinent' to elaborate them further, but in the present atmosphere of 'deeply
rooted prejudices' and 'intellectual cowardice' a true philosopher has no
choice but to lead her readers down the path of absolute right lest 'the
strong hold of prescription will never be forced by reason' and 'truth is lost
in a mist of words'.[153]

The mood in which Wollstonecraft undertook this enterprise was not,
she stressed, self-interested partisanship but rather the 'disinterested spirit'
of the truthseeker: 'I plead for my sex – not for myself.'[154] This did not
imply – nor would any eighteenth-century reader expect – a dispassionate
attitude. To 'reason deeply, when we forcibly feel', as she later wrote, was a
posture typical of the truly enlightened philosopher who, eschewing equally
the nitpicking pedantry of scholastics and the 'effete' persuasive arts of the
Burkean rhetorician, dedicates herself to truth in action.[155] Turning from
formal logic and courtly address to the heaven-sent powers of experience and
reflection,[156] the *Rights of Woman* (in a strikingly wordy passage), declares
itself concerned with 'things, not words!'

This is a rough sketch of my plan; and should I express my conviction with the
energetic emotions that I feel whenever I think of the subject, the dictates of
experience and reflection will be felt by some of my readers. Animated by this
important object, I shall disdain to cull my phrases or polish my style; – I aim at
being useful, and sincerity will render me unaffected; for, wishing rather to persuade
by the force of my arguments, than dazzle by the elegance of my language, I shall
not waste my time in rounding periods, or in fabricating the turgid bombast of
artificial feelings, which, coming from the head, never reach the heart. – I shall be
employed about things, not words![157]

As a statement of feminist authorial intent, Wollstonecraft's insistence
here on convincing by the 'force of my arguments' rather than seducing with
literary charm clearly set her at odds with all those who consigned women
writers to the realm of sentiment and 'flowery diction' while denying them
access to reasoned disputation. '[I]t requires great resolution to try rather
to be useful than to please' she wrote to Mary Hays in May 1792, and this
was particularly true for a female polemicist whose political purpose would
be undermined by the sweet-talking stratagems identified with feminine
writing.[158] Yet the *Rights of Woman* is often as florid as the 'sickly' writings
it condemns – and as emotive in its readerly address. A romantic eloquence
that is explicitly repudiated becomes Wollstonecraft's implicit rhetorical
strategy.

This purple tinge to Wollstonecraft's writing has troubled some of her
interpreters who, classifying it as linguistically feminine, emphasise the

contrast it presents to her 'masculinist' reverence for philosophical reason.[159] In fact the model (and target) for Wollstonecraft's more luxuriant prose was as much Burke as any female sentimental novelist; nor would she have accepted the distinction between philosophical discourse and authentic linguistic passion.[160] Throughout the *Rights of Woman* Wollstonecraft repeatedly insists that reason and feeling – that is, true feeling, as opposed to the 'bombast' of false sentiment – are always allied. Effective knowledge can never be achieved by cutting oneself off from emotional investments. Wisdom is not born from Olympian contemplation.

> The world cannot be seen by an unmoved spectator; we must mix in the throng, and feel as men feel, before we can judge of their feelings. If we mean, in short, to live in the world to grow wiser and better, and not merely to enjoy the good things of life, we must attain a knowledge of others at the same time that we become acquainted with ourselves – knowledge acquired any other way only hardens the heart and perplexes the understanding.
> I may be told, that the knowledge thus acquired, is sometimes purchased at too dear a rate. I can only answer that I very much doubt whether any knowledge can be attained without labour and sorrow...[161]

Here we see the division between thought and emotion not merely bridged but deliberately repudiated, in favour of what Wollstonecraft elsewhere described as the 'practical wisdom' acquired through sympathetic social intercourse. It would be tempting to describe this as a feminine philosophical posture, given its emphasis on the affective and experiential. But in fact what makes this philosophical programme so compelling is its simultaneous defiance of psychological and gender boundaries. Both the Parnassian masculine reasoner and the parochial feminine emotionalist here give way to the image of a mind engaged by the life it contemplates, seeking its meaning and destiny in identification with others. As Wollstonecraft said of Catharine Macaulay, she was a woman who wrote not only with 'sober energy and argumentative closeness' but also with that 'sympathy and benevolence' which give 'vital heat' to arguments.[162] A true philosopher's thoughts and words spark with a humane vitality that can never be acquired by reflection alone, but only by passionate embroilment in the drama of life.

As in the speeches and writings of other 1790s radicals, this was philosophy charged with radical purpose. Philosophers, Marx would pronounce a half-century later, had confined themselves to interpreting the world when the point was to change it. But for the radical *literati* of Wollstonecraft's day, interpretation and transformation were coterminous: the light of truth, as it radiated across the minds and hearts of humanity, was the great agent

of social revolution. It was the 'mental revolution' wrought by enlightened
ideas which was responsible for the demise of French tyranny, Tom Paine
explained in his *Rights of Man*: 'The mind of the nation had changed ... and
the new order of things has naturally followed the new order of thoughts.'[163]
A 'new spirit' had entered the world 'to organise the body politic', Wollstonecraft declared in her *History of the French Revolution*: 'Reason has, at
last, shown her captivating face ... and it will be impossible for the dark
hand of despotism again to obscure it's [sic] radiance ...'[164]

Today, in the wake of *marxisant* and counter-*marxisant* interpretations
of political change, this elevation of mind into the chief progenitor of revolution may appear naively intellectualist. At the time, however, it was a
perspective shared by virtually all political thinkers, radical and conservative. Burke's savage indictment of the 'philosophical politicians' of British
radicalism was mirrored by the radicals' own congratulatory self-image
as those 'few puissant and heavenly endowed spirits who are capable of
guiding, enlightening, and leading the human race ownward to felicity.'[165]
Enlightenment was a political path on which English 'jacobins', as Wollstonecraft and her radical associates became known, took up a vanguard
position. 'It was my first determination to tell all that I apprehended to be
truth,' Godwin wrote of his 1791 plan for the book which became *Political
Justice*, 'which by its inherent energy and weight, should overbear and annihilate all opposition and place the principles of politics on an immoveable
basis'.[166] Later he would reject such dreams as grandiose; but in the early
years of the Revolution there were few who did not share this vision, for
better or for worse.

The intellectual hubris responsible for the *Rights of Woman* drew breath
from this heady atmosphere. Reviewing Wollstonecraft's *A Vindication of
the Rights of Men* in 1791, one critic sneered that he had always been 'taught
to suppose that the rights of women were the proper theme of the female
sex'.[167] Now revolution emboldened Wollstonecraft to embrace this theme:
to bring philosophy to women's aid and thus become an 'assertrix of female
rights', a 'Gallic philosophess' as opponents dubbed her.[168] The figure of
the French *philosophe* had long been associated with irreligion, moral latitu-
dinarianism and sexual libertinage as well as political reformism. Now the
importation of these associations into British politics turned 'philosophy'
into a term of opprobrium. Yet, despite the growing censure, Wollstonecraft
emphatically endorsed this politicisation of intellect. Minds that were not
engaged with the 'general interests of the human race' were not properly
employed, she insisted. It was not abstract speculation but an 'affection for
the whole human race' that made her pen 'dart rapidly along' in support

of women's rights, she wrote at the beginning of the *Rights of Woman*.[169] What the true philosopher sought was not enlightenment for its own sake, but an intellectual torch that would lead humanity, *all* of humanity, from the darkness of servitude into freedom's dawn: a light of truth that would liberate the world by interpreting it.

* * *

'Feminism', I noted in the Introduction, is in some respects a problematic label to attach to Wollstonecraft's writings on women, since it appears to assimilate her ideas to a political tradition that did not acquire self-conscious existence until the international suffrage battles of the late nineteenth / early twentieth century. It was the architects of this tradition, we have seen, who made Wollstonecraft's *magnum opus* into western feminism's inaugural text. I have argued that the *Rights of Woman* was not a foundational work in this sense. Yet it undoubtedly marked a new stage in feminist advocacy, partly due to its radicalisation of women's claims, but also because of its symbolic stature. A book forged from a miscellany of overlapping 'philosophical' genres — educational reform literature; essays on manners; sermons; political and legal works; ethical treatises; histories of civilisation; gender polemic of an older '*querelle des femmes*' variety — was transformed by its times into a revolutionary manifesto. Pushed onto the stage of popular politics, Enlightenment prescriptions for improvements in women's status became translated into a women's-rights egalitarianism much more far-reaching than its antecedents. Subsequent generations of feminists then added further layers of interpretation to the text, resulting in a work that offers serious challenges to interpreters.

Thus even the apparently straightforward question — what is the goal of the *Rights of Woman*? — poses difficulties. The book names itself a vindication of rights, and subsequent rights-based feminist struggles make it tempting to read it in this light. Many recent commentators locate it within the natural-rights tradition. Yet after an opening salvo against the French government's exclusion of women from political citizenship, Wollstonecraft appears almost to lose interest in the question of rights, dwelling much more on women's duties than their entitlements. A promised second volume, dealing with women's legal status, never materialised. *The Wrongs of Woman, or Maria*, incomplete at Wollstonecraft's death, may have been intended to serve as this second volume, since it has a great deal to say about the legal disabilities of women, particularly those of wives. But, as in the *Rights of Woman*, Wollstonecraft's principal concern in *Maria* is less with the institutions that oppress women than with the experience of *being* female, with the emotional violence and intellectual debilitation on which feminine subjectivity is founded. To be 'born a woman' is to be 'born to suffer', the fictive Maria warns her infant daughter, and it is the saturation of female selfhood by this suffering, its permeation of every fibre of women's being, that preoccupies Wollstonecraft here and in her antecedent writings, including the *Rights of Woman*.[170]

The 'Author's Introduction' to the *Rights of Woman* describes the book as a 'treatise... on female rights and manners', and if the rights argument remains undeveloped, the question of female manners – their origins, character, consequences, and desperate need of reformation – is exhaustively explored.[171] Criticism of female manners was so prolific in the second half of the eighteenth century as to form an entire sub-genre of prescriptive literature. Wollstonecraft's treatment of the theme was both in tune with contemporary attitudes and sharply at odds with them. The point of disagreement, indicated at the outset, is plainly stated:

despising that weak elegancy of mind, ... and sweet docility of manners, supposed to be the sexual characteristics of the weaker vessel, I wish to shew that elegance is inferior to virtue, [and] that the first object of laudable ambition is to obtain a character as a human being, regardless of the distinction of sex...[172]

From here on, Wollstonecraft's book becomes an intricate exploration of the 'distinction of sex' and its ramifications for women's personal and social existence. 'I shall first consider women in the grand light of human creatures who, in common with men, are placed on this earth to unfold their faculties,' she declares, and only 'afterwards I shall more particularly point out their peculiar designation.'[173] But in fact it is what is 'peculiar' about women – the peculiar debasements and miseries that constitute modern Woman – which is the leitmotif of her entire feminist *oeuvre*. In a male-ruled society, Wollstonecraft insists, the difference between the sexes is largely 'factitious', an 'artificial distinction' imposed by education, social practices and cultural expectations. How can this fiction of difference be eliminated, or at least reworked in women's favour?

Wollstonecraft was not exclusively concerned with the minds and manners of individual women. The collective fate of her sex concerned her too, particularly as she became caught up in the tidal wave of political revolution. Part II turns to her vision of political change and its implications for women. But the heart of Wollstonecraft's feminism was not a campaigning agenda for improvements in women's status, but a complex critique of the impact of power relations on the feminine psyche. Born female, Maria 'feel[s] acutely the various ills my sex are fated to bear', evils which degrade [women] so far below their oppressors, as almost to justify their tyranny; leading at the same time superficial reasoners to term that weakness the cause, which is only the consequence of short-sighted despotism.[174]

Created men's peers, women are made their subalterns, and no real fellowship or love between the two sexes is possible until both have been restored to natural equality. It is to this goal, the replacement of artificial Woman with the human creature of God's creation, that the *Rights of Woman* principally devotes itself, rather than to the political rights named in its title.

As an exploration of the influence of power and oppression on the personality, the *Rights of Woman* was in good company. Enlightenment intellectuals were much preoccupied with the dynamics of human hierarchy. The perpetuation of entrenched inequalities through manners and 'education' (a concept much broader than at present, closer to our notion of 'socialisation') was a key issue for progressive opinion-makers, many of whom moreover shared Wollstonecraft's view of gender attributes as cultural artefacts, 'proper...social inventions' in Rousseau's words.[175] This sceptical approach to sexual differences fed into the wider project, so fundamental to Enlightenment, of replacing the idea of an innate, immutable human nature by one open to change and improvement: a project whose implications for women were most fully elaborated in the *Rights of Woman*, but adumbrated less systematically by many other philosophes both before and during Wollstonecraft's lifetime. The conclusions drawn – most notoriously in the case of Rousseau – were often far from feminist, but the intellectual terrain was one littered with feminist possibilities. As the leading critic of femininity, Wollstonecraft's arguments found their natural starting point then in the gender philosophies of her avant-garde predecessors and contemporaries, particularly, as we shall now see, in those of her two favourite male adversaries, Edmund Burke and Jean-Jacques Rousseau.

2

The chimera of womanhood

Wollstonecraft is usually depicted as an uncompromising rationalist, a stern advocate of Reason's rule over human affairs. '[T]he perfection of our nature and capability of happiness must be estimated by the degree of reason, virtue, and knowledge, that distinguish the individual, and direct the laws which bind society,' the *Rights of Woman* characteristically pronounced.[1] The tone is stringent, but the cerebralism is deceptive. What Wollstonecraft meant by reason is frequently misunderstood by modern critics, partly because they tend to view it through an overlay of nineteenth-century positivism; but also because, unlike the gradgrindian rationality that succeeded it, the Enlightened mind was constituted as much by feeling and fantasy as it was by the liberating powers of analytic cerebration. Concepts of subjectivity, as they developed over the course of the eighteenth century, increasingly focused on an ideal of personal authenticity founded on strong emotions and a lively imagination. Well before the Romantic poets began celebrating the energies of the fantasising psyche, a psychology of the inner life had evolved centring on the imagination as a fount of true selfhood. 'Believe me, sage sir,' Wollstonecraft wrote to her lover, Gilbert Imlay, in 1794, 'you have not sufficient respect for the imagination':

I could prove to you in a trice that it is the mother of sentiment, the great distinction of our nature, the only purifier of the passions – animals have a portion of reason, and equal, if not more exquisite, senses; but no trace of imagination, or her offspring taste, appears in any of their actions. The impulse of the senses, passions, if you will, and the conclusions of reason draw men together; but the imagination is the true fire, stolen from heaven to animate this cold creature of clay, producing all those fine sympathies that lead to rapture, rendering men social by expanding their hearts . . .[2]

This reverence for the imaginative faculty was relatively new to western thought.[3] From Aristotle on, European philosophy had regarded the imagination as one of the lower functions of mind: a messenger between sensation and reason, as Francis Bacon described it, capable only of translating sensible impressions received from the external world into mental images which were then delivered over to the jurisdiction of the mind's higher faculties of understanding and judgement. To the extent that the imagination went beyond this merely reproductive remit – for example, by chopping and combining impressions so as to form images of non-existent entities – it became a dangerous and delusory power, requiring the firm hand of reason to restrain it. Poets might celebrate the fantastic creations that imagination could generate, but such 'forms of things unknown'[4] were to be allowed free play only within explicitly fictive settings, and had no wider epistemological validity.

Yet by the second half of the eighteenth century the imagination had achieved an exalted position in the human mind. 'Perhaps there is nothing,' the bluestocking scholar Elizabeth Carter reflected in 1765,

which so indisputably distinguishes the human race from other animals as that power, which not confined by the appearances that offer themselves to the senses, nor by the deductions of the understanding, ranges through all the regions of possible existence:... which sometimes gives to external objects a brighter colouring of joy, and a softer shade of melancholy, and by an inexplicable union connects them with the affections of the heart: at others, magnifies and varies them till they become too vast and too complex for the grasp of the mind, which then most sensibly feels the natural greatness of its aims, and the limits of its present capacity.[5]

Regarded in this elevated light, the imagination became, in Ernest Tuveson's elegant formulation, 'a means of grace'.[6] As in previous centuries, the imagination was understood to receive from Nature those sensate impressions (particularly visual impressions) through which God's handiwork was perceived. But now its role was not merely to reproduce these impressions, but to transform them through processes of creative ideation which were seen as the essence of aesthetic genius. 'The fancy,' Hume explained, 'runs from one end of the universe to the other in collecting those ideas, which belong to any subject', which are 'thus collected by a kind of magical faculty of the soul' which is 'perfect in the greatest geniuses' but 'inexplicable by the utmost efforts of human understanding.'[7] When the mind is 'once enlarged by excursive flights, or profound reflection, the raw materials... arrange themselves,' Wollstonecraft later wrote.[8] It is those possessing such expanded faculties who are best able, through poetry or music or painting, to arouse the imaginations of less gifted people, so that they may share in the divine gift of aesthetic experience, and thus also be brought closer to God.

The routes by which theorists came to this new appreciation of the imagination varied, but behind them all lay the seventeenth-century revolution in epistemology. The displacement of the classical concept of Right Reason – the intellectual attunement of the human mind to eternal Truth – by the empiricist view of reason as the capacity to formulate judgements on the basis of sensory data, gave new significance to subjective consciousness. If all that can be known of the world, as Locke argued, are our impressions of it, then the experiencing self is the only repository of truth. This did not imply a solipsistic denial of external reality: internal perceptions, Locke believed, reveal by their reliability and predictability a correspondence to the natural order of things.[9] But the theory certainly encouraged subjectivism. To Joseph Addison for example, writing in *The Spectator* in 1712, Locke's revelation that light and colour are to be found not in the object viewed but in the mind of the viewer indicated that all human perception is fantasmatic. '[L]ost...in a pleasing delusion...we walk about like the enchanted hero of romance, who sees beautiful castles, woods, and meadows, and at the same time hears the warbling of birds, and the purling of streams; but, upon the finishing of some secret spell, the fantastic scene breaks up, and the disconsolate knight finds himself on a barren heath...'[10] As to why we dwell in this world of quixotic illusion, Addison's reply was typical of the age. God 'has given almost everything about us the power of raising an agreeable idea in the imagination; so that it is impossible for us to behold his works with coldness or indifference' and in order that we may be imaginatively drawn toward Him.[11]

The Supreme Author of our being has so formed the soul of man, that nothing but himself can be its last, adequate, and proper happiness. Because, therefore, a great part of our happiness must arise from the contemplation of his Being, that he might give our souls a just relish of such a contemplation, he has made them naturally delight in the apprehension of what is great or unlimited. Our admiration... immediately rises at the consideration of any object that takes up a great deal of room in the fancy, and, by consequence, will approve into the highest pitch of astonishment and devotion, when we contemplate his nature...[12]

The imagination, in other words, was a psychic pathway between humanity and the divine. This sacralised imagination, as Tuveson has shown, was a key player in eighteenth-century psychology. It was also, however, a difficult concept to sustain, requiring the drawing of a firm boundary between transcendent fantasy and other, less edifying varieties of extrarational mental activity such as hallucinations, madness, or masturbatory reveries.[13] The distinctions were in fact unsustainable, but the struggle to maintain them led to a strong re-affirmation of older hostilities toward the fantasising psyche. 'No man will be found in whose mind airy notions do not sometimes tyrannise, and force him to hope or fear beyond the limits of sober probability,' Samuel Johnson cautioned in his *Rasselas*. 'All power of fancy over reason is a degree of insanity.'[14] Even indulgence in daydreams could loosen moral inhibitions and addle the brain, it was warned – not to speak of the hazards of indiscrimate novel-reading. Only minds of genius could handle these mental intoxications; for the rest of humanity, sober reflection was an essential check on imaginative excess. 'The judgement,' as Edmund Burke noted with ambiguous approval, 'is for the greater part employed in throwing stumbling blocks in the way of the imagination, in dissipating the scenes of its enchantment, and in tying us down to the disagreeable yoke of our reason.'[15]

The imagination could escape reason's yoke because it occupied a dimension of mind beyond conscious cerebration. This idea – so profound in its consequences – was implicit in all eighteenth-century psychology, although concepts of the unconscious mind remained rudimentary. In Lockean theory, mental life was seen to consist not only in a brightly lit domain of perception/reflection but also in 'a murky land of ideas dormant in memory' beyond the control of conscious understanding.[16] This dark territory of our inner world, Locke had argued, intermittently erupts into consciousness via 'gangs' of mental associations that disturb thought and behaviour without the controlling intervention of reflection or intention: 'instantaneous associations', in Wollstonecraft's words, governed not by logical intelligence but by 'individual character... and over it how little power can reason obtain.'[17] In Locke's view these unconscious ideas were the root source of all prejudices and superstitions, and so fundamentally malign. And although later thinkers were prepared to argue that it was in this realm of the psyche that humanity's loftiest as well as lowest ideas and impulses originated, the fear of unconscious and hence uncontrolled thought remained a dominant theme.

Over the course of the eighteenth century this anxiety about the waywardness of extra-rational mental activity prompted reinforcement of the boundaries between imagination and fantasy. Fantasy, or fancy as it was more generally known, had long been identified with 'romantick' wish-fulfilling illusions. But whereas in previous centuries the imagination *per se* had been viewed in a similarly negative light, now the sublimities of the creative imagination were increasingly contrasted to the lower-order fictions of the merely fanciful mind – a division that was then, predictably, mapped onto the distinction between the sexes. 'The imagination in women is... more gay and sprightly than in men,' according to William Duff, author of the influential *Essay on Original Genius* (1767), 'but it is usually at the same time...less vigorous and extensive'.[18] The imagination in women was 'sprightly' and 'playful', James Fordyce (one of Wollstonecraft's literary *bêtes noires*) argued in 1776, while earlier in the century Addison had suggested that female fancy was better suited to the creative demands of needlework than to literary exertions.[19] The solemn spiritual aspects of the imagination, nearly all commentators agreed, were beyond women, whose relationship to religion was marked by fanciful 'enthusiasms' and quasi-magical su-perstitions (Wollstonecraft concluded the *Rights of Woman* with a fierce attack on women's passion for fortune-telling, mesmerism, and other im-pious 'delusions'). Women, Duff claimed, lack 'that creative power and energy of imagination, which is exerted in calling into existence things that are not, and in bestowing on shadowy forms all the colours of life and reality'.[20] Genuinely inventive fantasy was a prerogative of the male mind.

Duff's celebration of the generative capacities of the masculine imagi-nation neatly reversed the Renaissance view of the imagination as a faculty for imaging an external reality that existed independently of the perceiving subject.[21] According to this older view it was women, their minds ruled by vapours rising from their wombs, who were liable to delusions and phantasmagoria rather than imaginative apprehension of universal Truth.[22] Trapped in the corporeal, it had been claimed, women could not achieve the transcendence of subjectivity necessary for the imagination to function as a mirror of eternal verities. The displacement of this older imaginary version of Right Reason by the eighteenth-century imagination, source of original inspiration and aesthetic genius, might have had the effect of enhancing the status of feminine fancifulness; in the event, however, it led to a psychic re-mapping where creative Art was elevated to lofty heights far above the trivial exertions of lesser fantasists – notably women writers. The category of the artistic genius, as Christine Battersby has shown, while theoretically as open to the ploughman or the lady novelist as to educated well-to-do men, was almost invariably deemed the prerogative of the latter. Feminine genius, if not quite unthinkable, was seen as exceptional.[23] Rousseau, as so often in these matters, was most direct:

Women, in general...have no genius. They can succeed in little works which require only quick wit, taste, grace, and sometimes even a bit of philosophy and reasoning...But that celestial flame which warms and sets fire to the soul, that genius which consumes and devours...those sublime transports which carry their raptures to the depths of hearts, will always lack in the writings of women; their works are all cold and pretty as they are; they may contain as much wit as you please, never a soul...[24]

Here, as in most eighteenth-century aesthetic theory, the Promethean virility of imaginative genius revealed itself in its attunement to the Sublime – that thrilling domain of the wild and terrible associated with images of phallicised Nature (craggy mountains, surging seas, cascading waterfalls, dizzying heights and so on) and a general sense of overwhelmingness. This was in sharp contrast to the Beautiful (or the merely pretty, as Rousseau would have it) with its soft, shallow associations to the fanciful and the feminine. The distinction was hammered out by writer after writer – most elaborately by Kant, more crudely by Burke and Rousseau, and with greater or lesser subtlety by an army of their admirers. In Burke's influential *Philosophical Enquiry into the Origin of Our Ideas of the Sublime and Beautiful* (1757) the gendering of the categories was clear. Where the sublime is 'great, rugged, and negligent' the beautiful is 'small ... smooth, and polished'; sublimity inspires fear and admiration, while beauty inspires love:

There is a wide difference between admiration and love. The sublime, which is the cause of the former, always dwells on great objects, and terrible; the latter on small ones, and pleasing; we submit to what we admire, but we love what submits to us ...[25]

Beauty thus, Burke insists, inspires affection but seldom respect since it 'carries with it an idea of weakness and imperfection' of which beautiful women in particular are 'very sensible': 'for which reason, they learn to lisp, to totter in their walk, to counterfeit weakness and even sickness' in order to promote a sense of loveable deficiency. This, again, was in stark contrast to the 'vast power' of the sublime. 'Look at a man, or any other animal of prodigious strength, and what is your idea before reflection? Is it that this power will be subservient to you ...? No; the emotion you feel is, lest this enormous strength should be employed to the purposes of rapine and destruction ...' – a thrilling potency which unfortunately does not survive the domestication of the brute.[26] Once put to the plough (or confined to a genteel drawing room) an ox is 'spoil[ed] of every thing sublime, and ... immediately becomes contemptible.'[27]

The sublime imagination rises toward the magnificent and unfathomable, while the beautiful imagination wanders in pastoral landscapes, all domesticated and flowery. Such notions were so popular in the late eighteenth century that it was hard for any aspirant artist or critic to think outside them. Certainly the young Wollstonecraft couldn't, and in 1787 she wrote a tale exploring these themes. This story, 'The Cave of Fancy', which was left unfinished and published by Godwin only after her death, takes place in a sublime island landscape of towering mountains and terrifying

storms inhabited by a hermit named Sagestus who, as the story opens, is
rescuing a little girl from a shipwreck. The child is found weeping by the
corpses of her parents whose faces the sage studies with a careful eye, concluding that her mother was a 'truly feminine' woman (that is, charmingly
delicate, ignorant, and sentimental – a Burkean paragon) while her father
appears a dull but worthy man who 'was most conversant with the beautiful,
and rarely comprehended the sublime'.[28] The tale concludes with the life
history of a female spirit, another dweller in the cave, whose story begins in
beautiful fantasies of romantic love and ends on 'a wild and grand' hillside
at night where her soul 'escaped from this vale of tears': 'My reflections
were tinged with melancholy, but they were sublime,' she tells the rescued
child, 'I grasped a mighty whole...[and] [my] passion seemed a pledge of
immortality...'[29]

This was clearly an apprentice effort, echoing literary conventions, but
even here Wollstonecraft was beginning to display an inclination to re-work
conventional categories in unexpected ways. The female spirit of 'The Cave
of Fancy' is in fact, as we shall see, a proto-feminist whose sublimity points to
a moral stature rarely accorded women. Why should imaginative grandeur
be all on men's side, while women are consigned, like the shipwrecked
mother in the tale, to the pretty and the petty? The question, hovering
over Wollstonecraft's earlier writings, emerged clearly in the early 1790s
as, launching her career as a radical philosopher, she took on two of the
age's leading theorists of the imagination, Burke and Rousseau, in her two
Vindications.

A Vindication of the Rights of Men (1790), Wollstonecraft's rebuttal of
Burke's *Reflections on the Revolution in France* (1790), was one of the earliest shots fired in the pamphlet war that broke out in English political
circles following the French Revolution. Wollstonecraft's text, whose political themes will be discussed in more detail later, sets out a classic radical
defence of the liberal phase of the Revolution. Treating Burke as a representative spokesman for old-regime despotism, Wollstonecraft champions
the reformist initiatives of the new French government against his 'rusty,
baneful opinions', and censures British political elites for their opulence,
corruption, and inhumane treatment of the poor.[30] But the subversive
thrust of the *Rights of Men* derives not just from these overtly political arguments but from its satirical by-play with issues of imagination and gender.
Resurrecting the ideas of Burke's *Philosophical Enquiry*, Wollstonecraft slyly
turns its theses about the imagination and sexual difference against their
author, showing that in his *Reflections* Burke reveals himself to be, in his

own terms, a beautiful writer, with all the connotations of fanciful and denigrated femininity implied by this. The truly virile imagination, she shows, belongs to Burke's opponent (whose identity was not revealed until the second edition).[31]

* * *

As an exposé of political bad faith, the *Rights of Men* is a bracing read, sending a chilly breeze across the rhetorical fripperies of Burke's *Reflections* to reveal the shoddy illiberalities lurking behind them. Yet it is also a rather nasty text, with an unrelentingly *ad hominem* tone. Burke's Catholic background, his Irishness, his parliamentary pension, his unsympathetic attitude toward the madness of King George: all are held up to scorn. But it is Burke's linguistic femininity — that is, his 'wit', meaning his rhetorical eloquence and fanciful sentimentalism — that is the chief target of Wollstonecraft's contempt. In his *Philosophical Enquiry* Burke had identified wit with the imagination, and opposed both to the powers of judgement. 'Judgement is sublime, wit beautiful; and according to your own theory, they cannot exist together without impairing each other's power,' Wollstonecraft reminds him. 'The predominacy of the latter, in your endless Reflections, should lead hasty readers to suspect that it may, in a great degree, exclude the former.'[32] She compares him to a 'celebrated beauty' anxious 'to raise admiration on every occasion' through a display of 'witty arguments and ornamental feelings.' 'Even the Ladies, Sir, may repeat your sprightly sallies, and retail in theatrical attitudes many of your sentimental exclamations' — clearly a sign of intellectual bankruptcy. But then what else is to be expected from a man of such 'pampered sensibility'?

> ...you foster every emotion till the fumes, mounting to your brain, dispel the sober suggestions of reason. It is not in this view surprising, that when you should argue you become impassioned, and that reflection inflames your imagination, instead of enlightening your understanding.[33]

— exactly the accusation she was later to level against her own sex, in the *Rights of Woman*.

Exposing Burke as a sentimental fantasist — a common tactic among his opponents — was a disingenuous move, since fantasy was explicitly assigned a key role in his political vision. *Reflections on the Revolution in France* famously compared the art of politics to chivalry, 'that generous loyalty to sex and rank, that proud submission, that dignified obedience, that subordination of the heart' on which 'the glory of Europe' had once depended, but which was now giving way to the 'barbarous philosophy' of political democracy. 'The age of chivalry is gone, – That of sophisters, oeconomists, and calculators, has succeeded,' Burke mourned, and the result could be seen in the tragic triumph of reason over imagination:

Now all is to be changed. All the pleasing illusions, which made power gentle, and obedience liberal, which...incorporated into politics the sentiments which beautify and soften private society, are to be dissolved by this new conquering empire of light and reason. All the decent drapery of life is to be rudely torn off. All the super-added ideas, furnished from the wardrobe of a moral imagination, which the heart owns, and the understanding ratifies, as necessary to cover the defects of our naked shivering nature, and to raise it to dignity in our own estimation, are to be exploded as a ridiculous, absurd, and antiquated fashion.[34]

Seen in the cold light of democratic reason, in other words, the Emperor did indeed have no clothes – nor did the Empress. In 1789 the Parisian mob had invaded the royal apartments, forcing Marie Antoinette (so Burke claimed) to flee from her bed 'almost naked', stripped not only of her garments but also of the chivalric fantasies which sustained her prestige both as woman and queen. 'Little did I dream that I should have lived to see such disasters fallen upon her in a nation of gallant men, in a nation of men of honour and of cavaliers,' Burke lamented.[35] But cavaliership was dead, and honour for monarchs too – swept away by a regime in which 'a king is but a man; a queen is but a woman; a woman is but an animal; and an animal not of the highest order. All homage paid to the sex in general... is to be regarded as romance and folly.'[36]

Wollstonecraft's response to all this was predictably brisk. What kind of sensibility is it, she wants to know, that can be moved to tears by the downfall of queens 'whilst the distress of many industrious mothers...and the hungry cry of helpless babes' are scorned as vulgar sorrows unworthy of sympathy?[37] Chivalric homage to 'the sex in general' is a poor substitute for concern for actual women; moreover, such phoney veneration, far from honouring women

vitiates them, prevents their endeavouring to obtain solid personal merit; and, in short, makes those beings vain inconsiderate dolls, who ought to be prudent mothers and useful members of society.[38]

Again, it is Burke's predilection for beautiful fantasy over painful reality which is at fault here, since it is only by projecting his own states of mind into others that he is able to respond to them. As a *parvenu* yearning for prestige, Wollstonecraft implies, Burke's imaginative sympathies extend no further than the ranks to which he aspires. 'A *gentleman* of lively imagination must borrow some drapery from fancy before he can love or pity a *man*.

Misery, to reach your heart, I perceive, must have its cap and bells...'[39]
A romantic conservatism which robes servility in sentiment would in effect
transform all citizens into Burkean women – weak, degraded, garbed in false
loyalties and illusory hopes. 'Your politics and morals...' Wollstonecraft
tells him, 'would undermine religion and virtue to set up a spurious, sensual
beauty, that has long debauched your imagination...'[40] The virile alternative to this is to be found among those, like Richard Price, of 'enlightened
understanding' who labour 'to increase human happiness by extirpating
error.'[41]

There is a certain stoniness of political tone here which, as Marilyn Butler
has indicated, was characteristic of all the radical responses to Burke. In
adopting the language of high sentimentalism Burke drove his opponents
into 'an exaggerated posture of rationality' which often sat ill with their
own political passions.[42] But for a woman radical, burdened with the traditional associations between femininity, fantasy and emotionality, such
a stance offered more than just a corrective to conservative sensibilities.
Shouldering Burke with the romantic excesses usually attributed to women
freed Wollstonecraft to take to herself a position of rhetorical masculinity –
stern, stoical, reflective.[43] One difficulty with this move was that it left
untouched the division between feminine fancifulness and masculine rationalism which was to become a major target of her feminism. But a more
immediate problem lay in the conflict between idealised Reason and Wollstonecraft's own political imagination. For if Burke was merely a beautiful
fantasist, revelling in hyperbolic eloquence, what of the dreams of his democratic opponents? Burke had accused Richard Price and the other English
supporters of the Revolution of visionary extremism, of wanting to impose
'metaphysical' principles of popular government, and now Wollstonecraft
took it upon herself to respond to the charge:

I am not, Sir, aware of your sneers, hailing a millennium...nor did my fancy
ever create a heaven on earth, since reason threw off her swaddling clothes. I
perceive, but too forcibly, that happiness, literally speaking, dwells not here; – and
that we wander to and fro in a vale of darkness as well as tears. I perceive that
my passions pursue objects that the imagination enlarges, till they become only a
sublime idea that shrinks from the enquiry of sense...But these are only the trials
of contemplative minds, the foundation of virtue remains firm.[44]

If the 'sublime system of morality' which Price had advocated was at
present impractical in 'a world not yet sufficiently civilised to adopt [it]',
nonetheless 'the most improving exercise of the mind...is the restless
enquiries that hover on the boundary, or stretch over the dark abyss of

uncertainty...'[45] It is from action inspired by such visionary conjectures, Wollstonecraft goes on to show here and in her succeeding works, that a truly just social order will eventually result.

The imagination, then, is simultaneously invidious and emancipatory; a source of corruption and of virtue. This dual attitude towards fantasy runs throughout the *Rights of Men*, its ambiguities heightened by Wollstonecraft's fierce opposition to Burke's sentimental irrationalism. In common with most British moralists, Burke believed in the existence of a moral instinct, an innate moral sense which – according to his *Reflections* – directed human affairs to benign ends, without the intervention of abstract notions such as natural rights. A staunch moral realist herself, Wollstonecraft did not accept this idea, or its social implications: 'were these *inbred* sentiments faithful guardians of our duty when . . . slavery was authorized by law to fasten her fangs on human flesh . .?'[46] She *did* concede that rational reflection alone was unlikely to galvanise human beings into moral endeavour, but where Burke looked to atavistic instincts and unreasoned attachments as the foundations of political virtue, she looked to the striving psyche. 'The cultivation of reason damps fancy . . .' the *Rights of Men* explained, yet 'the blessings of Heaven lie on each side', for it is only with the combined impetus of desire and imagination that morality awakes.

Sacred be the feelings of the heart! concentrated in a glowing flame, they become the sun of life; and, without this invigorating impregnation, reason would probably lie in helpless inactivity, and never bring forth her only legitimate offspring – virtue. But to prove that virtue is really an acquisition of the individual, and not the blind impulse of unerring instinct, the bastard vice has often been begotten by the same father.[47]

It is true, the *Rights of Men* reminded its readers, that without the governance of reason the imagination can easily descend into 'horror and confusion' or even madness.[48] The strongest action of the imagination is in childhood, before 'reason clips the wing of fancy – [and] the youth becomes a man', and if a propensity to fantasise survives into adulthood (as in most women, and in Burke) it often points to mental infantilism: 'He who has not exercised his judgement to curb his imagination during the meridian of life, becomes, in its decline, too often the prey of childish feelings.'[49] Those who possess genius, however (particularly poetic genius) need not fear such a fate, for when a strong imagination is wedded to a great intellect it can range freely without falling into mere delusion. Indeed, the 'fine phrensy' of such minds must not be constrained by reason, lest their creative fires should be damped. 'Poets, and men who . . . possess the liveliest imagination, are most touched by the sublime,' as she later wrote, 'while men who have cold, enquiring minds, have not this exquisite feeling in any great degree, and indeed seem to lose it as they cultivate their reason.'[50]

It turns out then that it is not the presence of a really vigorous imagination which is Burke's problem but rather the absence of it. Lacking the 'genuine enthusiasm of genius', men like Burke – 'cold, romantic characters' – substitute instead a parade of fanciful sensibility which is as inauthentic as it is hyperbolic. The language of moral sentiment is adopted not as an expression of ethical conviction but because it is 'fashionable and pretty'.[51] As a political moralist, in other words, Burke is nothing more than a posturing narcissist – then, as now, a common enough political species, but one that puts Wollstonecraft in mind not of Burke's fellow parliamentarians, but instead, abruptly, of her own sex, or rather (taking further the reference to slave-owning as the height of moral perfidy) of the wives of West Indian planters who, after days spent inventing tortures for their 'captive negroes', then 'compose their ruffled spirits and exercise their tender feelings' by weeping over French novels.

How true these tears are to nature, I leave you to determine. But these ladies may have read your Enquiry concerning the origin of our ideas of the Sublime and Beautiful, and, convinced by your arguments, may have laboured to be pretty, by counterfeiting weakness.[52]

The first edition of *A Vindication of the Rights of Men*, we noted earlier, was published anonymously. It was only with the appearance of a second edition later in the same year that Wollstonecraft's authorship became known, much to the irritation of at least one male reviewer who complained that having assumed the writer was male he had treated the book unchivalrously.[53] But if this journalist didn't guess the author's sex, it's hard to imagine most other readers didn't, given the sudden sharp engagement with Burke's views on women that erupts into the text with no obvious bearing on matters to hand, and is anyway directed not at his *Reflections* but at his much earlier *Philosophical Enquiry*. Read, however, in the context of Wollstonecraft's underlying concern with issues of gender and imagination, these passages simply make explicit what is implicit throughout the *Rights of Men*: that at the heart of Burke's conservatism is a psychic femininity – a corrupt feminine eroticism – capable of turning male politicians into effeminate wits and women into legal prostitutes, dedicated to inspiring 'pleasing sensations' in men by 'systematically neglecting morals to secure beauty'. The 'debauched imagination' sacrifices the masculine sublimity of revolutionary democracy to the beauty of counter-revolutionary conformity – a perfect model of venal compliance.

As in the rest of the *Rights of Men*, the passages in which Wollstonecraft discusses Burke's views on women are addressed to him; but the condemnatory weight of her polemic falls heaviest on women themselves, or at least on those wealthy slave-beating ladies who, having read the *Philosophical Enquiry* (the caricature proceeds) are then textually seduced by Burke's panegyrics to female beauty.

You may have convinced them that *littleness* and *weakness* are the very essence of beauty; and that the Supreme Being, in giving women beauty in the most supereminent degree, seemed to command them... not to cultivate the moral virtues that might chance to excite respect... Thus confining truth, fortitude, and humanity, within the rigid pale of manly morals, they might justly argue, that to be loved, women's high end and great distinction! they should 'learn to lisp, to totter in their walk, and nick-name God's creatures'.[54]

Such women – '*little, smooth, delicate, fair* creatures' – are content to survive without reason or ethics, or even a soul (since Burke 'had not steered clear of the mussulman's creed' – a reference to the common misconception that Muslims denied that women possessed souls).[55] Designed only to arouse male desire, absorbed in their mission to please, such women must avoid all 'exalted qualities' such as 'fortitude, justice, wisdom' in order that

the affection they excite... should not be tinctured with the respect which moral virtues inspire, lest pain should be blended with pleasure, and admiration disturb the soft intimacy of love.[56]

The 'laxity of morals in the female world' to which such attitudes inevitably lead, Wollstonecraft concludes mordantly, 'is certainly more captivating to a libertine imagination than the cold arguments of reason, that give no sex to virtue.'[57]

But exactly whose libertine imagination is at stake here? Who is culpable: the witty, feminine Burke, or the narcissistic women influenced by him? Are eroticised women – 'authorised to turn all their attention to their persons, systematically neglecting morals to secure beauty' – a product of Burkean fantasy, or are they merely prurient fantasists themselves, locked in dreams of love?[58] The overt message of the *Rights of Men* is that the male sexual imagination is to blame, but the insistently idealising tone in which true masculinity is evoked (as contrasted to Burke's effeminacy), combined with the hostile tone in which women and Burke's womanliness are described, suggests otherwise. And other texts – notably the *Rights of Woman* but also Wollstonecraft's fictional works – give an ambiguous, sometimes very harsh, account of women's relationship to fantasy. 'Fine ladies, brimful of sensibility, and teeming with capricious fancies' are a constant target, particularly when they indulge in novel-reading. Wollstonecraft's first novel, *Mary, a Fiction*, opens with a portrait of the eponymous Mary's mother, a wealthy woman of fashion (modelled on Wollstonecraft's then employer, Lady Kingsborough) whose days are spent in front of her mirror or, when 'she could turn her eyes from the glass', in reading 'those most delightful substitutes for bodily dissipation, novels':

> She was so chaste, according to the vulgar acceptation of the word, that is, she did not make any actual *faux pas*; she feared the world, and was indolent; but then, to make amends for this seeming self-denial, she read all the sentimental novels, dwelt on the love-scenes, and, had she thought while she read, her mind would have been contaminated; as she accompanied the lovers to the lonely arbors, and would walk with them by the clear light of the moon.[59]

The 'romantic twist of the mind' that drew women into such onanistic reveries, the *Rights of Woman* claimed, led them to neglect home duties in favour of imaginary pleasures – 'and frequently in the midst of these sublime refinements they plump into actual vice'.[60] For female fantasists it seems, the path from sexy wishes to outright wantonnness was a slippery downhill run.

Hostility to the sexual imagination, particularly the female sexual imagination, was of course hardly unique to Wollstonecraft. Erotic inventiveness had always been the mind's most scandalous feature. To many eighteenth-century thinkers, the capacity of the 'hot and wild imagination' to generate desire – either through visual impressions of a titillating object or by manufacturing erotic images *ex nihilo* – seemed so dangerous that it was held to be diabolically inspired.[61] And even moralists who took a less alarmist view still tended to regard the lascivious mind rather than the lustful body as the principal instigator of sexual desire. Popular ideas about sensibility gave widespread currency to these notions, particularly in imaginative literature. The heroine of Fanny Burney's *Camilla* was typical of many distressed damsels in sentimental novels whose chastity was imperilled less by caddish would-be seducers than by their own wayward thoughts. Camilla, Burney assured her readers, was always perfectly virtuous in her conscious intentions, 'and when reflection came to her aid, her conduct was as exemplary as her wishes'.

But the ardour of her imagination, acted upon by every passing idea, shook her Judgement from its unsteady seat, and left her at the mercy of wayward Sensibility – that delicate, but irregular power, which now impels to all that is most disinterested for others, now forgets all mankind, to watch the pulsations of its own fancies.[62]

'Pulsations' here wonderfully conveys the libidinal energy of the erotic imagination, its ability, as Patricia Meyer Spacks puts it, to exert 'compelling force in favour of the autonomy of the inner self, despite the claims of "all mankind" '.[63] How threatening and yet how delicious these uncontrollable fantasies could be was an insistent theme in women-authored novels: so much so that in 1791, in a review of Elizabeth Inchbald's *A Simple Story*, Wollstonecraft complained that women novelists were effectively producing pornography. 'Why do all female writers, even when they display their abilities, always give a sanction to the libertine reveries of men?'[64] The 'stale tales' and 'meretricious scenes' conjured up by such writers, she went on to claim in the *Rights of Woman*, enflamed women's passions and corrupted their taste; but worst of all, they locked women into identification with heroines designed not to promote female self-worth but to satisfy that 'male prejudice that makes women systematically weak'. Reading themselves into sexual scenarios played out between dashing gallants and swooning coquettes, women succumbed not just to the seductions of the text but to the images of femininity inscribed in them. It was here, as Cora Kaplan has pointed out, that Wollstonecraft's strongest objection to romantic fiction lay:

as the path to conventional, dependent, degenerate femininity – to the positioning of the female self in the...role as 'object of desire'...As the narrative of desire washed over the reader, the thirst for reason was quenched, and the essential bridge to female autonomy and emancipation was washed out.[65]

This negative alignment between fantasy, fiction and sexuality, Kaplan argues, was characteristic of Wollstonecraft's view of female subjectivity, in which imaginative identifications feature only as degrading illusions. If the 'desire of being always women is the very consciousness which degrades the sex', as the *Rights of Woman* argued, then novels which led women to identify with hyper-feminine stereotypes were inherently debasing. The literary imagination which seduces women into such chimerical self-identity 'numbs the nerve of resistance to oppression'.[66]

However, this is only part of the story. For the fantasising mind may be potentially corrupting, but it is also generative of humanity's finest mental creations. 'I consider those minds as the most strong and original, whose imagination acts as the stimulus to their senses,' Wollstonecraft told Gilbert

Imlay.[67] Humdrum individuals might be gratified by animal pleasures and mass-market fantasies, but minds of real power throw their nets wider. 'An imagination of this vigorous cast can give existence to insubstantial forms, and stability to the shadowy reveries which the mind naturally falls into when realities are found vapid,' Wollstonecraft wrote, and the specific imagination she had in mind here was that of her intellectual hero, Rousseau.[68] 'Rousseau, respectable visionary!' the *Rights of Woman* eulogised, whose 'glowing pen of genius' evoked splendours unimaginable by ordinary mortals,[69] including fantasies of love directed not to lewd, corporeal objects but to 'grand, ideal' images. 'The lively, heated imagination,' Wollstonecraft wrote (in a passage revealing both her own and Rousseau's debt to Plato) 'draws the picture of love... with those glowing colours, which the daring hand will steal from the rainbow...':

It can then... imagine a degree of mutual affection that shall refine the soul, and not expire when it has served as a 'scale to the heavenly'; and, like devotion, make it absorb every meaner affection and desire. In each other's arms, as in a temple, with its summit lost in the clouds, the world is to be shut out, and every thought and wish, that do not nurture pure affection and permanent virtue.[70]

Wollstonecraft's attitude to Rousseau is usually described as militantly adversarial, and certainly her treatment of him in the *Rights of Woman* is very quarrelsome. As discipleships go, this was an exceptionally ambivalent one, full of disappointment and exasperation. But that Wollstonecraft *was* a Rousseauist is indisputable. 'I am now reading Rousseau's Emile....' she wrote excitedly to her sister from Ireland in 1787: 'He chuses [sic] a *common* capacity to educate – and gives as a reason, that a genius will educate itself.'[71] Six months later she announced the completion of *Mary: a Fiction*, 'a tale, to illustrate an opinion of mine, that a genius will educate itself'.[72] It was 'Rousseau's opinion respecting men' which she 'extend[ed] to women' she wrote in *The Rights of Woman*, in the midst of the argument with him that occupies so much of the text.[73] 'I have always been half in love with him,' she confided to her sister Everina in 1794.[74]

But if one half of Wollstonecraft loved Rousseau, the other half clearly identified with him. 'He rambles into that *chimerical* world in which I have too often wandered – and draws the usual conclusion that all is vanity and vexation of spirit,' she told Everina. 'He was a strange inconsistent unhappy clever creature – yet he possessed an uncommon portion of sensibility and penetration' – a condition with which Wollstonecraft was all too familiar.[75] Reading Rousseau, she immediately recognised a fellow 'Solitary Walker' – another of those restive spirits who 'lost in a pleasing enthusiasm... live in the scenes they represent; and do not measure their steps in a beaten track...'[76] As she absorbed his words, she mourned him; and unable to confront him in life, recreated him in her fictions as a wayward visionary to be admired, loved, and corrected by her female characters. Yet throughout her writings she also criticised the 'rampant' imagination which, 'breaking loose from [Rousseau's] judgement', had destroyed his personal peace.[77] '[H]ad his fancy been allowed to cool, it is possible that he might have acquired more strength of mind.... [and] enjoyed more equal happiness on earth,' she claimed – and again the echoes of her own difficulties are easily heard.[78] 'My imagination is forever betraying me into fresh misery,' she sighed to Godwin a year before her death.[79]

This complex identification with the century's foremost male theorist of gender can be heard throughout Wollstonecraft's *oeuvre*. 'I...love [Rousseau's] paradoxes,' she wrote at one point, and not the least paradoxical aspect of this encounter between the notorious exponent of female subordination and his leading feminist opponent is how within it a new vision of womanhood began to be forged.[80] The contradictions of the Rousseauist sexual imagination fuelled a radical fantasy of female emancipation. Betrayal by a beloved male mentor fired feminist aspirations (as it was to do in the case of neo-Freudian feminists almost two centuries later). This was not really the irony it appears to be: the embrace of new ideas, as Rousseau and Wollstonecraft both recognised, is always a love/hate story.

* * *

In 1790, reviewing Rousseau's *Confessions* for the *Analytical Review*, Wollstonecraft reprised his account of the genesis of his great romantic novel, *La Nouvelle Héloïse* (1761). Living in seclusion with no one but his working-class mistress for company, Rousseau had

> felt himself alone, his heart having no real object for his imagination to adorn... Then the fancy seized him of describing some of the situations and of indulging the flighty desire of loving, which he had never been able to satisfy, and with which he felt himself devoured.[81]

Transfixed by these erotic fantasies, Rousseau had 'directed all the warmth of his heart to one imaginary object' and created his fictive heroine, Julie d'Etange. As a romantic fantasy, Julie is supremely compelling; but also, to Wollstonecraft's mind, a dangerous figure, exemplifying the hazards of the 'inflamed' literary imagination.[82] Julie is a 'slave of love' invented by a man enslaved by desire.[83] '[B]orn with a warm constitution and lively fancy, nature carried [Rousseau] toward the other sex with such eager fondness that he soon became lascivious,' Wollstonecraft explained in the *Rights of Woman*.

Had he given way to these desires, the fire would have extinguished itself in a natural manner; but... [since] fear, delicacy, or virtue, restrained him, he debauched his imagination, and reflecting on the sensations to which fancy gave force, he traced them in the most glowing colours, and sunk them deep into his soul.[84]

The portrait of the degenerate fantasist – common to virtually all of Rousseau's eighteenth-century critics – is too lurid to convince, despite having originated with Jean-Jacques himself, whose *Confessions* revealed his inability to relate sexually to women except via masochistic fantasy.[85] In the *Confessions* this enthralment of erotic life to the imagination is presented as perverse: an occasion for another display of eerily complacent self-accusation of the kind that dominates the text. But in Rousseau's fictions, particularly *La Nouvelle Héloïse*, this primacy of fantasy over physical sexuality is presented not as pathological but as the essence of human erotic psychology.

La Nouvelle Héloïse, one of the most influential novels of the eighteenth century, is a very sexy story with almost no physical sex. Julie d' Etange and her lover, St Preux, have intercourse twice, and spend the rest of the novel interlocked in amorous fantasies that flower most excitingly in each others' absence. The 'world of fancy... the land of chimeras, is the only world worthy to be inhabited,' Julie explains to St Preux shortly before her death (in words repeated almost verbatim in Wollstonecraft's *Maria*), 'and such is the inanity of human enjoyments that, except that Being which is self-existent, there is nothing delightful but that which is not'.[86] Or as Rousseau later wrote in *Emile*: 'In love everything is only illusion. I admit it.'

But what is real are the sentiments for the truly beautiful with which love animates us and which it makes us love. This beauty is not in the object one loves; it is the work of our errors. So, what of it? Does the lover any the less sacrifice all of his low sentiments to this imaginary model?[87]

It is women, or rather fictions of women, who serve as these imaginary models to draw men away from corrupting passions toward the Beautiful and Good.[88] Julie is such a model – not only for St Preux but, in the end, in her Christ-like death, for humanity as a whole – and so too is Sophie, the heroine of Rousseau's other great fictional work, *Emile*. But in Sophie's case the myth has been formulated with a specific man in mind: the eponymous Emile. Prior to meeting Sophie in the flesh, Emile's teacher and moral guide,

known as his Mentor, presents him with a fantasy of the perfect Woman as
a channel for his masturbatory desires. Sophie, as it turns out, is this ideal
Woman, but whether she is real or merely a delusion shared by Emile and
the Mentor is not obvious – nor particularly important. For Sophie's role
in Emile's life is merely to *be* an illusion: a 'chimera' which Emile will prefer
'to the real objects that strike his eye'.[89] For what, Rousseau demands, is
'true love' anyway,

> if it is not chimera, lie, and illusion? We love the image we make for ourselves far
> more than we love the object to which we apply it. If we saw what we love exactly
> as it is, there would be no more love on earth.[90]

Here, as far as Rousseau was concerned, was the fantasmic reality of human desire – and, as far as Mary Wollstonecraft was concerned, the *fons et
origo* of female oppression. The forging of Julie and Sophie in the unholy fire
of Rousseau's sexual imagination reveals not only their own fantastic nature
but, Wollstonecraft argues, the fictionalising processes by which 'females . . .
are made women' throughout contemporary culture.[91] A chimera of
womanhood, rooted in erotic imaginings, has been created that entrances
both sexes – women in narcissistic self-admiration; men in objectifying
passion – to the point where real women disappear into its seductions.
Women are not allowed to *be* but rather 'always to *seem* to be this or that'
in scenarios of sexual illusion; the 'wife, mother and human creature . . .
swallowed up by the factitious character' of the coquette, mistress, or lover.[92]
The Rousseauist woman is a phantasm, and in this she exemplifies the
female dilemma.

* * *

Wollstonecraft's reiterated description of Rousseau's attitude toward
women as 'paradoxical' is a view shared by most commentators. How
could the man who insisted on women's subordination to men then go
on to condemn the French legal system for treating women as men's juridical inferiors? Why was the author of *Lettre à D'Alembert*, a hysterical
attack on women's impact on public life, so fervent in his praise of the
female patriots of antiquity? And above all, how could the creator of the
formidable Julie d'Etange, saintly heroine of *La Nouvelle Héloïse*, also have
created the sly and insipid Sophie of *Emile*, a girl so ethically shallow even
her author eventually gave up on her? Early in his career Rousseau was
employed as secretary to a Mme Dupin who intended to write a book on
female equality. Rousseau assisted her by assembling and annotating works
on women, many of them written from an egalitarian position.[93] An impressive quantity of such texts were available in mid eighteenth-century

France, and it is possible that an early essay by Rousseau on women's role in political life was written under their influence.[94] So there was nothing uninformed or naive in Rousseau's treatment of the woman question. Indeed, the famous concluding book of *Emile*, 'Sophie, or the Woman', is probably best understood as a conscious counterblast to feminist argumentation: which makes Wollstonecraft's swingeing indictment of it all the more telling.

Emile, or On Education, published in 1762, is the tale of a boy's intellectual and emotional formation at the hands of an omniscient Mentor who is responsible for every aspect of his pupil's life from birth to marriage. The Mentor's duty is to mould Emile into an exemplary man, and in doing so provide a model for human development under optimum psychological conditions. At the time of writing the book, Rousseau saw it as a recipe for a utopia of robust, clear-headed young men and their dutiful wives. But a later sequel, in which Emile and Sophie fall foul of wordly corruption, pointed to the tragic impossibility of such hopes.[95] Emile and Sophie, despite their author's aspirations for them, fail to be more than human, their downfall signalling an inevitable exile from Edenic bliss.

The role of the imagination in personal development is a central theme of the book. 'All of Emile's early rearing,' Alan Bloom has noted, 'is an elaborate attempt to avoid the emergence of the imagination... the faculty that turns man's intellectual progress into the source of his misery.'[96] As a child, Rousseau tells his readers, Emile is a savage, with a savage's mindless devotion to immediate needs. He is part of nature, existing in harmony with the physical world, with no thoughts of the future or regrets for the past. In his earlier *A Discourse on the Origins of Inequality* (1755) Rousseau had outlined a conjectural history of humanity in which this first phase of infantile development appeared as the state of nature, that primordial, pre-cultural and pre-linguistic stage of human history in which every individual is a 'world unto himself', motivated only by the instinctive egoism of self-preservation (*amour de soi*). At this earliest point in humanity's story, individuals are unable to distinguish self from other. There are no psychological boundaries, 'not the slightest notion of thine and mine', and the only affective ties are an empathetic pity or compassion based on identification.[97] (Rousseau often evoked the mother–child bond as the prototype of a compassionate relationship).[98] Copulation occurs instinctively and at random, without fantasy or emotion. 'Imagination, which wreaks such havoc among us, does not speak to Savage hearts; everyone peacefully awaits the impulsion of Nature, yields to it without choice... and, the need once satisfied, all desire is extinguished.'[99] This instinct-driven sexuality Rousseau (following Buffon and other Enlightened thinkers) described as 'physical' love, so as to distinguish it from the object-oriented 'moral' love which makes its appearance in the transition from savagery to civilisation.[100]

In this state of nature, the distinction between the sexes is biological but not psychological. Men and women lack all gender awareness; and this too is paralleled by the prepubescent phase of individual maturation in which sexual difference has yet to impress itself on subjective consciousness. We are, according to Rousseau, 'born twice . . . once for our species and once for our sex'. Prior to puberty 'children of the two sexes have nothing apparent to distinguish them . . . Everything is equal: girls are children, boys are children; the same name suffices for beings so much alike.'[101] Thus the small Emile 'does not feel himself to be of any sex . . . [m]an and woman are equally alien to him'.[102] He has no more feeling for women than for his dog, or his watch. But all children grow older; all savages evolve. The serpent of fantasy slithers into this pre-erotic Eden:

> . . . the senses are awakened by the imagination alone. Their need is not properly a physical need. It is not true that it is a true need. If no lewd object had ever struck our eyes, if no indecent idea had ever entered our minds, perhaps this alleged need would never have made itself felt to us, and we would have remained chaste without temptation, without effort, and without merit.[103]

The loss of this psychological chastity is the beginning of individual maturity, and the origin of human civilisation. As instinct gives way to imagination, men begin to develop sexual preferences. Comparing one woman to another, they generate ideal images of individual love objects. Women, or rather these idealised images of women, incite in them amorous passions in excess of their powers of gratification ('we exhaust our strength, yet never reach our goal'). This gap between what may be satisfied (the instinctive demands of physical love) and what is wanted (the fantasied objects of moral love) is the space in which insatiable desire arises.[104] It is this desire that forces men into speech (to state their wishes) and into the ferocious sexual rivalry that inaugurates the life of the competitive ego (*amour propre*). And it is this rivalry which in turn marks man's entry into civil society, into the realm of law, prohibition, taboo, which must be entered if individuals are not to annihilate each other in the unrestricted warfare of competing sexual claims.[105]

Thus humanity is delivered into the drama of incessant, unfulfilled yearning which to Rousseau is our inevitable fate – and our abiding tragedy. 'The real world has its limits; the imaginary world is infinite. Unable to enlarge the one, let us restrict the other, for it is from the difference between the two alone that are born all the pains which make us truly unhappy.'[106] Unrequited longing is the agonising lot of the fantasising mind. The Mentor hopes to spare Emile this unhappiness by curbing his imaginative life, particularly at puberty when masturbatory fantasies begin to arise – and '[o]nce he knows this dangerous supplement, he is lost'. He institutes twenty-four hour surveillance of Emile, including during his sleeping hours, to prevent his pupil from learning this fatal sexual 'substitute'.[107] But even these draconian measures prove insufficient. Desirous thoughts and images begin to appear, and these will destroy Emile unless drastic action is taken. What can be done? It is at this critical juncture that the advantage of fictional pupils over real ones becomes apparent, for if Emile's fantasies cannot be controlled, at least their object can. Sophie is the Mentor's solution: a fantasy of womanhood introduced into the narrative to serve as the 'imaginary object' of Emile's desires. Sophie is not intended to be Emile's peer; rather, she is what Woman must be if men are not to expire by their own hand. She is the chimera whom Emile will come to prefer to his own onanistic reveries and even, Rousseau assures us, to the real women that he meets. For were Emile to love an actual woman rather than a fantasmic one, disillusion and unhappiness would inevitably be his lot. 'When we stop loving, the person we loved remains the same as before, but we no longer see her in the same way. The magic veil drops, and love disappears. But, by providing the imaginary object, I am the master of comparisons...'[108]

Sophie, then, is literally a man-made woman, 'made to please and to be subjugated'.[109] She is intended to serve as the ideal complement to her fictive lover, and also as a counterexample to the educated upper-class women of late eighteenth-century France who, in Rousseau's view, had become a shocking source of moral disorder. Sophie is sweet, sexy, shy and deceitful; she is designed to stimulate Emile's passions while simultaneously harnessing them to the demands of family life and civic order. To herself, she is nothing, 'a fanciful kind of half being', as Wollstonecraft put it, whose entire intellectual and ethical subjectivity is lodged in her male partner. 'She ought' – the words are Wollstonecraft's – 'to sacrifice every other consideration to render herself agreeable to him: and let this brutal desire of self-preservation be the grand spring of all her actions...to fit which her character should be stretched or contracted...'[110] Sophie is Woman as she is 'created for man': never allowed to be more or other than the male fantasies she embodies.

Or so it would seem. But about halfway through Sophie's tale a second Sophie suddenly appears, an alter-Sophie 'so similar to Sophie that her story could be Sophie's without occasioning any surprise'.[111] This girl emerges in the narrative without explanation or warning, just before Emile and his future wife are due to meet. And this Sophie, unlike Sophie One, is a dreamer, a fantasist (and, like her inventor, a good Platonist) – a true Rousseauist, in other words, whose eruption into the novel seems to bewilder everyone, including Rousseau.

This second Sophie, Rousseau writes, was once a young woman of the same impeccable docility as the ur-Sophie, until one day when her disposition abruptly altered. 'She had moments of distraction and impatience; she was sad and dreamy; she hid herself in order to cry.'[112] Her health deteriorates; her parents become distracted; what has happened to the paragon child? The truth finally comes out. Sophie Two has fallen in love, not with Emile but with the eponymous hero of Fénelon's didactic romance, *Telemachus, Son of Ulysses*.[113] Like her author, this Sophie is consumed with love for someone who does not exist; her passion triggered – as Emile's is for her original – by an imaginative yearning toward one who will serve as her inner complement. '[W]hy cannot this someone exist, since I exist – I who feel within myself a heart so similar to his?'[114] Telemachus, with his princely merits, is a sublime object of desire, a 'charming model...imprinted...on her soul' – and this Sophie, devout lover of the Good, will settle for no less; is articulate and determined in her unrequitable passion; is, in other words, fully and truly human: or, as Rousseau put it, in his astonishing coda to this episode:

...in spite of the prejudices born of the morals of our age, enthusiasm for the decent and the fine is no more foreign to women than to men, and...there is nothing that cannot be obtained under nature's direction from women as well as from men.[115]

'Shall I bring this sad narrative to its catastrophic end?' Rousseau finally demands of his readers, painting a picture of a mother enraged, a father rendered cruel by disappointment, and poor Sophie Two 'even more attached to her chimera as a result of the persecution she has suffered for it' heading toward the grave. No, Sophie must be saved:

Let us render his Sophie to our Emile. Let us resuscitate this lovable girl to give her a less lively imagination and a happier destiny. I wanted to depict an ordinary woman, and by dint of elevating her soul I have disturbed her reason. I went astray...[116]

And so Sophie One reappears, to be whisked into marriage to Emile (with Fénelon replaced by *The Spectator* as her reading material). The Sophie who might have been, a Rousseau-Sophie, must die in order that the proper Woman may survive – more devoted than ever to home and family, sweetly attuned to her marital responsibilities, and above all attentive to her womanhood, never allowing it to be shadowed by any trace of sexual ambiguity. And in achieving all this, Rousseau insists, his resurrected Sophie is really nothing special. Neither Emile nor Sophie are 'prodigies'; but rather 'Emile is a man and Sophie is a woman; therein consists all their glory. In the confounding of the sexes that reigns among us, someone is almost a prodigy for belonging to his own sex.'[117]

Why is maintaining the difference between the sexes such a prodigiously difficult affair?

Book 5 of *Emile*, Sophie's story, opens with a disquisition on the nature of women: 'In everything not connected with sex, woman is man':

She has the same organs, the same needs, the same faculties... [But] in everything connected with sex, woman and man are in every respect related and in every respect different. The difficulty of comparing them comes from the difficulty of determining what is... due to sex and what is not.[118]

Identifying the boundary between men and women, even with the help of comparative anatomy, is difficult, Rousseau goes on, since 'in what they have in common, they are equal' and 'where they differ they are not comparable'; moreover there are many 'general differences' which 'do not appear connected with sex' but in fact are 'by relations which we are not in a position to perceive'.[119] None of this uncertainty however prevents Rousseau from insisting that it is 'one of the marvels of nature' that 'two such similar beings... are constituted so differently' that instead of serving as mere equivalents to each other they can be perfect complements.[120] Man and woman are two halves of a whole; in their union they make one 'moral person' in which woman is the inactive perceiver while man is the performer: a division whose advantages become most apparent in sexual intercourse where male initiatives are met by women's passive co-operation (or, better still, by just enough modest resistance to heighten male pleasure). Penile rule, in other words, is Nature's way, and 'once this principle is established, it follows that woman is made specially to please man' and must behave accordingly. Men, on the other hand, automatically please women merely by mastering them ('he pleases by the sole fact of his strength').[121] 'This is not the law of love...' Rousseau unnecessarily concludes, 'But it is that of nature, prior to love itself.'[122]

Wollstonecraft described this sort of reasoning as 'sophisticated', meaning sophistical, and we can see her point. 'If woman is made to please and to be subjugated, she ought to make herself agreeable to man,' Rousseau insists.[123] But what is agreeable to man is neither fixed nor lasting. 'Nature has given charms to women, and ordained that their ascendant over man shall end with their charms,' as Montesquieu (a great influence on Rousseau in these matters) had written, and throughout his writings Rousseau harped on the same theme.[124] '[N]o man ever insisted more on the transient nature of love,' Wollstonecraft pointed out, so how is it that the whole of a woman's life is to be dedicated to inspiring love's ardour?[125] Why should Sophie be made 'beautiful, innocent and silly... to make her the mistress of her husband, a very short time'?[126] The answer, which Wollstonecraft's critique of Rousseau hints at but never quite reaches, is that Sophie exists as a sexualised cypher not to gratify the ungratifiable – i.e. the fantasmic yearnings of male desire – but rather to provide Emile (and Emile's author) with an illusion of masterly control. Woman as an imaginary creation is a defence – and a woefully inadequate one, it turns out – against actual women in all their ontological ungovernability. All those sweet little Sophies, in their docile inanity, must triumph over their wayward alter-egos if emotional catastrophe is to be avoided.

What sort of catastrophe? Here Rousseau was explicit. As the endlessly tantalising object of male desire, Woman's 'violence is in her charms', and the result can easily be fatal.[127] For while men's sexual aggressivity is regulated by 'the moderation which nature imposes' on them, women's sexual capacities know no such limitation. Thus if women were not sexually restrained – either by force or through the imposition of artificial codes of sexual decorum – they would make impossible demands on the men who 'would finally be their victims and would see themselves dragged to death...'[128] Writing to the Encyclopedist D'Alembert to oppose his proposals for the introduction of theatres into Geneva, Rousseau warned of the dangers of plays which represent men in the thrall of women's romantic appeal.

Love is the realm of women. It is they who necessarily give the law in it, because, according to the order of nature, resistance belongs to them, and men can conquer this resistance only at the expense of their liberty. Hence, a natural effect of this sort of play is to extend the empire of the fair sex, to make women and girls the preceptors of the public, and to give them the same power over the audience that they have over their lovers.[129]

Women are inherently seductive; thus public displays of male susceptibility to women's attractions are invariably dangerous. Moreover, by drawing women out of their homes into a public space, the theatre corrupts them. 'There are no good morals [*moeurs*] for women outside of a withdrawn and domestic life,' Rousseau warns: a maxim observed in all well-ordered societies (like the classical republics) but constantly violated in Paris, where women gad about everywhere and where even the home is no longer sacrosanct.[130] 'Every woman at Paris,' Rousseau writes sourly (in an obvious reference to the *salonières*), 'gathers in her apartment a harem of men more womanish than she, who know how to render all sorts of homage to beauty' and the result is a breakdown of all sexual distinctions:

> . . . for this weaker sex, not in the position to take on our way of life, which is too hard for it, forces us to take on its way, too soft for us; and, no longer wishing to tolerate separation, unable to make themselves into men, the women make us into women.[131]

Such was the ghastly fate of metropolitan Frenchmen; now Rousseau's fellow Genevans seemed hellbent on going the same way. In a less corrupt world, women's natural sense of shame and timidity would prevent such disasters, but in Paris at least, Rousseau believes, all shame has fled. In fact he is not at all certain that shame and sexual timidity are more natural to women than to men. Female pigeons seem to feel such things, he points out, but without much conviction.[132] But even if it's true that such proper attitudes are not natural but merely social conventions, 'it is in society's interests that women acquire these qualities' Rousseau insists, since otherwise chaos will ensue.[133] Women will become men; men will become women; paternity will be uncertain; society's moral structure will disintegrate. Far better that men and women be kept rigidly segregated, even at the expense of the gossip and backbiting which goes on in exclusively feminine circles, or the drunken rowdiness of all-male environments. 'Never has a people perished from an excess of wine; all perish from the disorder of women.'[134]

The sexual distinction is precarious, then, precisely because it is designed to keep annihilatory disorder at bay. Physical differentiation is important (Rousseau was obsessed by aspects of it) but the chief responsibility for preventing sexual homogenisation rests not with biology but with psychology, with fantasy and desire. In a state of nature, both sexes are innocently physical beings, but once exiled from this Edenic savagery into the civilised world, women are as much estranged from Nature as men are, and no amount of pontificating about the joys of breastfeeding or the mating habits of pigeons can hide the artificiality of their condition. 'The male is male only at certain moments. The female is female her whole life or at least during her whole youth. Everything constantly recalls her sex to her', Rousseau wants to insist; but in fact it's all too evident that the 'everything' of femininity – the female body in its capacities and vicissitudes – is never sufficient to remind women of their sex, since given half a chance they begin to think and behave just like men.[135] 'Girls . . . ought to be constrained very early,' Rousseau instructed in *Emile*:

This misfortune . . . is inseparable from their sex, and they are never delivered from it without suffering far more cruel misfortunes. All their lives they will be enslaved to the most continual and most severe of contraints – that of the proprieties. They must first be exercised in constraint, so that it never costs them anything to tame all their caprices in order to submit them to the will of others . . . [T]each them above all to conquer themselves.[136]

A woman, to be acceptable, must bow to the 'tyranny of decorum', Julie tells her friend Claire in *La Nouvelle Héloïse;* she must veil herself in a *persona* of feminine submission which conceals and ultimately obliterates her inner reality.[137] Life for a woman is a performance in which there is no sneaking offstage. The theatre is dangerous to the Genevan populace precisely because it reveals the theatricality of the sexual *moeurs* on which civilised culture is based. For if the masks which disguised men and women's true natures were once removed – if women's sexual power and man's sexual yearnings stood fully revealed – 'the result would soon be the ruin of both, and mankind would perish by the means established for preserving it.'[138]

However: this is not just Woman's story. The realm of appearances to which women are confined is modernity as Rousseau understands and deplores it. The processes through which females become Sophies are those by which all men and women, born free and equal, are shackled into the bear-dance of modern society. Becoming a modern citizen – that is, entering into that condition of psychic and political unfreedom that characterises contemporary life – is for both sexes becoming Woman: a being deprived of all inner authority, whose life is one of duplicity and dependence. 'Do you want to know men? Study women,' Rousseau instructed D'Alembert, and 'women' it seemed were everywhere to be studied: in Paris, throughout European society (although perhaps not in England, a peculiarly masculine nation, Rousseau believed), but above all in the soul of Jean-Jacques himself, torn as he was between the virility of his independent intellect and the effeminacy of his dependent and often abject social relationships.[139] In 1728, impoverished and homeless in Turin, Rousseau went to work as a valet for the Countess de Vercellis who treated him with cold *hauteur*. 'She judged me less by *what I was* than by *what she had made* me; and since she saw in me nothing but a lackey, she prevented me from appearing to her in any other light'.[140] Perhaps no real man would have tolerated such dehumanising treatment, but Parisians – that is, modern citizens – and all women certainly must. In Paris every man 'must leave his soul, if he has one, at the door, and take up another with the colours of the house, as a lackey puts on new livery', just as all women must garb themselves in the dress of sexual vassalage.[141] 'A woman is always only too much what men want her to be' was the Mentor's verdict in *Emile*, and in this She becomes the paradigm of that alienated subjectivity – that chimera of being – which is the essence of modernity.[142] 'To speak always contrary to one's thoughts; to disguise all we feel; to be deceitful through obligation, and to speak untruth through modesty; such is the habitual situation of every young woman . . .', Julie sighs, but likewise every civilised man, in this mendacious world.[143]

But if modern life is a dystopia for both sexes, women's lot is nonetheless a peculiarly unhappy one. 'To what will we reduce women if we give them as their law only public prejudices? Let us not bring down so low the sex that governs us and honors us' Rousseau suddenly insists in *Emile*; for in France, as he informs his readers, 'the fair sex are . . . subjected in the greatest degree to the tyranny of the laws. Is it to be wondered that they so amply avenge themselves in the looseness of their manners?'[144] Seen in this light, women's 'irregularities' are 'less owing to themselves than our bad institutions'; or as Emile's Mentor confesses, '[a]midst our senseless arrangements a modest woman's life is a perpetual combat against herself'.[145] But these 'senseless arrangements' are precisely the ones Rousseau has ordered for Sophie, so in that case – 'why is the life of a modest woman a perpetual conflict?' The question is Wollstonecraft's; and 'I should answer,' she tells her readers,

that this very system of education [which Rousseau advocates] makes it so. . . . [for] when sensibility is nurtured at the expence [sic] of the understanding, such weak beings must be restrained by arbitrary means, and be subjected to continual conflicts . . .[146]

Sophies are made, not born.

* * *

In criticising Rousseau's representation of Sophie, Wollstonecraft never suggests that such women do not exist; indeed, if the *Rights of Woman* is to be believed, silly, guileful Sophies are pretty much the norm. Her attack on Sophie is directed not at her plausibility but at her genesis: at the 'artificial structure', as Wollstonecraft puts it, within which Rousseauist Woman is fabricated.[147]

All Wollstonecraft's writings are shadowed by Rousseau. But the most sustained critique of his views on women appears in the chapter of the *Rights of Woman* titled 'Animadversions on Some of the Writers Who Have

Rendered Women Objects of Pity, Bordering on Contempt'. The writers targeted here are the tribe of (mostly male) advice-givers – James Fordyce, John Gregory, Lord Chesterfield, *et al.* – whose 'pernicious...books, in which [they] insidiously degrade the sex whilst they are prostrate before their personal charms, cannot be too often or too severely exposed.'[148] The effect of placing Rousseau in this company is to make him appear less the great philosopher than another common-or-garden male supremacist; his Sophie no paragon of womanly virtues but merely the sort of domestic doll preferred by sexual traditionalists. Likewise, the critical strategy Wollstonecraft employs – reproducing long passages from *Emile*, interspersed with caustic commentary – seems designed to expose the affinity between Rousseau's 'partial opinions' on women and other varieties of old-world dogma mauled in similar fashion by enlightened philosophes. Wollstonecraft adopts this method, she states, because Rousseau's argument is made with 'so much ingenuity that it seems necessary to attack it in a more circumstantial manner', but the result, while certainly spirited, is occasionally rhetorically diminishing, reducing her from equal disputant to vituperative heckler.

However, *Emile does* deserve Wollstonecraft's particular attention: not just because of Rousseau's intellectual weight but because, more than any other creation of the eighteenth-century male imagination, the figure of Sophie exemplifies Woman as prescriptive invention, a masculine fantasy of the feminine. The rule governing Sophie's existence – 'to render herself agreeable to man' – is not only the 'grand spring of all her actions', as Wollstonecraft points out, but the imperative that *makes* her Woman: an 'iron bed of fate, to fit which her character should be stretched or contracted, regardless of all moral or physical distinctions'.[149] Sophie is contorted into the feminine position, and it is this Wollstonecraft seeks to expose: first by giving Rousseau plenty of textual rope with which to hang himself ('I have quoted this passage, lest my readers should suspect that I warped the author's reasoning to support my own arguments,' she remarks after reproducing his advice to women to foster men's desire by shamming unwilling submission to their advances), and then by offering her own account of the 'ignoble contrivances' by which little girls become Sophie-women.[150]

* * *

Are women the natural equals of men? In the *Rights of Woman*, Wollstonecraft raises the question only to refuse it. '[B]ecause I am a woman, I would not lead my readers to suppose that I mean violently to agitate the contested question respecting the quality or inferiority of the sex', her 'Author's Introduction' opens:

but as the subject lies in my way . . . I shall stop a moment to deliver, in a few words, my opinion – In the government of the physical world it is observable that the female in point of strength is, in general, inferior to the male. This is the law of nature; and it does not appear to be suspended or abrogated in favour of woman. A degree of physical superiority cannot, therefore, be denied – and it is a noble prerogative! But not content with this natural pre-eminence, men endeavour to sink us still lower, merely to render us alluring objects for a moment . . .[151]

At birth a female child has less physical potential than a male, but is there any other innate inequality – of mental capacity, or moral strength? Here Wollstonecraft insists on agnosticism, on the grounds that as long as women are 'treated as subordinate beings, and not as a part of the human species' it is impossible to know their natural condition: a stance that places her firmly outside the old *querelle des femmes*, with its stylised disputes over sex superiority, and takes her instead into an extended analysis of the psychological and cultural pressures that de-nature female children.

In early childhood, Wollstonecraft claims, every girl is 'a romp'. Like little Emile, who prior to puberty is psychologically genderless and is only awakened into virility via erotic fantasy, so little Sophies, according to the *Rights of Woman*, lack any discernibly feminine traits. In *Emile* Rousseau had offered as evidence of the natural coquettish of female children a tale of a girl who, happening to glance into a mirror while practising her handwriting, saw that drawing the letter 'O' placed her in an ungraceful attitude, and thereafter refused to write 'O's'. The anecdote, Wollstonecraft observes, has about as much credibility as those of 'the learned pig', but then what did Jean-Jacques know about little girls? 'I have, probably, had an opportunity of observing more girls in their infancy than J. J. Rousseau':

I can recollect my own feelings, and I have looked steadily around me . . . [and] I will venture to affirm, that a girl, whose spirits have not been damped by inactivity, or innocence tainted by false shame, will always be a romp, and the doll will never excite attention unless confinement allows her no alternative. Girls and boys, in short, would play harmlessly together, if the distinction of sex was not inculcated long before nature makes any difference. – I will go further, and affirm . . . that most of the women, in the circle of my observation, who have acted like rational creatures, or shewn any vigour of intellect, have accidentally been allowed to run wild . . .[152]

Running wild, a little girl has 'no sex to her mind', nor is her mind on sex until 'improper education . . . by heating the imagination' calls forth 'the desire connected with the impulse of nature to propagate the species' prematurely. And it is precisely this which happens all the time, as female children of nature are educated into little 'coquettes', the 'insignificant objects of male desire'.

How does this deformation occur? Like all Enlightened thinkers, Woll-stonecraft regarded human character as very pliable, particularly during childhood years. Post-Lockean psychology, with its emphasis on acquired habits of thinking, provided a compelling account of personality develop-ment, and in chapter 6 of the *Rights of Woman* Wollstonecraft mobilises this theory to explain how 'females...are made women of when they are mere children' through the acquisition of unconscious mental habits based on infantile sensory impressions. The shaping of character in both sexes, she argues there, results from a combination of innate disposition with 'habitual associations of ideas' laid down in the mind prior to puberty. Like Locke's 'gangs' of unconscious thoughts, these early associations 'lie by for use, till some fortuitous circumstance makes the information dart into the mind with illustrative force, that has been received at very different periods in our lives' in a process which 'can seldom be disentangled by reason':

One idea calls up another, its old associate, and memory, faithful to the first impressions, particularly when the intellectual powers are not employed to cool our sensations, retraces them with mechanical exactness.[153]

Subliminal pathways of this kind dominate the minds of both sexes. But whereas in men's adult life 'business and other dry employments of the understanding' tend to 'break associations that do violence to reason', thus freeing them to move along new psychic trajectories, women's lives offer no such opportunities for imaginative re-routing. '[T]reated like women, almost from their very birth', women become slaves not just to men but to unconscious mental patterns imposed on them in youth.[154]

Every thing that they see or hear serves to fix impressions, call forth emotions, and associate ideas, that give a sexual character to the mind. False notions of beauty and delicacy stop the growth of their limbs and produce a sickly soreness, rather than delicacy of organs; and thus weakened by being employed in unfolding instead of examining the first associations...how can they attain the vigour necessary to enable them to throw off that factitious character? – where find strength to recur to reason and rise superior to a system of oppression, that blasts the fair promises of spring? This cruel association of ideas, which every thing conspires to twist all their habits of thinking, or, to speak with more precision, of feeling, receives new force when they begin to act a little for themselves; for they then perceive that it is only through their address to excite emotions in men, that pleasure and power are to be obtained.[155]

Women's intellectual narrowness; their servile conformity to male opin-ions; their obsessive concern with appearance and fashion: all these reflect the 'habitual slavery to first impressions' which, by the time girls reach puberty, has locked them into a mindless libidinism. 'Supinely dream[ing] life away in the lap of pleasure', young women's imaginative lives, like their rational faculties, become langorous and routinised. Consigned to that passive sensualism in which desire is only the desire to be desired, the female imagination becomes a narcissistic ghetto that 'shap[ing] itself to the body, and roaming around its gilt cage, seeks only to adore its prison'.[156] The effect is a corruption so total that the entire personality is deformed. 'She was quite feminine, according to the masculine acceptation of the word' Wollstonecraft wrote of one woman who spent her days – in best Burkean fashion – flirting and lisping 'nonsense, to please the men who flocked around her': 'The wife, mother, and human creature, were all swallowed up by the factitious character which an improper education and selfish vanity of beauty had produced.'[157]

The harshness of the depiction reminds us of its origins in anti-elite caricature of a type exemplified by Rousseau's tirades against the women of the French urban upper class. Indeed, it was as a counterexample to the women of the Parisian *beau monde* that Rousseau created Sophie. Sophie hates flirtation and courtly manners, Rousseau assured his readers, and would scold young gallants if they complimented her in fashionable style. She even tells off Emile when he performs the chivalric gesture of kissing her dress. In such attitudes at least she is certainly a woman after Wollstonecraft's heart. But one of the most radical moves of the *Rights of Woman* is to turn on this paragon of homeloving bourgeois femininity to show that here too is a woman who, for all her ostensible virtues, is, in Wollstonecraft's words, 'grossly unnatural',[158] with her most unnatural feature the pleasure she takes from her submissive condition. For having passed through the educational regime of the Mentor, Sophie has become a slave without chains. Having internalised those 'habits of subordination' which are the essence of adult femininity, she subscribes to Women's Duty not as an obligation imposed on her from without but as the fullest expression of her inner nature. 'Considering the length of time that women have been dependent,' Wollstonecraft writes, 'is it surprising that some of them hug their chains, and fawn like the spaniel? "These dogs," observes a naturalist, "at first kept their ears erect; but custom has superseded nature, and a token of fear is becoming a beauty." '[159]

Thus cocky little girls are perverted into women. For Wollstonecraft, such corruption of Nature is monstrous, and a sin. For Rousseau, however, it is a social necessity – and not just for women. Men too must be shaped for communal life. 'Natural man is entirely for himself,' and this makes him dangerously unfit for civil society: 'Good social institutions are those that best know how to denature man, to take his absolute existence from him in order to give him a relative one and transport the *I* into the common unity...'[160]

Natural man is instinct-driven, ruled only by the internal demands of *amour de soi*. Social man, on the other hand, existing 'always outside himself', is 'capable of living only in the opinion of others and, so to speak, derives the sentiment of his own existence solely from their judgement.'[161] The *amour propre* of civilised man is a social creation, a veneer of self-esteem acquired under the assessing eye of the world: '[we are] forever asking others what we are, without ever daring to ask it of ourselves...'[162] So if it is 'women' who must always dwell in the realm of appearances, and forgo private beliefs for public orthodoxies; if it is 'women' whose honour depends less on their conduct than on their reputation; and if it is 'women' who must be ruled by opinion, rather than by their own powers of judgement – then to be 'women' is the destiny of Everyman. 'Little girls... can already be governed by speaking to them of what will be thought of them,' Rousseau writes in *Emile*. 'When the same motive is... suggested to little boys, it by no means has a similar empire over them... It is only by dint of time and effort that they are subjected to the same law.'[163]

Thus it is Sophie, not the stout-hearted Emile (much less his unbiddable author), who possesses the requisite civic personality. If 'the task of political hegemony is to produce the very forms of subjecthood which will form the basis of political unity', then such subjectivity for Rousseau is realised under the sign of Woman.[164] In *La Nouvelle Héloïse*, St Preux writes to Julie from Paris. His letters to her, she decides with some irritation, are 'trifling' compared to those sent to a male friend, which discuss political matters. But then, Julie concedes, why should she care about politics anyway?

Bound to respect the government, under which it is my fate to have been born, I give myself no trouble to enquire whether there are any better. To what end should I be instructed in the knowledge of governments, who have so little power to establish them?[165]

And to what end should men and women have personal ideals or private hopes, when these can only promote social instability? The independent self, whose core faculty is the imagination, is forever straining toward a vanishing horizon. Dreaming of the Ideal, such free spirits fail in their allegiance to the Real. Society must be protected from them; as indeed they must be protected from themselves. Fantasies must be restricted; dreams must be curbed; thoughts – particularly religious beliefs – must be policed. 'Always keep your children within the narrow circle of the dogmas connected with morality' Rousseau warns, since 'whoever combats [dogma]...is the disturber of order and the enemy of society.'[166] The 'reckless pride' of individual conviction – the pride, say, of a Sophie Two – dissolves social sentiment, leading to open dissent and factionalism. Private piety defies public orthodoxy, setting conscience against law. So Sophie is offered only the faith of her father and husband, which she has no right to question. 'Do not make your daughters theologians and reasoners', Rousseau urges, but ensure rather 'that in her belief she is enslaved by authority' – just as all men must be, if social peace is to be maintained.[167]

The properly reared woman, her individuality sacrificed to *le bien publique*, is civilised selfhood incarnate. Stripped of the importunate impulses and independent reasonings associated with virile manhood, she is the ideal subject of the General Will; but more than this, she is also the instrument by which male compliance to the demands of civility can be secured. After Sophie's marriage to Emile, the Mentor tells her that he is transferring his authority over Emile to her. Of course she must obey her husband, 'just as nature wanted it', but she must also act as his moral superintendent, exploiting her sexual power over him to become 'arbiter of his pleasures'. 'It will cost you some painful privations, but you will reign over him if you know how to reign over yourself...'[168] Sophie's 'chaste power' will tame Emile, for in moral matters 'it will always be the lot of your sex to govern ours'.[169] Dedicating his *Second Discourse* to his homeland of Geneva, Rousseau exhorted its 'citizen-women' to use their 'persuasive gentleness' to police the *moeurs* of Genevan men, and so 'preserve the love of the laws' in them; for

[w]hat man would be so barbarous as to resist the voice of honor and reason from the mouth of tender wife...? Therefore always be what you are, the chaste guardians of morals and the gentle bonds of peace, and continue at every opportunity to assert the rights of the Heart and of Nature on behalf of duty and virtue.[170]

This chaste moral governance – as embodied say in the divine Julie – is the benign face of feminine rule (and the theme that gave Rousseau his considerable reputation as a friend to womankind, seeking – as one French feminist put it – to 'reestablish [women] in their natural dignity').[171] Exercised irresponsibly, however, as in the Paris elite, female power is terrifyingly malign, destructive of individual men and social mores in general. '[W]hen...we are corrupted it is...the fault of women.'[172] Thus 'even if the timidity, chasteness, and modesty which are proper to [women] are social inventions' such qualities are so essential to social well-being that the woman who refuses to cultivate them 'offends good morals'.[173] Women's natural ascendancy must be limited and channelled if it is not to foment public disaster.

Nowhere in her quarrel with Rousseau does Wollstonecraft contest this overblown, paranoid account of female power; indeed her own ruminations on the theme tend to be even darker than his. The 'passions of men . . . have placed women on thrones', she writes, from where they rule with a frivolous cruelty degrading to themselves and the men in their thrall.[174] Resigning 'the natural rights which . . . reason might have procured them' women exploit their youthful beauty to become 'short-lived queens' with no thought of the reckoning to come.

Exalted by their inferiority (this sounds like a contradiction), they constantly demand homage as women, . . . [to be] treated like queens only to be deluded by hollow respect, till they are led to resign, or not assume, their natural prerogatives.[175]

The result has been a generalised corruption of family life and a 'fearful catalogue of crimes' in the public domain, particularly in those nations (like France) where women's sexual wiles have secured them significant political influence. 'When, therefore, I call women slaves, I mean in a political and civil sense; for, indirectly they obtain too much power, and are debased by their exertions to obtain illicit sway.'[176]

Women's erotic power was such a commonplace of eighteenth-century thought that the only startling element in Wollstonecraft's handling of the theme is its unremitting harshness. But then feminists had particular cause to loathe sexual subterfuge. A simpering coquette exploiting her sexual charms was enough to make any feminist gorge rise – especially when such behaviour was as grossly idealised as it was in the case of Rousseau's Sophie. The feminist critic who most influenced Wollstonecraft in this regard was Catharine Macaulay, who in her own 1790 rebuttal of *Emile* had savaged 'female allurement' as 'hostile to . . . rational manners'.[177] According to Rousseau, female coquetry was a necessary counterbalance to women's physical inferiority to men; but the damage it wrought was far too serious, Macaulay had insisted, to be defended on these grounds: 'By the intrigues of women, and their rage for personal power and importance, the whole world has been filled with violence and injury . . .'[178] The remedy, then, must be as far-reaching as the evil: 'power [must be taken] out of the hands of vice and folly' and women fully emancipated.

. . . when the sex have been taught wisdom by education, they will be glad to give up indirect influence for those established rights which, independent of accidental circumstances, may afford protection to the whole sex.[179]

The free woman, Macaulay contended, will have no need of illicit power, happy instead with those 'rational privileges' that are God's legacy. Imbued with the 'principles of true religion and morality', she will embrace chastity and modesty not as specifically feminine virtues but as 'indispensible [sic] qualities in virtuous characters of either sex'.[180] Such a woman – 'grave, manly, noble, full of strength and majesty' – will permit only God to legislate her conduct. And since to 'make the condition of slavery an unalterable law of female nature' is no part of the divine plan, Macaulay could foresee a time when such women would predominate, inaugurating an era of general virtue and happiness.[181]

For Catharine Macaulay, who was a sophisticated theologian, it was Christian providence that offered women the best promise of a life of dignity and fulfilment. It was this theocentric core of Macaulay's feminism, more than any other of its features, that won Wollstonecraft's wholehearted assent. Echoing Macaulay's call for a religious renewal among women, Wollstonecraft uses the *Rights of Woman* to set out a programme for female spiritual redemption, and then calls on Heaven for endorsement. 'Gracious Creator of the whole human race!' Wollstonecraft exhorts her Maker,

hast thou created such a being as woman, who can trace thy wisdom in thy works, and feel that thou alone art by thy nature exalted above her, – for no better purpose... [than] to submit to man, her equal – a being, who, like her, was sent into the world to acquire virtue? – Can she consent to be occupied merely to please him; merely to adorn the earth, when her soul is capable of rising to thee?[182]

Never short of an answer, she then replies to her own question: 'if [women] be moral beings, let them have a chance to become intelligent; and let love to man be only a part of that glowing flame of universal love, which, after encircling humanity, mounts in graceful incense to God'.[183]

Admirers of Mary Wollstonecraft are often reluctant to see her as a religious thinker. This should not surprise us. Appeals to God and virtue of the kind that dominate the *Rights of Woman* are pretty much a 'dead letter' to feminists now, one critic remarks; and if by dead letter is meant a failed communication, then it is certainly true that of all aspects of Wollstonecraft's thought it is her religious faith that has failed to speak to modern interpreters.[184] Most studies do no more than gesture toward it, and then usually to dismiss it as ideological baggage foisted on her by her times, with no positive implications for her views on women. *A Vindication of the Rights of Woman* is generally located in a tradition of Enlightenment humanism that is assumed to have been at least indifferent to religion, if not actively hostile to it.

So it is startling, on looking closely at the *Rights of Woman,* to find that it contains at least fifty discussions of religious themes, ranging from brief statements on one or other doctrinal point to extended analyses of women's place within a divinely ordered moral universe. Nor are these discussions in any sense peripheral to the main message of the text. If Wollstonecraft's faith becomes a dead letter to us, then so does much of her feminism, so closely are they harnessed together. The famous call for a 'revolution of female manners' in the *Rights of Woman* is first and foremost a summons to women to establish a right relationship with their Maker. 'In treating ... of the manners of women, let us, disregarding sensual arguments, trace what we should endeavour to make them in order to co-operate ... with the Supreme Being':[185]

...for ... if they be really capable of acting like rational creatures, let them not be treated like slaves; or, like the brutes who are dependent on the reason of man, when they associate with him; but cultivate their minds, give them the salutary sublime curb of principle, and let them attain conscious dignity by feeling themselves only dependent on God.[186]

It is through the exercise of 'a rational will that only bows to God' that women will achieve that self-respect on which inner freedom is founded. 'These may be Utopian dreams,' Wollstonecraft writes, but 'thanks to that Being who impressed them on my soul, and gave me sufficient strength of mind to dare to exert my own reason, till, becoming dependent only on Him for the support of my virtue, I view, with indignation, the mistaken notions that enslave my sex.'[187] It was thanks to God, in other words, that Mary Wollstonecraft became a feminist.

3

For the love of God

> ...an affection for mankind, a passion for an individual, is but an un-
> folding of that love which embraces all that is great and beautiful...
> (Mary Wollstonecraft, *A Short Residence in Sweden*)[1]

RELIGION AND FEMINISM

Wollstonecraft's family were inactive members of the Church of England, and according to her husband and biographer, William Godwin, she 're-ceived few lessons of religion in her youth'.[2] Nonetheless, for the first twenty-eight years of her life she was a regular churchgoer and her first published work, *Thoughts on the Education of Daughters*, was steeped in orthodox attitudes, advocating 'fixed principles of religion' and warning of the dangers of rationalist speculation and deism. For women in particular, the young Wollstonecraft argued, clear-cut religious views were essential: 'for a little refinement only leads a woman into the wilds of romance, if she is not religious; nay more, there is no true sentiment without it, nor perhaps any other effectual check to the passions'.[3] In the same year that *Thoughts* was published, however, Wollstonecraft stopped attending church, and by the time she produced her last book, *A Short Residence in Sweden*, she had performed an apparent *volte-face*, writing approvingly of free-thinkers who 'deny the divinity of Jesus Christ, and...question the necessity or utility of the christian system'.[4] The abandonment of Christian orthodoxy, however, only served to underline her commitment to what had become a highly personal faith. 'Her religion,' as Godwin wrote in his *Memoirs* of her shortly after her death, 'was almost entirely of her own creation. But she was not on that account less attached to it, or the less scrupulous in discharging what she considered as its duties.'[5]

At the time Godwin met Wollstonecraft she had not been a churchgoer for over four years. Nonetheless, on that occasion they managed to have a row about religion in which, as Godwin recalled, 'her opinions approached much nearer to the received one, than mine'.[6] When they met again, in 1796, Godwin was an atheist. This meeting was much more successful than the first: they became friends, then lovers, then husband and wife – and meanwhile went on disagreeing about religion. 'How can you blame me for taking refuge in the idea of a God, when I despair of finding sincerity here on earth?' Wollstonecraft demanded at one low point two months before her death.[7] At any rate, little as he would have wanted it, it was Godwin who had the last word, since after his wife's premature death it was left to him to produce an account of her religious beliefs in his *Memoirs*.

Wollstonecraft's religion, Godwin wrote, was 'in reality, little allied to any system of forms' and 'was founded rather in taste, than in the niceties of polemical discussion':

Her mind constitutionally attached itself to the sublime and the amiable. She found an inexpressible delight in the beauties of nature, and in the splendid reveries of the imagination. But nature itself, she thought, would be no better than a vast blank, if the mind of the observer did not supply it with an animating soul. When she walked amidst the wonders of nature, she was accustomed to converse with her God. To her mind he was pictured as not less amiable, generous and kind, than great, wise and exalted.[8]

This representation of Wollstonecraft's deity as a wishful mental projection owed too much to Godwin's own religious scepticism to be reliable.[9] Mary Hays's alternative depiction of Wollstonecraft's God as 'a being higher, more perfect, than visible nature' whom she 'adored... amidst the beauties of Nature, or... in the still hour of recollection', better captures Wollstonecraft's *credo*.[10] Both Godwin and Hays rightly stressed the central role of passion and fantasy in Wollstonecraft's theology. Both also – much less plausibly – represented her as indifferent to theological controversy. Her 'faith relied not upon critical evidence or laborious investigation', Hays claimed, which in Godwin's version became a depressingly condescending portrait of his wife's mind in action.[11] 'She adopted one opinion,' Godwin wrote, 'and rejected another, spontaneously, by a sort of tact, and the force of a cultivated imagination; and yet, though perhaps, in the strict sense of the term, she reasoned little, it is surprising what a degree of soundness is to be found in her determinations.'[12]

'She reasoned little...': and this of the woman who translated and reviewed theological works in three languages, was conversant with the major theological debates of her period, and who consistently argued that true religion was not a mere matter of enthusiastic sentiment but rather 'a governing principle of conduct, drawn from self-knowledge, and rational opinion respecting the attributes of God'.[13] This refusal to take Wollstonecraft seriously as a religious intellectual was symptomatic of the anxieties aroused in Godwin by his wife's *savante* status. But it was also indicative of an important shift of opinion in the eighteenth century, as religious belief became increasingly aligned with the feminine and both came under the rule of sentiment, what Godwin described as the 'empire of feeling'. In the second edition of his *Memoirs* Godwin revised his account of Wollstonecraft's 'intellectual character' so as to make some of these connections more explicit. The difference between the sexes, he argued there, corresponds to the psychological opposition between reason and emotion – and he and Wollstonecraft exemplified this divide, he being dominated by 'habits of deduction' while she enjoyed an 'intuitive sense of the pleasures of the imagination' which eventually aroused his own emotions as well: 'Her taste awakened mine; her sensibility determined me to a careful development of my feelings.'[14] So while the Philosopher could not follow his wife into her religious beliefs, he nonetheless became a convert to the deep sense of personal truth reflected in them, the 'fearless and unstudied veracity' of Wollstonecraft's womanly heart.

This portrait of the woman of sensibility (at one point Godwin called Wollstonecraft a 'female Werther') tells us less about Wollstonecraft than it does about prevailing sexual mores – and Godwin's haphazard efforts at keeping his wife's stormy history within them. This is not to deny that Wollstonecraft enjoyed donning the cloak of female Wertherism at times, but the idea of a uniquely feminine emotionality was anathema to her, a central target of her feminism. Religious sentimentality of the kind typically associated with women she particularly disdained. Drawing a line between this sort of 'irrational enthusiasm' and the deep emotions of the true believer was not easy, however, and Wollstonecraft worked hard at clarifying the distinction. Her ambiguous attitude toward sensibility (which has received so much attention from recent commentators) is best understood in this context, as part of her wider endeavour to define an authentic religious subjectivity.[15] What shape does a woman's inner life take when it is forged in a right relationship to her Maker? Wollstonecraft's first sustained attempt to answer this question can be found in the character of the philosophical Mary of her novel, *Mary, a Fiction*.

From her earliest youth, the fictive Mary is animated by what Wollstonecraft describes as 'enthusiastic sentiments of devotion':

Sublime ideas filled her young mind – always connected with devotional sentiments . . . The wandering spirits, which she imagined inhabited every part of nature, were her constant friends and confidants. She began to consider the Great First Cause, formed just notions of his attributes, and, in particular, dwelt on his wisdom and goodness.[16]

At night the adolescent Mary 'converses' with God and sings hymns 'of her own composing' until at times she almost hallucinates her Creator: 'only an infinite being could fill the human soul'.[17] At fifteen she decides to receive the holy sacrament and in order to prepare herself 'would sit up half the night' 'perusing the scriptures, and discussing some points of doctrine which puzzled her'. The oscillation between an almost ecstatic ardour and the fierce intellectualism of the student of theology vividly calls up the adolescent Wollstonecraft. In the life of the fictive Mary it climaxes in the great day of her first communion:

. . . she hailed the morn, and sung with wild delight, Glory to God on high, good will towards men. She was indeed so much affected when she joined in the prayer for her eternal preservation, that she could hardly conceal her violent emotions; and the recollection never failed to wake her dormant piety when earthly passions made it grow languid.[18]

But alas for bright young hopes: Mary's unloving parents contract her to a mercenary marriage from which she flees to female friendship and love of the invalid genius, Henry, whose eventual death leaves her with 'a heart in which there was a void, that even benevolence and religion could not fill' and the eager anticipation of an early death.[19] Her life having been one of unceasing affliction, Mary ends her narrative existence having learned to expect happiness nowhere but in God's kingdom. '[I]t is the office of Religion to reconcile us to the seemingly hard dispensations of providence,' she reflects heroically, 'and . . . no inclination, however strong, should oblige us to desert the post assigned us . . .'[20]

Mary is an irritating little saint. Her superior sensitivities and sighs of stoical resignation make this impious reader long for the ironies of a Fielding or an Austen. Yet as a vehicle for the young Wollstonecraft's proto-feminist aspirations, Mary embodies a powerful pro-woman dimension of the Christian tradition. Her struggles to extricate herself from the soul-destroying conventions of fashionable femininity – as represented by her mother and other elite ladies she meets in her travels – draw her toward a counter-ideal of true selfhood that is, in essence, genderless. 'Heaven had endowed her with uncommon humanity, to render her one of His benevolent agents,' Wollstonecraft writes of Mary; but this inner grace is not sex-specific.[21] The deiformity of humankind transcends profane bodily distinctions. 'Human nature itself, which is complete in both sexes, has been made in the image of God,' Saint Augustine had written, and thus in the spirit 'there is no sex'.[22] 'It be not philosophical to speak of sex when the soul is mentioned,' Wollstonecraft insisted.[23]

The appeal of this viewpoint to feminists has been strong and longstanding. Religion, as Simone de Beauvoir wrote with characteristic trenchancy in *The Second Sex*, 'cancels the advantage of the penis' – and although the vocabulary is not one an early modern woman would have used, the underlying egalitarian theme remained much the same.[24] Feminism, it is worth recalling, has for most of its history been deeply embedded in religious belief. Eighteenth and nineteenth-century western feminists were nearly all active Christians, and even the more secular varieties of feminism that emerged in western societies in the 1960s and 1970s still had significant undercurrents of religious belief. Obviously, the religions which have engaged feminists internationally over the centuries have been so varied that any attempt to offer a general account of them would be foolhardy. But given the centrality of Wollstonecraft to the self-image of western feminism, understanding her theology may give us more than local insights into the religious impulse as it has operated across the feminist tradition.

In Wollstonecraft's Protestant England, the spiritual equality of women had long been an important minority theme. Puritan sects in particular, with their fierce emphasis on the democracy of God's grace, had provided generations of female believers with a language of spiritual self-assertion; and even the Church of England had harboured godly feminists. 'Whatever...Reasons Men may have for despising Women, and keeping them in Ignorance and Slavery, it can't be from their having learnt to do so in Holy Scripture,' the High Anglican Mary Astell claimed in 1700, adding stoutly that 'the Bible is for, and not against us...'[25] Calls to a higher life – whether it meant an intensification of female piety in the home or even, as in the case of seventeenth and eighteenth-century women preachers, leaving their households to spread God's Word – was a route to enhanced self-esteem and moral status, and sometimes to the potential subversion of Female Duty. 'I chose to obey God rather than man,' one female preacher wrote on abandoning her husband in order to serve her Maker, and the appeal of such forms of religious obedience to many insubordinate female spirits is easily imagined.[26]

The religious revival which swept Britain from the 1730s on carried such aspirations in its wake, although with mixed results. The decline of the militant spirit which had fostered the revival, combined with stricter policing of sexual divisions within its ranks, led to women's claims often being pushed to the margins of the movement or outside evangelicalism entirely. Pauline strictures against the ministry of women were a staple of popular sermonising by the 1780s. So while the religious ardour of the fictive Mary is often revivalist in tone, by the time the book was written her bossy pronouncements on spiritual matters – so reminiscent of early Puritan women preachers – would certainly have been deemed improper by most evangelicals. 'The influence of religion is to be exercised with discretion [by women],' Hannah More warned in 1799, since '[a] female Polemic wanders almost as far from the limits prescribed to her sex, as a female Machiavel.'[27]

These fluctuations in the fortunes of female believers were accompanied by changing perceptions about the importance of gender in the Christian self. The soul may be sexless, but its earthly vehicles patently are not: a fact that acquired increasing weight over the course of the eighteenth century. From the mid century preachers of all stripes could be heard arguing that female religious feeling was intrinsically more powerful than that of men: a view reinforced by the idealisation of pity as the primary Christian sentiment. The cult of feminine sensibility, evident in both fiction and moral literature, derived largely from this source. Womankind, the Newcastle vicar John Brown explained in a sermon delivered in 1765, has a greater 'sensibility of pain' than men, and thus a greater capacity to empathise with the sufferings of others, while at the same time taking 'highest Delight...in a grateful Subordination to its Protector'.[28] These emotional predispositions, combined with the 'calmer' lives women lead, mean that while 'in man, Religion is generally the Effect of Reason' in women 'it may almost be called the Effect of Nature'.[29] Such innate piety, Brown concluded (on a note heard with increasing frequency over succeeding decades) gave women a uniquely authoritative role in moral life, since

a Mind thus gentle and thus adorned exalts subordination itself into the Power of Superiority and Command...the Influence and irresistible Force of Virtue.[30]

Women may be men's inferiors in social and political life, but in matters of the spirit they are preeminent. This line of argument worked well as a defence against women's secular claims. But it also posed some real hazards for sexual conservatives, particularly in its more militant formulations. In some respects *Mary, A Fiction* exemplifies these dangers. The fictive Mary, according to her author, is so strongly attuned to the needs and sufferings of others that for her no 'sensual gratification' can compare to the joy of feeling her 'eyes moistened after having comforted the unfortunate'.[31] This compassionate sensibility benefits everyone around her (although they remain disappointingly ungrateful) while at the same time bestowing an 'enthusiastic greatness' on Mary's soul. She 'glanced from earth to heaven', Wollstonecraft tells us, and 'caught the light of truth' which, like her author, she was then ever eager to shed on others – 'her tongue was ever the faithful interpreter of her heart'.[32] And why should

Mary keep silent, when heart and soul have so much to say? Christian militancy irresistibly posed the question, and even women ostensibly opposed to all that Wollstonecraft stood for, often found themselves responding to the call in unconventional ways. Hannah More may have held female polemicists to be ungodly, but this didn't prevent her from publishing tens of thousands of pious works exhorting women to use their superior moral influence against Satan, the slave trade, and French 'democratical' politics. Soon (although not in Wollstonecraft's lifetime) many women Evangelicals began explicitly linking doctrines of female moral leadership to demands for practical improvements in women's own political and legal status.

Being a proper Christian woman, then, was a paradoxical affair, bestowing important ethical prerogatives to be exercised only under conditions of psychological and practical submission. A woman, Rousseau had argued in *Emile*, should always defer to the religious views of her father or husband, and most women probably agreed – 'conforming', as Wollstonecraft put it, 'as a dependent creature should, to the ceremonies of the church which she was brought up in, piously believing that wiser heads than her own have settled that business...'[33] Certainly mainstream moralists were as likely to denounce women with independent religious views as they were to condemn the godless. The immensely influential handbook of advice to young women written by Dr John Gregory (and criticised by Wollstonecraft in the *Rights of Woman*) specifically counselled them against all religious study while at the same time emphasising that 'even those men who are themselves unbelievers dislike infidelity in *you*'. Lack of piety in women, Gregory noted, was taken as 'proof of that hard and masculine spirit, which of all your faults, *we* [men] dislike the most' while its presence was men's best security for 'that female virtue in which *they* are most interested', i.e. chastity.[34] James Fordyce similarly condemned any sign of intellectual independence in women while at the same time recommending public devotions as a way of displaying female face and form to most pleasing effect.[35] 'Why are women to be thus bred up with a desire of conquest?...' was Wollstonecraft's irritable response to all this: 'Do religion and virtue offer no stronger motives, no brighter reward?'[36]

Women conductbook writers by contrast tended to emphasise women's intellectual relationship to God, urging close study of the Bible and familiarity with major theological works. Women writers published biblical commentary, entered into public debate with male theologians, and wrote essays in which Female Duty was spelled out with fierce moral stringency. The brand of female devotion promoted by these women was as much a matter of mind as heart, and in this they were clearly spiritual sisters to Wollstonecraft's fictive Mary, and also to the redoubtable Mrs Mason of Wollstonecraft's *Original Stories* for children. Mrs Mason, a Christian propagandist with a formidable sense of her own self-worth, tells her little pupils that they must learn not only to love God but also to mimic Him. '[T]o attain any thing great,' she informs them, 'a model must be held up to our understanding, and engage our affections' in such a way that we learn 'to copy his attributes' and 'imitate Him'. 'We are his children when we try to resemble Him . . . convinced that truth and goodness must constitute the very essence of the soul . . .'[37] The tone is conventionally didactic, but to urge a little girl to find 'dignity and happiness' from mimicking God when the most to which she was generally meant to aspire was (in the words of the *Rights of Woman*) 'to model her soul to suit the frailities of her [husband]' was not just pious conventionalism.[38] This affirmation of women's capacity to apprehend and identify with the divine, expressed in nearly all female writings of the period, was so fundamental to women's sense of ethical worth, and so far-reaching in its egalitarian implications, that it can properly be described as one of the founding impulses of feminism.

The heroine of *Mary, a Fiction* is clearly indebted to these protofeminist elements of English Protestantism while at the same time rejecting evangelical extremism and Establishment reaction. 'The cant of weak enthusiasts have made the consolations of Religion . . . appear . . . ridiculous,' Wollstonecraft wrote to her sister in 1784, and by the time she wrote *Mary* this view was hardening into a wholesale condemnation of all varieties of Christian 'fanaticism'.[39] The fictive Mary begins her career, as we have seen, as a professing Anglican with an evangelical tinge. But as the novel progresses she becomes increasingly unorthodox. Like her author, she feels closest to God not in church but in the contemplation of His works, particularly 'the grand or solemn features of Nature' in which her sensitive heart delights. She does not scorn Scripture, but nor does she unthinkingly accept it, for 'her mind was not like a mirror' merely reflecting what was before it, but an instrument of rational criticism. Travelling in Portugal, she enters a Catholic church in the company of some 'deistical' Englishmen, and then:

Mary thought of both the subjects, the Romish tenets, and the deistical doubts; and though not a sceptic, thought it right to examine the evidence on which her faith was built. She read Butler's Analogy, and some other authors: and these researches made her a christian from conviction, and she learned charity, particularly with respect to sectaries; saw that apparently good and solid arguments might take their rise from different points of view; and she rejoiced to find that those she should not concur with had some reason on their side.[40]

Mary, in other words, is well on her way to becoming a typical Enlightenment intellectual, eschewing blind faith and evangelical purism in favour of 'rational religious impulses' and liberal toleration. The trajectory roughly followed Wollstonecraft's own. Four years before the publication of *Mary* she had moved with her sisters to Newington Green, north of London, to run a girls' school there. Newington Green had long been a hotbed of religious and political radicalism; its presiding spirit at the time of Wollstonecraft's arrival was Richard Price, minister to the local community of Rational Dissenters (or Unitarians, as they became known). Price and his fellow Unitarian, the Birmingham scientist and preacher Joseph Priestley, were leading figures in the English radical intelligentsia, and although Wollstonecraft never became a Unitarian she attended Price's chapel, studied his sermons (which however she deemed too 'profound' and 'controversial' for 'the generality', and so warned her young friend George Blood against reading them) and came to admire his personal and political integrity.[41] It was Burke's targeting of Price in his *Reflections on the Revolution in France* which helped galvanise Wollstonecraft into writing *A Vindication of the Rights of Men*. 'I am not accustomed to look up with vulgar awe, even when mental superiority exalts a man above his fellows; but still the sight of a man whose habits are fixed by piety and reason, and whose virtues are consolidated into goodness, commands my homage,' she told Burke, adding however that she was prepared to grant that Price's 'political opinions' were perhaps no more than 'Utopian reveries'.[42] The concession was probably tactical, since her own political views were by then at least as radical as Price's. Despite the 'bitter calumnies' of those who reviled his progressivism, Price was 'one of the best of men', she wrote shortly after his death, in the *Rights of Woman*.[43]

Rational Dissent was a variety of Protestant Nonconformity forged by and for the *avant-garde* educated middle class. The most cerebral of the Nonconformist sects, Rational Dissent offered its adherents a bracing brew of Lockean psychology, Newtonian cosmology, rationalist morality and reform politics. Its creed was anti-trinitarian (the divinity of Christ was denied) and its deity was a benign Supreme Being with a judicious regard for all His creatures and no taste for hellfire. Calvinism, with its savagely anti-humanist ethos, was repudiated in favour of a vision of mankind as essentially good and inherently perfectible. 'We must get entirely clear of all the notions...of original sin...[to] leave room for the expansion of the human heart,' Wollstonecraft wrote in 1794.[44]

In common with all Nonconformists, Rational Dissenters were subject to the Test Acts – discriminatory laws barring them from holding office under the Crown or in municipal corporations, and from taking degrees at Oxford and Cambridge. The struggle to repeal the Acts, which lasted many decades, was at its height when Wollstonecraft was attending Price's chapel, and the political stridency with which it infused the Unitarians' rhetoric clearly struck a chord in their young fellow-traveller. The analogy between the oppression of women and the penalties suffered by Dissenters was readily drawn, and Wollstonecraft herself drew it in the *Rights of Woman* (where she also claimed however that both Dissenters and women were psychologically deformed by their secondary status).[45] But more important for her feminism was Unitarianism's emphasis on private reasoned judgement as the foundation of true religion: a position to which the circumstances of Dissenters and women gave real political bite. The fictive Mary's cool weighing of doctrinal choices, and her insistence that all religious beliefs (including those of 'sectaries', i.e. Dissenters) be respected, reflected this viewpoint – its radicalism heightened in this instance simply by having a woman hold it. By 1790 Wollstonecraft was prepared to be more explicit. 'I look into my own mind,' she wrote *contra* Burke:

> my heart is human, beats quick with human sympathies – and I FEAR God...I fear that sublime power, whose motive for creating me must have been wise and good; and I submit to the moral laws which my reason deduces from this view of my dependence on him. – It is not his power that I fear – it is not to an arbitrary will, but to unerring *reason* I submit.[46]

'[T]o act according to the dictates of reason,' she wrote further on, 'is to conform to the law of God.'[47]

This appeal to the inner authority of the individual believer was at the heart of all varieties of Enlightened theism. '*Intra te quaere Deum*' Basil Willey has noted, was the motto of the age:

> look for God within thyself. And what exactly would you find when you looked within? Not the questionable shapes revealed by psycho-analysis, but something much more reassuring: the laws of God and Nature inscribed upon the heart...[48]

The will of God, as Rousseau wrote in his immensely influential credo of the Vicar of Savoyard, is 'written by nature with ineffaceable characters in the depth of my heart. I have only to consult myself...'[49] Wollstonecraft's fictive Mary, contemplating scenes of public devotion, observes that true religion 'does not consist in ceremonies' but in doing good and loving God. She, like her author, experiences her deepest religious emotions during moments of solitary contemplation, when the absence of all loved ones makes her particularly 'sensible of the presence of her Almighty Friend'.[50]

Rational Dissent did not go so far as this in rejecting religious observance, but its political case for toleration was founded on the same reverence for personal conviction. 'Every man ought to be left to follow his conscience because then only he acts virtuously,' Price argued.[51] No earthly power has authority over our private judgement, and no restriction on conscience is ever legitimate. 'Liberty,' Price wrote in his 1758 *Review of the Principal Questions and Difficulties in Morals* (with which Wollstonecraft was clearly familiar) is 'the power of *acting* and *determining*: And it is self-evident, that where such a power is wanting, there can be no moral capacities.'[52] Liberty and reason, Price went on, 'constitute the capacity of virtue'; or as Wollstonecraft put it: 'the conduct of an accountable being must be regulated by the operations of its own reason; or on what foundation rests the throne of God?... Liberty is the mother of virtue.'[53] Only those able to think and act for themselves will win a place by God's throne. Emile's Sophie may have been willing to allow him to legislate for her in religious matters, or Milton's Eve be prepared to defer to Adam's spiritual authority – 'God is thy law, thou mine: to know no more / Is women's happiest knowledge and her praise' Eve warbles away – but against these models of feminine self-abnegation Wollstonecraft invoked the Protestant imperative for direct dealing with one's Maker. If no priest may stand between creature and Creator, why should a mere man stand between a woman and her God?

For if it be allowed that women were destined by Providence to acquire human virtues, and, by the exercise of their understandings, that stability of character which is the firmest ground to rest our future hopes upon, they must be permitted to turn to the fountain of light, and not forced to shape their course by the twinkling of a mere satellite. [54]

Only a soul 'perfected by the exercise of its own reason' is 'stamped with the heavenly image', but 'man ever placed between [woman] and reason, she is always represented as only created to see through a gross medium' and so is estranged from her own moral potential. This alienation from grace is the nadir of female oppression, since it denies to women that inner mirroring of God's sublimity which is every soul's proper achievement. Universal reason is God's gift to all, the sign of His presence within, but men's jealous claims to reason's prerogatives would damn women to spiritual ignorance, and so flout God's plan. If the Father of All Creation smiles equally on all His offspring, who are men to raise themselves to a higher position in His sight? 'Let us then, as children of the same parent... reason together, and learn to submit to the authority of reason...' Wollstonecraft urges her readers. For 'they alone are subject to blind authority who have no reliance on their own strength. They are free – who will be free!'[55]

Seen in this light, women's emancipation is not only a *desideratum* for this life, but the prerequisite for women's eternal salvation. This emphasis in Wollstonecraft's feminism on secular gains as a means to spiritual goals is possibly one of the most difficult to appreciate today, yet her writings are suffused with it. The line of argument is clear. If the human soul were not immortal – if our brief existence invariably terminated at death – then female oppression, however censurable in itself, would be only one more of those infinite woes which make up our lot in this vale of tears. Social revolution throws into relief the injustice of women's subordinate status and offers opportunities for change; but it is the prospect of life beyond all such mortal contrivances which makes women's sufferings as a sex wholly reprehensible – for in enslaving women on earth men have also been denying them heaven. Rational Dissent held mortal existence to be a probationary state, a trial period, from which the souls of the virtuous alone would emerge into eternal bliss. Wollstonecraft consistently endorsed this view, and then pointed out its implications. For if women are disallowed the conditions necessary for the acquisition of virtue, then 'how [they] are to exist in that state where there is neither to be marrying nor giving in marriage, we are not told':

For though moralists have agreed that the tenor of life seems to prove that *man* is prepared . . . for a future state, they constantly concur in advising *woman* only to provide for the present. Gentleness, docility, and a spaniel-like affection are, on this ground, consistently recommended as the cardinal virtues of the sex; and disregarding the arbitrary economy of nature, one writer has declared that it is masculine for a woman to be melancholy. She was created to be the toy of man, his rattle, and it must jingle in his ears whenever, dismissing reason, he chooses to be amused.[56]

But 'if morality has an eternal foundation' then 'whoever sacrifices virtue, strictly so called, to present convenience . . . lives only for the passing day' at the expense of futurity. To propitiate men, women neglect absolute morality in favour of the relative merits – chastity, humility, diffidence – assigned to their sex, and the result is their spiritual nullification. 'I wish to sum up what I have said in a few words,' Wollstonecraft wrote in conclusion to the third chapter of the *Rights of Woman*, in what could well serve as a *coda* to the entire text: 'for I here throw down my gauntlet, and deny the existence of sexual virtues . . . For man and woman, truth . . . must be the same.'[57]

Here indeed is the puritan voice, stiff with ethical rigour. Moral absolutism of this kind has always had strong appeal for feminists, wary of the laid-back pragmatism of elite sophisticates and hostile to the traditionalist morality of Burkean conservatives. It is all very well, as Wollstonecraft told Burke, for those in power to preen themselves on the possession of moral instincts which are somehow, mysteriously, always in accord with the *status quo*; for the unenfranchised, however, the assertion of ethical imperatives that transcend and potentially subvert the moral commonsense of an age is a powerful weapon against established authority. 'It is time to separate unchangeable morals from local manners' she insisted in the *Rights of Woman*, to bring all humanity under God's law.[58] But as far as women are concerned,

the fanciful female character, so prettily drawn by poets and novelists, demanding the sacrifice of truth and sincerity; virtue [to them] becomes a relative idea, having no other foundation than utility; and of that utility men pretend arbitrarily to judge, shaping it to their own convenience.[59]

Where there is no absolute standard of right, power maintains its own codes of expedience. Men, like all despots, seek grounds for their rule in precept and custom, so that the ruled appear duty-bound to obey. Wollstonecraft's line of attack against this authoritarianism further revealed her debt to Rational Dissent, and in particular to its anti-voluntarist view of the respective obligations of God and mankind. Anti-voluntarist theology, at its simplest, holds that the power of God is constrained by His goodness; or as Price put it, in his *Review of Morals*, God's sovereign authority derives 'not merely from his almighty power' but from the 'infinite excellencies of his nature as the foundation of reason and wisdom'.[60] Worship, in other words, is not blind submission to an omnipotent force, for (in Wollstonecraft's words) 'what good effect can the latter mode of worship have on the moral conduct of a rational being?'[61] Conservatives like Burke might believe cringing deference to be authority's due, but Wollstonecraft was having none of this. She worshipped God, she told Burke in the *Rights of Men*, not for His omnipotence but for the divine perfections which human virtues mimic. It is not arbitrary might but Virtue itself to which she submits:

Submit – yes; I disregard the charge of arrogance, to the law that regulates his just resolves; and the happiness I pant after must be the same in kind, and produced by the same exertions as his – though unfeigned humility overwhelms every idea that would presume to compare the goodness which the most exalted created being could acquire, with the grand source of life and bliss.[62]

We love God because He deserves our love, not because He commands it; and the fruit of this worship is that 'enlightened self-love' which is every believer's entitlement.

This emphasis on *esteem* as the key element in religious devotion had important extratheological implications. For if it is not power but virtue that elicits respect in the divine sphere, why should this not also be true of intimate human relationships? 'It were to be wished,' Wollstonecraft writes, 'that women would cherish an affection for their husbands, founded on the same principle that devotion [to God] ought to rest upon' – which sounds shockingly retrograde until one realises exactly what she is saying. Husbands should be loved inasmuch – and only inasmuch – as they possess virtues capable of inspiring wifely respect. 'No other firm base is there under heaven – for let [women] beware of the fallacious light of sentiment; too often used as a softer phrase for sensuality.'[63] It is neither power nor romantic enthusiasm which should tie women to their menfolk, but only shared love of the Good.

The appeal of such arguments to women of independent-minded temperament is readily imagined, and Rational Dissent contained many such. Most in Wollstonecraft's day were not explicitly feminist, and some – notably Anna Barbauld, of whom more later – publicly opposed Wollstonecraft's ideas. But the network of likeminded believers in which Unitarian women moved was one of the most sexually liberal of the period, and increasingly hospitable to female aspirations. Within a quarter century of Wollstonecraft's death it was Unitarianism that was providing many intellectual leaders for nascent English feminism.[64]

Yet despite these affinities, Wollstonecraft's relationship to Rational Dissent was not uncritical. On several occasions she explicitly distanced herself from Dissenting culture, describing their chapels as too homely, their sectarianism as too narrow, and their general attitude to life as one of 'prim littleness'.[65] More important, her attitude toward religious feeling was very unlike theirs. That our access to God is through reason rather than mindless faith or overheated enthusiasm was certainly as central to her theology as to Rational Dissent, but the idea of reason operative in her writings was not the rather chilly deductive faculty found in most Unitarian preachings – which she frequently criticised as 'cold, instrumental' reason – but a much more libidinised, imaginative drive toward the True and the Good derived from Rousseau and the Christian Platonist tradition. For Wollstonecraft, to know God is not merely to appreciate him, in the Unitarian fashion, but to adore Him – and this not only because His perfections inspire adoration but because the epistemic impulse toward Him is essentially imaginative and erotic in character. The love Wollstonecraft had for her Maker, according to Mary Hays, was a 'delicious sentiment', a 'sublime enthusiasm' fuelled by a 'fervent imagination, shaping itself to ideal excellence, and panting after good unalloyed'.[66] For Wollstonecraft, *eros* was the core of the religious experience.

Scattered references throughout Wollstonecraft's *oeuvre* signal her awareness of the platonic roots of this ideal. If women are merely to be loved
for their 'animal perfection', she rebuked Burke in 1790, then 'Plato and
Milton were grossly mistaken in asserting that human love led to heavenly'; but if one accepts the platonic view that love of the divine is 'only an
exaltation of [earthly] affection' then women too must be loved for their
rational virtues rather than their physical attributes.[67] The feminist twist
was new, but the general argument had its source in what James Turner, in
his fine study of Christian sexual theorising, has described as the 'Christian-
isation of the Platonic *Eros*' to be found in Augustine and many varieties of
post-Augustinian theology, leading up to Milton.[68] 'Thy affections are the
steps; thy will the way;' Augustine had written, 'by loving thou mountest,
by neglect thou descendest.'[69] Desires that ascend toward God are to be
radically distinguished from those that descend toward earthly things, yet
both are designated as *eros* – the love which links humanity to the divine.
Those moralists who would disdain earthly affections, Christian Platonists
therefore argued, are in fact apostates, denying their connection to God.
'They... who complain of the delusions of passion,' Wollstonecraft wrote,
'do not recollect that they are exclaiming against a strong proof of the
immortality of the soul.'[70]

This valorisation of love points to an abiding tension within Christian morality where sexual love has always functioned as the key trope
for relations between God and His church, and marriage as the central
metaphor for the consummation of all things, but where love's physical
expression, with a few heretical exceptions, has either been condemned
in toto or confined to the marital bed. Christian Platonism, with its celebration of earthly affections as the vehicle for transcendent devotion, elevated this ambivalence into a theological principle. In the late seventeenth
century a group of churchmen known as the Cambridge Platonists argued that love 'issuing forth from God centres itself within us, and is the
Protoplastick virtue of our beings'; 'man is the instinct of love'.[71] In the
1690s one of these theologians, John Norris, engaged in a lengthy correspondence with the feminist writer Mary Astell (later published as *Letters
Concerning the Love of God*) in which they agreed that no mere mortal
could ever gratify the soul's desires: ' 'Tis true, a Sister Soul may give somewhat better Entertainment to our Love than other creatures can,' Astell
wrote, 'but she is not able to fill and content it' since it was only love of
God which could be 'secured from Disappointment, Jealousy, and all that
long Train of Pain and Grief which attends Desire' when it seeks earthly
objects.[72] Astell herself never had a sexual relationship, hoping instead to

spend her days in all-women communities united by 'love... breathing forth it self in flames of holy desires after GOD': an unrealised vision of a life dominated, we may suppose, by sublimated homoerotic desire.[73]

Astell's theological and feminist writings, very influential in her lifetime, were barely remembered by Wollstonecraft's day. The influence of Norris and other Cambridge Platonists, however, was still felt in liberal intellectual circles, particularly in the Rational Dissenting academies where their works were closely studied.[74] A strong Platonist element was discernible in Unitarian thought, especially in Richard Price's moral philosophy and in the writings of Anna Barbauld, the leading Unitarian woman writer who, as we shall see further on, was also an eloquent defender of the religious eros.[75] The mid-century Unitarian Platonist, David Hartley, in his highly influential *Observations on Man* (1749), had praised what he dubbed theopathy – love of God – in terms similar to Wollstonecraft's. '[W]e are led by the Love of good men to that of God, and back again by the Love of God to that of all his Creatures in and through him. The Love and Contemplation of [God's] Perfection and Happiness will transform us into his Likeness, into the image of him in which we were first made.'[76] There is no direct evidence of Hartley's influence on Wollstonecraft, but given the admiration with which his ideas were regarded by enlightened intellectuals, it is hard to imagine that she was not aware of them.

But the main impetus behind the propagation of the platonic *eros* in the eighteenth century came from poetry and fiction, and above all from Milton's classic celebration of sacred love in *Paradise Lost*. In the Miltonic Eden, Adam, confronted with Eve, finds himself yearning for more than intimations of the divine, and is scolded by the archangel Raphael:

> What higher in her society thou find'st
> Attractive, human, rational, love still;
> In loving thou dost well, in passion not,
> Wherein true Love consists not; love refines
> The thoughts, and heart enlarges, hath his seat
> In Reason, and is judicious, is the scale
> By which to heav'nly Love thou may'st ascend,
> Not sunk in carnal pleasure...[77]

Wollstonecraft quoted these lines repeatedly, as did scores of other eighteenth-century English writers gripped by Miltonian high romance.[78] Samuel Richardson's Clarissa even expired for this ideal. But it was Rousseau, also a passionate *devoté* of Milton, who purveyed these ideas to the largest audience through his immensely popular novels. 'The true philosophy of lovers is that of Plato,' he told his readers in the introduction to *La Nouvelle Héloïse*.[79] 'There is no true love without enthusiasm, and no enthusiasm without an object of perfection, real or chimerical,' Emile's Mentor instructs his pupil, while St Preux tells Julie that it is the 'perfect union of [our] souls which connects the most perfect, the most harmonious unity, with ties an hundred times more sacred'.[80] Julie fervently endorses this, asking her lover to 'consult your own breast' for true morality, since there he will find that 'sacred fire which hath so often inflamed us with love for the sublimest virtue', a 'sacred enthusiasm' which 'passions may defile, but can never efface'.[81] She marries the god-like Wolmar and becomes a mother, but still feels her heart sigh 'after something of which it is entirely ignorant':

my desiring soul seeks an object in another world; in elevating itself to the source of sentiment and existence, its languor vanishes... [and] obtains a new existence in the immensity of the Supreme Being...[82]

As she is clearly too good to live, Julie (like her prototype, Richardson's Clarissa) then dies and goes to where her perfect love can find its perfect object in the heavenly 'mansions of the blessed'.[83]

Wollstonecraft read *Emile* in 1787 and the *Confessions* either the same year or just before (when she first read *La Nouvelle Héloïse* is not recorded). And it was in 1787 that the theme of transcendent love first appeared in her work, in the final section of her unfinished tale, *The Cave of Fancy*. The narrative on which the *Cave* concludes is the life-history of the cave-dwelling female spirit, as told to the rescued child, Sagesta. The story is torturously complicated – plotting was never one of Wollstonecraft's strong points – but it centres on the love which, as a mortal woman, the spirit had felt for a married man prior to her own marriage. By the time of her wedding, she believes she has managed to repudiate this illicit passion, but the day itself is marked by an epiphany. Sitting alone 'on the brink of madness' (the spirit tells Sagesta) 'a strange association was made by my imagination' between the story of Galileo 'who when he left the inquisition, looked upwards, and cried out, "Yet it moves"' and her own overwrought state. 'in an agony I exclaimed, "Yet I love"'.[84] The analogy is clumsy, but the point Wollstonecraft is making is clear enough. For just as Galileo tried to turn men's eyes away from the illusions of the merely empirical to the reality of the heavens, so the erotic history of the fictive spirit is a progress from romantic illusion to a higher and truer Love. Like the men who inhabited Plato's allegorical cave, the spirit once dwelt in a world of shadows and phantoms. As a mortal woman, she tells Sagesta, she 'adored virtue':

and my imagination, chasing a chimerical object, overlooked the common pleasures of life; they were not sufficient for my happiness. A latent fire made me burn to rise superior to my contemporaries in wisdom and virtue... [85]

She had looked to 'the fairy land' of romantic love to satisfy these desires, but the hard lessons of life combined with her own virtuous disposition eventually lead her to recognise that such 'scenes of fancy' are dangerous delusions which must be abandoned. Piety shows her the path. Tied to a husband whose 'religion was coldly reasonable, because he wanted fancy' she looks in her own mind and finds 'opinions... graven with a pen of brass', the 'seeds of eternal happiness'. She clings fast to these new convictions, knowing them valorised by God. The imagination which had once generated a 'devouring flame' of forbidden desire now draws her away from the illusions of worldly passion toward heavenly Love. 'Worthy as the mortal was I adored, I should not long have loved him with the ardour I did, had fate united us, and broken the delusion the imagination so artfully wove,' she concludes:

His virtues... would have extorted my esteem; but he who formed the human soul, only can fill it, and the chief happiness of an immortal being must arise from the same source as its existence. Earthly love leads to heavenly, and prepares us for a more exalted state; if it does not change its nature, and destroy itself, by trampling on the virtue, that constitutes its essence, and allies us to the Deity.[86]

What little Sagesta must learn, in other words, is that for women, as for men, true love is found only in amorous communion with God.

The struggles of the female spirit were Wollstonecraft's first attempt to depict the psychological turmoil of women caught between customary attitudes and inner imperatives. Here, as in her later writings, it is the erotic imagination that propels women into that realm where profane passion transmutes into sacred rapture. Wollstonecraft's attitude toward sexuality has been criticised by modern scholars for its self-denying asceticism. Removed from its religious context, her view of sex in the *Rights of Woman* seems relentlessly negative. Yet while it is true that concupiscence is derogated in the *Rights of Woman*, eroticism in its wider sense is certainly not. Far from turning away from erotic desire, Wollstonecraft persistently celebrates it as the dynamic core of human subjectivity, the perfectibilist drive powering the personal ego. This eroticism, however, has its true source in the fantasising mind, not in the body, and its ultimate direction must be heavenward. A soul in love has only one right object. 'I see the sons and daughters of men pursuing shadows, and anxiously wasting their powers to feed passions which have no adequate object,' she writes:

To see a mortal adorn an object with imaginary charms, and then fall down and worship the idol which he had himself set up – how ridiculous!...Would not all the purposes of life have been much better fulfilled if he had only felt what has been termed physical love? And, would not the sight of the object, not seen through the medium of the imagination, soon reduce the passion to an appetite, if reflection, the noble distinction of man, did not give it force, and make it an instrument to raise him above this earthly dross, by teaching him to love the centre of all perfection...?[87]

The 'deification of the beloved object' in erotic love is a shadowy intimation of our love of the Deity; the erotic imagination is implanted in us by God to lead us toward Him. If directed exclusively toward mortal objects, the imagination becomes – the term Wollstonecraft used to describe both Rousseau and Burke's fantasies about women – 'debauched': delusional, corrupting, and invidious particularly in its consequences for women. When directed toward the divine, however, it illuminates the soul and 'afford[s] a glorious hope, if not a foretaste, of what we may expect hereafter'.[88]

Throughout its very long history, this ideal had been almost entirely androcentric: male spirit transcending the temptations of the female flesh. As a chief site of earthly corruption, the female body would be supervened by masculine moral aspirations. Rousseau's Emile, put to the test by his Mentor, gives a fine demonstration of such sublimatory prowess, while Sophie, who is capable of no such ethical grandeur, must have her passions restrained by harsh cultural conventions. Wollstonecraft was more than ready to agree with Rousseau that under present conditions women were too morally enfeebled to turn their desires to God – 'suspended by destiny... they have neither the unerring instinct of brutes, nor are allowed to fix the eye of reason on a perfect model' – but

[s]upposing...for a moment, that women were, in some future revolution of time, to become, what I sincerely wish them to be, even love would acquire more serious dignity, and be purified in its own fires...[89]

A free woman's passions, like her intellect, would then be transfigured by her inner grace. The female spirit of the *Cave of Fancy* was Wollstonecraft's earliest stab at imagining such a woman. A second, better-realised attempt, came in *Mary, A Fiction*, whose heroine has moral ardour in abundance and a sexual history designed to test it.

Throughout most of *Mary, A Fiction*, the heroine – like her author at the time of the novel's composition – is a virgin. She and her young husband, whom she meets on the day she is forced to marry him to secure an inheritance, part immediately after the ceremony and remain separated until the penultimate chapter. The man Mary loves, the fascinating Henry, touches her soul but never her body, and expires before anything more untoward can occur. And when, after Henry's death, Mary finally does join her husband it is only to deliver herself to him in a fugue of despair: 'when her husband would take her hand, or mention anything like love, she would instantly feel a sickness, a faintness at her heart, and wish... that the earth would open and swallow her'.[90] In the end it is religion only which makes life 'supportable', and Mary is left with her only 'gleam of joy' being the thought that 'she was hastening to that world *where there is neither marrying*, nor giving in marriage'.[91]

The message is direct: a loveless marriage can produce only sexual revulsion. Yet when it comes to Mary's feelings for Henry, Wollstonecraft's position is much hazier. That Henry is loved passionately is obvious, but the source and nature of this passion is much more ambiguous. It is at this point in the text, as the protagonists recognise their mutual attraction, that Wollstonecraft's prose, never particularly lucid throughout the novel, becomes virtually incomprehensible. The reason for this incoherence may become apparent, however, when we look at the ideas with which she was struggling. Here is her account of the moment when Mary realises the strength of her feeling for Henry, at the point when he has just told her of his fatherly affection for her, his wish to view her as his 'darling child'. Mary is overwhelmed: 'He had called her his dear girl... My child! His child, what an association of ideas! If I had a father, such a father! – She could not dwell on the thoughts, the wishes which obtruded themselves. Her mind was unhinged, and passion unperceived filled her whole soul.'[92]

The reader barely has time to draw breath from this extraordinary passage before Mary tackles Henry directly about her views on love. Henry has previously told her of his own propensity toward romantic fantasy – 'my fancy has too frequently delighted to form a creature that I could love, that could convey to my soul sensations which the gross part of mankind have not any conception of' – and now Mary reciprocates with an account of her own 'flights of the imagination' and the 'tumultuous passions' which give them wing.[93] In her case, however – and here Wollstonecraft ties together the enthusiastically devout young theologian with the loving woman – these passions are divinely inspired and divinely directed. The erotic imagination is directed toward mortal man only as a 'faint image' of a much greater love. She begins her peroration with a quotation: 'Milton has asserted, That earthly love is the scale by which to heavenly we may ascend' and then elaborates:

The same turn of mind which leads me to adore the Author of all Perfection – which leads me to conclude that he only can fill my soul; forces me to admire the faint image – the shadows of his attributes here below; and my imagination gives still bolder strokes to them. I know I am in some degree under the influence of a delusion – but does not this strong delusion prove that I myself 'am of *subtiler essence than the trodden clod*'[94]; these flights of imagination point to futurity; I cannot banish them.

The tone then alters:

Every cause in nature produces an effect; and am I an exception to the general rule? have I desires implanted in me only to make me miserable? will they never be gratified? shall I never be happy? My feelings do not accord with the notion of solitary happiness. In a state of bliss, it will be the society of beings we can love, without the alloy that earthly infirmities mix with our best affections, that will constitute great part of our happiness.[95]

'With these notions can I conform to the maxims of worldy wisdom?' she concludes by demanding, in what amounts to a virtual manifesto for the rights of the heart as against the 'cold dictates of worldly wisdom'. She ends with a terrific flourish: 'My conscience does not smite me, and that Being who is greater than the internal monitor, may approve of what the world condemns...'[96]

Mary is plainly a romantic martyr; but what precisely has she been doing that God condones while the world condemns? Propositioning Henry? Celebrating her freedom from her husband? Or simply embracing the inevitable suffering of a tender spirit in a cynical world? Or should the post-Freudian reader also begin to speculate about the alignment between her love of Henry, with all his fatherly affection for her, and love of the Divine Father (into whose hands, Wollstonecraft tells us, Mary eagerly delivers her soul)? Clearly Wollstonecraft herself did not know; and her wretched heroine, bewildered by misfortune, can only conclude on a sigh: 'the world...is ever hostile and armed against the feeling heart!'[97]

Mary, Wollstonecraft wants her readers to understand, is rather too much the romantic enthusiast. Loving Henry, she is 'unhinged' by emotions so overwhelming that they blank out 'every other remembrance and wish'. 'I know I am in some degree under the influence of a delusion,' she mournfully reflects. Yet her stance is not apologetic. 'You may tell me I follow a fleeting good, an *ignis fatuus*; but this chase, these struggles prepare me for eternity,' she tells Henry, quoting Corinthians: 'when I no longer see through a glass darkly I shall not reason about, but *feel* in what happiness consists'.[98] Mary knows that love, illusory and unrealisable in its earthly form, will transmute into the verities of eternal bliss.

This movement of love toward the divine re-appeared as a major theme in the *Rights of Woman* four years later and remained a significant element in Wollstonecraft's writings until her death. To see why we must now turn to her views on sexuality, and in particular to the key role assigned to the religious imagination in the formation of female sexual subjectivity. This returns us to her relationship with Rousseau, whose platonic-erotic vision inspired in his leading feminist disciple a sexual philosophy almost as complex and paradoxical as his own.

EROS AND EQUALITY

Sex pervades the *Rights of Woman*. The text is so erotically preoccupied, so charged with sexual imagery, that at times it verges on the pornographic. Like a pornographer too, the language in which Wollstonecraft talks sex – particularly female sex – is charged with fruity disgust. 'Women subjected by ignorance to their sensations, and only taught to look for happiness in love, refine on sensual feelings... [until] frequently in the midst of these sublime refinements, they plump into actual vice.'[99] From childhood on, women's 'senses are inflamed, and their understandings neglected' until they are rendered 'systematically voluptuous', the willing 'slaves of casual lust'.[100] The picture is so overblown as to be grotesque, and although Wollstonecraft frequently pauses to remind her readers that this unhappy condition has been culturally foisted on women, the negative force of the images overrides the causal explanation.

Men, despite Wollstonecraft's insistence that they are 'more under the influence of their appetites than women' get somewhat gentler treatment.[101] But when the two sexes merge the result is mutual corruption. 'The depravity of the appetite which brings the sexes together' is condemned *tout court*, inside marriage as well as out. 'Nature must ever be the standard of taste, the gauge of appetite – yet how grossly is nature insulted by the voluptuary' which is redeemable only – and barely – by the natural requirements of reproduction.'[102] 'The feelings of a parent mingling with an instinct merely animal, give it dignity' by mixing 'a little mind and affection with a sensual gust'; but once children have arrived the duties of parenthood are incompatible with further erotic indulgence.[103]

In order to fulfil the duties of life, and to be able to pursue with vigour the various employments which form the moral character, a master and mistress of a family ought not to continue to love each other with passion. I mean to say, that they ought not to indulge those emotions which disturb the order of society, and engross the thoughts that should be otherwise employed... I will go still further, and advance, without dreaming of a paradox, that an unhappy marriage is often advantageous to a family, and that the neglected wife is, in general, the best mother... [104]

In a good marriage, lust soon evaporates. Husbands and wives become celibate companions; friendship replaces desire. Where this does not happen a wife is 'rendered licentious' and unfit for maternal duty; if widowed, her appetites probably drag her to an early grave. [105] In a woman of virtue, on the other hand, the 'natural death of love' occurs early, leaving her to concentrate on her children; if widowed, she remains morally immaculate, seeking no new sexual partner. 'In the bloom of life,' Wollstonecraft tells us, such a woman 'forgets her sex – forgets the pleasure of an awakening passion, which might again have been inspired and returned... Her children have her love, and her brightest hopes are beyond the grave...' [106]

Even for an age of intensifying sexual restrictions, this was pretty nasty stuff: Wollstonecraft at her most disheartening. And it is views like these that, unsurprisingly, have led many modern scholars to brand her a sexual puritan. The *Rights of Woman*, Cora Kaplan has eloquently and influentially argued, 'expresses a violent antagonism to the sexual, it exaggerates the importance of the sensual in the everyday life of women, and betrays the most profound anxiety about the rupturing force of female sexuality'. [107] Mary Poovey, in her major study of Wollstonecraft's relationship to eighteenth-century sexual ideology, makes a similar argument, pointing out that Wollstonecraft's sexual outlook was heavily inflected by the repressive codes of propriety characteristic of the new middle class. [108] In one sense this is clearly right. Both in spirit and content, much of Wollstonecraft's anti-erotic rhetoric can easily be recognised as part of the eighteenth-century middle-class project to enhance its standing by contrasting its sober-minded decency to the moral laxity of the idle rich. The image of the eroticised woman to be found throughout Wollstonecraft's writings is therefore, as we saw earlier, both polemical and class specific: a caricature of aristocratic womanhood common to virtually all middle-class morality literature. The opulent lady of leisure lying in her bed surrounded by lapdogs, French novels and male admirers – a favourite image of the *Rights of Woman* – may have been a figure to which women of the middling sort occasionally aspired, but it bore little relation to the reality of their lives. This is occasionally made clear in the *Rights of Woman* itself, as when Wollstonecraft describes the middle-class housewife as a 'square-elbowed family drudge'. [109] But the mobilisation of such images in her book must nonetheless give pause. Why is female sexuality so denigrated by Wollstonecraft, and what implications did this have for her feminism?

The answer to the first question lay partly in contemporary sexual attitudes. At a time when the line between vicious and virtuous sexual behaviour in women, particularly middle-class women, was becoming drawn so rigidly that even to admit to sexual feelings was to risk disgrace, Wollstonecraft's views were pretty much the norm. 'Men were the wooers, women the wooed', and an assertive female sexuality which threatened this pattern was absolutely prohibited in all but the lowest and highest levels of society.[110] A woman must not only obey her husband, as one cleric declared, but must also bring 'unto him the very Desires of the Heart to be regulated by him so far, that it should not be lawful for her to will or desire what she liked, but only what her husband should approve and allow.'[111] The alternative to this, as Rousseau warned, was carnal and familial chaos, but also the collapse of the male/female division which is (or must be – Rousseau frequently slipped from natural facts to cultural imperatives) a distinction between the subject and object of sexual passion. '[T]he audacity of one sex and the timidity of the other', he wrote, establishes the naturally predatory dynamic of the sexual sphere.[112]

In fact, as we have seen, like nearly all eighteenth-century moralists Rousseau was not at all confident about female sexual diffidence. For centuries women had been regarded as the more carnal sex, inveterate nibblers at forbidden apples whose appetites required the sternest checks. In the course of the eighteenth century this notion was increasingly countered by its antithesis: far from wallowing in fleshly delights, women were seen to possess a sense of physical shame so powerful that it set absolute inner limits on their sexuality. Chastity as a prohibitive code could therefore give way to chastity as a subjective principle, a defining feature of the feminine personality, with unchaste women pushed beyond the pale of true womanhood.[113] The natural whoredom of the entire sex was thereby expunged, only to reappear in the figure of the whore herself: the Mary Magdalen who by bearing the burden of female sexual depravity made possible the de-eroticisation of the rest of the Christian sisterhood.

This sexual sanitisation of women, which reached its apotheosis in the Victorian period, was still a relatively new development in the late eighteenth century, and one feminists viewed with marked ambivalence. On the one hand, the excision of physical desire from the female character, if accompanied by greater male self-restraint, offered the promise of conjugal unions based on established affections rather than transient passions. This companionate marital ideal, originating in puritan preachings of the previous century, had long served as an important counter to women's sexual chatteldom, so it's hardly surprising to find the *Rights of Woman* drawing on this tradition.[114] 'A man, or a woman, of any feeling, must always wish to convince a beloved object that it is the caresses of the individual, not the sex, that are received and returned with pleasure; and that the heart, rather than the senses, is moved,' Wollstonecraft writes.[115] Compared to the 'modest overflowings of a pure heart' the 'feverish caresses of appetite' are 'but sin embracing death'.[116]

The argument had strong appeal for feminists, who knew all too well the price paid by women for unregulated sexual behaviour. Throughout the eighteenth century dark dramas of seduction and ruin, such as are portrayed in Wollstonecraft's *Maria*, showed the heartbreaking effects of the sexual double standard. But for most women it was the more prosaic experience of too frequent pregnancies, hazardous births (such as the one that killed Wollstonecraft herself) and venereal disease which made sex at least as dangerous as pleasurable. Companionate love offered the hope of a husband whose affectionate respect for his wife might override his carnal appetites: an attractive prospect, no doubt, to many overburdened mothers of large families. To secure a 'husband's respect before it is necessary to exert mean arts to please him and feed a dying flame' so that 'friendship and forbearance take place of a more ardent affection', as Wollstonecraft recommended, probably seemed a wife's best recipe for domestic happiness.[117]

On the other hand, as Wollstonecraft noted, the prescriptive writers who promulgated the idea of innate female chastity were usually less concerned with the reality of feminine virtue than with its appearance, particularly when it came to eligible young women whose success in the marriage market depended as much on their appeal to male erotic appetites as on their own reputation for sexual abstinence: a slice of sexual *realpolitik* which most moralists implicitly acknowledged. The route out of this conundrum lay in the concept of feminine 'modesty', a behavioural code combining overt sexual innocence with covert sexual provocation. Women, particularly young women, were meant to blush and simper at male attentions, displaying an incomprehension of erotic intentions so improbably excessive that it served as further inducement to masculine ardour. Again it's Rousseau's Sophie who provides a classic instance of this, in a description quoted in full by Wollstonecraft:

Her dress is extremely modest in appearance, and yet very coquettish in fact: she does not make a display of her charms, she conceals them; but in concealing them, she knows how to affect your imagination. Everyone who sees her will say, There is a modest and discreet girl; but while your are near her, your eyes and affections wander all over her person, so that you cannot withdraw them; and you would conclude, that every part of her dress, simple as it seems, was only put in its proper order to be taken to pieces by the imagination.[118]

'Is this modesty?' Wollstonecraft demands. 'Is this a preparation for im-mortality?' In fact, she concluded, a girl educated to such behaviour was better suited for an 'Eastern harem' than respectable wifehood.

In place of such cynical coquetry Wollstonecraft insists on a de-eroticised standard of modesty for both sexes. 'Modesty – Comprehensively Consid-ered, and Not as a Sexual Virtue', as chapter 7 of the *Rights of Woman* is titled, denotes a purity of mind and body which 'never resides in any but cultivated minds' and so is utterly distinct from the false winsomeness of a Sophie.[119] The modest woman – and man – is chaste not from worldly considerations but in loving conformity to 'that God who requires more than modesty of mien', and on whose own virtues human conduct must be modelled.[120] The body of both sexes, Wollstonecraft sternly reminds her readers, is a sacred temple that must not be wantonly sullied. Thus while '[a]s a sex, women are more chaste than men', this does not release men from the requirement to behave morally; nor – controversially – does it imply that unchastity is more vicious in women than in men.[121] In her *Letters on Education*, Catharine Macaulay had repudiated the misogynist dogma that a single sexual experience was all it took to transform a virgin into a wanton:

no such frail beings come out of the hands of Nature. The human mind is built of nobler materials than to be easily corrupted; and with all their disadvantages of situation and education, women seldom become entirely abandoned till they are thrown into a state of desperation by the venomous rancour of their own sex.[122]

Reviewing the *Letters* in 1790, Wollstonecraft didn't even dare to quote these remarks, only nervously commenting that 'till the minds of women are more enlarged, we should not weaken the salutary privileges which serve a substitute...for rational principles'.[123] But two years later the *Rights of Woman* approvingly repeated Macaulay's words, and echoed her indict-ment of the sexual double standard which originated, Macaulay claimed, in 'women having been considered...mere property of the men...[with] no right to dispose of their own persons'.[124]

It is this historic subalternity of women, Macaulay and Wollstonecraft both stress, that is responsible for female sexual wiliness. Far from being swept up by erotic passion, most women, Wollstonecraft writes, 'have such perfect power over their hearts as not to permit themselves to fall in love till a man with a superior fortune offers'.[125] The need to marry for money and security permits women to experience romantic desire only vicariously, principally through novel-reading. Deprived of genuine erotic attachments, locked inside a narrowly narcissistic world, women's pleasures become trivially masturbatory. 'By fits and starts they are warm in many pursuits; yet this warmth, never concentrated into perserverance, soon exhausts itself; exhaled by its own heat...'[126] Safe in her boudoir, a woman might sigh over the agonies of a Clarissa, and pant for a rapacious Lovelace; but such 'caprices of fancy' are as slight and ephemeral as the minds harbouring them. '[S]uch tales...would force sweet tears of sensibility to flow in copious showers down beautiful cheeks, to the discomposure of rouge, etc. etc....' Wollstonecraft wrote of the mother of the heroine of *Mary, A Fiction*, whose only real love-objects were her dogs.[127] She 'had none of those feelings which are not easily analysed' was the damning verdict, any more than did the fictive Mary's 'truly feminine' friend, Ann, for whom it was never great and challenging things but merely soft and pretty ones that were attractive. Romantic love such as the heroic Mary experiences is beyond such women, since sublime ardour of this order requires the strong imagination, fierce emotions, and disdain for worldly considerations which are no part of the typical feminine psyche. 'She is a romantic creature, you must not copy her, miss' a lady of fashion warns her daughter on meeting Mary.[128]

* * *

Female sexuality is too sensuous, too worldly, too self-absorbed for the visionary grandeur of erotic love: here is one message of Wollstonecraft's writings. Erotic love in women is delusive, corrosive of emotional and moral boundaries, emotionally disintegrative: here is another. Prior to 1793, Wollstonecraft had little experience on which to base either view. A frustrating, probably unconsummated, romance with the artist Henry Fuseli had ended in humiliation; other flirtations had come to nothing. Plagued by a 'full heart' of restless intensity (which produced a plethora of somatic symptoms) and a mortifying envy of sexually attractive women, Wollstonecraft seems nonetheless to have found the intemperance of erotic desire disturbing and frightening. A woman in love seeks paradise on earth, and that quest – unless redirected heavenward – must surely end in disaster: not only disillusion and loss but a virtual annihilation of self, a collapse of personal identity. 'I cannot live without loving,' the fictive Mary weeps after parting from the dying Henry, ' – and love leads to madness'.[129] Either love must die or Mary must, seemed to be the message: and six years later that was exactly how Wollstonecraft herself, abandoned by her lover Gilbert Imlay, was to view matters. 'I have loved with my whole soul, only to discover that I had no chance of return – and that existence is a burthen without it,' she wrote to Imlay a month after her second suicide attempt.[130]

The trials of love afflict all women, but to feminists they offer particularly savage ironies. Wollstonecraft was thirty-three when she met Imlay:

a professional writer celebrated across Europe for her freethinking radicalism. 'Independence I have long considered as the grand blessing of life,
the basis of every virtue,' she had written in the *Rights of Woman*, 'and
independence I will ever secure by contracting my wants, though I were
to live on a barren heath.'[131] Talent and hard work had brought her material independence, but with Imlay she encountered wants which could
be neither contracted nor controlled. She was literally over-joyed: both by
him and her own newly discovered sensualism. They met, in Paris, in April
1793; by August Wollstonecraft was pregnant. 'I like to see your eyes praise
me;' she wrote to him rapturously, 'and, Milton insinuates, that, during
such recitals, there are interruptions, not ungrateful to the heart, when the
honey that drops from the lips is not merely words.'[132]

At first, Imlay appears to have been as captivated as his lover (although
occasionally made uneasy by her 'quickness of feeling'). But his real passion,
Wollstonecraft soon discovered, was money. Having left America, where
he had fought in the revolutionary army, heavily in debt, he was now eager
to seize the opportunities generated by the chaos of the French economy.
He threw himself into commercial ventures which increasingly absorbed
his attention, taking him away from Paris for extended periods. These
separations were terrible for Wollstonecraft, who in his absence fell into
a slough of misery that threatened to drown her. Terrified, she nagged
away at him, complaining of the infrequency of his letters and becoming
abject whenever she thought his epistolary tone too cool. '[L]et me, in the
sincerity of my heart, assure you, there is nothing I would not suffer to
make you happy,' she wrote to him at the beginning of 1794, 'My own
happiness wholly depends on you.' Her life before him had been so full of
sorrow, she told him, that 'left to myself' it was easy for her to believe that
their happiness together was merely a passing dream: fears reinforced by his
seeming reluctance to spend time with her and their new baby daughter.
'[T]ell me when I may expect to see you, and let me not be always vainly
looking for you, till I grow sick at heart.'[133]

Still in the midst of this anxious turbulence, however, the feminist eye
remained open, its clear gaze fixed on the male character. She had 'begun to
form a new theory respecting men,' she wrote to Imlay with teasing affection
in 1793, but within the year experience was lending theory an increasingly
bitter edge. 'You know my opinion of men in general;' she wrote to him at
the end of 1794, 'you know I think them systematic tyrants... When I am
thus sad, I lament that my little darling, fondly as I doat on her, is a girl.'[134]
She pondered what lay behind men's ill-treatment of their sexual partners,
and in particular wondered over men and women's different erotic needs.
She knew he was having other affairs, and couldn't understand why. 'You

have a heart, my friend,' she informed him at one point, 'yet, hurried away by the impetuosity of inferior feelings, you have sought in vulgar excesses, for that gratification which only the heart can bestow.'[135] This 'ignoble way of thinking' disappointed her, since it revealed a crassness typical of merely ordinary men. 'The common run of men, I know, with strong health and gross appetites, must have variety to banish *ennui*, because the imagination never lends its magic wand, to convert appetite into love,' she wrote to him in 1795. 'Ah! my friend,' the letter continued:

you know not the ineffable delight, the exquisite pleasure, which arises from a unison of affection and desire, when the whole soul and senses are abandoned to a lively imagination, that renders every emotion delicate and rapturious. Yes; these are emotions, over which satiety has no power... [emotions which] appear to me to be the distinctive characteristic of genius, the foundation of taste, of that exquisite relish for the beauties of nature, of which the common herd of eaters and drinkers and *child-begeters* [sic and her emphasis], certainly have no idea.[136]

The note of emotional superiority must have been profoundly irritating. '[I]t is the rarest thing in the world, to meet with a man with sufficient delicacy of feeling to govern desire,' she primly informed him. But for this man it was *she* who was consumed by an ungovernable desire which ultimately became an agony of self-destructive humiliation. No suggestion to Imlay that they two should transfer their devotions from each other to God – far from it. 'My friend – my dearest friend – ' she writes, 'I feel my fate united to yours by the most sacred principles of my soul...'[137] And for the fate that followed, the loss of Imlay, not even religious faith could console her. 'I have not found a guardian angel, in heaven or on earth, to ward off sorrow or care from my bosom,' she told him, for '[u]niting myself to you... I leaned on a spear, that has pierced me to the heart.'[138]

Wollstonecraft only just survived this heartbreak. In 1794 she followed her lover from Paris to Le Havre (where Fanny was born in May) and from there back to London, where she desperately hoped they might finally establish a home. But in London Imlay was busier than ever with commercial schemes and new girlfriends. 'I have not only lost the hope, but the power of being happy...' Wollstonecraft wrote to him, 'My soul has been shook, and my tone of feelings destroyed.'[139] She was 'nothing', she told him. She swallowed a dose of laudanum, but was soon discovered by her maidservant, who managed to rouse her. '[G]rief has a firm hold of my heart,' she wrote to him miserably.[140]

It was at this low juncture that Imlay, shaken by the suicide attempt but also desperate to get her out of his hair, proposed that she should go to Scandinavia on a business trip for him. An astonishing suggestion to the mother of a small baby, one might think: but Imlay knew his lover. Wollstonecraft immediately agreed, and left – Fanny and her French maid, Marguerite, in tow – within a week. The task she had undertaken, to win compensation for a valuable cargo stolen by the Norwegian captain of Imlay's ship, was demanding, and she spent nearly four months at it: travelling to remote and unfamiliar destinations to meet and bargain with officials, studying local customs, enjoying strange landscapes and risky sea journeys. The adventure, despite a stream of melancholy letters to Imlay, revived her; but the return to London was devastating. Imlay had another new mistress, an actress. On getting this news (from her cook), Wollstonecraft went to Putney Bridge, soaked her clothing, and threw herself into the Thames. Only the arrival of some passing watermen saved her. 'Mistaken in the object of her attachment, imputing to him qualities which, in the trial, proved to be imaginary,' Godwin wrote in his *Memoirs*, '[Mary] proceeded to stake her life upon the consequences of her error...'[141] Even after reluctantly surviving this second bid for death, she continued to persecute Imlay with pleas for reconciliation, until finally illusion dissipated and hope died. 'I now solemnly assure you, that this is an eternal farewell,' she wrote in her last letter to him, 'I part with you in peace.'[142]

'Love,' Wollstonecraft had written with fierce disapproval in the *Rights of Woman*, 'is...an arbitrary passion, and will reign like some stalking mischiefs, by its own authority, without deigning to reason.'[143] When she wrote this – in her 'virginal period', as Ellen Moers has dubbed it – the mischief was mostly theoretical.[144] But by the end of 1795 Wollstonecraft had had a very full education in love's dangers and pains. If to the author of the *Rights of Woman* sexual love was a principal source and symptom of female abjection, now, four years later, Wollstonecraft knew herself to *be* such an abject woman, as hostage as any other to the irrationalisms of the heart. 'Half the sex, in its present infantine state, would pine for a Lovelace,' she had sneered in 1792, just before falling for a man who, if not quite a Richardsonian rake, was certainly no paragon either.[145]

'You know best whether I am still preserving the remembrance of an imaginary being,' she told Imlay at the close of the affair.[146] But in the end it was she who gradually allowed this knowledge to take hold, over months of agonising self-reflection. 'On examining my heart,' she wrote to him in July 1795, 'I find that it is so constituted, I cannot live without some particular affection – I am afraid not without a passion...'[147] 'Love is a want of my heart.'[148] She brooded on the unhappy childhood in which the 'simple pleasures that flow from passion and affection, escaped me', and saw how in loving Imlay she had endowed him with imaginary charms.[149]

Yet even as she lost him, she learned to give sanction to the passions he had aroused. 'I know what I look for to found my happiness on,' she told him as they moved apart, which was certainly more than her younger self could have said.[150] A friend in Paris during this period reported overhearing an exchange in which a Frenchwoman boasted to Wollstonecraft that she had never experienced sexual desire. '*Tant pis pour vous, madame,*' was the immediate reply, '*c'est un défaut de la nature.*'[151]

And then, within months of the final rupture with Imlay, Wollstonecraft was calling on her old acquaintance, Godwin, and lending him a copy of *La Nouvelle Héloïse*. It was bold for a woman to take the initiative in this way, but then boldness came easily to Wollstonecraft. Very soon they were lovers. Here was a man, a 'tender affectionate creature', a sweet and 'sapient Philosophership', in whose arms she finally found that warm reciprocity for which she yearned.[152] 'I am never so well pleased with myself, as when I please you,' she told Godwin, and please each other they certainly did.[153] Their correspondence in the fourteen months between July 1796 and her death in September 1797 crackles with erotic delight. 'If the felicity of last night has had the same effect on your health as on my countenance, you have no cause to lament your failure of resolution,' she writes in November 1796, 'for I have seldom seen so much live fire running about my features as this morning when recollections – very dear, called forth the blush of pleasure, as I adjusted my hair.'[154]

She loved being wifely, she told Godwin as she sorted his household linen, and it was this very homeliness of their romance – the snug blend of domestic busyness, and mutual affection for little 'Fannikins', with arguments over literary matters, shared friendships with other radical intellectuals, and of course the sexy nights, plenty of sexy nights – that began to give her the emotional security she craved. Crises of confidence still occurred. 'I am not well – I am hurt – But I mean not to hurt you,' she wrote after one miserable episode. 'Consider what has passed as a fever of your imagination; one of the slight mortal shakes to which you are liable – and I – will become again a *Solitary Walker.*'[155] But Godwin knew how to reassure her. 'Well! well – it is almost gone – I mean all my unreasonable fears... which you have routed,' she wrote cheerily later the same day. 'Now will you not be a good boy, and smile upon me...'

* * *

Love hurts and heals, delights and destroys. But more than this: love invents us, as the poets say, because it is through love fantasies and choices that our selves are made. '[H]ave I desires implanted in me only to make me miserable?' the heroine of *Mary, a Fiction*, struggling with her doomed love for Henry, cries out; and the answer the novel gives is – yes: desire, unless sublimated into sacred love, must inevitably end in anguish.[156] 'Why am I thus forced to struggle continuously with my affections and feelings?' Wollstonecraft wrote desperately to Imlay while en route to Sweden.[157] But now the repudiation of earthly love for heavenly seemed a less ideal option. Travelling around Scandinavia, Wollstonecraft recorded many devotional thoughts, but with a significant shift in emphasis. Galloping across mountain meadows, struggling alone up cliffside paths, she revelled in the strength and health of her body, and – 'open[ing] my bosom to the embraces of nature' – sent her soul 'to its author' in a reverential move that divinised both the natural world and her own physicality.[158] Self-denying asceticism had given way to a newly sacralised sensualism. A particularly lyrical passage in her letters, written from Tonsberg, in Norway, evokes this new mood very clearly, as she describes waking from a nap on the hillside by the bay.

Balmy were the slumbers, and soft the gales, that refreshed me, when I awoke to follow, with an eye vaguely curious, the white sails, as they turned the cliffs, or seemed to take shelter under the pines which covered the little islands that so gracefully rose to render the terrific ocean beautiful. The fishermen were calmly casting their nets; whilst the seagulls hovered over the unruffled deep. Every thing seemed to harmonize into tranquillity – even the mournful call of the bittern was in cadence with the tinkling bells on the necks of the cows, that, pacing slowly one after the other, along an inviting path in the vale below, were repairing to the cottages to be milked. With what ineffable pleasure have I not gazed – and gazed again, losing my breath through my eyes – my very soul diffused itself in the scene – and, seeming to become all senses, glided in the scarcely-agitated waves, melted in the freshening breeze . . . I pause, again breathless, to trace, with renewed delight, sentiments which entranced me, when, turning my humid eyes from the expanse below to the vault above, my sight pierced the fleecy clouds that softened the azure brightness; and, imperceptibly recalling the reveries of childhood, I bowed before the awful throne of my Creator, whilst I rested on its footstool.[159]

Nature, God, and physical sensation here merge into an eroticism that, radiating from her imagination and body, diffuses itself across natural Creation, and then returns to remind her of her recent sexual history – and her continuing sexual vitality. The paragraph that follows directly addresses her absent lover. 'You have sometimes wondered, my dear friend,' she tells Imlay, 'at the extreme affection of my nature – But such is the temperature of my soul.'

For years have I endeavoured to calm an impetuous tide – labouring to make my feelings take an orderly course. – It was striving against the stream. – I must love and admire with warmth, or I sink into sadness. Tokens of love which I have received have rapt me in elysium – purifying the heart they enchanted. – My bosom still glows...[160]

The young romantics of Wollstonecraft's circle loved Wollstonecraft's Scandinavian letters, and it's easy to see why. Their lyrical pantheism deeply appealed to romantic sensibilities.[161] More conventional readers, however, professed themselves shocked by the *Short Residence*, one even going so far as to argue that 'we may date her lapse from that dignity of character which distinguished her' to her northern travels when

she discarded all faith in christianity... From this period she adored [God]... not as one whose interposing power is ever silently at work on the grand theatre of human affairs, causing eventual good to spring from present evil, and permitting nothing but for wise and benevolent purposes; but merely as the first great cause and vital spring of existence.[162]

The charge of deism, and occasionally even of atheism, was to be repeated regularly over the years. The accusation was false: Wollstonecraft never abandoned her faith in a personal God. But now her spiritual quest took her past all brands of Christianity, even Rational Dissent, into the realm of 'animated nature', that sphere of sacralised unity between Self and Other in which believers experience their Maker in the subjective resonances of His natural works. At their most exaltant, these moments of divine rapture drew Wollstonecraft back in time – to childhood devotions, to her love for Fanny Blood, to her passion for Imlay – and forward, with hopeful excitement, to the future. And finally to death itself, which she viewed with a mixture of terror and anticipatory awe. 'I cannot bear to think of being no more – of losing myself –' she told Imlay,'... nay, it appears to me impossible that I should cease to exist, or that this active, restless spirit, equally alive to joy and sorrow, should only be organized dust...'[163] But seeing the 'noble forests' near Frederikstad in Sweden, and observing the 'grey cobweb-like appearance' of the oldest trees whose 'fibres whitening as they lose their moisture' gave the impression of 'imprisoned life... stealing away', she wrote: 'I cannot tell why –'

but death, under every form, appears to me like something getting free – to expand in I know not what element; nay I feel that this conscious being must be as unfettered, have the wings of thought, before it can be happy.[164]

Wollstonecraft found some happiness while still in life's fetters. But perhaps these reflections indicate why on her deathbed 'not one word of a religious cast fell from her lips'.[165] Certainly it was true that her religion was not one, in Godwin's words, 'calculated to be the torment of a sick bed', and if instead it proved a final comfort to her, this was not revealed to her atheistical husband.[166] Her last written words, scribbled just before Mary Godwin's birth, contained no pieties, but only an echo of her mother's stoical sigh – 'a little patience, and all will be over'.[167]

* * *

If, as William James once claimed, 'the gods we stand by are the gods we need and can use, the gods whose demands on us are reinforcements of our demands on ourselves and on one another', then the primary demand we make of ourselves, each other and our gods, I have been suggesting, is the demand for a self-identity that is psychically and culturally viable.[168] How such a viable subjectivity is established is in part – but only in part – a matter for history. Clearly the components of selfhood change over time – does it for example include a soul? – but the fundamental psychological processes through which self-identities are forged, I am proposing, are ubiquitous and constant. It is these processes that give persuasive weight to religion's universalist claims: not the claim of this or that religion to the exclusive possession of universal truth, but rather the capacity of all religions, as James suggests, to speak to the demands of being human.

We are of course all human in different ways; but for all of us the vicissitudes of love play a decisive part in our self-formation. 'I have examined myself with more care than formerly,' Wollstonecraft wrote to Imlay after her first suicide attempt, 'and find, that to deaden is not to calm the mind – Aiming at tranquillity, I have almost destroyed all the energy of my soul...'[169] This energy of heart and soul – what Freud was later to call libido – not only attracts us to others, mortal or divine, but forms us in the images of our loved ones. As children we turn to our father and mothers with an idealising passion that moulds us in their fantasised contours. This worshipful identification with deified parents – every child's personal gods – are the threads from which our subjectivity is woven: and in this sense Wollstonecraft's preference for divine images over human ones was no more exotic or archaic than the unconscious ego itself, built on the history of its *amours*. We all become what we have adored.

As life progresses, these originary love-fantasies mingle with adult passions that are often – for some people, all too often – far from ideal. Reflecting on her misery with Imlay, Wollstonecraft realised that it was the evaporation of the imaginary perfections with which she had invested him that was a major source of her pain. Similar patterns of idealisation and disillusion had appeared in earlier relationships, particularly in her romantic friendship with Fanny Blood. Earthly love, it seemed, was inevitably a fool's paradise; and it was from this dark sense of blighted hopes, Mary Poovey has suggested, that Wollstonecraft's religiosity stemmed. In 'promising consolation for earthly disappointments,' Poovey writes, 'religion sanction[ed] the very feelings [in Wollstonecraft] that, when directed to other people, always seem[ed] to end in pain'.[170] Or as Wollstonecraft put it, in the *Rights of Men*, '[W]hen friends are unkind, and the heart has not the prop on which it fondly leaned, where can a tender suffering being fly but to the Searcher of hearts?'[171] In the wake of Imlay's desertion it was to God ultimately that she looked for consolation since He at least (unlike mortal friends, she rebuked Joseph Johnson, who had made some poorly-received observation on her situation) 'never disregarded an almost broken heart'.[172]

That religion brought Wollstonecraft emotional comfort is therefore plain; but as an explanation for her faith this is insufficient. For what the author of the *Rights of Woman* sought in the divine was not just consolation for earthly disappointments but a revolutionised ethical subjectivity. In her writings Wollstonecraft characterised love's inventions as fantasies, chimeras, which in their profane version result only in moral corruption and female sexual exploitation. The male erotic imagination transforms biological sexual difference into a rigid division between male sexual possessor and female possessed, and then concocts a female image to fit the scenario. Women, economically dependent and intellectually degraded, immerse themselves in mythic Woman to the point where their subjectivity disappears into the image. A female self is created so saturated by masculine fantasy that it appears to lack any independent moral personality – or even a soul.

Against this, Wollstonecraft insisted on the possibility of a female moral subjectivity founded in amatory identification with God. In place of their present abject moral status, women would acquire those sacred virtues that in Wollstonecraft's writings were often represented as masculine attributes enlarged and perfected, but also appeared as the gender-neutral attributes of a deity known (in stock rational-religious fashion) as the 'Supreme Being', 'Creator' or 'Image'. 'The mind of man is formed to admire perfection,' Wollstonecraft wrote to her sister Everina in 1784, 'and perhaps our longing after it and the pleasure we take in observing a shadow of it is a faint line of that Image that was first stamped on the soul.'[173] Adoring and identifying with the divine is the true foundation of self-respect, she wrote in the *Rights of Men*, for 'what can make us reverence ourselves, but a reverence for that Being, of whom we are a faint image?'[174] Men have seen women merely as projections of their own desires; but now it is to God's all-seeing gaze that women must turn their own. 'It is not sufficient to view ourselves as we suppose that we are viewed by others...' she wrote in the *Rights of Woman*, 'We should rather endeavour to view ourselves as we suppose that Being views us who seeeth each thought ripen into action, and whose judgement never swerves from the eternal rule of right.'[175]

As the basis of a pro-woman ethics, this was an argument with serious advantages. Launching moral claims from the highest possible ground is always good tactics. But it was also a stance that carried stiff penalties. Divine perfection is a cruelly exacting standard of moral worth. Wollstonecraft's moral absolutism and transcendent romanticism may have fostered a vision of feminine dignity that shone against the murk of fashionable manners – but at a price. All her life, she was a ruthless self-critic. Letters to intimates, particularly in early adulthood, reveal a painful blend of self-pity, self-dislike and guilty contrition. 'I am sick with vexation – and wish I could knock my foolish head against the wall, that bodily pain might make me feel less anguish from self-reproach,' she wrote to Joseph Johnson after one unfortunate incident.[176] Remonstrating with Imlay, some of the worst recriminations were reserved for herself, for the 'querulous humours' and 'caprices of sensibility' with which she 'plagued' him. 'Surely it is hell; to despise one's self!' she exclaimed to Johnson.[177] Hellish enough indeed for her to attempt self-murder, twice over.

If the passions of religion are, in part at least, responses to love's failures, then in Wollstonecraft's case it was a failure of self-love that proved critical. If, as I have argued, identification with deified parents is a crucial stage in self-formation, it is also the case that such divinised images have a very dark side, bringing with them inflated images of personal evil. Idealisations are twinned by denigrations; internalised gods become inner devils. The polarities are universal, but tend to exert the most tenacious hold where the gap between ideal and reality is widest. Children who grow up with ordinary affection can usually learn to do without absolute goodness/badness, in themselves as well as in those around them; children without love, however, have nothing to clasp but grandiose images of it. 'Could she have loved her father or mother, had they returned her affection,' Wollstonecraft wrote of the fictive Mary's religiosity 'she would not so soon, perhaps, have sought out a new world', with the clear implication that miserable childhoods incline individuals toward piety.[178] The point was obviously autobiographical. The child of a petty dictator ('his orders were not to be disputed; and the whole house was expected to fly, at the word of command') and an unloving, 'intolerably peevish' mother, what realistic images of love did Wollstonecraft have to comfort and to shape her?[179]

If becoming a self means taking on a gendered subjectivity that is invariably ambiguous and conflictual, then erotic life is where these psychic difficulties are most strongly experienced. What is at stake in love, as Wollstonecraft discovered, is not only who we have but who we are. A love directed away from other people toward a transcendent, perfect object can seem to bypass these painful issues of personal identity. Loving God, we need be only what He requires of us: our right selfhood is immanent in Him. For a woman like Wollstonecraft, so poorly equipped for love's ardours, the idea had an appeal that never disappeared. But by the end of her life she had come to a new accommodation with her erotic wishes and passions. Perhaps motherhood assisted her in this; certainly her relationship with Godwin did. Love acquired new meanings in her life, and so in her final years she began to grapple with an alternative perspective on erotic fantasy that drew her to new and challenging conclusions.

* * *

In 1798 Godwin published the novel Wollstonecraft had been writing at the time of her death – *The Wrongs of Woman, or Maria*. *Maria* is a gothic tale of love and betrayal in which the author, having resurrected the Mary of her first novel, sets her on another stony path. Just as Mary's story was intended to counter dominant representations of women by portraying a female 'genius' of independent mind, so Maria's history is 'of woman, [rather] than of an individual', and of Woman moreover not as she should be but as she is. 'I have...endeavoured to pourtray [sic] passions [rather] than manners,' Wollstonecraft wrote.[180]

Maria is a particularly poignant close to Wollstonecraft's intellectual career, since many of its themes show her thought moving in radically new directions. We shall look at these intellectual innovations later. But in the theme which concerns us here – women's relationship to fantasy – the novel does in fact feel like a culmination, a final autocritique. Wollstonecraft never fully resolved her attitude toward the imagination, but in the course of her career she came to a much deeper understanding of how erotic fantasy functioned in the female psyche. Nowhere in *Maria* is it suggested that the fictionalising desire that transforms ordinary men into romantic heroes should be redirected toward a divine destination: *eros* in its religious form virtually disappears. What remains, however, are the internal conflicts and external pressures which lead women into amorous idealisations – and the price those idealisations exact. What appeared as a solution to the subjective dilemmas of womankind in *Mary, a Fiction* and the *Rights of Woman* – the anchoring of female intellect and imagination in the love of God – had by the end of Wollstonecraft's life begun to give way to a much more difficult option: the recognition that some inner dilemmas are not amenable to complete resolution.

Maria is a 'philosophical' novel, one designed to educate and persuade rather than to entertain. 'In many instances I could have made the incident more dramatic,' Wollstonecraft explained in her preface, but that would have been 'to sacrifice my main object, the desire of exhibiting the misery and oppression, peculiar to women, that arise out of the partial laws and customs of society.'[181] To a modern reader the book's Gothic settings, cat-and-mouse pursuit of Maria by her husband, and heart-palpating romance offer drama enough. But the larger literary point – the sacrifice of narrative pleasure to political purposes – was an important one for the writers of Wollstonecraft's circle, nearly all of whom, in the course of the 1790s, had produced novels of this polemical stripe. The most influential of these had been Godwin's *Caleb Williams* (1794); the most overtly feminist, next to *Maria*, Mary Hays's *Emma Courtney* (1796). Politicised fiction was a particularly apt vehicle for feminists, given women's high profile in novel-writing and the private, domestic character of female oppression. The sentimental view of women purveyed by the popular novel was, as we have seen, a particular target of feminist wrath: what better way to tackle this than by offering counter-images? Thus Hays's *Emma Courtney* had offered its readers a female protagonist who, in contrast to the sugary perfection of most fictive heroines, was as 'liable to the mistakes and weaknesses of our fragile nature' as any other individual.[182] Likewise Wollstonecraft's Maria who, as the novel's preface emphasises, is not a heroine 'born immaculate... to act like [a] goddes[s] of wisdom', but a woman whose heroism emerges only under pressure, through a remorseless train of cruelly testing 'events and circumstances'.[183]

* * *

Like the heroine of Wollstonecraft's first novel, *Mary, A Fiction*, Maria is an heiress whose wealth makes her prey to the selfishness of others. A lout named George Venables deceives her about his true character and inveigles her into marriage. Once wed, Maria soon discovers that Venables is a hard-drinking wastrel who cares for nothing but her money. She tolerates him with saintly forebearance until finally he tries to prostitute her to one of his friends, at which point she flees with their baby daughter in her arms. Venables hunts her down, as is his legal right, and has her imprisoned in a lunatic asylum, which is where the novel opens. The metaphorical significance of these events for the general condition of her sex is made explicit: 'Was not the world a vast prison,' Maria broods in her cell, 'and women born slaves?'[184] The manifold ways in

3 Mary Godwin by John Opie, 1797.

which men and institutions enslave women are the 'wrongs' which the novel then sets out to explore, cataloguing miseries ranging from rape and prostitution to economic exploitation and the inequities of the marriage law. The indictment of a patriarchal order is fierce, comprehensive, and exceptional in its social radicalism. But alongside this political critique runs the thorny problem of women's own contribution to their enslavement, and in particular how romantic dreams forged in conditions of intellectual and cultural subalternity can become nightmares of self loss, self debasement.

In personal traits, Maria is almost a replica of the earlier Mary, possessing the same 'ardent imagination', delicate sentiments and unfailing sympathy. She is very clever, but 'the thoughtfulness which resided on her brow did not take from the feminine softness of her features; nay, such was the sensibility which often mantled over it, that she frequently appeared, like a large proportion of her sex, only born to feel'.[185] She is also childlike in her manner, with an 'infantine ingenuousness' which occasionally leads people to under-rate her intellect. This childishness is a crucial sign, as it is throughout Wollstonecraft's writings, of emotional authenticity: we are to understand that this is Woman not as society wants her to be but as nature made her. It is also important as the dimension of the personality in which religious feeling resides. This idea, that piety belongs to the infantile part of the self, was heralded in Wollstonecraft's letters from Scandinavia and also in a later essay on poetry; in *Maria* it appears when she is reminiscing about a return to the village of her childhood where she revisited the local church.

I recollected with what fervour I addressed the God of my youth: and once more with rapturous love looked above my sorrows to the Father of nature. I pause – feeling forcibly all the emotions I am describing; and (reminded, as I register my sorrows, of the sublime calm I have felt, when in some tremendous solitude, my soul rested on itself, and seemed to fill the universe) I insensibly breathe soft, hushing every wayward emotion... [186]

This is one of the few times religion appears in the novel, and the elegiac quality of the memory shows the reader that the adult Maria is even less a churchwoman than the heroine of *Mary*. She is certainly, like her predecessor, an inveterate fantasist, but her imaginings tend less toward God than 'ideal phantoms of love and friendship'.[187] Languishing in her asylum cell, she spends her time in solitary reverie until eventually encountering a fellow prisoner – another disciple of Rousseau, again named Henry – who prior to their actual meeting lends her some books via the asylum wardress. On opening the volumes, Maria finds they have been scribbled with marginalia 'written with force and taste'. Her heart begins to throb with 'sympathetic alarm' as she reads these jottings 'over and over again'...

and fancy, treacherous fancy, began to sketch a character, congenial with her own, from these shadowy outlines... What a creative power has an affectionate heart! There are beings who cannot live without loving, as poets love; and who feel the electric spark of genius, wherever it awakes sentiment or grace.[188]

The erotic imagination has caught Maria in its toils. She can now think of nothing but Henry Darnford, waits by the window to see him, quizzes the wardress about him, and then, becoming ashamed of her behaviour, rebukes herself with the thought of 'how difficult it was for women to avoid growing romantic, who have no active duties or pursuits'.[189] Meanwhile the howls of lunatics are all about her, including the wails of a woman suffering from post-partum psychosis. Maria, whose own baby has been ripped from her arms by her husband's agents, hears the voices with terror, thinking how 'a mental convulsion...like the devastation of an earthquake, throws all the elements of thought and imagination into confusion' until 'we fearfully ask ourselves on what ground we ourselves stand'. She wonders if Darnford is mad too, and wishes that she was so that she could 'escape from the contemplation of it'.[190] She teeters on the brink of a mental crisis, for which the final push comes from – where else? – Rousseau. Darnford lends her *La Nouvelle Héloïse*. Maria has read the novel before but now (in words lifted directly from Rousseau's text) 'it seemed to open a new world to her – the only one worth inhabiting'. Her overwrought mind immediately plunges her into a romantic scenario with Darnford as St Preux and she as the adored Julie. '[P]ity, sorrow, and solitude all conspired to soften her mind, and nourish romantic wishes' until under the spell of this dream, she takes Darnford as her lover. 'A magic lamp now seemed to be suspended in Maria's prison, and fairy landscapes flitted around the gloomy walls' as she opens her arms to him and 'felt herself, for once in her life, treated like a fellow creature'. 'We see what we wish, and make a world of our own,' Wollstonecraft tells her readers; 'Maria now, imagining that she had found a being of celestial mould – was happy...'[191]

But the moment of sublime felicity is brief; the serpent awaits. For Darnford, the novel repeatedly hints, is a philanderer in the Imlay mould, temporarily transformed into a romantic hero by the power of Maria's imagination. The story to which Wollstonecraft alludes to make this point is the Pygmalion myth: 'Maria's imagination found repose in portraying the possible virtues the world might contain,' Wollstonecraft writes. 'Pygmalion formed an ivory maid, and longed for an informing soul. She, on the contrary, combined all the qualities of a hero's mind, and fate presented a statue in which she might enshrine them.'[192] At first Darnford is inspired to act up to this glorified image, but as the two lovers become better acquainted and Maria's transformative vision starts to wane, his real character begins to reveal itself. 'A fondness for the sex often gives an appearance of humanity to the behaviour of men, who have small pretensions to the reality,' Wollstonecraft tells the reader ominously, and all five conclusions which she sketched for the book involve Darnford's betrayal of Maria. 'Divorced by her husband —' one of these outlines reads, 'Her lover unfaithful — Pregnancy — Miscarriage — Suicide.'[193]

The perils of erotic illusion, we saw earlier, were a standard feature of eighteenth-century fiction. But here Wollstonecraft's exploration of these dangers as part of a wider female tragedy — 'the wrongs of woman' — adds a radical dimension to the conventional viewpoint. We have seen how throughout the century concepts of fantasy were split between positive and negative poles: the imagination as both a sublimely creative force, a means of grace, but also as the malign propagator of soul-destroying delusions. The fictive Mary of Wollstonecraft's first novel experiences her romantic fantasies as split in this way, with love of Henry leading to potential madness while love of God directs her toward eternal bliss. Maria shares all Mary's torments, but in her case the desiring self, divided by and against her erotic imaginings, finds no transcendent route out of the conflict. Her dreams, like Wollstonecraft's love of Imlay, turn out to be tragic delusions, but ones to which no sacred or subliminatory solution is proffered.

However, it is not only the solution which has changed but also the problem — and with it Wollstonecraft's image of female subjectivity. For now the sexual content of romantic fantasy is no longer evaded or condemned. Maria acknowledges erotic desire and, when she decides the time is right, acts upon it. Her code of emotional authenticity leads to a radical revision of conventional morals. 'When novelists or moralists praise as a virtue, a woman's coldness of constitution, and want of passion; and make her yield to the ardour of her lover out of sheer compassion, or to promote a frigid plan of comfort, I am disgusted,' Maria writes in her journal (written as a letter to her lost daughter):

They may be good women, in the ordinary acceptation of the phrase ... but they want that fire of the imagination, which produces *active* sensibility, and *positive* virtue ... Truth is the only basis of virtue; and we cannot, without depraving our minds, endeavour to please a lover or husband, but in proportion as he pleases us.[194]

The only sexual act of which she is truly ashamed, she tells her daughter, is going to bed with her husband after she knew his true character. During her miserable marriage, plenty of other men had made advances to her, but having discovered that 'I could not coquet with a man without loving him a little ... and ... should not be able to stop at the line of what are termed *innocent freedoms*', she had refused them all — until events brought Darnford onto the scene.[195] To him, as she tells the court where Darnford is eventually tried for seduction and adultery, 'I voluntarily gave myself...' for '[w]hile no command of a husband can prevent a women from suffering for certain crimes, she must be allowed to consult her conscience, and regulate her conduct, in some degree, by her own sense of right'.[196] The judge condemns such 'French principles', sternly reminding her that

if women were allowed to plead their feelings, as an excuse or palliation of infidelity, it was opening a flood-gate for immorality. What virtuous woman thought of her feelings?[197]

As a defence of women's sexual self-entitlement, these passages sounded a more radical note than was to be heard again in feminist circles for almost a century. The problem with Maria's erotic imagination is therefore not its eroticism – for 'the real affections of life, when they are allowed to burst forth, are buds pregnant with joy and all the sweet emotions of the soul' – but the fantasmic substitution of the ideal for the real which in her case (that is, in Everywoman's) turns out to be a doomed attempt to make psychological gold out of mere dross.[198] For Maria too is the daughter of a tyrannical father and unloving mother who blight her childhood with 'petty cares... continual restraint... unconditional submission to orders'.[199] Befriended in childhood by a paternal uncle, a clever man made melancholy by disappointed love, she has been taught to prefer the pleasures of the imagination to the miseries of daily existence. 'Endeavouring to prove to me that nothing which deserved the name of love or friendship, existed in the world' her uncle (another Rousseau facsimile) had given Maria books which, together with his conversation, 'animated my imagination.... to make me form an ideal picture of life', so imbuing her mind with that 'romantic turn' that, blinding her to reality, leads her into her disastrous attachment to George Venables and all that follows from it.[200]

Maria's need for love, her early lack of it, and her idealising imagination – here represented as a fateful corruption – have all conspired toward her downfall. But as the novel moves toward its finale, a shift occurs. Having known Darnford for some time, Maria finds that with him she does 'not taste uninterrupted felicity; there was a volatility in his manner which often distressed her' so that although he remains – for a while at least – 'the most tender, sympathising creature in the world', Maria starts to perceive his deficiences.[201] She is becoming, in effect, dis-illusioned. At this point she determines (partly inspired by Darnford's masculine 'decision of character') to 'eradicate some of the romantic notions, which had taken root in her mind' and look life in the eye. The effect, as Wollstonecraft describes it, is transformative:

4　William Godwin by James Northcote.

Maria... discovered virtues, in characters, she had before disregarded, while chasing the phantoms of elegance and excellence, which sported in the meteors that exhale in the marshes of misfortune. The heart is often shut by romance against social pleasure; and, fostering a sickly sensibility, grows callous to the soft touches of humanity.[202]

Never having known love, Maria has fantasised its perfect embodiment while overlooking genuine merit and affection in those about her. But now her travails have brought her to a new awareness of emotional realities. Wollstonecraft's tone in all this is often as conventionally censorious as any other middle-class moralist inveighing against female mental waywardness. But set alongside her passionate defence of female feeling, the critique of fantasy lends new depth to her account of female subjectivity. For what Maria achieves in her painful education is not redemption, nor a translation of earthly desires into heavenly devotion, but courage realistically to evaluate herself and others. Rather than a new relationship with God, she acquires a new relationship with herself. Young people who 'do not sigh after ideal phantoms of love and friendship, will never arrive at great maturity of understanding', Wollstonecraft wrote, but

if these reveries are cherished, as is too frequently the case with women, when experience ought to have taught them in what human happiness consists, they become as useless as they are wretched. Besides, their pains and pleasures are so dependent on outward circumstances, on the objects of their affections, that they seldom act from the impulse of a nerved mind, able to choose its own pursuit.[203]

Those who are prisoners of fantasy's objects are never free to tackle experiences as they arise: to 'nerve' the mind to life as it is and might become, and then make choices on that basis. Travelling in Scandinavia, full of heartbreak, Wollstonecraft found herself once more taking 'refuge from sorrow in a strong imagination' –

the only solace for a feeling heart. Phantoms of bliss! ideal forms of excellence! again inclose me in your magic circle, and wipe clear from my remembrance the disappointments which . . . experience rather increases than damps . . .[204]

– but now these visions have no direction or purpose beyond the immediately consolatory. A few days earlier, walking through some pine groves in the evening, she has felt a rapture which in this instance reminds her not of God but of the creative energy of the human mind. 'How often do my feelings produce ideas that remind me of the origin of many poetical fictions,' she writes, for '[i]n solitude, the imagination bodies forth its conceptions unrestrained, and stops enraptured to adore the beings of its own creation. These are moments of bliss; and the memory recalls them with delight.'[205]

Fantasy is to be valued, then, as the poetic dimension of mental life, the realm of original genius and sublime invention. The visions with which we people our solitude are precious evidence of imaginative vitality. But if we cling too tightly to these images we lose the inner freedom that nourishes them: blissful dreams become psychic shackles. For women in particular, their minds twisted by 'romance', this is an omnipresent hazard. But what is the alternative? In *Maria* we see Wollstonecraft beginning to explore the

possibility of a woman empowered by her own mental and moral resources. Uncorrupted female nature becomes sufficient guarantee of ethical
worth. The move was, implicitly at least, anti-theistic, yet alongside there
appeared a clear re-affirmation of the divine *logos*. In the months that
Wollstonecraft was drafting *Maria* she was also writing an essay, 'On
Poetry'. The bulk of this essay, published in *The Monthly Magazine* six
months before her death, is a conventional celebration of the 'native wildness and simplicity' of poetic genius, with an accompanying attack on
Augustan formalism ('the silken wings of fancy are shrivelled by rules').[206]
But in searching for the sources of creative inspiration, Wollstonecraft finds
a key originating impulse, once again, in mortal love, which in turn 'leads to
devotion':

> grand and sublime images strike the imagination – God is seen in every floating
> cloud, and comes from the misty mountain to receive the noblest homage of an
> intelligent creature – praise. How solemn is the moment, when all affections and
> remembrances fade before the sublime admiration which the wisdom and goodness
> of God inspires... and the world seems to contain only the mind that formed, and
> the mind that contemplates it![207]

Here, as in all her previous writings, the erotic imagination remains
the faculty uniting self to the sacred. Creative originality is literally the
God within. Like her sexual philosophy, Wollstonecraft's contribution to
romanticism has been much analysed in recent decades. Her emphasis on
the affective and imaginative roots of authentic artistry – and her personal
claim to original genius, in the teeth of those who would deny women
creative originality – mark her out as a pioneer of romantic individualism,
it has been suggested: a woman whose 'daring project' was to put her faith
in 'powers... drawn from her own inwardness, without the mediation of
the tight social world'.[208] But while self versus the world was certainly a
Wollstonecraftian motif, the untrammelled subjectivity implied by such
interpretations misses the crucial point: that for Wollstonecraft the truly
creative spirit, like the soul of a truly emancipated woman, remained one
bound by the love of God.

* * *

Love as a creative, redemptive force carried particular meanings for a feminist. However, within the radicalism that nurtured Wollstonecraft's feminism, love's transformative potential was by no means restricted to women.
Love was an important player in late eighteenth-century British politics.
1790s political arguments were shot through with the language of passion and attachment, from Burke's famous panegyric to familial love as

the foundation of a good polity to the jacobin humanitarianism which was central to Wollstonecraft's civic ideals.[209] To conservatives and radicals alike, love was not just a private emotion but a public commitment. For conservatives, love of one's family, one's nation, one's monarch, were the bonds linking individuals to the public weal; for radicals, by contrast, love was a force transcending such narrow allegiances, drawing the heart away from 'partial affections' towards humankind in general.[210] It was a 'godlike affection' for humanity, Wollstonecraft claimed in 1790, that inspired the architects and supporters of the French Revolution. 'Universal benevolence' (the phrase most often used to describe this ideal) was a leading tenet of Rational Dissent and in 1789, addressing the theme of patriotic sentiment, Richard Price spelled the principle out. 'Our Lord and his Apostles...' he sermonised in his famous *Discourse on the Love of Our Country* (in a passage singled out for praise by Wollstonecraft),

have recommended that universal benevolence which is an unspeakably nobler principle than any partial affections. They have laid such stress on loving all men, even our enemies, and made an ardent and extensive charity so essential a part of virtue, that the religion they have preached may, by way of distinction from all other religions, be called the Religion of Benevolence... The noblest principle in our nature is the regard to general justice, and that good-will which embraces all the world.[211]

Preached by a Christian minister, the notion may seem far from subversive; but this was a Christian love very unlike conventional religious charity. The shift from the latter to the former was a critical move for Wollstonecraft. The heroine of *Mary, A Fiction* is a woman of boundless, one might say compulsive, benevolence, incessantly offering gifts to the poor, unsought advice and assistance to her social inferiors, and so on. Mary is an overbearing philanthropist, but she is no radical.[212] By the time Wollstonecraft wrote her two *Vindications*, however, this kind of do-gooding, aiming at alleviating suffering while leaving the political and social roots of misery untouched, was disdained: 'The rich and weak... find it pleasanter to... justify oppression than correct abuses... If the poor are in distress, they will make some benevolent exertions to assist them; they will confer obligations, but not do justice.'[213] The benevolence Wollstonecraft now praised – 'humanity' or 'public spirit' as she also dubbed it – was the sort that, stiffened by a passion for equality and freedom, impelled its possessor to 'do justice' to his/her fellows. The French Declaration of Rights was 'calculated to touch the humane heart', she claimed.[214] By contrast, instinctual compassion of the Burkean variety, disassociated from any rational commitment to universal entitlements, was mere empty sentimentality: 'in my eye all feelings are false and spurious, that do not rest on justice as their foundation, and are not concentred by universal love'.[215]

Love as an agent of human liberation may seem very distant from the aspirations and passions marking Wollstonecraft's sexual history, but in the turbulent world of 1790s politics the two spheres became closely aligned. Thrust into the arena of revolutionary politics, Wollstonecraft's vision of love as an agent of psycho-ethical reformation coalesced with radical dreams of a world free from selfishness and malevolence, where all 'would over-flow with the diffusive soul of mutual philanthropy, and generous, undivided sympathy...'[216] Caught up in the hopes unleashed by the French Revolution, *eros* became the emotional engine of a revolutionary-utopian programme.

PART II

Feminism and revolution

'Who will pretend to say, that there is as much happiness diffused on this globe as it is capable of affording? as many social virtues as reason would foster, if she could gain the strengh she is able to acquire even in this imperfect state; if the voice of nature was allowed to speak audibly from the bottom of the heart, and the *native* unalienable rights of men were recognised in their full force...?'

(Wollstonecraft, *A Vindication of the Rights of Men*)[1]

'The reformer's love of humanity, which has so much hatred in it as well as love, fermented within her.'

(Virginia Woolf, *Mary Wollstonecraft*)[2]

4

Wollstonecraft and British radicalism

In November 1789 Richard Price delivered a political sermon, *A Discourse on the Love of Our Country*, to the Society for Commemorating the Revolution of Great Britain. Printed as a pamphlet, it was reviewed by Wollstonecraft the following month in the *Analytical Review*, where she applauded its 'truly eloquent' case for an enlightened patriotism based on universal love, and endorsed its criticisms of the British constitution.[3] The review concluded by quoting Price's closing remarks, a jubilant paean of praise for what Wollstonecraft rather coyly referred to as 'a late event in a neighbouring kingdom'. 'What an eventful period is this!' Price had told his audience:

I am thankful that I have lived ... to see thirty millions of people, indignant and resolute, spurning at slavery, and demanding liberty with an irresistible voice; their king led in triumph, and an arbitrary monarch surrendering himself to his subjects ...

Be encouraged, all ye friends of freedom, and writers in its defence! The times are auspicious. Your labours have not been in vain. Behold kingdoms, admonished by you, starting from sleep, breaking their fetters, and claiming justice from their oppressors! Behold, the light you have struck out, after setting America free, reflected to France, and there kindled into a blaze that lays despotism in ashes, and warms and illuminates Europe.[4]

Price's *Discourse*, delivered less than four months after the fall of the Bastille, was British radicalism's first welcoming salvo to the French Revolution. Within a year it had been countered by Burke's *Reflections*, so triggering a war of words that raged across British politics for half a decade. At its height this 'revolution controversy', as it is known to modern historians, embroiled scores of writers many of whom – like Wollstonecraft – were new to public political debate. By the time the conflict ended, with some four hundred works published, Britain had experienced what Alfred Cobban has described as its 'last real discussion of the fundamentals of politics': 'Issues as great have been raised in our day, but it cannot be pretended that they have evoked a political discussion on the intellectual level of that inspired by the French Revolution'.[5]

To we citizens of the second millennium – accustomed to spin-doctored politicking – perhaps the most startling feature of this ideological conflict would have been its face-to-face intimacy. The men and women who responded to the philosophical call to arms of 1789–95 were not, for the most part, isolated thinkers but members of close-knit intellectual communities. On the radical side, most of the leading propagandists were published by Joseph Johnson, whose list in the 1790s was a roll-call of prominent radical intellectuals: Wollstonecraft, Paine, Godwin, Joseph Priestley, Thomas Holcroft, Joel Barlow, Mary Hays, Richard and Maria Edgeworth, William Blake, Thomas Beddoes, John Horne Tooke, Anna Barbauld, a dozen or so more. Parties of these men and women met frequently, often at Johnson's home, to explore new ideas and debate political strategies. There were some close personal connections on the conservative side too, and occasionally affinities even crossed the political divide, as they did in the case of Paine and Burke who in the 1780s had enjoyed strolls together in the countryside.[6]

Prior to 1789, the world of informed opinion inhabited by these men and women had been markedly tolerant, a culture of ideas sufficiently confident and expansive to allow for lively disagreements of all kinds. After 1790, and particularly after 1792, this open-mindedness vanished under the triple pressures of developments in France, war and – more important than either – the spread of popular radicalism throughout large sectors of the British working population. The revolution had sent a shudder of political hope through the ranks of what Wollstonecraft described as that 'numerous class of hard working mechanics' who, denied all political entitlements, were yet being taxed to the hilt to 'pay for the support of royalty when they can scarce stop their children's mouths with bread'.[7] Radical sentiment among such men – craftsmen, shopkeepers, schoolmasters, small employers, poor clergymen – was not new, but the associations they (and a much smaller number of women) created in the 1790s were unprecedented in popularity and militancy.[8] The London Corresponding Society, with its one penny subscription and 'Members unlimited', was the most important, but by 1793 it had been joined by similar societies in over twenty towns and cities across the nation. Meanwhile Ireland rumbled with rebellion. Authorities everywhere took alarm. 'A very general spirit of combination exists amongst all sorts of labourers and artisans, who are in a state of disaffection...' one frightened justice of the peace wrote from Lancaster in 1791, while from Sheffield the Deputy Adjutant-General, sent out by the government to investigate the state of nation, reported widespread reform activity in 1792 among 'the lowest mechanics': 'Here they read the most violent publications, and comment on them, as well as on their correspondence not only with the dependent Societies in the towns and villages in the vicinity, but with those...in other parts of the kingdom,' he warned.[9]

This book does not deal with this popular democratic agitation. Other historians have told very well the story of the courageous men and women who in 1791–3 battled for political rights that we now take for granted.[10] Wollstonecraft was never a grassroots campaigner of this sort, nor were most of her associates. This was less a matter of higher social origins – most of the writers in the Wollstonecraft/Godwin circle, like many LCS activists, were from modest *petit bourgeois* or artisan backgrounds – than of circumstance and personal disposition. Men and women accustomed to wielding their pens for meliorative aims naturally resorted to the printed word in times of conflict, and it was for their words that they soon found themselves pilloried and persecuted. Wollstonecraft's *Rights of Men*, the first published reply to Burke, initially attracted nothing worse than sneering jibes from conservative reviewers, some of whom even commended its author's intelligence; but with the publication of the hugely influential second part of Paine's *Rights of Man* (1792) the last traces of polite debate disappeared, to be replaced by savage counter-propaganda and overt repression.

Paine, who was in France when the second part of the *Rights of Man* was published, was convicted for seditious libel *in absentia*. Public assemblies were banned; reform writings proscribed; *habeus corpus* suspended; leading radicals seized, tried for treason and in some cases transported. John Frost, a radical attorney, went to prison for being overheard declaring 'I am for equality...Why, no kings!' in a London coffeehouse.[11] Among radical intellectuals it was Paine (who was regularly burnt in effigy) who was the chief target of this counter-revolutionary offensive, but other writers came in for their share of anti-publicity as well – and sometimes worse. Neither Wollstonecraft nor Godwin were ever physically threatened by the loyalist thugs who, encouraged by local magistrates, marauded through towns and cities, attacking known radicals, but other leading reformers were.[12] Joseph Priestley watched as his home was burnt and his library scattered to the winds by a 'Church and King' mob in 1791; he then fled to America. 'I cannot give you an idea of the violence with which every friend of liberty is persecuted in this country,' he wrote despondently to a friend in 1793.[13] But by then republican terrorism in France and the outbreak of war were sapping British radical confidence. Liberty's face that had shone so brightly in 1789–92 was once again obscured by oppression and xenophobia, leaving many radical philosophers bitterly disillusioned. Government-sponsored repression – 'Pitt's Reign of Terror', as Fox dubbed it – finished the task. By the end of 1795 – the year that Wollstonecraft left France for good, having personally witnessed the horrors perpetrated by the 'beast' of jacobin dictatorship – the great revolution debate was effectively over.[14]

Wollstonecraft was no mere spectator of revolution, watching its dramas unfold at a safe distance. Like other British radicals who went to Paris in the early 1790s to witness events there first-hand, she consorted regularly with leading members of the National Convention. Soon after her arrival in late 1792 she was preparing policy proposals for the Convention's education committee.[15] By the spring of 1794 she was clandestinely shipping chapters of her *An Historical and Moral View of the Origin and Progress of the French Revolution* to Johnson, much against the advice of her fellow expatriate, Helen Maria Williams, who urged her to burn the manuscript: 'and to tell you the truth,' Wollstonecraft wrote to Everina, 'my life would not have been worth much, had it been *found*.'[16] If Imlay had not taken the precaution of registering her as his wife with the American Embassy, she might well have found herself in prison – as Helen Maria Williams herself did for six months – or even on the scaffold. '[D]eath and misery, in every shape of terrour [sic], haunts this devoted country,' she wrote to Everina in March 1794.[17]

Yet even at the height of the Terror, Wollstonecraft declared herself 'certainly...glad' to be in France during 'the most extraordinary event that has ever been recorded'.[18] And it is there that we must see her – gaping at Louis's carriage as it passed her window en route to his trial;[19] slipping in blood flowing across the cobbles of the Place de la Revolution;[20] fainting at news of friends' beheadings;[21] putting her points to the education committee just months before its key member, Condorcet, fled the jacobin terrorists – before we can begin to grasp what a radical politics really meant to her. France was the site not only of Wollstonecraft's most passionate sexual love but also of her profoundest political romance. In the end, neither Imlay nor the Revolution were to live up to her initial expectations; yet neither disappointment, however bitter, could wholly erode her energetic, demanding faith in herself and her fellow creatures. Five years before going to France, Wollstonecraft had fretfully asked of a clerical friend why God bestowed exceptional abilities on some individuals when life was so inhospitable to the talented: 'refinement [,] genius...produce misery in this world...Why then do they at all unfold themselves *here*? If useless, would not the Searcher of hearts...have shut them up 'till they could bloom in a more favorable climate?...Surely *peculiar* wretchedness has something to balance it!'[22] Now, in the struggle to create a just society, she had found the answer to her puzzle, one that nothing – not the Robespierrist 'monster' nor any other development that 'disgrac[ed] the struggle of freedom' – could ever fully divest her.[23]

Thus far in this book I have focused on Wollstonecraft as a philosopher in the sense that liberal Britons gave to the term for most of the eighteenth century: that is, as an abstract reasoner of enlightened disposition, concerned to comprehend and elucidate general truths. Now I turn to Wollstonecraft as a philosopher in the specific meaning of the 1790s, that is, as a proponent of revolutionary democracy, one of those 'philosophising serpents' (in Horace Walpole's typically vicious phrasing) responsible for formulating and disseminating the principles of the French Revolution.[24] In her fine summary analysis of the Revolution controversy, Marilyn Butler has urged that its radical works be read not as the 'discrete *oeuvres* of autonomous authors' but as elements in a 'collective literary enterprise': 'Study of the Revolution controversy as a whole reveals the artificiality of the practice, common among philosophers and critics, of examining an isolated book out of its context.'[25] The meaning of texts like the *Rights of Woman*, Butler reminds us, resides as much in their times, their political intentions, and their audiences' expectations as in individual authorial intentions: in other words, in their status as 'philosophical' propaganda. From the moment Wollstonecraft published the *Rights of Men* her status shifted from literary lady to radical *philosophe*, an intellectual insurgent of the kind that so frightened and enraged political conservatives. 'No Philosophers!' was reputedly the cry of the mob that burned down Priestley's home, and it is in the fearsome glow of this historical moment – overheated to the point of conflagration with excitement, hope, fear – that Wollstonecraft's political writings must be read.

* * *

Radicalism in 1790s Britain was a rich brew of disparate political traditions and aspirations. Commonwealth radicalism jostled for ideological space with economic liberalism and religious millennialism, while working-class activists from the London Corresponding Society shared patriotic meeting halls with lower middle-class bluestockings and Unitarians. Seasoned parliamentary reformers – veterans of the Wilkes campaign and other electoral battles – mingled with Pantisocratic poets and Spencean communitarians busy with schemes for a New Age of unparalleled bliss. The air vibrated with perfectibilist ambitions; so much so that at one point Price, who in the 1780s had served as a government financial adviser, found himself wondering whether 'a scheme of government may be imagined that shall by annihilating property and reducing mankind to their natural equality, remove most of the causes of contention and wickedness'.[26] The Revolution wrenched open the political imagination until all that was right seemed possible; all that was wrong simply doomed. 'Whatever is loose must be shaken,' Anna Barbauld decreed in 1790, 'whatever is corrupted must be lopt away; whatever is not built on the broad basis of public utility must be thrown to the ground...'[27]

Given their diversity of outlooks, pinning a single political label on these men and women, as some historians have wanted to do, seems misguided. Hostile contemporaries dubbed them all 'jacobins' which, despite its inaccuracy (nearly all British radicals, if they supported a French revolutionary faction at all, endorsed the programme of the Girondins and strongly opposed the 'sanguinary ferocity' of the jacobins) was accepted as a badge of honour by many radicals.[28] Although it was 'fixed upon us, as a stigma, by our enemies', John Thelwall wrote, he embraced the jacobin tag precisely because of its negative connotations for British conservatives. 'The crime of the [British] Jacobin,' he told readers of his 1796 *Rights of Nature*, 'is that he looks forward to a state of society more extensive in its refinements – more perfect, and more general in its improvements, than any which has yet been known': a definition sufficiently vague to encompass what he described as the 'many different opinions' about the nature and extent of political change to be found among British jacobins.[29]

Despite its innovatory claims, the radicalism of the 1790s had a long pedigree. An extra-parliamentary political opposition had existed in Britain – rooted in Country Toryism on the one hand, and residual 'Good Old Cause' radicalism on the other – since the early decades of the eighteenth century. In the 1760s the sustained campaign of criticism waged by these politicians against the Whig establishment had begun to evolve into a coherent programme for parliamentary reform.[30] Country phillipics against court corruption steadily gave way to radical-Whig demands for a rebalancing of constitutional power in favour of the disfranchised majority of property owners. Invigorated by American republicanism and the strident campaigning of John Wilkes's supporters, during the 1770s and 1780s this reform platform became increasingly democratic and plebian, winning substantial support from the middle and lower classes. By 1789 popular radicalism had become a familiar feature of the British political landscape.

Most of the pamphleteers on the pro-French side of the Revolution debate belonged to this radical-Whig tradition, their rhetoric infused with its vocabulary of popular liberties and historic entitlements. The reforms they urged – the reduction of court influence over parliament; a limited broadening of the electoral franchise; rectifying the 'abuses' of place and patronage – were, for the most part, moderate and ameliorative rather than revolutionary.[31] But during the heady early years of the Revolution this reformist agenda found itself, for a time at least, enmeshed with much more visionary aims. 'A spirit is abroad,' Wollstonecraft prophesied in 1792, 'to break the chains that have hitherto eaten into the human soul, which bids fair to mould the body politic in a more proportional form...than has yet been seen on earth', and it was with anticipations of this order that she, Godwin, Thomas Holcroft, Mary Hays and likeminded associates took up their pens in defence of French *liberté* and universal social justice.[32]

In a memoir of Holcroft written in 1816, William Hazlitt described the Godwin/Wollstonecraft circle as 'ardent...Utopian[s]', and this is surely right – but in ways that are more complex than might first appear.[33] To modern ears, the word 'utopian' strikes a slightly cracked note, resonant of New Age visions and similar post-modern pipedreams. But the political optimism of British jacobinism was as toughly reasoned as it was imaginative. The glorious future portended by the Revolution was not some rhapsodical dream but the inevitable outcome of human strivings for 'improvement', brought to consummation through a steady process of historic advance. Most in the Wollstonecraft/Godwin circle understood this evolution in providential terms. The unfolding of the human *telos* was interpreted as a divinely led movement toward that predestined state of 'ideal excellence... [and] unsullied bliss' promised in scripture, a veritable paradise on earth.[34] Seen through this lens, the revolutions in America and France appeared to herald not only a global libertarian upheaval but also the arrival of the divine millennium, as foretold in *Revelations*. 'The *events* of human life, when *properly* considered, are but a series of *benevolent providences*...' Catharine Macaulay wrote in response to Burke's *Reflections*:

Has Mr Burke never heard of any millennium, but that fanciful one which is supposed to exist in the Kingdom of the Saints? If this should be the case, I would recommend to him to read *Newton on the prophecies*...some passages in the Revelations point out a period of time when the *iron* sceptre of *arbitrary* sway shall be broken; when *righteousness shall prevail* over the whole earth, and a *correct* system of equity take place in the conduct of man.[35]

Richard Price and Joseph Priestley likewise regarded their turbulent times as the prophesied Last Days preceding God's earthly reign. The progress of political reform in America and Europe, Price told a London audience in 1787, showed 'the world outgrowing its evils, superstition giving way, antichrist falling, and the Millennium hastening'.[36] The following year, writing in a similarly adventist vein, Wollstonecraft depicted the heroine of *Mary, a Fiction* as eagerly anticipating 'the great day of judgement… when all worldly distinctions will fade away, and…the Lord Omnipotent will reign'[37]. Such touches were rare for Wollstonecraft, however, for whom a genuinely millennialist outlook seems to have had little appeal. But if Christian apocalypse played less part in her political imaginings than in those of some of her associates, her vision of revolution was no less sacralised. Witnessing the 'chaos of vice and follies' that constituted French politics in 1793–4, she nevertheless looked beyond these to better prospects:

…these evils are passing away; a new spirit has gone forth, to organise the body-politic;…Reason has, at last, shown her captivating face, beaming with benevolence; and it will be impossible for the dark hand of despotism again to obscure it's [sic] radiance, or the lurking dagger of subordinate tyrants to reach her bosom. The image of God implanted in our nature is now more rapidly expanding; and, as it opens, liberty with maternal wing seems to be soaring to regions far above vulgar annoyance, promising to shelter all mankind.[38]

Whatever the sufferings of the present – these words were written as war was accelerating and the tumbrils rolling – God's promise remains secure, and mankind's future with it.

When it came to questions of immediate political strategy, however, Wollstonecraft's stance was more pragmatic, and she often warned of the dangers of utopian thinking. To advocate, as some French revolutionists had done, a 'perfect system of government' for a civilisation not yet sufficiently evolved to sustain such a polity is 'destructive to society', she wrote in her history of the Revolution: a position she emphasised further when, discussing the debates surrounding the drafting of the French Declaration of Rights, she made a point of distinguishing the activities appropriate to a philosopher, 'who dedicates his exertions to promote the welfare, and perfection of mankind, carrying his views beyond any time he chooses to mark', from those of a practical politician, 'whose duty it is to attend to the improvement and interest of the time in which he lives, and not sacrifice any present comfort to a prospect of future perfection.'[39] Confusing the two, as ardent reformers were wont to do, risked intensifying the miseries of the oppressed, and thus 'affording to despotism the strongest arguments to urge in opposition to the theory of reason'.[40] Extending the 'grand principles of liberty' to people not prepared to receive them could only foment wretchedness and anarchy.[41] Successful change is evolutionary and gradual:

An ardent affection for the human race makes enthusiastic characters eager to produce alteration in laws and governments prematurely. To render them useful and permanent, they must be the growth of each particular soil, and the gradual fruit of the ripening understanding of the nation, matured by time, not forced by an unnatural fermentation.[42]

Yet these pragmatic conclusions – first glimpsed, we must recall, not over some London dinner table but in terrorist France – implied absolutely no curtailment of Wollstonecraft's own perfectibilist expectations. True civilisation may be attainable only in slow, laborious stages rather than by 'sudden revolutions', but this was 'not a discouraging consideration': 'Our ancestors have laboured for us; and we, in our turn, must labour for posterity... The first inventor of any instrument has scarcely ever been able to bring it to a tolerable degree of perfection... Can it be expected, that the... most important and difficult of all human improvements... will not require the same gradations, and advance by steps equally slow to that state of perfection necessary to secure the sacred rights of every human creature?'[43] It is the 'premature execution' of 'sublime theories' that is the problem, she insisted – not the ideals themselves.[44] Rather than attempting to construct a perfect society *ex nihilo*, radicals must synchronise their efforts with historic progress, and so bring human happiness to full fruition.

5

Perfecting civilisation

'What then is to hinder man, at each epoch of civilisation, from making a stand, and new modelling the materials that have been hastily thrown into a rude mass, which time alone has consolidated and rendered venerable?'
(Wollstonecraft, *A Historical and Moral View of the Origins and Progress of the French Revolution*)[1]

The enthusiasm with which Wollstonecraft and other British radicals greeted the French Revolution was as much philosophical as emotional, prompted by 'metaphysical' ideas about human nature and prospects of the sort that Burkean conservatives found so distasteful. The future being born in France was not some chimerical El Dorado, but an anticipated liberation from tyranny and injustice. Christian providentialism, as we have seen, was one way of conceptualising such a deliverance; intersecting with this, however, was a more secular interpretation of mankind's advance. From the mid seventeenth century, enlightened thinkers had begun envisioning human history as evolving through a series of fixed stages, beginning in an original condition of primitive savagery and progressing through increasingly sophisticated modes of life until reaching the refined societies of western Europe: 'civilisation', as European modernity was dubbed in the 1760s. The 1770s and 1780s had seen a plethora of these universal histories, particularly in Britain where they had served to reinforce popular faith in national progress.[2] Wollstonecraft's familiarity with the genre is evident throughout her writings, but its influence is most apparent in her history of the French Revolution, which opens with the classic philosophic claim that, viewed with a properly analytic eye, the Revolution revealed itself as 'neither produced by the abilities or intrigues of a few individuals; nor the effect of sudden and short-lived enthusiasm' but as

the natural consequence of intellectual improvement, gradually proceeding to perfection in the advancement of communities, from a state of barbarism to that of polished society, till now arrived at the point when sincerity of principles seems to be hastening the overthrow of the tremendous empire of superstition and hypocrisy, erected upon the ruins of gothic brutality and ignorance.[3]

The likely end-point of this civilising process was a matter of dispute among Enlightenment theorists, but as far as most British *philosophes* were concerned it had already achieved fulfilment in their own commercial society. The politely businesslike manners of capitalist Britain were the pinnacle of genteel civility, it was claimed, to which all ruder peoples and nations should aspire. This bourgeois-triumphalist reading of modern history found some echoes in Wollstonecraft's writings, but generally she rejected it as too 'partial' a vision. Until the benefits of civilisation had been extended across all ranks and both sexes, society would not have fulfilled its promise. 'For all the advantages of civilisation cannot be felt, unless it pervade the whole mass, humanising every description of men – and then it is the first of blessings, the true perfection of man.'[4]

'True civilisation', then, remained in prospect. What then of contemporary society, 'things as they are' in Godwin's famous phrase?[5] How was the present to be appraised? Like most utopian projections, Wollstonecraft's perfectibilist visions served a critical as well as predictive function, highlighting the iniquities of the present by contrasting them to future glories. Viewing the world as it was from the vantage point of what it would become, showed it to be a very bad place indeed. The opening lines of the *Rights of Woman* set the tone.

After considering the historic page, and viewing the living world with anxious solicitude, the most melancholy emotions of sorrowful indignation have depressed my spirits, and I have sighed when obliged to confess, that either nature has made a great difference between man and man, or that the civilization which has hitherto taken place in the world has been very partial.[6]

The civilisation 'of the bulk of the people of Europe' is a matter of 'unsightly ignorance', 'slavery', and 'unheard-of misery', Wollstonecraft insists further on: an assessment which, despite occasional upbeat valuations to the contrary, remained fairly constant over the years.[7] 'Let us examine the catalogue of the vices of men in a savage state, and contrast them with those of men civilized;' she wrote in 1794, '[and] we shall find, that a barbarian, considered as a moral being, is an angel, compared with the refined villain of civilised life.'[8] The verdict, markedly Rousseauist, is meant to apply to both sexes, but – as in Rousseau's writings – is pronounced with particular severity against women, who 'in general... have acquired all the follies and vices of civilization, and missed the useful fruit'.[9] Here and there some enlightened progress is discernible, particularly in France where the polite 'social intercourse which has long subsisted between the sexes' has produced 'a more general diffusion of knowledge than in any part of the European world'.[10] But overall Wollstonecraft's judgement is damning. 'That the society is formed in the wisest manner, whose constitution is founded on the nature of man' is a self-evident truth, but the denatured way of life promoted in civilised European societies has reduced humankind, especially womankind, to a level well below the savage: 'Civilised women are... so weakened by false refinement, that, respecting morals, their condition is much below what it would be were they left in a state nearer to nature.'[11]

This negative estimate marked a crucial moment in Wollstonecraft's engagement with Enlightenment thought. If it is true, as Karen O'Brien has persuasively argued, that the whole of Wollstonecraft's non-fictional *corpus* can be read as an 'ambitious and unified attempt to adapt Enlightenment history and sociology to a radically critical analysis of modern culture' then it was the figure of civilised Woman that held centre-place in this project, but in such a denigrated guise that her progressive potential was made to seem almost nugatory.[12] This too was in the spirit of the age. Enlightenment philosophes were by no means undivided in their attitude toward modernity. Self-congratulatory commendations of contemporary society vied with gloomy Gibbonesque predictions of civilised corruption and downfall. Philosophical optimists competed with Jeremiahs prophesying a general implosion of moral values. Woman, with her premodern ignorance and prejudices (particularly her religious prejudices) and hyper-modern manners, became an important focus for these competing perspectives, her status in civilised nations seen as an index of both cultural progress and collective decline. As an enlightened social critic, Wollstonecraft inevitably found herself caught up in these complex ideas with, from a feminist perspective, some very troubling consequences.

* * *

That women played a major role in the civilising process was a matter of general agreement in the eighteenth century. Nearly all enlightened historians linked the advance of civilisation to parallel transformations in women's role and status. In its most popular version – a veritable *idée fixe* among educated Britons – the connection was seen as a wholly beneficent one, with women experiencing a steady improvement in their condition as society evolved from rudeness to refinement. Philosophical historians as diverse as Montesquieu, Helvetius, John Millar, and William Alexander traced women's rise from the brutal enslavements of barbarism, when they had been valued only as childbearers, through to the respectful affection accorded them in commercial societies.[13] As one Evangelical populariser of these ideas, Thomas Gisborne, wrote: 'When nations begin to emerge from gross barbarism, every new step which they take towards refinement is commonly marked by a gentler treatment, and a more reasonable estimation of women; and every improvement in their opinions and conduct respecting the female sex, prepares the way for additional progress in civilisation.'[14] Women were thus the chief beneficiaries of civilisation, but also the chief civilisers, their gracious manners serving to tame and refine their menfolk. The 'empire of women' that Rousseau had detected and condemned in polite culture was thus explicitly endorsed by these modernisers; after all, as David Hume demanded, what 'better school for manners' could there be 'than the company of virtuous women':

where the mutual endeavour to please must insensibly soften the mind, where the example of female softness and modesty must communicate itself to their admirers, and where the delicacy of that sex puts every one on his guard, lest he give offence by any breach of delicacy?[15]

To adapt oneself constantly to the standards and sensibilities of others: here indeed was the essence of genteel civility, rather campily recommended to men by James Fordyce as 'a certain flowing urbanity'. 'I do not mean,' he hastily added, 'that the men I speak of will become feminine; but their sentiments and deportment will contract a grace.'[16] But fear of what such sweet decorum might imply for men frequently raised its head. '[M]odern politeness... runs often into affectation and foppery,' Hume admitted.[17]

Civilisation was women's 'golden age', enthusiasts declared.[18] As a cultural myth, the idea had powerful attractions, particularly for the aspirational middle class; but it also had plenty of critics. One didn't need to be a card-carrying Rousseauist to worry that men polished into politeness by feminine hands might be emasculated by the process. Nor was the female touch *per se* always well regarded. Women's easy sympathy; their natural chattiness and sociability; their willingness to adapt themselves to the needs of others and the demands of reputation; their elegance, wit, and good taste in furniture: here surely were the personal requirements of a civilised culture? Possibly, critics responded, but what about women's hypocrisy and false sentimentality; their vanity and obsession with fashion; their insatiable taste for gossip; their unthinking compliance with public opinion and the demands of reputation? Here too was the civilised personality, seen with a much colder eye. Not only Wollstonecraft but many British thinkers, including some usually regarded as the most enthusiastic modernists, viewed all this mannerly artifice with dismay. The glossy gentility of a commercialising society brought all the old anxieties about the debilitating effects of 'luxury' – that quintessentially feminine vice – bubbling to the surface. Womanliness as the civilising influence could all too easily tip over, it seemed, into a feminising corruption. '[T]he delicate sensibility required in civilised nations sometimes destroys the masculine firmness of the character', Adam Smith admitted, while the Reverend John Brown, a hugely influential mid century social critic, complained that Britain's commercial prosperity had produced a nation steeped in 'vain, luxurious, and selfish effeminacy.' 'Our manners,' Brown thundered, 'are degenerated into those of Women'.[19]

This fear of a cultural decline into the feminine – audible throughout eighteenth-century social commentary – was particularly marked in discussions of empire and nation, where over the course of the century anxieties about national moral degeneration and the decline of patriotic spirit became pressing and strident.[20] Commercial success and imperial expansion had fostered a citizenry, John Brown claimed, given over to a 'rage of Pleasure and unmanly Dissipation'.[21] As in the last days of the Roman empire, civic virtue and military valour had collapsed into 'effeminacy', a word that in political writings usually referred to that fatal softening of national muscle induced by the emasculating delights of idleness and luxury.[22] Far from praiseworthy, genteel society was here condemned as the chief source of a moral malaise that, according to the radical James Burgh, had by the mid century infected even the 'trading part of the nation' until they too had become 'enervated and effeminate'.[23] To modernisers celebrating the era as one of feminine advancement, the response from these critics then was plain: if this effete dereliction equalled modern civilisation, then 'women' were welcome to it.

This representation of corrupting excess as feminine was far from new. From antiquity onward, luxury had been strongly associated with female sensuality and avidity. To Augustine, luxury was 'this vice of women'; in the Middle Ages it was personified as Dame Luxury.[24] Condemned throughout history for their love of opulence and show, women in Hanoverian Britain were regularly indicted for their passion for lace and ribbons and other luxury items. More important, as the focus of male concupiscence Woman herself appeared as the luxury object *par excellence*, and it was in this guise that she posed the greatest threat to masculinity, weakening it both physically and psychically. Desiring women too much, too luxuriously, automatically depleted manliness (the effeminate man, until the late eighteenth century at least, was one who enjoyed women to excess). A detailed account of this history, with its fascinating entanglement of erotic fantasy, gender expectations, and consumer attitudes, is beyond the scope of this study. But its influence on Wollstonecraft's critique of civilised femininity is readily apparent.

One of the most important jeremiads against luxurious effeminacy issued in the course of the eighteenth century was Rousseau's condemnation of the Parisian *beau monde*, that female-ruled world of salons and theatres whose male denizens, Rousseau insisted, had been emasculated by *politesse*. To Rousseau, French elite civility was inherently unmanning. The theme's strong appeal to Wollstonecraft was apparent in her attacks on old-regime France, that 'nation of women'[25] as she derided it in her history of the Revolution. The metaphor pleased her so much that she elaborated it relentlessly. The French, a 1793 letter from Paris complained, are vain, superficial, addicted to the pleasures of the moment. 'On all sides they trip along, buoyed up by animal spirits... like motes in a sunbeam, enjoying the passing ray.' '[E]very thing has conspired' to make them the 'most sensual people in the world' and 'what can render the heart so hard, or so effectually stifle every moral emotion, as the refinements of sensuality'?[26] The French imagination is merely 'passive' while their 'evanescent emotions' are 'more lively than strong'; their 'great susceptibility of disposition leads them to take an interest in all the sensations of others' which are then however 'forgotten almost as soon as felt'... and so on and on, a veritable catalogue of all those feminine traits that Wollstonecraft despised.

More ingenious than profound in their researches; more tender than impassioned in their affections; prompt to act, yet soon weary; they seem to work only to escape from work, and to reflect merely how they shall avoid reflection. Indolently restless, they make the elegant furniture of their rooms, like their houses, voluptuously handy. Every thing, in short, shows the dexterity of the people, and their attention to present enjoyment.[27]

This theme of effete French degeneracy was such a favourite of English xenophobes that playing on it eventually made Wollstonecraft uneasy: 'The frequent repetition of the word French, appears invidious...' she acknowledged to Johnson, for 'are we not all of the same stock?'[28] Those who generalised about national character in this fashion usually failed to 'discriminate the natural from the acquired difference', she later observed.[29] But the feminist pay-off from the analogy made it impossible to resist. For if, like the French, all 'men who have been placed in similar situations [to those of women], have acquired a similar character', the implications for women were plain.[30] For while women's follies were generally attributed to inborn inferiority, the womanly ways of old-regime Frenchmen – Wollstonecraft spells the message out laboriously – were demonstrably not innate but in-culcated: 'Lewis XIVth [sic] ... spread factitious manners, and caught ... the whole nation in his toils; for ... he made it the interest of the people at large, individually to respect his station and support his power'[31]; 'the morals of the whole nation were destroyed by the manners formed by the government'.[32] Like luxurious ladies of fashion, the French had been per-verted into femininity. '[M]ade feeble, probably, by the same combination of circumstances, as has rendered [women] insignificant' Frenchmen had learned to embrace their 'silken bonds' and so become 'effeminated'.[33]

Wollstonecraft's inventiveness here is impressive. For having exposed civilised Woman as an artefact of patriarchal culture – a creature so en-slaved by convention that even her moral responses are vitiated into shal-low compliance – she now translates this into a historical psychology of oppression *tout court*, interpreted through the female condition. 'A man' she writes in 1790, '[is] changed into an artificial monster by the station in which he was born': a formula so rich in feminist possibilities that in the *Rights of Woman* it appears as a systematic comparison between women and all those persons, high as well as low, male as well as female, implicated in relations of dominance and servitude.[34] As with the effete Frenchmen of her *Historical and Moral View*, the argument in the *Rights of Woman* is run through a series of representative analogies. Clergymen – a constant target of Wollstonecraftian invective – are trained into 'blind submission' by the church to the point where they even acquire a 'servile dependent gait', while professional soldiers – 'idle superficial young men' who 'flutter' about the country towns showing off their finery and flirting with local girls – are '[l]ike the *fair* sex ... taught to please, and ... live only to please':

[M]ilitary men ... are, like [women], sent into the world before their minds have been stored with knowledge or fortified by principles. The consequences are similar; soldiers acquire a little superficial knowledge, snatched from the muddy current of conversation, and, from continually mixing with society, they gain what is termed a knowledge of the world; and this acquaintance with manners and customs has frequently been confounded with a knowledge of the human heart ... The conse-quence is natural; satisfied with common nature, they become a prey to prejudices, and taking all their opinions on credit, they blindly submit to authority.[35]

'Where is then the sexual difference,' Wollstonecraft sums up, 'when the education has been the same?'[36] But the leading comparison in the *Rights of Woman* is between women and the rich: '[W]ealth and female softness equally tend to debase mankind, and are produced by the same cause', she explains, that is, by the 'blessings of civil governments, as they are at present organized'.[37] And to support her argument she offers no less an authority than Adam Smith:

When do we hear of women who, starting out of obscurity, boldly claim respect on account of their great abilities or daring virtues? Where are they to be found? 'To be observed, to be attended to, to be taken notice of with sympathy, complacency, and approbation, are all the advantages which they seek.' – True! my male readers will probably exclaim; but let them, before they draw any conclusion, recollect that this was not written originally as descriptive of women, but of the rich. In Dr Smith's Theory of Moral Sentiments, I have found a general character of people of rank and fortune, that, in my opinion, might with the greatest propriety be applied to the female sex. I refer the sagacious reader to the whole comparison...[38]

Like clerics, soldiers, and elite frenchmen, the rich are disabled not by natural weakness but by those denaturing circumstances for which women's dependent, degraded situation is the unhappy prototype: 'For if, excepting warriors, no great men... have ever appeared amongst the nobility, may it not be fairly inferred that their local situation swallowed up the man, and produced a character similar to that of women, who are *localized*, if I may be allowed the word, by the rank they are placed in by *courtesy*?'[39]

As sites of character deformation, gender and rank are homologous, both operating to reduce individuals to moral nullities, puppets of the power relations they inhabit. From a variety of enlightened theorists, but particularly from Montesquieu and Rousseau, Wollstonecraft had learned how hierarchical relationships degrade all parties to them, with the most powerful usually the most morally debilitated.[40] 'Birth, riches, and every extrinsic advantage that exalt a man above his fellows, without any mental exertion, sink him in reality below them... till the bloated monster has lost all traces of humanity...'[41] Here again, women made monstrous by chivalric homage provide the leading paradigm: 'They lose all simplicity, all dignity of mind, in acquiring power, and act as men are observed to act when they have been exalted by the same means.'[42] Most Enlightenment thinkers venerated education as the royal road to social improvement, but Wollstonecraft was not convinced: 'till society be differently constituted, much cannot be expected from education', particularly not in the case of women to whom sexual prerogatives have proven so 'intoxicating',

that until the manners of the times are changed, and formed on more reasonable principles, it may be impossible to convince them that the illegitimate power, which they obtain, by degrading themselves, is a curse, and that they must return to nature and equality, if they wish to secure the placid satisfaction that unsophisticated affections impart. But for this epoch we must wait – wait, perhaps, till kings and nobles, enlightened by reason, and, preferring the real dignity of man to childish state, throw off their gaudy hereditary trappings: and if then women do not resign the arbitrary power of beauty – they will prove that they have *less* mind than man.[43]

Women, soldiers, churchmen, the rich, old-regime Frenchmen: all re-side on the dark side of civilisation, that bleak social landscape where 'freedom... has been bartered for splendid slavery... [and] the pleasure of commanding flattering sycophants, and many other complicated low cal-culations of doting self-love, have all contributed to overwhelm the mass of mankind.'[44]

The picture is so gloomy that it seems to belie Wollstonecraft's political hopefulness. Yet elsewhere, and repeatedly, she reaffirmed her revolutionary optimism. '[S]ociety seems to have arrived at that point of civilization,' she wrote in 1794, 'when it becomes necessary for governments to meliorate it's [sic] condition, or a dissolution of their power and authority will be the consequence'.[45] Observing a certain lack of public spirit in Norway in 1795, she assured her readers that popular political awareness would soon generate a higher level of social conscience: 'The french revolution will have this effect.'[46] Everywhere ordinary working people were becoming less blindly submissive, she contended. Conservatives for whom the Revolution's tragic history demonstrated the impossibility of large-scale reform got no backing from her; nor did those philosophers who had argued 'that there is only a certain degree of civilization to which men are capable of attaining, without receding back to a state of barbarism'.[47] After all, if God has seen fit 'to call into existence a creature above the brutes, who could think and improve himself', how could His benign intentions for this creature, 'designed for perfect happiness', be doubted?[48] Wrong as things may now be, they must inevitably come right: only the ignorant or impious could deny it.

This conviction – the leading article of Wollstonecraft's radicalism – took her to the heart of the corruption/progression antimony haunting eighteenth-century thought. If present-day civilisation is a perversion of God's purpose, or at best its partial realisation, how is true progress ever to be secured? Rousseau, civilisation's leading critic, had lost all hope of human improvement – or so Wollstonecraft believed; and it is in responding to Rousseau's presumed pessimism that the grounds of her own optimism are spelled out. The argument runs over several early pages of the *Rights of Woman*. 'Impressed by... the misery and disorder which pervaded society, and fatigued with jostling against artificial fools,' Rousseau, she writes, argued for a return to the 'brutal' state of nature, mankind's 'golden age of stupidity'.[49] As a man sensitive to human suffering, Rousseau had been right to be repelled by the evils of the times, but wrong in his diagnosis of them:

Disgusted with artificial manners and virtues, the citizen of Geneva, instead of properly sifting the subject, threw away the wheat with the chaff, without waiting to inquire whether the evils which his ardent soul turned from indignantly, were the consequence of civilisation or the vestiges of barbarism. He saw vice trampling on virtue ... [and] talents bent by power to sinister purposes, and never thought of tracing the gigantic mischief up to arbitrary power, up to the hereditary distinctions that clash with the mental superiority that naturally raises a man above his fellows.[50]

It is not civilisation *per se* that generates corruption and injustice, but arbitrary, hereditary government. 'Let us investigate the causes which have produced this degeneracy [in civilised nations], and we shall discover, that they are those unjust plans of government, which had been formed by peculiar circumstances in every part of the globe.'[51] Thus where Rousseau (Wollstonecraft believed) had posited regression to savagery as the solution to civilised degeneracy, the true remedy lay with democratic political progress. It is 'the pestiferous purple which renders the progress of civilisation a curse' and

... had Rousseau mounted one step higher in his investigation ... his active mind would have darted forward to contemplate the perfection of man in the establishment of true civilization, instead of taking his ferocious flight back to the night of sensual ignorance.[52]

This misperception of Rousseau as a back-to-nature primitivist was shared by nearly all commentators, admirers and critics alike, in the late eighteenth century. Perhaps it is only with the benefit of hindsight that Rousseau's despairing advocacy of modernity can be fully appreciated. Perhaps too the idea of an age of prelapsarian innocence had particular appeal in a period when growing minority prosperity was being achieved through increased majority hardship. Wollstonecraft, who loathed inequality so much, certainly felt the tug of primitivist nostalgia, although in her case the appeal was offset by a (slightly guilty) preference for the culturally up-to-date, and – more important – by a powerful rejection of history. It is this antihistorical stance that fuels her quarrel with Rousseau, as it had her earlier opposition to Burke. Why idealise the past, as she had demanded of Burke, when all it reveals are 'dark days of ignorance' and the 'grossest prejudices'?[53] Historical legacies are the curse of civilisation, not its redemption. In his *Memoirs*, Godwin described how Wollstonecraft's early 'respect for establishments' had been 'undermined' by the French Revolution.[54] In fact her regard for established power institutions had been dealt such a body-blow that all she now saw in their historic record was despotism, misery and ruin. 'The first social systems were certainly founded by... individuals wishing to fence round their own wealth or power, and make slaves of their brothers to prevent encroachment. Their descendants have ever been at work to solder the chains they forged...'[55]

Wollstonecraft was not a sophisticated historian. Her indictment of past despotisms, although passionate, was far from precise, gesturing vaguely toward bygone times variously described as 'feudal', 'barbaric', or 'gothic'. But if the chronology is murky, the underlying political message is clear enough. Inequality and injustice are archaic rubbish of the past – a 'rust of antiquity... which ignorance and mistaken self-interest have consolidated' – that must now be jettisoned.[56] Contemporary society heaves with its democratic future, but realising this potential requires that status distinctions be discarded as outmoded relics, with neither legitimacy nor sanction.[57] The imperative applies with particular force to the sexual distinction, a leftover from those 'ferocious ages' of female enslavement anatomised by Enlightened historians.[58] Women's eroticised manners and prerogatives are decadent remnants of old-world despotism; likewise men's conjugal authority, which Wollstonecraft scorns as an archaism unacceptable in a modern body politic: 'The *divine right* of husbands, like the divine right of kings, may, it is to be hoped, in this enlightened age, be contested without danger.'[59] Given the 'gloom of despotism' that she everywhere discerned, the hope was somewhat disingenuous, but the darkness, she assured her readers, was steadily receding, and 'as sound politics diffuse liberty, mankind, including woman, will become more wise and virtuous.'[60] Thus instead of despairing because their ambitions cannot be immediately realised, 'advocates of truth and reason' must simply think long term, and 'should not relax in their endeavours to bring... more equal freedom, and general happiness to mankind.'[61]

* * *

Pragmatic reformism coupled to perfectibilist aspirations was Wollstonecraft's recipe for a just society. The agenda, spelled out most clearly in her writings on France, also shaped her view of British politics. The *Rights of Men*, her most typically jacobin text, offers a stock radical critique of the miseries wrought by an elite-dominated, unrepresentative government on a populace without the rights or means to influence the political process. The oppression of the working poor is a leading theme, and the language, for the most part, is radical-Whig. Thus, the House of Commons is 'a bear garden... contain[ing] a dead weight of benumbing opulence and... ignoble ambition', whose 'clogged wheels of corruption' are 'continually oiled by the sweat of the laborious poor, squeezed out of them by unceasing taxation'.[62] The common people of Britain are 'oppressed by the influence of their own money, extorted by the venal voice of a packed representation'.[63] The proposals for rectifying this situation – political representation; reform of the taxation and game laws; abolition of naval impressment – were orthodox radical remedies. Yet looking past these, Wollstonecraft allows her mind to wander along more utopian paths, toward an England where all large estates have been sub-divided into small farms, transforming the country into a garden society 'more inviting than Eden' where 'springs of joy [would] murmur on every side'.[64] Why should not such a vision be realised, she demands, since it would give so much more happiness than the rich estates of the present, full of their 'sweeping pleasure grounds, obelisks, temples' where 'every thing is cherished but man'?

At work here, as in all of Wollstonecraft's political writings, was an absolute egalitarianism, one aiming to eliminate not only political/juridical hierarchies but (as a reviewer of the *Rights of Men* warned) to 'bring all to the most perfect equality, and, by establishing absolute democracy, annihilate every species of subordination'.[65] It was here that the influence of Rousseau, particularly his *Second Discourse* (that 'admirable work on the origins of inequalities amongst mankind', as Wollstonecraft described it), left some of its most radical traces.[66] Throughout her political career, the leading test of a good society for Wollstonecraft was the level of equality attained there, since 'the more equality there is established... the more virtue and happiness will reign in society'.[67] In fact without equality 'there can be no society; – giving a manly meaning to the term', since without it there can exist none of those virtues – personal or public – on which happy societies are founded.[68] Possessing, or wanting to possess, more than other people corrupts and depletes the individual; personal ambition displaces social instincts and self-respect disintegrates. True self-love, by contrast, is always egalitarian because it is founded on that love of one's fellows which to Wollstonecraft, as to her coadjutors, was the core of the virtuous ego.

Wollstonecraft's passion for equality is often taken for granted by modern readers. Two centuries of lipservice to egalitarian ideals from western politicians have made it hard to recall just how radical these principles were in their early enunciations. In her own day, they identified Wollstonecraft with what conservatives and moderate reformers alike excoriated as the dangerous 'levelling' principles of Paine and his plebian followers, whose advocacy of natural rights and natural equality were interpreted as implying a wish to return to a primitive state of society where property was held in common and rank unknown.[69] In the case of Paine, the charge was largely false; in Wollstonecraft's case too, it was panicky and prejudicial – but with more truth behind it.[70] How much truth we will see in a moment, but first it is worth pausing to contrast contemporaries' view of 1790s egalitarianism with the common (at one time near-unanimous) twentieth-century image of Wollstonecraft as a bourgeois ideologue committed to the values and interests of middle-class women. On this reading, equality for Wollstonecraft was not – as her eighteenth-century audience believed it to be – the elimination of 'every species of subordination' but merely a levelling of sex-status differentials at society's middle rung; a reformist adjustment permitting women of her own background, as one critic typically puts it, to 'catch up with men in the system'.[71]

What is the evidence for this interpretation? Labelling Wollstonecraft and her fellow radicals as 'bourgeois' fails to convey either their material situation or social self-perception. For a start, it implies a level of affluence very few possessed. Rich these men and women may have been in mind and energy, but as journalists, pamphleteers, literary professionals of all sorts, they were anything but fat of purse, inhabiting a world where income was dependent entirely on skill (not capital), and where social or political influence were attainable, if at all, solely through the exercise of talents or trade.[72] If there was a single economic viewpoint to be found among them, it was not bourgeois-aspirational but that much older spirit of artisanal 'independency' that, in an economic world still largely governed by preferment and patronage, automatically placed them at odds with elite values. This was at least as true for jacobin women, nearly all of whom earned their own livings through writing, as it was for booksellers like Joseph Johnson, dissenting ministers like Price, journalists like Thomas Christie and Godwin, or artisans-turned-authors like Paine (a former staymaker), Thomas Holcroft (a former shoemaker and strolling player) and William Blake (an engraver). Like the men, women radicals were first and foremost hard-pressed self-employed workers, and it was this – rather than some notional 'bourgeois' status – that gave their politics an edge of go-getting individualism. Genius's laurels won freehanded, without incurring 'feudal' obligations, was a key point of thorny pride. 'A degree of exertion, produced by some want, more or less painful, is probably the price we must all pay for knowledge,' Wollstonecraft wrote from Scandinavia: 'How few authors or artists have arrived at eminence who have not lived by their employment?'[73]

Poised between the propertied and labouring classes, dependent on their wits for survival, these radicals were not, as is sometimes argued, the temporarily revolutionary face of a rising bourgeois elite, but a very specific cultural grouping living at the margins of – and often in direct collision with – mainstream middle-class Britain. Burke's description of jacobinism as 'the Revolt of the enterprising talents of a country against its Property' captures very well this complicatedly oppositional relationship between radical philosophes and the well-heeled circles in which Burke himself found such favour.[74] In a world where 'respect is the shadow of wealth, and commonly obtained ... by a criminal compliance with the prejudice of society', these were independent professionals striving to live virtuously, that is, in accordance with their own demanding principles of radical integrity – and to remould their society to that end.[75]

If a class tag is wanted for this, Raymond Williams's choice of petty bourgeois is probably the most satisfactory, not least because, by signalling the gap between these writers and the large commercial bourgeoisie, it helps to illuminate their equivocal pronouncements about middle-classness.[76] The notion of an ethically superior 'middle station' or 'middle rank' (terms used far more often by Wollstonecraft and her contemporaries than 'middle class') had been popular throughout the eighteenth century.[77] As the golden mean between opulence and indigence, middling life was lauded as the repository of all those virtues – enterprise, independence, personal and public probity – so conspicuously absent among both the wealthy and the impoverished. 'One rule remains,' the Poet Laureate versified in 1762, 'Nor shun nor court the great, Your truest center is the middle state'; or as Richard Price put it a quarter century later: 'the happiest state of man is the middle state between the savage and the refined, or between the wild and the luxurious state.'[78] The *Rights of Woman* addresses itself to middle-class women because they are, Wollstonecraft declares, in the 'most natural' state, that is, neither corrupted by extreme wealth nor corroded by the malignities of poverty. But it is middle-class men for whom Wollstonecraft reserves her warmest praise:

Abilities and virtues are absolutely necessary to raise men from the middle rank of life into notice; and the natural consequence is notorious, the middle rank contains most virtues and abilities. Men have thus, in one station, at least an opportunity of exerting themselves with dignity, and of rising by the exertions which really improve a rational creature ...[79]

These middling men, Wollstonecraft enthuses, are so preoccupied with 'business, extensive plans ... [and] excursive flights of ambition', that for them – unlike idle, listless women – marriage is only a secondary concern, and 'pleasure ... [a] mere relaxation' rather than a debilitating way of life.[80] Strong in mind and liberal in outlook, it is men like these to whom Britain

owes its relatively advanced position in the Europe-wide struggle against
entrenched privilege.[81] And it is in them that Wollstonecraft seems to rest
women's hopes, calling on them to 'generously snap our chains.'[82] This
done, '[l]et there be then no coercion *established* in society, and the common law of gravity prevailing, the sexes will fall into their proper places'.[83]
Women's freedom, it would seem, is coterminous with the triumph of an
entrepreneurial age.

Read in isolation, passages like these would certainly seem to support
the interpretation of Wollstonecraft as a bourgeois thinker. Viewed in relation to her radical philosophy as a whole, however, a very different picture
emerges. For against such pronouncements must be set her perfectibilist
commitments, her abiding faith in a future when all partial interests and
sectional loyalties would dissolve into Universal Benevolence and communal happiness. It is striking how as Wollstonecraft traversed the decade of
revolution her utopianism *and* her realism simultaneously deepened, as if
the horrors of 1793/4 merely girded her loins for larger changes to come.
The evils performed in the name of *liberté* simultaneously enlarged and
toughened her radicalism, imbuing it with a more sophisticated awareness of the obstacles, structural as well as political, confronting reformers.
Preparing the times for perfection was a harder task than she had imagined,
one requiring a longer radical reach. One key manifestation of this evolving perspective was her increasingly critical view of commercial civilisation.
A bourgeois manhood applauded in 1792 was by 1795 condemned as the
spearhead of a new economic despotism. The shift of perspective was not
as great as it might seem, since the men of enterprise eulogised in the *Rights
of Woman* were not in fact commercial bourgeoisie but members of the
traditional middling sectors of professionals and small tradesmen. But the
overall radicalisation of outlook is unmistakable.

* * *

Wollstonecraft's leftward shift can perhaps best be traced through her reflections on the ideal society. Wollstonecraft rarely indulged in explicit
utopian speculations, partly no doubt because of her reservations about
premature social remodelling, but also because such thinking would have
seemed dangerously 'enthusiastic' to her contemporaries, reminding them
of the sectarian radicalism of the previous century. 'I am not, Sir, aware of
your sneers, hailing a millennium...' she had told Burke in 1790, 'nor did
my fancy ever create a heaven on earth, since reason threw off her swaddling
clothes'.[84] But if her ambitions were not literally paradisical, the outline
images she offered of a 'world perfected' placed it well within the Christian utopian tradition. Imagining the way of life most conducive to virtue

and happiness, the *Rights of Woman* depicts a society of small, independent farmers and domestic craft enterprises, all with sufficient resources for modest comfort but none with a surplus large enough to encourage idleness. As in most Christian utopias, this is seen as a pastoral society (in post-revolutionary France, Wollstonecraft hoped, Paris would 'crumble' as its enlightened populace abandoned it for the 'charms of... agricultural recreations') unburdened by gross economic inequalities or caste distinctions. 'Why cannot large estates be divided into small farms? these dwellings would indeed grace our land... [i]f society was regulated on a more enlarged plan; if man was contented to be the friend of man...'[85]

For an already existing example of such a society, Wollstonecraft – like most British radicals – looked to America, the first of the world's nations to be governed entirely 'on the basis of reason and equality'.[86] Charmed by Imlay's accounts of life on the western frontier, in 1793 she began making plans to return there with him. The scheme died with their relationship; but even as this prospect evaporated another model society, this one nearer to hand, hoved into view. This was Norway, whose people – the 'most free community I have ever observed' – Wollstonecraft encountered in 1795, living a life of Rousseauist simplicity on Europe's northern fringe.[87]

Wollstonecraft's Scandinavian travels, undertaken in a mood of amorous melancholia and with the outrages of terrorist France still vivid in her mind, afforded her much-needed space in which to ponder her emotional life, but also a perfect opportunity to refine her views on human progress by comparing life in Europe's 'most polished' nations to conditions in its 'half-civilised' hinterland: a task she approached with that combination of fact-finding zeal and philosophic presumption so characteristic of Enlightened social explorers. Entering Norway, she found herself in a country of modest farms and small towns whose unsophisticated, independent-minded inhabitants immediately won her delighted approval. Of one community of backwoodsmen she wrote admiringly – in terms strongly reminiscent of some New World traveller encountering a tribe of noble savages – that they seemed to possess all the attributes of the fabled 'golden age': 'independence and virtue; affluence without vice; cultivation of mind, without depravity of heart; with "ever smiling liberty"; the nymph of the mountain'.[88] Staying with townsfolk, she was pleased to find them tolerant or even freethinking in their religious beliefs, and – thanks to an uncensored press – remarkably uninihibited in their political opinions.[89] The Norwegian legal system was mild, she reported, while its government – a popular monarchy – was very responsive to public feeling. Even Norwegian transport was exemplary: 'I have never met with better... post-horses.'[90]

As her sojourn in the country continued, this enthusiasm dimmed somewhat. Norway had no university, she discovered, and scientific curiosity was
almost moribund.[91] Middle-class Norwegian women were 'artlessly kind'
but also vulgar and uncultivated, and their menfolk stank of tobacco.[92]
Everyone ate too much.[93] Dining in the homes of local dignitaries, she
soon wearied of the endless food, the pipe fumes, the clumsy small-talk.
Even the rough beauty of the landscape began to bore her until, with some
embarrassment, she found herself pining for London (and feeling less censorious about French sophistication).[94] The life of a Rousseauist primitive
wasn't for her, she decided.

But despite these reservations, the nation's democratic character continued to impress. The sub-division of the countryside into small freeholds
had led to 'a degree of equality... which I have seldom seen elsewhere', and
endowed Norwegian farmers with a truly 'manly' temperament, 'for not
being obliged to submit to any debasing tenure, in order to live, or advance
themselves in the world, they act with an independent spirit.'[95] Even the
existence of a small merchant elite could not warp this egalitarian social
fabric since, obliged by inheritance laws to divide their wealth among all
their children (with boys receiving twice as much as girls), the property of
this class 'has not a chance of accumulating till overgrown wealth destroys
the balance of liberty'.[96] The result was that she 'never... heard of anything
like domineering, or oppression, excepting such as has arisen from natural
causes.'[97] Unsurprising then, to find that the Norwegians were nearly all
(despite fierce loyalty to their own, democratic-minded prince) republican
sympathisers and keen supporters of the French Revolution – so keen indeed, that 'they excuse every thing... [and] I could hardly persuade them
that Robespierre was a monster'.[98]

This image of a small-producer society, its wealth sufficiently dispersed
to ensure rough equality, had dominated British radical utopian imaginings throughout the eighteenth century. In the 1790s it found expression
not just in Wollstonecraft's writings but in Tom Paine's agrarian reform
programme, in the rural arcadia proposed by the Newcastle schoolmas-
ter Thomas Spence, and – closest to Wollstonecraft – in the Pantisocratic
scheme hatched by the young Samuel Coleridge and Robert Southey who,
inspired by Godwin's anarcho-communism, in 1794 decided to build New
Jerusalem on the banks of the Susquehanna River in Pennsylvania. The
plan was aborted, but the choice of America as its site reflected radicals'
view of the new republic as a land of uncorrupted virtue; a nation whose
people, as Wollstonecraft wrote, were characterised by such perfect 'equality... integrity, simplicity' that, at a time when most of Europe was 'palsied

by oppression', they seemed almost 'another race of beings, men formed to enjoy the advantages of society, and not merely to benefit those who governed.'[99] True civilisation really was possible, Wollstonecraft (and many other jacobin intellectuals) believed, for America's 'independent and hardy yeomanry' were in the process of building it.[100]

Wollstonecraft's most enthusiastic comments on America were made as she and Imlay planned their new life there. By late 1794, as Imlay's philandering and financial preoccupations were undermining their relationship, she was writing more critically about the republic and its commercial-minded citizenry. Warnings about the destructive influence of commerce on social relations became frequent, and bitterly personal. Writing to Imlay in December 1794, she told him how such she detested his 'commercial face'. Why chase after more money than was needed to keep 'the pot boiling', she demanded, when pursuing it inevitably 'debases the mind, and roots out affection from the heart?'[101] Why sacrifice so much for riches when merely avoiding poverty was surely enough?[102] If this was the American way, it was not for her. Mulling these matters while rescuing Imlay's business affairs in Norway, she hooked personal reflections onto a larger critique of commercial modernity. Under 'whatever point of view I consider society', she wrote, 'it appears, to me, that an adoration of property is the root of all evil'; and then, on a prescient note:

England and America owe their liberty to commerce, which created a new species of power to undermine the feudal system. But let them beware of the consequence; the tyranny of wealth is still more galling and debasing than that of rank.[103]

By the end of Wollstonecraft's life this attitude had overtaken any earlier admiration for *le doux commerce*. The critique was already taking shape in 1793 when, speculating as to whether the French Revolution would ever lead to a new 'purity of manners', she reflected that 'if the aristocracy of birth is levelled with the ground, only to make room for that of riches, I am afraid that the morals of the people will not be much improved by the change, or the government rendered less venal'.[104] The 'narrow principle of commerce which seems every where to be shoving aside *the point of honour* of the *noblesse*' offered 'little' for the future, she 'hesitantly' told Joseph Johnson; but soon the hesitant note disappeared to be replaced, in the final pages of her history of the Revolution, with a strong indictment of the effects of commercial advance, the 'most pernicious' of which

is it's [sic] producing an aristocracy of wealth, which degrades mankind, by making them only exchange savageness for tame servility, instead of acquiring the urbanity of improved reason. Commerce also, overstocking a country with people, obliges the majority to become manufacturers rather than husbandmen; and then the division of labour, solely to enrich the proprietor, renders the mind entirely inactive.[105]

The effects of such developments, she went on – obviously glancing toward Adam Smith's Britain – is to turn 'whole knots of men... into machines, to enable a keen speculator to become wealthy; and every noble principle of nature is eradicated by making a man pass his life in stretching wire, pointing a pin, heading a nail'.[106] Far from being advantaged by these new work processes, the working poor are debilitated even further, as their enervating labours 'impede that gradual process of improvement, which leads to the perfection of reason, and the establishment of rational equality'.[107] Moral depravity and communal corruption do not disappear with antique despotisms, in other words, but find invidious new forms through modernisation itself.

To describe these sentiments as anti-capitalist would be only partly accurate. Wollstonecraft was no economist; nor could she foresee the leviathan that industrial capitalism, then a minority player on the economic stage, would become. Like many intellectuals, her disdain for the commercial spirit had more than a whiff of high-minded snobbishness about it. Writing about economic conditions in pre-Revolution France, she praised the attempts of Turgot and other economists to unshackle French commerce from government control, while at the same time urging the revolutionary government to intervene directly in France's business affairs so as to reduce the gap between wealth and poverty.[108] Rich versus poor, rather than capital versus labour, remained for her, as for all radicals, the main economic divide. She was never an absolute opponent of private property, although at times veering in that direction. 'The only security of property that nature authorizes and reason sanctions is, the right a man has to enjoy the acquisitions which his talents and industry have acquired; and to bequeath them to whom he chooses,' she argued in stock radical-Lockean fashion in the *Rights of Men*, while simultaneously condemning primogeniture, that 'everlasting rampant' against the advance of talents and virtue.[109] 'I am afraid that all men are materially injured by inheriting wealth,' she wrote to Godwin, on a more levelling note, in 1797,[110] while two years earlier the plight of underpaid custom-house officers in Norway prompted her to remark that 'Much public virtue cannot be expected till every employment... has a salary sufficient to reward industry, whilst none are so great as to permit the possessor to remain idle. It is this want of proportion between profit and labour which debases men...'[111] Her favourite targets, like most radicals, were men she regarded as economic parasites: speculators, stockjobbers, greedy merchants (like Imlay) engaged in war profiteering. 'The interests of nations are bartered by speculating merchants,' she wrote from Hamburg, after observing the activities of businessmen there. 'My God! with what *sang froid* artful trains of corruption bring lucrative commissions into particular hands...'[112] She also expressed concern about the character and impact of large-scale industry, but here her unease did not go beyond anxieties common at the time. Reviewing a 1792 pamphlet about child-labour in the cotton mills she noted indignantly that

Mistaken, indeed... must be principles of that commercial system, whose wheels are oiled by infant sweat, and supine the government that allows any body of men to enrich themselves by preying on the vitals, physical and moral, of the rising generation! – These things ought to be considered.[113]

Registering such evils, and recoiling from them, does not make Wollstonecraft a proto-socialist, but it does demonstrate a link between her thought and social radicalisms to come. The socialist movement that emerged in Britain in the 1820s was strongly indebted to the jacobin utopians, especially to Godwin whose indictment of private property was much more systematic and comprehensive than his wife's. The communist principle was openly endorsed by some of Godwin's acolytes – including Thomas Holcroft (whose novel *Anna St Ives* featured a working-class communist among its chief protagonists) and the young Pantisocrats – but the only evidence of Wollstonecraft holding similar views appeared in some remarks she made to Southey about the French communist Gracchus Babeuf and his 'Conspiracy of Equals'. Praising Babeuf as the 'most extraordinary' individual she had ever met, she expressed regret about the failure of his attempt to impose a 'system of total equalisation' on the French economy, which 'would have rendered any return to common systems impossible, and excited insurrection all over Europe. But Babeuf did not set sail till the tide had set in against him.'[114] Whether Southey reported her accurately cannot be known, but the sentiments certainly fit with the passion for 'equalisation' evident in all her writings on France. 'Nature having made men unequal, by giving stronger bodily and mental powers to one than to another,' she wrote in her history of the Revolution, 'the end of government ought to be, to destroy this inequality by protecting the weak' while on the next page of the same work: 'It appears to be the grand province of government, though scarcely acknowledged, so to hold the balance, that the abilities or riches of individuals may not interfere with the equilibrium of the whole.'[115] No *laissez-faire* for Wollstonecraft here: what equality requires, the polity must provide, since it is only on this basis that general happiness and virtue may thrive.

* * *

Building a truly civilised society required all human beings to fulfil their God-given potential. Thus far, Wollstonecraft judged – echoing a host of critics – her own sex had shown little sign of this. Modernisers who believed otherwise, who praised women's elevating social influence, were dismissed as gallant sentimentalists. Women's artificial manners, corrupt morals, and luxurious tastes made them an insidiously anti-progressive force. Whether this injurious role was a residue of the uncivilised past or a function of the civilising process *per se* was left unspecified by most critics. In Wollstonecraft's writings, the emphasis tended to be placed on the recidivist elements in women's behaviour and social status; but her conviction that a further stage of civilised progress was yet to come meant that the denunciation of the female condition as a 'gothic' relic could as easily apply to contemporary society ('partial civilisation') as to preceding ages.

To a modern reader, what is so striking about these criticisms is their remoteness from any lived female experience. In Wollstonecraft's writings, as in most eighteenth-century works on feminine manners, modern Woman is a figure of sensational unreality. A preening narcissist, obsessed with appearance and fashion; a voluptuous hedonist, wallowing in sybaritic excess; an enervated emotionalist, strung out on frail nerves and overwrought sensibilities: the pages of the *Rights of Woman* are so crammed with caricatures like these that the reader, looking up from them, finds it hard to recall the more mundane reality, that in 1792 the vast majority of British women were not rich dilettantes but poor women who spent their days labouring in field or home, tending their children, worrying about bread prices, rents, unwanted pregnancies. Wollstonecraft knew this too, yet it was to be some years before the shadow cast by emblematic Woman over her writings began to fade. Thus, in her history of the French Revolution, apart from some stock-radical criticisms of female influence in the Bourbon regime, she has virtually nothing to say about the lives and experiences of Frenchwomen, despite having lived among them for nearly two years. Similarly, American women, praised in the *Analytical Review* for the frank openness of their manners, otherwise appear only as the epitome of what she came to regard – thanks mostly to Imlay – as a particularly nasty commercial society. As 'the land of liberty and vulgar aristocracy, seated on her bags of dollars', America, she wrote, displayed a 'national character' unique in human history: 'a head enthusiastically enterprising, with cold selfishness of heart'.[116] And for the prototype of this cold selfishness, she offered the women of the American cities, whose prudery, ignorance, ostentation and chilly frivolity were such as to throw 'leaden fetters on their charms'.[117] On the other hand, travelling across Scandinavia she carefully documented female working conditions, marital lives, and cultural habits. 'Still harping on the same subject, you will exclaim –' she wrote to Imlay, as she reported on the sexual exploitation of lower-class Danish women, 'How can I avoid it, when most of the struggles of an eventful life have been occasioned by the oppressed state of my sex...'[118]

Wollstonecraft's difficulty in dragging this 'same subject' out from under the weight of symbol constructions of femininity was at its most acute when she turned to the question of civic rights. The status of women in political life was not a new concern in the late eighteenth century. Political thinkers of all stripes had previously addressed the issue, but in discourses so dominated by feminine stereotypes that actual women went virtually unnoticed. The 1790s was a critical moment in this regard. Caught up on a wave of revolutionary hope, women acquired new political expectations and new platforms from which to express them. Emblematic Woman came face to face with the female citizen, a novel political phenomenon, and feminism took on a new character and militancy. The final chapters explore this development; but first let us return to Wollstonecraft's social world to meet some of the other women – feminist and non-feminist – involved in 1790s radicalism.

6

Gallic philosophesses

Vigorous minds are with difficulty restrained within the trammels of authority; a spirit of enterprise, a passion for experiment; a liberal curiosity, urges them to quit beaten paths, to explore untried ways, to burst the fetters of prescription, and to acquire wisdom by an individual experience.

(Mary Hays, *Memoirs of Mary Wollstonecraft*)[1]

The female presence in the jacobin intelligentsia was small and, apart from Wollstonecraft, of minor public influence. The only woman radical prior to the 1790s to have enjoyed any real political prestige was Catharine Macaulay, who died in 1791 while the revolution debate was still in its early stages. Of the other women writers contributing to the radical side of the controversy – Helen Maria Williams, Charlotte Smith, Anna Barbauld, Mary Hays, Mary Robinson, Eliza Fenwick, Elizabeth Inchbald, Amelia Alderson, a few lesser figures – only three or four (Williams, Smith, Barbauld, possibly Hays) acquired reputations as radical thinkers outside leftwing circles. Anti-jacobin propagandists, keen to exploit the disreputability of such goings-on, sometimes made a fuss: 'Our peasantry now read the Rights of Man on mountains, and moors, and by the way side...,' T. J. Mathias wailed in a widely read pamphlet: 'Our *unsexed* female writers now instruct, or confuse, us and themselves in the labryinth of politicks, or turn us wild with Gallick frenzy.'[2] But unlike on the conservative side, where Hannah More's presence loomed very large indeed, radicalism was for the most part a staunchly masculine affair. Jacobin men endlessly celebrated their political virility, with Paine praising the 'gigantic manliness' of the new American republic while 'John Thelwall never tired of recommending the "manly energies of reason", "manly firmness", and "the powerful energies of manhood" '.[3] 'You think little of... manly confidence, and manly spirit,' Godwin accused a fellow radical who was losing heart over political developments in France, 'and only wish that mankind were well asleep'.[4]

Recent studies of the 1790s have tended to portray them as years of gender ferment, so it is worth recalling just how limited and temporary a flowering of feminist ideals occurred over this period. Sexual egalitarians were thin on the ground in plebian reform organisations, and outside the Wollstonecraft/Godwin circle even the radical intelligentsia could summon up only minority support for feminist principles. Nonetheless, over the course of the decade the 'rights of women' progressed from an easily dismissed, almost risible stance – the *ne plus ultra* of radical extremism – into a widely acknowledged, if highly controversial, element in popular democratic thinking. Records from London debating clubs, which in the 1790s were generally open to both sexes, show that by the final years of the century Wollstonecraft's ideas had become a favourite topic for popular disputation. Feminist voices were occasionally heard in these debates, like that of the 'Young Lady' who in 1797 wrote to the London Forum urging discussion of Wollstonecraft's views on women's mental equality and stating that for her part, she would 'give her hand to no man who will not declare he believes the Understandings of Women to be equal to those of Men'.[5] Meanwhile, in other British towns and cities coteries of reform-minded men and women, usually Rational Dissenters, circulated copies of the *Rights of Woman*. In 1795 one London Corresponding Society activist, on tour through the provinces, met several radical women of this kind, including a Chatham woman who, after praising the *Rights of Woman*, proffered him a short lesson in feminist politics: 'A *female* legislature, Sir, would never have passed those horrid Convention Bills, or abrogated the dear prerogative of speech':

There was nothing, she thought, to which women were not competent; and she strongly censured our sex, for first depriving them of every source of intelligence, and then reproaching them for their levity and discretion! She had truth and reason on her side; I therefore heartily concurred in the justice of her remarks.[6]

No doubt detailed local studies of radicalism would produce more such women – and male sympathisers, like Gale Jones – busy evangelising for women's rights. 'I have observed', George Dyer, a Cambridge radical poet, wrote hopefully in 1792, 'that the most sensible females,when they turn their attention to political subjects, are more uniformly on the side of liberty than the other sex':

... The truth is, that the modes of education and the customs of society are degrading to the female character; and the tyranny of custom is sometimes worse than the tyranny of government. When a sensible woman rises above the tyranny of custom, she feels a generous indignation; which, when turned against the exclusive claims of the other sex, is favourable to female pretensions; when turned against the tyranny of government, it is commonly favourable to the rights of both sexes. Most governments are partial, and more injurious to women than men.[7]

Dyer, who in the same year included the *Rights of Woman* among works to be used to educate the working class in radical principles, was, like Gale Jones, one of a few jacobin men to make feminist issues a personal priority.[8] The highest concentration of such men, unsurprisingly, were to be found among Wollstonecraft's intimates. In 1792 her close friend Thomas Holcroft published his *Anna St Ives*, a novel featuring a gorgeous heiress of Wollstonecraftian opinions who, allied with a lower-class lover, pits herself against old-world hypocrisy and prejudice. Another friend, Thomas Beddoes, in the same year published a tract on female educational reform that was set, at his insistence, by a woman compositor.[9] The young Robert Southey, who became acquainted with Wollstonecraft in the mid 1790s, later spoke of his great respect for her, and celebrated her in verse.[10] Other close male associates offered similar admiration and solidarity.[11] If, as Godwin claimed, Wollstonecraft 'trampled on those rules which are built on the assumption of the imbecility of her sex', she clearly knew the right men to do it among.[12]

* * *

Despite being a minority phenomenon then, female jacobinism was important both for its impact on radical thought and, more significant perhaps, as a portent of larger things to come. Wollstonecraft is usually seen as an individual pioneer. But setting her among her fellow radical *literatae*, the first coterie of women intellectuals to intervene in British reform politics, gives a truer sense of her historic significance. The involvement of this little 'Amazonian band' in the major political controversy of the day was an unprecedented development. Yet during the next century, as feminism expanded from an avant-garde intellectual position into a mass political movement, Britain was to hear much from such women. The fears expressed by 1790s conservatives about the subversive influence of jacobinical philosophesses may have been partisan and exaggerated – but as premonitory forebodings they were to prove more than justified.

Wollstonecraft's personal history too is usually regarded as idiosyncratic. Placed among her fellow female *philosophes*, however, her career looks fairly typical of their very atypical lives. Like her, nearly all came from middling backgrounds ranging from the shabbily genteel to the comfortably prosperous. Most were self-educated, having had only the rudimentary schooling usual for women. The majority were religious Nonconformists:

usually Rational Dissenters or, like Wollstonecraft, Dissenting sympathisers. Nearly all at some stage were married and had children, but this was usually where their claims to conventional femininity ended. Some had illicit lovers; some were deserted wives; very few enjoyed happy, stable marriages. None remotely conformed to received images of eighteenth-century womanhood, which partly reflects the inaccuracy of the stereotype but also the powerfully dissident quality of their lives and personal choices as well as their politics.

Some were women of considerable literary repute. Elizabeth Inchbald (1753–1821) was a highly regarded playwright and novelist whose life began quietly enough, on an East Anglian farm. But an early passion for the theatre drew her from home, aged nineteen, to try her luck on the London stage. Alone and vulnerable, she married a man seventeen years her senior (already the father of two illegitimate daughters) who died several years later, leaving her destitute. Never very successful as an actress, Inchbald now turned her hand to playwriting, at which she did much better; by the end of the 1780s she was well established as a dramatist and novelist, and financially secure. She never married again, but not for lack of trying, at one time unsuccessfully angling for a proposal from Godwin. An unrequited passion for the actor John Philip Kemble likewise came to nothing, and she ended her days in a Catholic residence for women.[13]

The career pattern, with its recourse to professional writing following a failure of male financial support, was repeated again and again. Eliza Fenwick (?–1804), one of Wollstonecraft's closest friends, was the wife of a hack writer whose fecklessness drove her into novel-writing to feed her family. In 1800 her husband abandoned her, forcing her to take up schoolteaching abroad, first in the West Indies and then in America where she died in 1840.[14] A similar trajectory was followed by Charlotte Smith (1749–1806) who, despite coming from a landed family, was compelled to take up writing to support her many children after her spendthrift husband had landed them all in debtors' prison. She too did well, although money always remained a problem. 'Charlotte Smith . . . is writing more volumes . . . for immediate subsistence,' a sympathiser wrote in 1801, 'She is a woman full of sorrows . . . One of her daughters . . . has to come to her mother, not worth a shilling, and with . . . three young children.'[15]

Like Smith, the poet and novelist Mary Robinson (1758–1800) also spent some time in a debtors' prison thanks to a husband's profligacy. Robinson, another of Wollstonecraft's intimates, was a merchant's daughter who, after parting from the wayward lawyer she had married at fifteen, went on to a brief but highly successful career as an actress and courtesan. Performing

'Perdita' in *A Winter's Tale* in 1779, she captivated the Prince of Wales who kept her as his mistress for about a year. When he moved on to a new *inamorata* she blackmailed him and then took up with a series of his political cronies, including Charles Fox and Richard Sheridan. In the early 1780s, while travelling in a coach to Dover, Robinson suffered a miscarriage that left her permanently paralysed. Her then-lover, a military *roue* named Tarleton, remained by her side, attending her and spending her literary earnings, until 1798, when he married an heiress half his age. In the same year, Robinson published her main feminist work, *Thoughts on the Condition of Women, and on the Injustice of Mental Subordination*;[16] two years later, shortly before her death aged forty-two, she wrote a brief, self-exonerating memoir explaining how she had 'ever been the reverse of volatile and dissipated': 'Alas! of all created beings I have been the most severely subjugated by circumstances...'[17]

As with Wollstonecraft herself, thrust into poverty by an errant father and later abandoned by the father of her illegitimate daughter, what is at first glance so striking about these women is their vulnerability to male absence or delinquency. A friend's description of Charlotte Smith as 'chained to her desk like a slave to his oar, with no other means of subsistence for herself and her numerous children' was applicable, at different life stages and to differing degrees, to virtually all of them.[18] What a closer look makes apparent, however, is the exceptional entrepreneurial acumen they brought to bear on these difficult circumstances. Victims of men or bad fortune they might have been, but they also knew a lucrative opportunity when they spotted it, and having made their way into the world of popular publishing proceeded to plough the literary field through every available furrow: novels (Inchbald, Robinson, Hays, Williams, Alderson, Fenwick); plays (Inchbald, Fenwick); short stories (Alderson, Robinson); poetry (Robinson, Barbauld, Williams); works for children (Fenwick, Barbauld, Smith); history (Williams, Smith) biography (Hays); book reviews (Inchbald, Hays); theatre criticism (Inchbald); political journalism (Hays, Williams); religious and didactic essays (Hays, Barbauld); translations (Inchbald, Robinson, Hays, Williams); and edited anthologies (Barbauld, Hays, Inchbald). Booksellers were solicited; fees negotiated; fellow writers consulted. 'You have talents, cultivate them, and learn to rest on your own powers,' the radical heroine of Mary Hays's novel, *Emma Courtney*, was instructed: a good sum-up of the life philosophy of these diligent, toughminded women.[19]

All were overjoyed by the outbreak of the French Revolution, writing poems in its praise, attending gatherings to honour visiting *citoyens*, occasionally even addressing public meetings.[20] Helen Maria Williams rushed off to Paris in 1790 to join in the first Bastille day celebrations and remained there for the rest of her life. Her *Letters Written From France in the Summer of 1790*, published by Johnson, were so popular back in England, despite their staunch republicanism, that they incurred sharp rebukes from rightwing competitors. 'The study, my dear madam, which I place in the climax of unfitness,' the novelist Laetitia Matilda Hawkins scolded her, 'is that of *politics*; and so strongly does it appear to me barred against the admission of females, that I am astonished that they ever ventured to approach it'. Women should either 'enjoy in peace the traditional creed of their fathers' or, failing that, maintain a discreet silence.²¹ Reverend Richard Polwhele, in a particularly mealy-mouthed piece of invective, condemned Williams (along with Wollstonecraft, Barbauld, Robinson, Hays and Smith) as one of the 'unsex'd.... female advocates of Democracy in this country' who 'though they have had no opportunity of imitating the French ladies, in their atrocious acts of cruelty; have yet assumed a stern serenity in the contemplation of those savage excesses'.²² Hawkins and Polwhele, like most of the anti-jacobin propagandists churning out lurid accounts of the immoralism and Amazonian freakishness of radical women, were hack sensationalists. But liberal-minded Britons too often found women political writers unsettling. The disquiet hovered over the revolution debate, intensifying as counter-revolutionary feeling strengthened. 'But women it is said have no business with politics —' Charlotte Smith wrote boldly at the high point of British radicalism, in the preface to her novel *Desmond* (1792):

Why not? — Have they no interest in the scenes that are acting around them, in which they have fathers, brothers, husbands, sons, or friends engaged? — Even in the commonest course of female education, they are expected to acquire some knowledge of history; and yet, if they are to have no opinion of what *is* passing, it avails little that they should be informed of what *has passed*, in a world where they are subject to such mental degradation; where they are censured as affecting masculine knowledge if they happen to have any understanding; or despised as insignificant triflers if they have none.²³

Other radical women too insisted on having their political say, demanding their right (in Elizabeth Inchbald's words) '[t]o think, to argue, to decide, to write/To talk, undoubtedly — perhaps, to fight.'²⁴ But by the end of the decade, with revolutionary hopes gone sour and Wollstonecraft everywhere slandered, female confidence foundered. In 1798 Mary Robinson bitterly condemned British society for its persistent cold-shouldering of progressive-minded women as 'masculine' beings 'too formidable... to be endured, much less sanctioned'.[25] 'Such is the force of prejudice, the law of custom, against woman,' she complained bleakly, that while a woman 'is expected to *act* like a philosopher' she is 'not allowed to *think* like one': an accusation that took on even greater weight in the early decades of the nineteenth century.[26]

Even at the height of popular radicalism, however, explicit feminism of the 'Wollstonecraft school' attracted only limited support among women writers. Conservative women like the Evangelical propagandist, Hannah More, damned the *Rights of Woman* outright (More refused to read it on the grounds that even its title was too 'fantastic and absurd')[27] while liberals like Anna Seward and the bluestocking Hester Chapone gave it only a qualified endorsement.[28] Nor did radical women award it a unanimous thumbs-up. Of the women discussed here, only Mary Hays and Mary Robinson were thorough-going Wollstonecraftians while others, like Elizabeth Inchbald, treated her ideas with wary respect spiked, occasionally, with satirical irony. Inchbald's 1793 comedy, *Everyone Has His Fault*, opened with the following, delicately ambivalent, verse:

> The *Rights of Women*, says a female pen
> Are, to do everything as well as Men.
> I grant this matter may be strained too far,
> And Maid 'gainst Man is most uncivil war;
> I grant, as all my City friends will say,
> That Men should rule, and Women should obey...
> But since the Sex at length has been inclin'd
> To cultivate that useful part – the mind; –
> Since they have learnt to read, to write, to spell; –
> Since some of them have wit, – and use it well; –
> Let us not force them back with brow severe
> Within the pale of ignorance and fear,
> Confin'd entirely to domestic arts,
> Producing only children, pies and tarts.[29]

Amelia Alderson and Helen Maria Williams expressed similarly ambivalent sentiments, with Alderson, seven years after Wollstonecraft's death, publicly mocking her feminism in a novel.[30] Only one female member of the radical intelligentsia, however – Anna Barbauld – openly opposed Wollstonecraft's ideas during her lifetime. But since Barbauld was probably the most respected woman writer to take up cudgels for the radical cause, her antagonism to feminism was particularly significant.

Anna Barbauld (1743–1825) was one of eighteenth-century Britain's foremost women poets, and a leading spokeswoman for enlightened Dissent.

A controversial figure outside progressive circles, her prolific political and religious writings took her too near the borders of feminine propriety to wholly escape moralising censure. Her response to those who charged her with stepping 'out of the bonds of female reserve' was never to criticise convention, however, but only to insist that her own situation was 'peculiar, and . . . would offer no rule for others'.[31] In the 1780s and nineties she inhabited the Bluestocking milieu, but with none of the feminine partisanship manifested by other Blues; and when two attempts were made to involve her in female initiatives – by Elizabeth Montagu, in the establishment of a 'college for young ladies', and by Maria Edgeworth, in a journal written and edited by women – she turned both down flat, to Montagu insisting that women had no need of higher education while Edgeworth was told that 'to write professedly as a female junto [sic] seems in some measure to suggest a certain cast of sentiment, and you would write in trammels'.[32] Meanwhile her poetry celebrated the joys of feminine submission: 'Your best, your sweetest empire,' she reminded her women readers, 'is – to PLEASE.'[33]

The refusal to be trammelled by female solidarities is an old tune for high-achieving women, still sung by plenty today. In Barbauld's case, however, it intersected with other aspects of her history in interesting ways. As the daughter of a leading Dissenter, she was raised and educated in one of the most advanced intellectual circles of provincial England. Her father John Aikin, a tutor at Warrington Academy in Lancashire, taught her literature and languages, including the classics (other bluestockings were often impressed by her Latin and Greek). With the encouragement of her brother John, Anna began publishing poetry in 1773 and then, in the same year, co-authored a book of essays with him, *Miscellaneous Pieces in Prose*. Shortly after the publication of *Miscellaneous Pieces*, John Aikin attended a dinner party with Charles Fox, who expressed his admiration for the book. 'I particularly admire your essay, *Against Inconsistency in our Expectations*,' Fox told him. 'That,' Aikin said, 'is my sister's.' 'I like much your essay, *On Monastic Institutions*,' Fox tried again. 'That is also my sister's.' Fox said no more about the book.[34]

In 1774 Anna (prompted, her brother later claimed, by the invidious influence of *La Nouvelle Héloïse*) married Rouchemont Barbauld, a student at Warrington. In later years he became acutely psychotic, but until then they had a successful partnership with Rouchemont preaching to Dissenting congregations while Anna taught school and wrote. By the 1780s, when Wollstonecraft met her, Barbauld was well established as a poet, essayist, children's writer, and religious controversialist. By the end of the 1780s she was deeply involved in the campaign against the legal disabilities of

Dissenters, publishing one tract whose tone was so uncompromising that it prompted Horace Walpole to brand her 'that virago Barbauld', while another critic expressed his shock that a woman had penned it. '[I]n soft bosoms dwells such mighty rage?' he wanted to know.[35]

Like all her fellow Unitarians, Barbauld greeted the outbreak of the French Revolution with enormous enthusiasm.[36] By 1793 her view of French politics had become much bleaker, but she bitterly opposed the war, and never entirely abandoned her earlier radicalism.[37] One of her finest works, the prophetic poem *Eighteen Hundred and Eleven*, was so uncompromising in its criticisms of political and social corruption in Britain that it met with a public outcry and accusations of sedition: a reception that so distressed the now-aging Barbauld that she never published anything of political substance again.

Why did such a vigorous radicalism falter when it came to her own sex? The question cannot be confidently answered. But Barbauld's democratic instincts were always weaker than most of her fellow jacobins, and she had none of Wollstonecraft's Rousseauist passion for equality. 'Levelling' notions were as unwelcome to her as to any anti-jacobin propagandist. 'It is the fault of the present age, owing to the freer commerce that different ranks and professions now enjoy with each other,' a 1773 essay complained, 'that characters are not marked with sufficient strength: the classes run too much into each other':

There is a cast of manners peculiar and becoming to each age, sex and profession...Each is perfect in its kind. A woman as a woman: a tradesman as a tradesman. We are often hurt by the brutality and sluggish conceptions of the vulgar; not considering that some there must be to be hewers of wood and drawers of water, and that cultivated genius, or even any great refinement and delicacy in their moral feelings, would be a real misfortune to them.[38]

Here, in this bland defence of cultural hierarchy, is one possible explanation of her persistent repudiation of female intellectualism, although the truculence with which she refused to support any expansion of women's education (warning Elizabeth Montagu that a university for women was likely to create '*Precieuses* or *Femmes Savantes*' rather than 'good wives or agreeable companions') also suggests an unease with her own capabilities common to many eighteenth-century learned women.[39] But the most revealing text, as far as Barbauld's anti-feminism is concerned, is one that makes no mention of women: her 1790 *Address to the Opposers of the Repeal of the Corporation and Test Acts*. This tract, a very effective blast at the Dissenters' parliamentary enemies, grounds the case for abolition of the Test

Acts on the 'inalienable right' of all men to full membership in the polity, regardless of religious affiliation. The Dissenters, Barbauld insists, 'wish to bury every name of distinction in the common appellation of citizen'. 'It is you,' she told the opposers of repeal, 'who by considering us as aliens, make us so. It is you who force us to make our dissent a prominent feature in our character.'[40] The argument so clearly rehearses Wollstonecraft's later 'wild wish' in relation to the sexual distinction that it serves as an important reminder of Wollstonecraft's own debt to Dissenting politics. The tension between this humanist drive to dissolve all distinctions into a common civic status, and the feminist pressure to take political cognisance of women's 'alien' status and disabilities, haunted Wollstonecraft's radicalism; in Barbauld's case, it resulted in a decisive rejection of all gender-based initiatives. Women *as* women had nothing of which to complain, Barbauld insisted, and thus no common cause to unite them. For literary women to form a 'corps' in order to further women's joint interests was 'absurd and ridiculous' Maria Edgeworth was told, in their correspondence over Edgeworth's proposal to establish a women's journal. Moreover, Barbauld reminded Edgeworth, '[t]here is a great difference between a paper written *by* a lady, and *as* a lady': a distinction so impossible to sustain (despite efforts by generations of literary women to do so) that it pretty well sums up the woman writer's predicament.[41]

It was these views, one imagines, that pushed Barbauld into open opposition to Wollstonecraft, although envy of the younger woman's confident displays of intellectual authority may also have played a part. With the publication of the *Rights of Woman*, where Wollstonecraft had irritably reprinted one of Barbauld's silliest poems praising women's subordination, the two woman directly clashed, with Barbauld then dashing off another poem in response to Wollstonecraft's criticism. This poem, 'The Rights of Woman', is a desperately arch depiction of the female struggle for sexual conquest, in which 'blushes and fears' serve as a woman's 'magazine of war' until finally romance overcomes her, and she discovers that 'separate rights are lost in mutual love'.[42] What Wollstonecraft made of the work is unrecorded, but as far as Barbauld was concerned the differences between them (although there doesn't seem to have been any personal animosity) outweighed any sense of common cause. In 1804, when Edgeworth came forward with her suggestion of a women's magazine, Barbauld pointed out that Hannah More's conservatism meant she wouldn't be willing to write with Edgeworth or herself, 'and we should probably hesitate at joining Miss Hays, or if she were living, Mrs Godwin'.[43] Seven years after Wollstonecraft's death, Barbauld wanted nothing to do with radical feminist philosophers.

Yet – in one of those ironies that litter women's history – it was Barbauld who, in the course of a long and stormy career as a professional contro-versialist, managed to tread on more masculine toes than nearly any other woman writer of the age. On the political front, only Wollstonecraft and Catharine Macaulay proved greater irritants to male conservatives, while as a religious writer Barbauld showed herself to be one of Rational Dissent's most formidable pugilists, willing even to tackle her mentor Priestley. In 1775 and again in 1792 she published tracts championing the cause of re-ligious emotion against what she criticised as the mechanical 'systematic spirit' of Priestley and other philosophical Dissenters. 'Let us not be super-stitiously afraid of supersitition,' she provocatively urged before mounting a robust defence of the application of the language of love to religious devotion.

The truth is devotion does in no small degree resemble that fanciful and elevated kind of love which depends not on the senses. Nor is the likeness to be wondered at, since both have their source in the love of beauty and excellence. Both are exceeding prone to superstition, and apt to run into romantic excesses. Both are nourished by poetry and music, and...both carry the mind out of itself, and powerfully refine the affections from everything gross, low and selfish.[44]

The argument, with its neo-platonic celebration of the erotic dimension of religious experience, appalled Priestley and, later, Gilbert Wakefield, who insisted that religious truth had nothing to do with mere sentiment.[45] Mrs Barbauld, Wakefield sneered, wrote as a '*Platonic visionary*' consumed with the 'flame of enthusiasm'.[46] Wollstonecraft, however – at whom Wakefield's charge could more justly have been directed – reprinted passages from Bar-bauld's 1775 tract in her *Female Reader*, praising it as having done 'honour to a female pen'.[47]

In 1792 this important quarrel was taken up again by Mary Hays who, writing in response to the same Wakefield tract as Barbauld, defended public worship and religious sentiment in terms similar to Barbauld's. The wrangle (in which Wakefield, despite snippily referring to his female opponents as 'Amazonian' and 'Viragos', was forced to respond point-by-point to Hays's and Barbauld's arguments) reminds us that in 1792 it was still religion that was the main arena of female public discourse. Like Barbauld and Hays, most jacobin women were Rational Dissenters and those who weren't – like Wollstonecraft and Mary Robinson – usually mixed in Rational Dissenting circles. The proto-feminist dimension of leftwing protestantism makes this connection unsurprising, but even here, as Barbauld's example shows, attitudes were divided. In fact of the radical *literatae* we have met, only Mary Hays combined Dissenting activism with zealous women's rights advocacy – which makes the contrast between her position and that of Anna Barbauld particularly interesting.

Mary Hays, Wollstonecraft's closest female associate, came into radical politics through her friendship with Godwin. They met after she wrote to him in 1794, asking to borrow a copy of *Political Justice*, and became regular correspondents. The relationship, particularly in its early stages, was uneven, with Hays ardent in her discipleship while Godwin was more restrained in his admiration. But there was certainly mutual esteem and, as Hays's confidence grew, intellectual comradeship. Each read and commented on the other's work, and although Hays sometimes complained that Godwin was a 'savage-hearted and barbarous critic' she generally appreciated his candour. 'The time you spare from your numerous avocations for the perusal of my scribbles I feel a real obligation...' she told him, 'your friendship is my pleasure and my boast'.[48] Forthrightness several times led to feelings being hurt ('in tête-a-tête I must be simple, honest and ingenuous, and fairly say anything that occurs to my mind,' Godwin told her huffily after she took umbrage at 'what was meant for a very cursory remark'), but over the years they shared their intimate joys and sorrows as well as joint philosophical concerns.[49] In her twenties Hays had been engaged to a fellow Dissenter who died before their wedding. Now, in her early thirties, she fell passionately in love with a Cambridge radical, William Frend, whose ambiguous reaction to her overtures inspired her 'philosophical romance', *Memoirs of Emma Courtney*. Godwin advised and consoled Hays over her love for Frend while she in turn engineered a very successful meeting between him and Wollstonecraft after earlier unhappy encounters. Realising, soon after, that her two mentors had become lovers, Hays at first reacted badly: 'She has owned to me that she cannot endure to see others enjoy the mutual affection from which she is debarred,' Wollstonecraft told Godwin.[50] But when Wollstonecraft told Hays of her pregnancy, Hays urged Godwin to marry her, and was finally rewarded with a happy little note giving her the news which 'you should rather learn from us than any other quarter'.[51] She remained close to both until Wollstonecraft's death, but then became estranged from Godwin, possibly because she disapproved of his re-marriage.

Like Barbauld and Wollstonecraft, Hays had a pronounced taste and talent for controversy. Her dispute with Wakefield earned her praise for sound reasoning 'unsophisticated by scholastick learning and drawn without prejudice from the source of truth'.[52] Sermons written by her were preached by the leading Dissenter John Disney at the Unitarian Essex

Street Chapel.[53] Over the course of the 1790s her increasingly close association with Wollstonecraft condemned her in the eyes of conservatives,
but progressive critics continued to admire her writings for their 'good
sense and liberal principle'.[54] Her book-length feminist polemic, *Appeal to
the Men of Great Britain in Behalf of Women*, was published anonymously
in 1798, but by then the cold winds of political reaction were beginning
to chill even her radicalism. A memoir of Wollstonecraft written shortly
after her death praised Wollstonecraft's views without reservation, but a
second memoir published in 1800 was less enthusiastic, and in 1803, when
she published her six-volume *Female Biography*, Wollstonecraft's name was
omitted from Hays's three hundred-strong list of female worthies.[55] In the
last forty years of her life she published little of note, and died forgotten and
disregarded.

Hays is an easy figure to ridicule. Small, declamatory, effusively sentimental, in early adulthood she performed her life like an erotic soap-opera,
Rousseau's Julie in burlesque. While in theory rejecting the codes that imposed sexual passivity and abstinence on unmarried women, in practice she
comported herself in the classic manner of frustrated spinsterdom, flutter-
ing and bridling at the least hint of sexual transgression. An unannounced
visit by Godwin, when he inadvertently caught sight of her dressing before
the fire, sent her into an orgy of blushing apology.[56] Her self-publicised
passion for Frend, followed by other unsuccessful flirtations, was a gift to
contemporary satirists, as were her ardent, clumsy manners and the wig she
apparently sported. A living caricature of a 'learned woman', she aroused
complex responses in other women writers anxious not to be tarred by her
reputation. The novelist Elizabeth Hamilton, no intellectual slouch herself, took Hays as her model for a cruel portrait of a learned woman in her
anti-jacobin fiction, *Memoirs of Modern Philosophers*.[57] Coleridge couldn't
stand her – 'to hear a thing, ugly and petticoated, exsyllogise a God with
cold-blooded precision...! I do not endure it' – and even close friends, including Wollstonecraft, sometimes lost patience.[58] 'Pray do not make any
more allusion to painful feelings, past and gone –' Wollstonecraft snapped
at her in 1796, probably in response to some particularly extravagant display
of mournful sentiment, '... for who has not cause to be miserable, if they
allow themselves to think so?'[59]

Yet Hays was in many respects the boldest of the feminist jacobins.
Demure she may not have been – nor pretty, unlike her mentor – but what
she lacked in conventional feminine virtues she made up for in intellectual
adventurousness (as well as being an enthusiastic Rousseauist she was one
of Helvetius's leading English admirers) and political imagination. And her

Emma Courtney, while awkwardly plotted and stylistically haphazard, is a novel of extraordinary daring, offering a passionate yet nuanced defence of female eroticism.

Emma Courtney, published in 1796, tells the unhappy history of a bright young middle-class woman of extreme sensibility and radical sentiments. Like her author, Emma is a 'free thinking', 'free speaking' spirit possessing a 'mind pervaded with republican ardour' and a 'bosom glowing with the virtues of patriotism'; more conventionally, her desires are 'impetuous', her imagination is 'unrestrained', and her 'tastes [are] all passions': the requisite attributes for a romantic heroine.[60] Under the pressure of oppressive social conventions – here is the jacobin message of the book – these latter characteristics are twisted into romantic delusion. Emma loves a young man, Augustus Harley, whom she hopelessly idealises. Having (in common with Wollstonecraft's *Maria* and many other female fictional creations of the day) imbibed Rousseau's *La Nouvelle Héloïse*, Emma transforms Harley into her St Preux, and worships him to the point of erotomania.[61] As in Wollstonecraft's *Maria*, the tale ends in dis-illusionment, as Emma recognises that the 'ideal object' of her adoration is merely another flawed human being. In contrast to the ambiguous conclusions of *Maria*, however, Emma's 'tender and fervent excess' of sexual imagination is unequivocally defended by Hays as indicative of her full humanity, her 'sublimely improvable mind'.[62] And since it is 'the individuality of an affection [that] constitutes its chastity' even an offer made by Emma to cohabit with Harley outside marriage is presented as morally defensible.[63] The problem with Emma, in other words, lies not with her erotic personality, but with a world that cannot tolerate its full expression. The novel's criticism on this score extends beyond mainstream society to radical philosophers like Godwin, as represented by Emma's mentor, Mr Francis, whose insistence that hearts must be ruled by reason is condemned by Emma as a doctrine concocted in defiance of the realities of the human character. 'Are not passions and powers synonimous [sic] – or can the latter be produced without the lively interest that constitutes the former? Do you dream of annihilating the one – and will not the other be extinguished? With the apostle, Paul, permit me to say – "I am not mad, but speak the words of truth and soberness." '[64]

Even now, *Emma Courtney* is a rather alarming read. The crazed obsessiveness of Hays's heroine, her self-annihilating abjection in the face of erotic rejection, can still induce queasiness in a modern reader. For here of course, despite Hays's ambiguous pathologisation of it, is the real stuff of sexual passion, displayed in all its mad glory. '[M]y heart flutters – I breathe with difficulty –' Emma, astoundingly, sighs as she implores Harley to take her into his bed, '*My friend – I would give myself to you –*'[65] And although Hays claimed that Emma Courtney's story was 'calculated to operate as a *warning*, rather than as an example', it is impossible not to read it now – as its eighteenth-century readers certainly did – as a celebration of the unbridled libido, the excess characterising all human sexuality.[66] The robust refusal of Hays's heroine to define herself *against* this excess contrasts starkly with the asceticism of Wollstonecraft's early writings; yet it was clearly inspired by Wollstonecraft's own unembarrassed display of romantic fixation in her *Short Residence in Sweden* (published just before Hays's novel was written). The defence of the romantic imagination that is central to Hays's book is expressed in terms virtually identical to those of the *Short Residence*, while on at least one occasion Emma Courtney quotes directly from Wollstonecraft's text. 'It is necessary for me to love and admire, or I sink into sadness,' she tells Mr Francis, in words borrowed (slightly inaccurately) from one of Wollstonecraft's most touching missives to Imlay.[67]

Read as a gloss on the *Short Residence*, then, *Emma Courtney* makes scandalously explicit the valorisation of women's eroticism implicit in Wollstonecraft's later works. But Hays's novel is also important for another reason, as the only jacobin text to begin to explore the limitations of 1790s radicalism when applied to women's lives and interests. Story-telling as a vehicle for radical-philosophical instruction – Hays's stated aim in *Emma Courtney* – was Godwin's particular forte, and in her preface, Hays praised Godwin's 1794 tale of one man's struggle against injustice, *Caleb Williams*, as 'masterly'.[68] Yet it is the masculine biases of Godwinian radicalism, as revealed both in *Caleb Williams* and in Godwin's own letters to her, at which Hays directs her feminist reproof, delivered through an epistolary dialogue between Emma and Mr Francis. Mr Francis – a severe man of perfectibilist opinions and abstemious habits – has no time for feminine frailities or diffidence, and scolds Emma whenever he spots such weaknesses. He lectures her on the 'resolution, and perserverance' needed to achieve reason's triumph over her heart's 'moon-struck madness'.[69] But the leading principle on which he insists is the imperative for absolute autonomy. Emma, Mr Francis instructs, must learn to lean on herself alone:

[T]he first lesson of enlightened reason, the great fountain of heroism and virtue, the principle by which alone man can become what man is capable of being, is independence. May every power that is favourable to integrity, to honour, defend me from leaning upon another for support!... The system of nature has perhaps made me dependent for the means of existence and happiness upon my fellow men taken collectively; but nothing but my own folly can make me dependent upon individuals.[70]

Emma considers this prescription for what 'man can become' and then, in a splendid access of self-assertion, flies out at her adviser:

Why call woman, miserable, oppressed and impotent, woman – *crushed and then insulted* – why call her to *independence* – which not nature, but the barbarous and accursed laws of society, have denied her? *This is mockery!* Even you, wise and benevolent as you are, can mock the child of slavery and sorrow![71]

What Francis/Godwin has failed to see, Emma goes on, is how the present 'customs of society', which 'have enslaved, enervated, and degraded woman', have corrupted intimate relations.[72] 'From the miserable consequences of wretched moral distinctions, from chastity having been considered as a sexual virtue,' Emma tells him, 'all these calamities have flowed': men 'rendered sordid and dissolute', women 'degraded', and those few finer individuals in possession of 'the dangerous gifts of fancy and feeling' left with no deserving object for their ardour.[73] How can women of 'elevated minds', handicapped as they are by destructive conventions, rise above such evils? 'I perceive my extravagance... [and] ardent excesses', but under these debilitating conditions how could female passions be other than unruly? 'While the institutions of society war against nature and happiness, the mind of energy, struggling to emancipate itself, will entangle itself in error,' Emma bleakly concludes.[74]

Criticising Godwin in this way was not just taking on any radical thinker. By the mid 1790s Godwin had become jacobinism's representative intellectual, New Philosophy incarnate: a status owed partly to the influence of his most famous work, *Political Justice*, but also to the efforts of anti-jacobin propagandists who found that his views, particularly his opposition to private property and marriage, made him an ideal target for scaremongering and satire.[75] He was admired by his fellow jacobins and revered by the young romantic poets; among women who knew him well, however, his stature fell short of iconic. Like Hays, these women respected his ideas, but his almost parodically masculine style of thought – dry, mechanical, hyper-rationalist – tickled them, as did his ponderous manner and obvious sexual naiveté. His anti-marriage stance, which occasioned so much outrage in rightwing quarters, seems mostly to have amused them, particularly intimate female friends like Amelia Alderson and Elizabeth Inchbald who clearly regarded it as intellectual posturing. They referred to him as 'the Philosopher' and teased him about the 'chilliness' of his rationality. 'Oh thou ungrateful, unfeeling, cruel, insulting, barbarous man, or to sum up thy iniquities in one word, thou Philosopher –' one anonymous letter-writer (probably a young Warwickshire friend, Sarah Parr) wrote in particularly fey mood, 'I am so angry that I could marry thee in downright spite...'[76]

The irreverence was not incidental. Among radicals, personal relations were to be run along the same democratic lines as political life. Applied to male/female relations, this meant replacing the artificial refinements of polite society with an open, egalitarian camaraderie: the 'simplicity and generosity of republican manners', as George Dyer eulogised them.[77] The key word here was 'simplicity', which to the men and women of the Wollstonecraft/Godwin circle meant all those virtues – sincerity, honesty, a Rousseauist artlessness – excluded from the 'gaudy' circles of elite society. So whereas among the *bon ton* 'decorum is to supplant nature, and banish all simplicity', among Wollstonecraft's associates it was the frank display of 'simplicity and independence of mind' – in men and women alike – that earned social kudos.[78] What all this really added up to was a particularly uncompromising version of Enlightenment ideals at their most revisionist. The enlightened project of a world transformed by free thought and humane sentiment was practically enacted by British jacobins as a radical social etiquette.

* * *

In November 1791 Godwin was invited to dinner at Joseph Johnson's. The guest of honour was Tom Paine, whom Godwin admired but had never previously met. Wollstonecraft, with whom Godwin was also unacquainted, was to be there too, but since a quick glance into her *Vindication of the Rights of Men* had revealed some irritating stylistic infelicities, Godwin was unenthusiastic about encountering its author. 'I had...little curiosity to see Mrs Wollstonecraft,' he later wrote, 'and a very great curiosity to see Thomas Paine.' But Paine, as it turned out, was 'no great talker', and Wollstonecraft was. 'I, of consequence, heard her,' he recalled, 'very frequently when I wished to hear Paine.' He and Wollstonecraft 'touched on a considerable variety of topics' and disagreed about all of them (with Paine reduced to occasionally throwing in 'some shrewd and striking remarks'). Debate ranged over religion, monarchy, and 'the characters and habits of certain eminent men', particularly Voltaire whom Godwin admired while Wollstonecraft emphatically did not. Wollstonecraft was censorious and high-handed, which annoyed Godwin so much that seven years later the memory still rankled. Yet even at the time his irritation was tempered with a startled admiration, as he noted what a 'person of active and independent thinking' this disputatious female philosopher was.[79]

An inauspicious start to a romance, but otherwise a typical evening in the radical social calendar. The Wollstonecraft/Godwin circle, as Mark Philp, William St Clair and others have shown, was a highly convivial grouping, constantly meeting for stimulating chat and to test ideas out on each other.[80] Letters from 1789 on show Wollstonecraft dining or tea-drinking with friends on a near-daily basis, usually in someone's home (women were not generally welcome in pubs or coffee-houses – the main sites of radical sociability) or at Joseph Johnson's. 'When I lived alone I always dined on a Sunday, with company in the evening, if not at dinner, at St P[aul's Churchyard]' she told Godwin, 'Generally also of a Tuesday, and some other day at Fuseli's. I like to see new faces, as a study – and since my return from Norway...I have dined every third Sunday at Twiss's, nay oftener, for they sent for me, when they had any extraordinary company.'[81] Women friends, especially Mary Hays and Mary Robinson, were visited regularly, as too were some male intimates – Thomas Holcroft, John Opie, William Roscoe – whom she usually saw *à deux*. (Holcroft was also a close friend of Godwin's, but she had an agreement with Godwin that they both met him separately.) Dinners – despite her dislike of cooking – were provided, often it seems to the same coterie of close associates.[82] 'Will you, my dear Mrs Reveley,' Maria Reveley was asked, 'dine with us next wednesday, to meet the same party as you did before, with the addition of Mr Godwin[?]'[83]

Conversation on these occasions seems to have been exceptionally un-inhibited; sometimes – as at Wollstonecraft's and Godwin's first meeting – rebarbative or even openly quarrelsome. Absolute candour was the rule, no matter what the consequences. Like so much else in radical life, this code originated with Rational Dissent. To the Dissenting mind, *sapere aude* was not just an intellectual injunction but a spiritual obligation, and even radicals who departed from a theistic viewpoint retained the truth-seeking imperative.[84] 'When will the world learn that the unlimited utterance of all thoughts would be virtuous?' Holcroft's Anna St Ives demanded of a friend: 'How many half-discovered half-acknowledged truths would then be promulgated; and how immediately would mistake, of every kind, meet its proper antidote!'[85]

For a woman, sincerity of this order required exceptional self assertive-ness. Again, jacobin fiction shows the ideal in action. Anna St Ives, the reader soon discovers, expects to be heard on any subject she chooses to address, including sex, insisting all the while that those subjected to her orations must 'consider only the words, not the girl by whom they are spo-ken'.[86] When her would-be lover, Coke Clifton, tries to derail her moral seriousness with teasing gallantries, Anna is affronted: 'Nay, nay, no com-pliments; I will not be interrupted.'[87] Mary Hays's Emma Courtney is sim-ilarly indifferent to feminine conversational conventions, shocking those around her by taking long – unaccompanied – disquisitional strolls with her philosophic mentor, Mr Francis. At dinner with an elegant group of gentlemen and ladies, including a Jamaican planter, Emma contends vigorously against West-Indian slavery, war, and other social evils until some of the guests protest at such unladylike 'sermonising'. 'That some of the gentlemen, present, should object to a woman's exercising her discriminating powers, is not wonderful,' Emma coolly responds, 'since it might operate greatly to their disadvantage.'[88]

For a woman to dispute abstract matters with men, particularly politics, was culturally proscribed. Yet, like her fictive heroine, Hays had no hesitation about expressing her opinions; nor of course did Wollstonecraft, whose difficult first encounter with Godwin was succeeded by others where the two of them batted about their views on self-love, sympathy, and 'perfectibility, individual and general'.[89] Godwin, who in his *Memoirs* apologised for the occasionally 'Amazonian' tone of Wollstonecraft's writings, often found her manner on these occasions strident and humiliating.[90] Other radical men, however – perhaps more confident with women – greatly enjoyed her company. Robert Southey and Coleridge both thought she possessed great powers of conversation (unlike her pedantic husband)[91] and even political opponents were sometimes seduced: 'her conversation and manners... we may from personal knowledge affirm, were generally fascinating,' a journalist for the conservative *Critical Review* admitted.[92]

Women who presented themselves as the discursive equals of men were sure to be accused of linguistic manliness. Friends tried to fend off such charges: Wollstonecraft's conversation, while 'spirited' was 'yet not out of her sex', one insisted.[93] She herself however remained unconcerned, sometimes even bragging about her verbal virility. A Danish naval man whom she met during her Scandinavian travels, over dinner 'told me bluntly that I was a woman of observation, for I asked him *men's questions*'.[94] More riskily, in the *Rights of Woman* she boasted about conversations with unspecified 'artists' (probably Henry Fuseli) and 'medical men' (likely her friends Thomas Beddoes and George Fordyce) with whom she had 'conversed, as man with man' on 'anatomical subjects, and... the proportions of the human body', yet was 'never reminded by a word or a look of my sex [or] of the absurd rules with make modesty a pharisaical cloak of weakness' – concluding from this, a touch over-optimistically, that 'in the pursuit of knowledge women would never be insulted by sensible men.... if they did not by mock modesty remind them that they were women...'[95]

Women should deal with men 'as man to man', with no trace of sexual self-consciousness or coquetry. This was of course a central message of the *Rights of Woman*, and many radicals, men as well as women, took it very seriously. Holcroft's fictional Anna St Ives might be a jaw-dropping beauty, but she is also shown to be a passionate puritan who eschews any sexual element in her relations with men. Flirting, even with the man Anna adores, is disdained, and any woman engaging in it regarded with contemptuous pity. Another male admirer of Wollstonecraft's, the jacobin novelist Robert Bage, delivered a similar message. 'Whilst [women] think of their charming figures... Mrs Wolstonecraft [sic] must write in vain,' one male character in Bage's 1796 novel *Hermsprong* explains to another. 'And when will they think less of them?' the interlocutor wants to know, to which the patronising response is, 'When they are better taught.'[96]

To what extent did radical practice conform to these stern precepts? Describing the London circles to which she and Wollstonecraft belonged, Mary Hays emphasised their highminded intellectualism (which lent Wollstonecraft's mind its 'masculine tone').[97] Similarly, Helen Maria Williams, reminiscing in later years about the little community of radical Britons in revolutionary Paris, recalled the earnestness of social life there:

We indulged little in common society chitchat. The women seemed to forget concern to please, and the men thought less about admiring them... In that salon there was something better than gallantry. What appeared most were mutual esteem and a shared interest in the great issues of the day.[98]

However: since Williams (who was gorgeous and, according to Fanny Burney, 'excessively affected') was at this time in the middle of an adulterous love affair with a fellow expatriate, John Hurford Stone (and Hays similarly embroiled in her romantic attachment to William Frend) what was meant here by 'mutual esteem' perhaps required clarifying.[99] Eschewing sexual wiles in favour of emotional authenticity did not necessarily imply sexual abstinence. In 1791 Wollstonecraft praised the chaste innocence of republican manners in America (where '[m]en and women mix together' to '[discuss] subjects that interest the whole race' while still 'respecting the marriage vow') while at the same time pursuing her romance with Henry Fuseli, a married man.[100] A little over a year later – 'still a Spinster on the wing' – she was off to France, where the divorce law had just been liberalised, to try her chances. 'At Paris, indeed, I might take a husband for the time being, and get divorced when my truant heart longed again to nestle with its old friends,' she wrote archly to William Roscoe, 'but this speculation has not yet entered into my plan.'[101] Planned or not, within six months she was Imlay's lover, and very soon an expectant mother, without a breath of apology for either. 'Let them stare!' she wrote defiantly to Imlay after an encounter with two women who had scrutinised her big belly. 'I told the good women...simply that I was with child: and let them stare!...all the world may know it for aught I care!'[102]

* * *

Charges of sexual delinquency were repeatedly levelled at radicals by conservative propagandists. The reform of the French divorce law in 1792, which for a brief period harnessed the progress of the Revolution to the advancement of women's interests, inspired a wave of scurrilous allegations against the architects of Revolution and their British supporters. Godwin's attack on marriage in *Political Justice* intensified these criticisms; but the real onslaught came with his *Memoirs* of Wollstonecraft and the posthumous publication of *Maria*, with its frank endorsement of adulterous passion. The revelation of the Imlay *affaire* inevitably turned the fictive Maria's vindication of unwed love into an implicit defence of Wollstonecraft's behaviour, to the discomfort of many of her erstwhile associates. There were limits, apparently, even to radical tolerance. This had in fact already become apparent at the time of Wollstonecraft's marriage when, faced with this irrefutable evidence that she was not Imlay's legal wife (something she had never hidden, but many chose to ignore), several of her circle, including Elizabeth Inchbald and the actress Sarah Siddons, promptly dropped her. To Amelia Alderson, who stood by her, Wollstonecraft wrote how sorry she would be to lose some of these friends (particularly Siddons, who had been an intimate), 'but my conduct in life must be directed by my own judgement and moral principles...I am proud perhaps, conscious of my own purity and integrity; and many circumstances in my life have contributed to excite in my bosom an indignant contempt for the forms of the world...'[103]

Exploring the part played by love in Wollstonecraft's career, we have seen how over the course of her adult life a transcendent erotic ideal, rooted in Christian Platonism, gradually gave way to a complex affirmation of physical love between the sexes. The trajectory had its own psychological and intellectual logic, but also a certain cultural momentum. Revisionary attitudes toward sexuality were not freefloating. When Wollstonecraft chose to become Imlay's lover, she was leaning on her own integrity, as she said, but also on a variety of traditions that sanctioned such behaviour. The Parisian venue of the romance was crucial. French Enlightenment antagonism to Catholic sexual mores endowed French radicalism with a much spicier flavour than its relatively pious British equivalent (a fact harped on by Burke and other British conservatives, who charged the *philosophes*, Rousseau in particular, with having promulgated a love-philosophy 'without gallantry...of metaphysical speculation, blended with the coarsest sensuality').[104] Wollstonecraft's arrival in France coincided with the highpoint of sexual liberalisation there, with legal divorce readily available, nuns and priests permitted to wed, and hostility to unwed mothers and illegitimate children temporarily diminished. Conservatives damned the 'wanton freedom' encouraged among women by these reforms: a charge that, judging by Wollstonecraft and Helen Maria Williams, as well as the thousands of Frenchwomen who rushed out to divorce their husbands as soon as the law permitted, had some foundation.

Prior to leaving for France, Wollstonecraft had already had some tutelage in sexual libertarianism from the Swiss artist Henry Fuseli. Fuseli, now best remembered for his 'Sturm und Drang' painting, was forty-seven when he and Wollstonecraft met in 1788: a small, self-important dandy known for his volatile temper. The son of a Protestant Zurich family, as a young man Fuseli had been ordained as a minister, but a political fracas over a corrupt judge resulted in his expulsion from the city. After wandering Europe for a while he ended up in London. Here, with the help of Joseph Johnson, he survived as a writer and occasional tutor until turning – very successfully – to painting. His pictures, with their surreal imagery and histrionic eroticism, were widely admired, and by the time Wollstonecraft met him he was a member of the Royal Academy and an established figure on the London art scene. He was also married, to a beautiful artists' model named Sophia Rawlins.[105]

As a young man, Fuseli had had amorous adventures with both sexes. Whether he and Wollstonecraft ever actually became lovers is unknown: Godwin's account, in his *Memoirs*, strongly implies not, and biographers have followed him. In the absence of clear evidence either way, and given Godwin's truth-telling compulsion, it seems likely that the relationship remained unconsummated. But Wollstonecraft clearly adored him, and given the intensely eroticised atmosphere with which Fuseli surrounded himself – with his stacks of pornographic drawings, and calculatedly obscene language – the passion must have been wonderfully heady stuff for a pious young sexual neophyte.

Admirers saw in Fuseli a 'new type of hero', a 'free man who gives full rein to his passions...to pave the way for the modern spirit of Enlightenment'; or as Fuseli himself put it, in a typical piece of promotional posturing, a 'philosopher [who would] damn all sects', a 'genius [who would] despise all restraints'.[106] In fact his radicalism seems to have amounted to little more than a penchant for satirical criticism and *épatant* sensationalism. His philosophical reflections consisted largely of sub-Rousseauist maunderings, and even his misogyny, which was strong, was expressed in secondhand Rousseauisms.[107] Thus he aphorised:

In an age of luxury women have taste, decide and dictate; for in an age of luxury woman aspires to the functions of man, and man slides into the offices of woman. The epoch of eunuchs was ever the epoch of viragos.[108]

Woman, he declaimed elsewhere 'fondles, pities, despises and forgets what is below her; she values, bears and wrangles with her equal; she adores what is above her' – which presumably was meant to explain Wollstonecraft's devotion to him. For her part, after three years of pining she became desperate, and proposed to Mrs Fuseli that she should join husband and wife in a domestic *menage à trois*. Sophia Fuseli, unsurprisingly, turned the suggestion down flat, and the relationship ended.

That Fuseli's influence on Wollstonecraft was either profound or lasting seems unlikely. '[H]e had little sympathy with feminism,' one of his interpreters has remarked – clearly an understatement.[109] But the image of renegade genius he projected was very attractive to a young woman just starting to flex her own unusual talents, while his unbuttoned sexual language and imagery must have contrasted excitingly with the idealistic moralism of most London radicals. The 'exalted, fervid imagination' evoked by the *Rights of Woman*, that 'sketched ... dangerous pictures' of love with 'those glowing colours, which the daring hand will steal from the rainbow' is meant to be Rousseau's, but the painterly imagery also hints at Fuseli, as perhaps does the sacralised eroticism pervading the text.[110] That the misogynistic tone of Wollstonecraft's book owed something to his influence is possible too; certainly none of her post-Fuseli writings conveyed the same lacerating contempt for women.

But if Fuseli himself was no feminist, this was not true of enlightened libertinage in general, which as an intellectual tradition had a long and important, if rather thorny, relationship to pro-woman thinking. This is a history that remains to be explored in depth, stretching back to seventeenth century *libertins erudits* like Pierre Bayle; through Voltairean freethought and the old-regime world of 'philosophical pornography' so wonderfully evoked by Robert Darnton; into Wollstonecraft's day and well beyond: into nineteenth-century utopian socialism, with its important sexual-libertarian element, and the libertine feminism of late nineteenth-early twentieth-century free-love campaigners.[111] Wollstonecraft's place in this lineage is difficult to interpret, partly because the trajectory itself has yet to be mapped, but also because her personal responses to it are largely unrecorded (her letters to Fuseli seem to have been destroyed). The only real insight into her attitude comes in her last novel, *Maria*, whose male protagonist, Henry Darnford – Gilbert Imlay's fictive incarnation – is made to voice the enlightened-libertine position. From their correspondence it is clear that Imlay had from time to time lectured Wollstonecraft on free-love principles: in *Maria* the arguments re-appear in a letter from Darnford to the heroine:

Darnford returned the memoirs to Maria, with a most affectionate letter, in which he reasoned on the 'absurdity of the laws respecting matrimony, which, till divorces could be more easily obtained, was,' he declared, 'the most insufferable bondage.' Ties of this nature could not bind minds governed by superior principles; and such beings were privileged to act above the dictates of laws they had no voice in framing, if they had sufficient strength of mind to endure the natural consequence. In her case, to talk of duty, was a farce, excepting what was due to herself. Delicacy, as well as reason, forbade her ever to think of returning to her husband: was she then to restrain her charming sensibility through mere prejudice?

The arguments, Wollstonecraft goes on to warn the reader, 'were not absolutely impartial, for . . . he felt he had some interest in her heart'.[112] And in fact in Maria's history, as in Wollstonecraft's with Imlay, libertine philosophy ultimately translates into female abandonment and despair.

British radicalism – earnest, pious – gave small encouragement to libertinage in theory or in practice. What little sexual heterodoxy did appear in Wollstonecraft's circle was usually, as we shall see, ethically motivated. Domicile in revolutionary Paris, however, certainly took its toll. As well as Wollstonecraft and Helen Maria Williams, at least three British jacobin men from Wollstonecraft's network – Thomas Christie (Wollstonecraft's colleague on the *Analytical Review*), John Hurford Stone (Williams's lover) and, famously, William Wordsworth – enjoyed extramarital liaisons while in France. Unlike French radicals, however, these men had no well-established intellectual rationale for such behaviour; and for a woman to act likewise was very deviant indeed. Seeing Wollstonecraft for the first time at a Paris *soirée*, accompanied by little Fanny, the Irish revolutionary Archibald Hamilton-Rowan was disconcerted. '[A friend] whispered to me that she was the author of the Rights of Woman. I started. "What?" I said within myself, "This is Miss Mary Wollstonecraft parading about with a child at her heels, with as little ceremony as if it were a watch she had just bought at the jeweller's." So much for the rights of women, thought I.'[113] Later Hamilton-Rowan became a close friend of Wollstonecraft's. But his initial disapproving reaction was to be echoed in radical male responses to Godwin's *Memoirs* which, as one previous admirer put it, 'lowered her not a little in my Esteem'.[114]

Viewed from another angle, however, British reform politics revealed some exceptionally permissive sexual attitudes and behaviour. To see this, we need to look away from the jacobin intelligentsia, with its middling/plebian standards of respectability, to the radical-Whig aristocracy dominated by Charles Fox. Despite its anti-elitism, the Wollstonecraft/Godwin circle abutted quite closely onto the world of Fox and his coadjutors where sexual codes were famously lax. Fox and his closest male cronies were notorious for their indifference to marital convention, as were two of their women associates: Georgiana, the Duchess of Devonshire, and her sister Lady Duncannon who in the 1780s and nineties managed to chalk up between them two marriages, seven affairs (including two probable lesbian ones on the part of the Duchess, one of them a *menage à trois* involving her husband), and nine children, three of them illegitimate. There is no evidence that Wollstonecraft and the Duchess of Devonshire ever met, but they did have at least one close friend in common: Mary Robinson, to whom Georgiana acted as patron, assisting her first onto the stage and then into publication[115]. Robinson's own alliances with Fox, the Prince of Wales, and Sheridan – all intimates of Georgiana's – barely raised an eyebrow in the Duchess's racy world; what is more interesting is that they apparently did her no harm in Wollstonecraft's milieu either, pointing to more flexible standards than those dictated by radical code-setters.[116]

Aristocratic sexual freedom was pleasure-oriented rather than principled. For elite progressives like Georgiana and Fox, sexuality was not a field of conviction politics. This sharply distinguished them from the tiny number of sex reformers in Wollstonecraft's circle for whom erotic freedom, like all lifestyle issues, was an intensely serious business. Thomas Holcroft's stance in *Anna St Ives* was typical. Taking up the anti-marriage arguments advanced in Godwin's *Political Justice*, Holcroft puts them into the mouth of Anna's working-class beau, Henley, who, outlining the Godwinian programme to his beloved, explains how in a perfect society marriage would be abolished. Would not this leave women exposed to male libertinism? Anna wants to know. Henley concedes the point, saying that as long as the world is full of 'bad, foolish, and dishonest' men, women must retain the little protection marriage affords; but in an ideal future marriage would be replaced by consensual unions created and terminated as couples chose. 'Of all the regulations which were ever suggested to the tyranny of selfishness, none perhaps to this day have surpassed the despotism of those which undertake to bind not only body to body but soul to soul, to all futurity...'[117] Holcroft explicitly described this as a 'levelling system', and the echoes of seventeenth-century sectarian radicalism were easy to hear.[118] The Godwinian poets with their Pantisocratic schemes for communal living, brought similar traces of puritan sexual utopianism onto the 1790s scene, as did William Blake's lyrical vision of a New Jerusalem free from sexual fear and repression. But it was Godwin's sexual heterodoxies that were most influential, and the key focus of public opprobrium.

Whether the anti-jacobins who accused Godwin of promoting 'whoredoms' ever actually read *Political Justice* seems unlikely, since it is difficult to imagine how sex ('the propensity to intercourse of the sexes' in the book's lumbering prose) could be made to appear less enticing than it does in Godwin's work. Listed, along with hunger, as one of those 'unfortunate passions...[that] with the progress of perfectibility...would soon become obsolete', its eradication in a better world is eagerly awaited:

Reasonable men then will propagate their species, not because a certain sensible pleasure is annexed to this action, but because it is right the species should be propagated; and the manner in which they exercise this function will be regulated by the dictates of reason and duty.[119]

In a perfected society marriage, that 'most odious of all monopolies', would soon disappear along with all other forms of private property, to be replaced by temporary unions motivated solely by the imperatives of reproduction: a reform which, in a reason-governed society, would cause no grief or rivalrous conflict among men (women's feelings apparently not being deemed worthy of consideration) since 'we shall all be wise enough to consider...sensual intercourse as a very trivial object.' In later editions of his book Godwin modified these arguments slightly, acknowledging sexual attraction as a possible factor in the formation of alliances and suggesting that sexual choices are likely to be long term. But his general position remained puritanical and implicitly anti-woman.

What did Wollstonecraft make of all this? There are hints that she found it ridiculous. She frequently twitted her lover, sometimes tenderly, sometimes irritably, about his 'icy Philosophy'. Rational '*esteem*' was too 'cold' a description of what she felt for him, she insisted, and did not he too feel something rather warmer?[120] Writing to him after one particularly happy evening when he had seemed to be 'opening your heart, to a new born affection, that rendered you very dear to me', she couldn't resist poking fun: 'There are other pleasures in the world, you perceive, beside those known to your philosophy.'[121] For herself, she enjoyed playing a wifely part, 'though you have so little respect for the character', and began hinting at marriage well before becoming pregnant, partly no doubt because of the strength of her feeling for him but also, as she later told Amelia Alderson, for more prosaic reasons: because her evenings were too lonely, because she wanted someone 'bound to me by affection' to help with Fanny, and because she wanted to shed Imlay's name.[122] Her pregnancy sealed matters since she was determined, in Godwin's words, not 'to incur that exclusion from the society of many valuable and excellent individuals, which custom awards in cases of this sort'.[123] In the event her marriage had precisely this effect. Death forestalled further humiliations, only to be followed by Godwin's *Memoirs* which brought down on her memory all the ill-repute she had sought to avoid.

To live as a free woman in an unfree world was impossible, Wollstonecraft discovered. 'Perfect confidence, and sincerity of action is, I am persuaded, incompatible with the present state of reason.'[124] The dilemma, common to all radical philosophesses, was particularly acute for a famous feminist whose life was made a public test of her principles. Male politicians are usually spared this scrutiny, or at least judged less harshly. Sure of the integrity of her own desires, Wollstonecraft nonetheless encountered much censure for acting on them.[125] This was hardly surprising. As a feminist revolutionary, the changes Wollstonecraft sought were as much personal and private as publicly political. Urging emancipation from crippling social conventions, she practised what she professed – and paid a predictable price for it. Most people, she reflected at one point, choose to play their role in life 'by rote',

and those that do not, seem marks set up to be pelted at by fortune; or rather as sign-posts, which point out the road to others, whilst forced to stand still themselves amidst the mud and dust.[126]

The image, characteristically self-dramatising, conveyed more than she could have foreseen about her longterm fate. But the passive martyrdom it evoked was wholly fictive. Passivity was never Wollstonecraft's mode; and in any case the 1790s were hardly a time for stoical quiescence. From 1789 until her death, Wollstonecraft's political world was in constant, often frantic motion. The oppositional intelligentsia that she had entered in the mid 1780s, an untutored young iconoclast with a budding feminist consciousness and an appetite for controversy, was, by 1791, embroiled in an unprecedented ideo-political conflict, and Mary Wollstonecraft was at the heart of the turbulence.

7

Woman versus the polity

In February 1793, two months after arriving in Paris, Wollstonecraft sent Joseph Johnson the first in a proposed series of on-the-spot reflections on the prospects for French civilisation (no more of these were written). Since her arrival Louis XVI had been executed and war with Britain declared. The economy was in a state of collapse; food rioters surged through the Paris streets; the Vendée rumbled with civil war. Even as Wollstonecraft was writing to Johnson, constitutional proposals were being put before the National Convention by the Girondins – the party supported by most of the Revolution's British fellow-travellers – only to be summarily rejected by the Jacobins, who were on the brink of seizing power. The Terror was months away. In her letter to Johnson Wollstonecraft referred only obliquely to these developments, choosing instead to 'calmly... consider the stage of civilisation in which I find the French' in order to 'throw some light' on their place in history. 'Before I came to France,' she wrote

I cherished, you know, an opinion, that strong virtues might exist with the polished manners produced by the progress of civilization; and I even anticipated the epoch, when, in the course of improvement, men would labour to become virtuous, without being goaded on by misery. But now, the perspective of the golden age, fading before the attentive eye of observation, almost eludes my sight; and, losing thus in part my theory of a more perfect state, start not, my friend, if I bring forward an opinion, which at the first glance seems to be levelled against the existence of God! I am not become an Atheist, I assure you, by residing at Paris: yet I begin to fear that vice, or, if you will, evil, is the grand mobile of action...[1]

The note of disenchantment is marked, but also, in one respect at least, disingenuous. The discovery, announced here, that evil can serve as the chief stimulus to progress, was not in fact new for Wollstonecraft: indeed *A Vindication of the Rights of Woman* had opened with this very proposition. God has made mankind with the capacity and inclination for wrongdoing, she had argued there, precisely in order that 'the passions should unfold our reason, because he could see that present evil would produce future good'.[2]

It is in struggling with our most 'lawless' impulses that individuals acquire the moral strength on which virtue is founded. '[W]hen the passions are justly poized (sic), we become harmless, and in the same proportion useless,' her *Letter on the French Nation* explained:

The wants of reason are very few, and, were we to consider dispassionately the real value of most things, we should probably rest satisfied with the simple gratification of our physical necessities, and be content with negative goodness: for it is frequently, only that wanton, the Imagination, with her artful coquetry, who lures us forward, and makes us run over a rough road, pushing aside every obstacle merely to catch a disappointment.[3]

Driven by the impassioned imagination, humanity pursues happiness along roads which in France were proving very rough indeed. Yet without this incessant striving, however chimerical its goals, there would be only stasis, death-in-life, the one truly impermissible state. In earlier years Wollstonecraft had brooded much on the futility of human aspirations. Frustrated joys and limitless sorrows were the destiny of all mankind, was the doleful message of *Mary, A Fiction*, with no promise of happiness except in eternity. With the fall of the Bastille, however, this mood of Christian resignation was abruptly abandoned. *A Vindication of the Rights of Men* marked the shift. That 'both physical and moral evil' are part of God's plan no one can doubt, Wollstonecraft argued there, but merely to resign oneself to the perpetuation of such evils is an abdication of moral responsibility. To preach to the oppressed the virtues of 'humility, and submission to the will of Heaven', as Burke did in his *Reflections*, was an impiety as well as a 'contemptible hard-hearted sophistry'. 'It is, Sir,' she told Burke, '*possible* to render the poor happier in this world, without depriving them of the consolation which you gratuitously grant them in the next. They have a right to more comfort than they at present enjoy...'

the business of life of a good man should be, to separate light from darkness; to diffuse happiness, whilst he submits to unavoidable misery. And a conviction that there is much unavoidable wretchedness, appointed by the grand Disposer of all events, should not slacken his exertions: the extent of what is possible can only be discerned by God.[4]

True, 'practical', virtue consists in meeting evil not with despair or resignation but with meliorative action. Viewed from this angle, the problem worrying the faithful since Job – why does a benevolent and omnipotent God allow evil to flourish? – became answerable in heroically optimistic terms: all prevailing miseries and injustices were divinely willed to instigate reformative endeavour, and thus, in Joseph Priestley's words, to 'gradually conduc[t]' human affairs 'to a more perfect and glorious state'.[5] Human passions and the malfeasance to which they give rise are not contrary to the divine purpose, but intrinsic to it; for why would God have endowed us with unruly desires and the capacity to act on them, Wollstonecraft demanded, unless these were meant to facilitate His plan? 'Firmly persuaded that no evil exists in the world that God did not design to take place, I build my belief on the perfection of God.'[6]

In a fascinating article, Daniel Robinson has explored the roots of Wollstonecraft's religious optimism in Enlightenment theology, particularly Leibniz's *Theodicy*.[7] A more immediate source, however, which Robinson does not discuss, was Rational Dissent, where radical theodical views of the kind propounded in Wollstonecraft's *Vindications* were commonplace. The transition from the quietist stoicism of Wollstonecraft's early writings to the activist message of her 1790s works was undoubtedly influenced by the politicised account of Providence adumbrated by Price, Priestley and other radical Unitarians. So too was her image of the political reformer as one who, encountering oppression and injustice as 'part of the system', would always 'endeavour to alter what appears to him to be [evil], even while he bows to the Wisdom of his Creator, and respects the darkness he labours to disperse'.[8] Evil demands emendation, and it is from this that great changes are born.

Underpinning this radical theodicy was a strongly positive view of the part played by the passions in the development of virtue. In nations as in individuals, freedom to act on 'grand passions', Wollstonecraft insists, is a *sina qua non* of moral maturation.[9] Just as men and women, when young, learn to distinguish moral truth from error not by conforming to prescriptive edicts but by performing impassioned, often ill-judged, actions, so too in the lives of nations, the free exercise of the passions is a precondition of genuine progress, whatever its initial cost. Receiving reports, while still in London, of the prison massacres in France, Wollstonecraft wrote to her friend William Roscoe urging him 'not to mix with the shallow herd who throw an odium on immutable principles, because some of the mere instrument [sic] of the revolution were too sharp. – Children of any growth will do mischief when they meddle with sharp-edged tools. It is to be lamented that as yet the billows of public opinion are only to be moved forward by the...squally gusts of passion...'[10]

But by the end of 1793, as the guillotine did its work, odium seemed the only possible response. 'The French will carry all before them,' Wollstonecraft wrote to her friend Ruth Barlow (risking the censors) in July 1794, 'but, my God, how many victims fall beneath the sword and the

Guillotine! My blood runs cold, and I sicken at thoughts of a Revolution which costs so much blood and bitter tears.'[11]

The decline of the French Revolution into horrors so 'calamitous' that they could not 'fail to chill the sympathizing bosom' tested even Wollstonecraft's political optimism.[12] Typically, however, her response to these adversities was not despairing but interrogative, to turn a 'cool eye of observation' on this 'grand theatre of political changes'.[13] The result was her *Historical and Moral View . . . of the French Revolution*, an anti-Burkean interpretation of developments in France to the end of 1789. The initial stages of the Revolution, which Burke had exorciated as a 'strange chaos of levity and ferocity . . . all sorts of crimes jumbled together with all sorts of follies', in Wollstonecraft's account became a series of heroic struggles to wrest the French polity from the stranglehold of a corrupt court.[14] By the end of her narrative, however, with the Versailles crowd driving Louis back to Paris, the tone had become much darker, as the revolutionists began to display those symptoms of effete depravity so characteristic of the French: 'the concomitant of that servility and voluptuousness which for so long a space of time has embruted the higher orders of this celebrated nation'.[15] Earlier we saw how, in tracing the impact of absolutism on French culture, Wollstonecraft repeatedly described these effects as feminising. So 'emasculated' had Frenchmen been by courtly *politesse*, so hyper-refined into polished uniformity, that 'like most women, [they] may be said to have no character distinguishable from that of the nation'.[16] Turning from the *ancien regime* to the revolution itself, the *Historical View* now set out to demonstrate that it was precisely this debilitating psychological legacy that bore major responsibility for all those 'terrible follies' committed in liberty's name.

The character of the french, indeed, had been so depraved by the inveterate despotism of ages, that even amidst the heroism which distinguished the taking of the Bastille, we are forced to see that suspicious temper, and that vain ambition of dazzling, which have generated all the succeeding follies and crimes . . . The morals of the whole nation were destroyed by the manners formed by the government. – Pleasure had been pursued, to fill up the void of rational employment; and fraud combined with servility to debase the character; – so that, when they changed their system, liberty, as it was called, was only the acme of tyranny . . .[17]

'This observation', Wollstonecraft sums up, 'inforces [sic] the grand truth on mankind, that without morality there can be no great strength of understanding, or real dignity of conduct.'[18] The French, like the female sex, must undergo inner change before their liberationist aims can be realised.

That a transformation of subjectivity was required to complete the civilising process was, as we have seen, one of the leading propositions of the *Rights of Woman*. Intense passions rightly directed are the *primum mobile* for good, Wollstonecraft argued there; but passions in women have been perverted from their higher purposes, left mired in selfishness and vice. Love especially, which should be general and spiritual – 'a glowing flame of universal love, which, after encircling humanity, mounts in graceful incense to God' – has in women remained exclusive and sensual, a 'narrow affectio[n], to which justice and humanity are often sacrificed'.[19] As a result, women possess no heroic sympathies, no public spirit. They 'find politics dry,' Wollstonecraft writes, 'because they have not acquired a love of mankind by turning their thoughts to the grand pursuits that exalt the human race, and promote general happiness'.[20] Deprived of civil rights and confined to family concerns, women 'have their attention naturally drawn from the interest of the whole community to that of the minute parts, though the private duty of any member of society must be very imperfectly performed when not connected with the general good'.[21] Their sense of justice is therefore very underdeveloped compared to that of men, and although they display much florid sentimentality, genuine feelings of benevolence or friendship – the affective cement of a good society – are 'very faint' in them, sacrificed to their absorption in their own (and their family's) interests. 'The exclusive affections of women,' Wollstonecraft declared, in a revealing analogy

seem indeed to resemble Cato's most unjust love for his country. He wishes to crush Carthage, not to save Rome, but to promote his vain-glory; and in general, it is to similar principles that [women's] humanity is sacrificed...[22]

It was for ambitions of just this vainglorious kind that Wollstonecraft now condemned French revolutionists, describing them as 'an effeminate race of heroes' caught up in 'disgusting conceit and wretched egotism'.[23] 'It is time,' she exhorted her readers, 'that a more enlightened moral love of mankind should supplant, or rather support, physical affections' so that 'the heroes of the present generation, still having their monsters to cope with, will labour to establish... rational laws throughout the world'.[24] Here, in this truly world-historic conflict, we see once again the divided self of Wollstonecraftian psychology, struggling with desires and fantasies that, rightly directed, lead to the Good, but without proper moral orientation, sink into vice and apathy. The struggle is simultaneously cosmic and immediate; it is also – as Wollstonecraft's denunciation of French manners makes plain – a gendered battle whose 'monsters' wear very feminine faces.

What France, and indeed the world, emphatically needs less of is Woman, the quintessence of selfish, anti-social sentiment. Locked in their petty, frivolous existence, women, like effete Frenchmen, are crassly egoistical, caring little for national concerns and even less for human welfare *in toto*. '[N]ot taught to respect public good', they possess no sense of public duty, and regard politics as merely another arena in which to pursue private advantage. Excluded from formal political power, they exploit sexual charm to achieve illicit influence, with devastating results: for the 'box of mischief thus opened ... what is to preserve private virtue, the only security of public freedom and universal happiness?'[25] In a male-dominated polity, women are a morbidly noxious presence, corrupting not only their intimates but the whole of the social body.

That women's confined lives and familial preoccupations were inimical to the cultivation of patriotic sentiment was widely agreed in the late eighteenth century. 'The master of a family is immediately connected with his country: his wife, his children, his servants, are immediately connected with him, and with their country through him only. Women accordingly have less patriotism than men,' Lord Kames wrote in 1774, or as another essayist put it, 'A man to [a woman] is more than a nation'.[26] To most commentators this seemed good reason, or pretext, to exclude women from political life; for Wollstonecraft, however – in one of her typical feminist revisions of intellectual commonplaces – it served as a key plank in her case for women's rights:

Contending for the rights of woman, my main argument is built on this simple principle, that if she be not prepared by education to become the companion of man, she will stop the progress of knowledge and virtue; for ... the love of mankind, from which an orderly train of virtues spring, can only be produced by considering the moral and civil interest of mankind; but the education and situation of woman at present shuts her out from such investigations.[27]

The logic here was clear, and the conclusion – '[l]et women share the rights, and she will emulate the virtues of man; for she must grow more perfect when emancipated' – politically impeccable.[28] But the antinomy between Woman and public-spiritedness on which the case was built was both clichéd and dangerous. In particular, the attack on female political influence – with its high-voltage imagery of 'vile and foolish' women delivering themselves over to powerful male voluptuaries in exchange for political favours – was a hackneyed anti-royalist theme that, at the time Wollstonecraft was writing the *Rights of Woman*, was being regularly pressed into service by French opponents of women's rights: which is perhaps why she chose to employ it, seeking to turn hostility against 'boudoir politics' into support for women's full, responsible citizenship.[29] But if so, the poetics of political life, the shaping of political vocabularies by gendered metaphors of power and desire, made directing such themes to feminist ends an extremely hazardous business.

* * *

Had Wollstonecraft been formulating her views outside history, in some airless realm of abstract rumination, their misogynist inflections would have mattered less. But the political world to which she delivered her case for female civic equality in 1792 – pushing it directly under the nose of a leading architect of the new French Constitution – was one already saturated in negative representations of political womanhood. French radicalism, as Dorinda Outram and others have shown, was fiercely hostile to the feminine presence in politics. The revolution, Outram observes in her impressive study of French radical mentalities, *The Body and the French Revolution*,

defined its difference from the old regime partly in terms of a difference in the impact of women on politics. In the rhetoric, the monarchy was par excellence a regime characterized by the corruption of power through the agency of women. Boudoir politics...were seen both as a cause of the weaknesses of the old regime, and as a justification for the Revolution itself.[30]

As the Revolution progressed, this misogynist idiom increased to the point where 'the entire struggle for the achievement of legitimacy, for the creation of a new legitimate public embodied by the Revolutionary governing class' became 'predicated not on an inclusion of the female, but on its exclusion' which 'posed great problems for any woman seeking public authority'[31]. The revolution, it was perceived, would succeed only 'if the niche formerly occupied by women's vice was taken over by male virtue.'[32] In 1789 the National Assembly adopted the distinction, first proposed by Abbé Sieyes, between active and passive citizens, the latter comprising women, children, foreigners and all those 'who contribute nothing to the maintenance of the public establishment'.[33] In 1791 women were formally denied political rights by the new French Constitution, despite Talleyrand's admission to the Convention that '[i]f we acknowledge that [women] have the same rights as men, they must be given the same means to make use of them'.[34] But the Declaration of the Rights of Man permitted abstract rights to be overriden by considerations of public utility, and on this basis, Talleyrand insisted, women were rightly excluded from the polity. Submitting his report on national education to the government, Talleyrand spelled out a Rousseauist programme of female education aimed entirely at preparing women for *la vie interieure*, with no preparation for public duties:

It seems incontestable to us that the common happiness, especially that of women, requires that they do not aspire to exercise rights and political functions. One must seek their best interest in the will of nature. Is it not obvious that their delicate constitutions, their peaceful inclinations, the many duties of maternity, constantly distance them from *habitudes fortes* . . . [L]et us teach them the real measure of their duties and rights. That they will find, not insubstantial hopes, but real advantages under the empire of liberty; that the less they participate in the making of the law, the more they will receive from it protection and strength; and that especially when they renounce all political rights, they will acquire the certainty of seeing their civil rights substantiated and even expanded.[35]

These attitudes did not go unchallenged. In Paris, women and men of the *Confederation des amis de la verité* vigorously promoted women's cause. Girondin ideologues like Condorcet and Etta Palm d'Aelders published tracts demanding full civic rights for women, while the extraordinary butcher's daughter, Olympe de Gouges, denounced women's detractors while presenting herself as an ideal revolutionary citizen and a 'great man'[36]. Across France, revolutionary women's clubs, ostensibly confined to auxiliary functions, provided occasional platforms for feminist propagandists. But the weight of opinion, at least among revolutionary opinion-formers, was strongly anti-egalitarian. In 1791 Prudhomme used his influential newspaper, *Revolutions de Paris*, to campaign against female participation in government: 'You take care of your household government,' he instructed the president of one women's club, 'and let us take care of the republic; let the men make the revolution.'[37] In 1793 he and likeminded *citoyens* urged the new Republic to shut down the women's clubs. Women's political associations were banned later that year; in 1795, in a general crackdown on the popular revolution following the defeat of the Jacobins, women were prohibited from attending political meetings, and even from parading in the streets in groups larger than five.[38] These restrictions were essential, wave after wave of government leaders insisted, to save the virtue of the Republic: a virtue that, by the end of the revolutionary decade, had revealed itself as emphatically, exclusively virile. 'For whom has liberty and equality been established?' the feminist writer Fanny Raoul demanded in 1801: '[for] men . . . It is for them, and for them alone, that political society has been made; women have no part in it.'[39]

The French revolution dramatised political gender divisions to a degree not to be experienced in Britain until the suffrage campaigns of the late nineteenth century. But the anti-feminine bias so marked in French politics was also apparent in British radicalism both before and during the 1790s. The first popular campaigners for parliamentary reform, the Wilkite radicals of the 1760s and 70s, fêted their own 'manly patriotism' while issuing scurrilous diatribes against effeminate aristocrats.[40] To Tom Paine, the British House of Lords appeared a 'seraglio of males' led by men who were mere 'counterfeits of wom[e]n'.[41] Political virtue and vice were sexualised through a series of symbolic connections linking heterosexual manliness to a life of public duty and setting both against the effete public conduct of the rich, 'especially their "extravagant submission" to women'.[42] Nor, as we have seen, were feminists adverse to such rhetoric. It was the power of women in 'all the courts of Europe', according to Catharine Macaulay, that had filled 'the whole world...with violence and injury'.[43]

Why was this misogynist element so prevalent in eighteenth-century radicalism? Scholars addressing this question usually point to the influence of the classical republican tradition, with its hyper-virile imagery of citizenship.[44] From the Graeco-Roman republics onward, the ideal republican citizen had been seen as a heroic warrior/statesman, a selfless Brutus whose dedication to public duty outweighed his private interests: an ideal which, in its *macho* austerity, had not only excluded women's traditional qualities but tended to associate these, particularly physical weakness and emotionality, with political inefficacy and improbity. A landowner whose wealth insulated him from corrupting influences, republican man was a stoical, high-minded independent who spent his political life as an equal member of the civic fraternity. In his private domain, however, this freedom-loving patriot was absolute master, wielding inviolable power over his wife, children and servants. In his person, then, political and patriarchal power interlocked to produce an image of masculine authority that, to its adherents, appeared natural, timeless and unassailable. Virility and political potency were one, and womanhood another: no imagined unity was possible.[45]

In Wollstonecraft's day this civic ideal still enjoyed tremendous currency in republican America, and in some French revolutionary circles. In Britain too it put real pressure on men of the political class right up to the 1790s; but here it had also acquired a distinctly archaic air. British commercial gentlemen were not cut in the mould of warrior-patriots. They were less inclined to wage war themselves than to pay others to do it; nor, by and large, did they view themselves as custodians of the public good in the way that classical citizens were meant to do. Public life, with its jostling elites and petty factionalism, was no longer idealised as the chief arena for the display of *virtu*; nor was the pursuit of private gain generally condemned as antithetical to the public interest. Increasingly, the good citizen was seen simply as the good man: the gentleman of property and propriety who respected his superiors, behaved decently to his inferiors, was kind to women and children, and paid his debts. Such men, it was felt, were the stuff on which Britain's greatness was based, and higher notions of civic virtue increasingly fell by the wayside. An alternative masculine ideal, gentler and more egoistical than the antique variety, pushed oldfashioned civic manliness aside.[46]

This shift must not be overstated. The political reform movement that emerged in Britain after 1760 had powerful undercurrents of republican sentiment flowing into it from the Commonwealth radicalism of the previous century. But it was an ideological stream so much diluted by other radical influences that by the 1790s, as Mark Philp has shown, republicanism, as a distinctive political stance, had virtually disappeared from British radical circles.[47] Of the feminist radicals, Catharine Macaulay was a republican, and an important one, yet she was far from purist in this commitment, preferring instead to blend republican ideals with natural-rights arguments and a Christian interpretation of political virtue.[48] Wollstonecraft was not a classical republican, nor were any of her close associates.[49] Yet residues of the tradition remained readily detectable in British jacobin writings, including Wollstonecraft's – not least in the persistent masculinisation of political virtue and manners. The admiration expressed by British radicals for that popular icon of American republicanism, George Washington, signalled the continuing yet declining influence of republican manly ideals. To inhabitants of the young American republic, Washington appeared to symbolise a heroic future; to British radicals, however, his inspirational example seemed more like a twilight glow from a dying age. '[T]he days of true heroism are over,' Wollstonecraft wrote, on a characteristically elegiac note:

when a citizen fought for his country like a Fabricius or a Washington, and then returned to his farm to let his virtuous fervour run in a more placid, but not a less salutory stream. No, our British heroes are oftener sent from the gaming-table than from the plough; and their passions have been rather inflamed by hanging with dumb suspense on the turn of a die, than sublimated by panting after the adventurous march of virtue in the historic page.[50]

British manliness wasn't what it used to be, and even a feminist could mourn the change. Elsewhere, however, Wollstonecraft eulogised Washington (along with Christ and Milton) as a paragon of masculine 'modesty'.[51] Other radicals praised him for his gentleness and emotional sensibility. Political heroes, it seemed, were softer creatures than previously;

some had even been known to cry.[52] Meanwhile female radicals, particularly in France, were celebrating women's political seriousness and, when necessary, bellicosity. The good citizen was becoming, in Olympe de Gouges's words, 'an amphibious animal', a political androgyne: or, as Wollstonecraft would have it, a universal 'human creature' in whom sex, like other 'artificial distinctions', had lost all political relevance.[53]

This erosion of gender distinctions in political life and thought – to the point where, Paul Langford tells us, 'defenders of masculine superiority were becoming genuinely concerned about the threat to their cause' – gave real force to Wollstonecraft's egalitarian wishes.[54] It also stimulated a powerful backlash. Never before had women, particularly women of the lettered middle class, so closely resembled men in their cultural experience, intellectual sophistication, and political aspirations, and the result was a strenuous male struggle to shore up the sexual boundaries that history (and feminism) were undermining. The rearguard action was made more difficult, however, by a further assault on masculine prerogatives from another direction: natural-rights philosophy.

From its inception, natural-rights theory had presented the rights-bearing individual as undifferentiatedly human. Unlike historic rights, over which they took precedence, divinely bestowed abstract rights were always and everywhere universal. '[T]here are rights which men inherit at their birth, as rational creatures, who were raised above the brute creation by their improvable faculties,' Wollstonecraft instructed Burke in her *Rights of Men*, 'and... in receiving these, not from their forefathers but, from God, prescription can never undermine natural rights.'[55] It was this 'fundamental truth' of which she sharply reminded Talleyrand in the *Dedication* to the *Rights of Woman* when, after quoting back to him his own admission that, 'according to abstract principles', women could not be excluded from political rights, she demanded to know:

If so, on what does your constitution rest? If the abstract rights of man will bear discussion and explanation, those of woman, by a parity of reasoning, will not shrink from the same test; though a different opinion prevails in this country, built on the very arguments which you use to justify the oppression of women – prescription.[56]

Employed thus, natural-right was such a powerful legitimator of feminist demands that it was only by wheeling in ancillary criteria for citizenship (such as 'common utility') that French politicians had been able to resist women's claims. The position, for revolutionary moralists, was doubly compromising, since to exclude any group from a polity defined by natural-law principles was to 'act like a tyrant' and 'tyranny, in whatever part of society it rears its brazen front, will ever undermine morality'.[57] Virtue as well as justice demanded that women's God-given entitlements should be acknowledged, whatever the cost to masculine pride and prestige.

Wollstonecraft, despite her sometime reputation for it, was not a systematic natural-rights thinker. Her writings are strewn with references to rights, but most are cursory. Like most British radicals, natural-rights was for her not a primary intellectual commitment but one of a quiverful of intellectual weapons to be kept sharp and handy for contestation. 'The rights of men' were 'grating sounds' that set the 'teeth [of the rich] on edge', she sneered at Burke pugnaciously in 1790, 'the impertinent enquiry of philosophic meddling innovation'.[58] She knew her Locke, and even better her Price, but made no attempt to replicate their careful explications of natural-law tenets.[59] What mattered to her were the equalitarian gains to be made from these ideas, and the mental distance they placed between enlightened 'political science' and old-world prejudices. Wollstonecraft's philosophical commitments were instrumental and strategic, not narrowly theoretic; nor would it have worried her in the least that ideas now deemed incompatible – such as a 'liberal' emphasis on personal rights versus a 'republican' emphasis on public obligations – were in her writings promiscuously blended. Jacobin theorists, as Philp has argued, were not creedal conformists, concerned to proselytise a party line, but men and women engaged in 'a developing political practice whose principles... [were] as much forged in the struggle as they [were] fetched from the arsenal and brought to it'.[60] In a hopeful, adversarial context, ideas could take on meanings quite different from those intended by their inventors (or those imposed by latter-day academic interpreters).

* * *

Womanliness, in both sexes, as a political ill for which manliness – again, in both sexes – was the cure: this notion, so common within eighteenth-century radicalism, was to prove exceptionally longlasting. Traces of it persisted well into the twentieth century. There were powerful reasons for this, beyond mere sexism. As a criterion of political entitlement, manliness was far more inclusive than birth or wealth, even with its exclusion of half of humanity. As a weapon against the claims of the already-powerful, civic manliness played a vital democratic role; yet in its wake came new structures of political belonging, ones that for the first time made gender a passport to insider status. Never before the drafting of the 1791 French constitution had any European government explicitly identified biological manhood as a qualification for citizenship. Never before had any government *needed* to do so, since governance had never been sufficiently open to non-elite individuals of either sex to make it necessary to exclude some of them. Nor, prior to the rise of the British parliamentary reform movement, had it occurred to anyone that a case for popular suffrage could be made on the basis of general male rights over women. Yet it was precisely in these terms that radicals from the 1760s on argued for the broadening of the franchise, to include all those who had proprietorship over wives, daughters, and children.[61] 'Every man,' James Burgh wrote in his influential *Political Disquisitions*,

has what may be called a property, and unalienable property. Every man has a life, a personal liberty, a character, a right to his earnings, a right to a religious profession and worship according to his conscience etc, and many men, who are in a state of dependence upon others, and who receive charity, have wives and daughters, in whom they have a right.[62]

Working men needed greater political power, Burgh went on, in order that they might protect 'their lives, their personal liberty, their little property...and the chastity of their wives and daughters'.[63]

Other leading male reformers made similar arguments, and either ignored women's claims or dismissed them out of hand.[64] Not all radical men were so sex-partisan: in 1795 the Norwich radical journal, *The Cabinet*, published two letters, apparently from men, in support of adult female suffrage, while in 1798 the Westminster Forum, a popular London debating club, sponsored a discussion over whether women should be elected to Parliament.[65] The ultra-radical Thomas Spence included female suffrage in his scheme for a communist Britain. The claim made by Charles Fox in a 1797 speech to Parliament that '[i]n all the theories and projects of the most absurd speculation, it has never been suggested that it would be advisable to extend the elective franchise to the female sex', was therefore erroneous; the general point of Fox's speech, however, that women should be disqualified from the right of election by virtue of their dependence on men, probably enjoyed near-universal acceptance.[66] Fox's motive in making this argument was not to scupper a possible feminist campaign – a likelihood too remote to worry any politician – but to undermine the case for universal male enfranchisement by showing that, like women, working-class men were incapable of exercising rational, independent political choice. The terms in which he made this comparison – pointing out that if 'the superior classes of the female sex of England' were deemed unfit for political rights, how could the 'lowest class of men' be thought capable of wielding them? – was an interesting foretaste of later female suffrage arguments. It also strikingly contrasted to the position adopted by Wollstonecraft in the *Rights of Woman* where, after 'dropping a hint' that 'women ought to have representatives, instead of being arbitrarily governed without having any direct share allowed them in the deliberations of government', she immediately tied this to the question of male working-class enfranchisement, pointing out that 'as the whole system of representation is now, in this country, only a convenient handle for despotism, they [women] need not complain' since they were as well represented as all the working men 'whose very sweat supports the splendid stud of an heir-apparent, or varnishes the chariot of some female favorite who looks down on shame'.[67] Why should a woman fare any better than an 'honest mechanic' whose sole property 'is in his... arms' and whose 'native dignity' is so often outraged by unjust laws and oppressive taxes?[68]

This sensitivity to popular suffering and entitlements was by no means constant in Wollstonecraft's writings. But the strength of radical impulse it signalled was very important. British radicalism was too diffuse and ideologically entangled to be divided along clear left/right lines. But on a spectrum of reform opinion, Wollstonecraft's views can be seen to occupy a more radical position – more 'democratical' as she would have said – than many of her jacobin compatriots. The significance of this for her feminism, however, was not to become fully apparent until her final work, *Maria*, where the figure of emblematic Woman finally began to give way to the predicaments and entitlements of actual women. But intimations of this shift were plentiful earlier on, particularly in her writings on female citizenship which, while still displaying the influence of older misogynist views, simultaneously mounted an exceptionally bold challenge to radical male supremacism.

8

The female citizen

Polemics against female political 'meddling', while paranoid and hyperbolic, had some foundation. Women had long influenced British political life although never, with the exception of queens, on a formal basis. The most significant female political presence in the eighteenth century was to be found, unsurprisingly, on the aristocratic stage to which parliamentary politics were largely confined. Here women were often key players, manoeuvring their menfolk into advantageous positions, negotiating alliances between competing families and factions, hostessing political gatherings. Most of this was backstage work and so condemned as 'illicit influence' and 'petticoat government' by reformers. Yet many of these elite women – most notably the Duchess of Devonshire, who publicly campaigned for Charles Fox in 1784 – were sophisticated political actors from whom important feminist lessons might have been drawn, had anyone cared to do so. Wollstonecraft, whose political circles overlapped with the Duchess's, never publicly commented on her activities, while women politicians themselves, constant targets of scurrilous abuse from rival factions, were generally keen to stress their feminine propriety. It was only her passionate concern for the public interest that induced her to budge from her family fireside, the Duchess intermittently (and implausibly) insisted. '[A] woman has no business in these things,' she wrote in the wake of some particularly vigorous campaigning, 'unless very sure of serving La Patrie...'[1]

Women were also present at the plebeian end of political life. Poor women, particularly small traders and market women, were a common sight in the eighteenth-century political crowd: cheering or jeering candidates at the electoral hustings, attacking unpopular local politicians, participating in anti-Catholic riots and other 'mob' actions. During the early years of the Revolution, the Paris streets saw a lot of such women, most famously in the October 1789 march that brought Louis XVI from Versailles to Paris. Replying to Burke's description of the Versailles marchers as 'unutterable abominations of the furies of hell, in the abused shape of the vilest of women', Wollstonecraft commented drily, 'Probably you mean women who gained a livelihood by selling vegetables or fish, who never had any advantages of education...'[2] But in her history of the Revolution she too dismissed these women as 'refuse of the streets' who had acted, she claimed, as stooges of the duke of Orleans and his henchmen in the Jacobin clubs.[3] 'That a body of women should put themselves in motion to demand relief of the king, or to remonstrate with the assembly respecting their tardy manner of forming the constitution, is scarcely probable; and that they should have undertaken the business, without being instigated by designing persons... is a belief which the most credulous will hardly swallow,' was her depressing verdict.[4]

Wollstonecraft's fear and dislike of the *menu peuple* of revolutionary Paris was shared by all English Girondin sympathisers. But her assumption that women of the labouring poor were incapable of acting on their own initiative was also of a piece with her view of oppression as debilitating, rather than radicalising. 'The being who...endures injustice...will soon become unjust, or unable to discern right from wrong', the *Rights of Woman* warned.[5] And so it was that the poor women of Paris, made desperate by 'want of bread', became easy puppets of the *sans-culottes* leadership while, at the top end of the social spectrum, aristocratic women, 'not allowed any civil rights' of their own, sought 'justice by retaliation' through unlicensed political influence.[6] The 'servitude [that] debases the individual' made these women – rich and poor alike – an invidious public presence.[7]

Turning away from these women, the *Rights of Woman* puts in their stead the model female citizen: well-instructed, independent-minded, and drawn from the middle rather than the upper ranks since it is women from this relatively modest station who 'appear to be in the most natural state'.[8] The portrait is composite, but its outlines are clear enough. A woman of means 'sufficiently above abject poverty not to be obliged to weigh the consequence of every farthing', this is no rich lady of leisure but a humble homemaker whose sole luxury, Wollstonecraft tells us, is her impeccable cleanliness.[9] Orderly and vigorous, she performs all the day-to-day house-work herself, except possibly the roughest tasks for which she might employ a single servant. A dedicated mother, she suckles and tends her children without the assistance of a wet-nurse; as they grow older, she is their primary educator and moral mentor as well as their chief protector. In addition to all this, she is also likely to be remuneratively employed – as a shopkeeper, a farmer, a midwife, or even a doctor.[10] In the little leisure time left to her, she enjoys tending her garden and reading experimental philosophy and other enlightening literature. Living in strict monogamy with a husband who is her equal companion, not her master, this woman is as cheerful as she is wise and frugal, and all that is further required are a few finishing touches – such as a little extra money for books and charitable donations – to render her situation 'the happiest as well as the most respectable ... in the world'.[11]

The inner life of this paragon is characterised by reason, piety, self-respect, and, above all, by that love of humanity which for Wollstonecraft was the *sina qua non* of good citizenship. The right-minded citizenness is the woman who, her natural sympathies elevated into universal benevolence, equates her personal interests with the general good. She is, in other words, a true patriot in the jacobin sense, that is 'a citizen of the world' who, committed to universal justice and happiness, purveys this ideal to others – in her case, to her children. For 'if children are to be educated to understand the true principle of patriotism, their mother must be a patriot', meaning she must have acquired that love of mankind which is the affective basis of virtuous public life, and the engine of human progress.[12]

Duty wedded to right is Wollstonecraft's formula for all this. '[A] right always includes a duty, and I think it may, likewise, fairly be inferred that they forfeit the right, who do not fulfil the duty.'[13] As rights-bearing citizens, women have duties to undertake, public services to render, a civic mission to perform. Unlike in more conventional renderings of this idea – as for example in Evangelical propaganda, where the notion of a specifically feminine mission of moral and social redemption was becoming increasingly popular – these are radical duties, ones with a strong revolutionary-utopian aim. What Wollstonecraft emphatically is *not* urging on women is any sacrifice of their needs to some imaginary, elite-defined public good, à la Burke. Fictitious communalities of this sort are simply tyrannies.[14] 'The happiness of the whole must arise from the happiness of the constituent parts, or the essence of justice is sacrificed to a supposed grand arrangement.'[15] But nor do good governments exist merely to service and protect individual interests. Rooted in humane passions, and serving as vehicles of divine purpose, political communities are more than the sum of their parts, since it is with their egalitarian-democratic potential that humanity's prospects ultimately rest.

The main ethical underpinning of this position, as we have seen, was the radicalised version of neighbourly love purveyed by leftwing Protestants, particularly Richard Price. But echoes of republican thinking were clearly audible too. As a model of political virtue, Christian altruism was readily applicable to women; republican ideals of public service, on the other hand, were so intractably masculinist that in evoking them Wollstonecraft immediately ran into difficulties. Chapter 9 of the *Rights of Woman*, where these themes are most fully elaborated, shows her struggling to feminise manly civic virtues, with little success. The quality she values most, independence, is given various, sometimes conflicting, meanings. But the classical image of the citizen as a soldier-statesman also tempts her. Could women offer such virile services to the polity? No feminist could avoid the question, not only because feminists were constantly accused of trying to masculinise women, but also because women's presumed unfitness to 'take the field... [as] soldiers, or wrangle in the senate' was regularly cited by anti-feminists as a rationale for denying them civic status.[16] Some earlier defenders of women, such as the anonymous author of the 1739 tract, 'Woman Not Inferior to Man', had insisted that women could run nations and armies as effectively as men: 'The military art has not mystery in it beyond others, which Women cannot attain to...'[17] But the argument had been ridiculed by Rousseau and other male supremacists.

I know that, as a proof of the inferiority of the sex, [Wollstonecraft writes] Rousseau has exultingly exclaimed, How can they leave the nursery for the camp! – And the camp has by some moralists been termed the school of the most heroic virtues; though, I think, it would puzzle a keen casuist to prove the reasonableness of the greater number of wars that have dubbed heroes.[18]

As it happens, Rousseau had written warmly of bellicose female patriots like the famous Spartan mothers who, the story had it, had rejoiced at the death of their sons in victorious battle.[19] Wollstonecraft, who detested Spartan aggressivity, couldn't share this enthusiasm; but nor was she inclined to give up female military heroics entirely, at least not for the right occasions: 'if defensive war, the only justifiable war... were alone to be adopted as just and glorious, the true heroism of antiquity might again animate female bosoms.'[20] Having issued this startling suggestion, however – one never further elaborated – she hastens to assure her readers that she is not advising women 'to turn their distaff into a musket':

I only recreated an imagination... by supposing that society will some time or other be so constituted, that man must necessarily fulfil the duties of a citzen [sic], or be despised, and that while he was employed in any of the departments of civil life, his wife, also an active citizen, should be equally intent to manage her family, educate her children, and assist her neighbours.[21]

Abandoning warrior-women, Wollstonecraft opts for a gender-specific civic ideal. As citizens, women have 'different duties to fulfil', duties prescribed – and circumscribed – by their familial role.[22] A woman, the *Rights of Men* explained, has a special part to play in 'the social compact', which is to 'superintend her family and suckle her children'.[23] Women enter the polity not just as rights-bearing human beings but as wives and mothers; and it is to enable them to become better wives and mothers – and thus better citizens – that they need improved education, equal legal status, and political rights. Women's public contribution is composed of private responsibilities, but 'to render [women's] private virtue a public benefit, they must have a civil existence in the State, married or single'.[24] For while a 'wife.. [who] neither suckles nor educates her children, scarcely deserves the name of a wife, and has not right to that of a citizen', to make a wife into a good citizen requires more than propriety and convention:

to render her really virtuous and useful, she must not, if she discharge her civil duties, want, individually, the protection of civil laws... [for] take away natural rights, and duties become null.[25]

Packaging rights with duties in this fashion was standard for eighteenth-century moral-political thinkers The rights bestowed by God were not discretionary liberties to be exercised as one pleased, but moral powers, 'granted for a purpose... namely, that of contributing to an overall moral order'.[26] Every right/power entailed a duty to exercise the right properly; conversely, every duty entailed a right, that is, a power to act: and it was here that Wollstonecraft's rights rhetoric found its key point of attack. For while women were exhorted to attend to their domestic obligations, they were seldom allowed the powers necessary to properly perform them. Without better education, an improved cultural standing, and political entitlements, women would never be successful wives and mothers. 'The only method of leading women to fulfil their peculiar duties,' Wollstonecraft sums up, 'is to free them from all restraint by allowing them to participate in the inherent rights of mankind.'[27]

Deriving women's egalitarian claims from their family responsibilities was to become such a key tactic of nineteenth and early twentieth-century feminists that it is easy to read Wollstonecraft's arguments – as most commentators have done – as a prequel to this. First-wave feminism's much-criticised endorsement of a separate domestic sphere for women would seem to have found a major precedent in Wollstonecraft's image of the homemaker-citizen. It was this interpretation of the *Rights of Woman* that was favoured by late Victorian feminists like Millicent Fawcett.[28] The reading, however, is only partly accurate: first because Wollstonecraft's account of female citizenship is embedded in a wider revisionary thesis about the relationship between political and personal morality which she applies equally to men; second, because there is another line of argument running through the *Rights of Woman*, a counter-argument strongly subversive of separate-spheres thinking. The result is a less coherent account of female citizenship than interpreters have generally assumed, but one with greater imaginative reach, and more radical implications.

* * *

Incorporating private merits into the civic ideal was not, to Wollstonecraft's mind, a sex-specific move. The personal virtues that would generate true public spirit in women would have the same happy effect on men. '[I]f you wish to make good citizens, you must first exercise the affections of a son and a brother. This is the only way to expand the heart; for public affections, as well as public virtues, must ever grow out of the private character.'[29] It is the role of 'a husband, and a father, [which] forms the citizen imperceptibly, by producing a sober manliness of thought, and orderly behaviour...'[30] Sobriety, self-restraint, dignity, chastity – modesty, as Wollstonecraft collectively dubs these excellencies – 'must be equally cultivated by both sexes', and equally mould their political consciousness.[31] '[I]t is vain to expect much public or private virtue until both men and women grow more modest... [and] treat each other with... humanity and fellow-feeling.'[32]

> Chastity, modesty, public spirit, and all the noble train of virtues, on which social virtue and happiness are built, should be understood and cultivated by all mankind, or they will be cultivated to little effect... Why then do philosophers look for public spirit? Public spirit must be nurtured by private virtue, or it will resemble the factitious sentiment which makes women careful to preserve their reputation, and men their honour. A sentiment that often exists unsupported by virtue, unsupported by that sublime morality which makes the habitual breach of one duty a breach of the whole moral law.[33]

Rooting public spirit in private virtues in this way was not, contrary to some recent arguments, intellectually novel.[34] Protestant radicalism had always regarded personal righteousness as the foundation of a virtuous and just polity. Having said this, however, it is important to recognise how Wollstonecraft's formulation of the private/public connection differed from less reform-minded versions. If it is true, as J. G. A. Pocock and others have claimed, that the eighteenth century saw a shift in civic ideals away from self-sacrificial *virtu* and valour to the less austere virtues of a well-mannered commercial gentleman – busy contributing to Britain's wealth and power through the polite pursuit of his private interests – then this relatively weak notion of political meritoriouness is emphatically *not* what Wollstonecraft has in mind.[35] British jacobinism, with its call for universal justice and freedom, expected much more from its citizens of the world than this; nor was private virtue of the Wollstonecraftian variety remotely equitable to codes of propriety. 'Local manners', Wollstonecraft insists, are the antithesis of 'unchangeable morals'.[36] It is from God, not convention, that standards of human virtue derive, just as it is His path to universal happiness down which humanity must inexorably travel. In public as in private life, the true citizen is not just a law-abiding worthy but a divinely inspired activist, a standard-bearer for eternal justice and right.

Infusing family life with reformative political purpose would appear to incorporate female concerns into this radical civic project. If children are to become good patriots, their mother must be capable of inculcating them with libertarian-patriotic ideals, Wollstonecraft insists, repeating a notion popular in republican America, and also in revolutionary France where by 1792 Rousseau's sentimental image of the mother as political educator, training up baby citizens for *le patrie*, had become a favourite piece of radical orthodoxy. 'Republican motherhood', as this ideology has been labelled, may (or may not – historians are in some dispute) have been an important force in the shaping of political attitudes among American and French women.[37] But to assign it a key role in Wollstonecraft's thought, as some interpreters have done, is unjustified.[38] Certainly the *Rights of Woman* contains hints of such a notion. But the insistent finger-wagging about maternal responsibilities to be found there is driven mostly by the book's anti-elitism. The innumerable ladies of fashion that waltz through its pages, hugging lapdogs in preference to their children and refusing to breastfeed for fear of diminishing their sexual allure, are the main target of Wollstonecraft's good-mothering strictures. When the discussion becomes less polemically focused, that is, when she turns to women of her own class, her attitude toward domestic life takes a more equivocal turn. Family affections receive mixed reviews. The primary allegiance to the 'little platoon' of family celebrated by Burke and other conservatives is sometimes endorsed, but more often condemned as egoistically anti-social. Like other jacobin intellectuals, Wollstonecraft was fiercely anti-empire and anti-nationalist, regarding imperial ambitions and national loyalties as grossly selfish. In her history of the French Revolution, this 'false patriotism' is equated to family love which, like national chauvinism, owes more to 'selfish passions, than reasonable humanity'. The example she cites here, tellingly, is the soldier-citizenry of the classical republics whose 'much-extolled patriotism' she derides as 'vain glory and barbarity':

[l]ike the parents who forgot all the dictates of justice and humanity, to aggrandize the very children whom they keep in a state of dependence, these heroes loved their country, because it was their country, ever showing by their conduct, that it was only a part of a narrow love of themselves.[39]

Like personal greed masking itself as dedication to national prosperity (another favourite critical butt), devotion to family interests is mere self-aggrandisement, she declared in the *Rights of Men*, and 'the mind must have a very limited range that thus confines its benevolence to such a narrow circle'.[40] The particular family ties targeted here were those of the landowning aristocracy for whom kinship bonds were inseparable from 'sordid calculations' of inheritance and property management.[41] But the familial chauvinists bearing the main brunt of the assault are women – middle class as well as elite – whose kin loyalties are derogated as 'narrow prejudice' and whose sequestration in home life is represented as trivialising and debilitating.[42] '[I]mmured in their families groping in the dark' women acquire no 'greatness of mind nor taste', nor do they experience any of those humane emotions from which civic spirit derives. Even the paragons among them – 'good managers and chaste wives' – are rendered narrow and philistine: 'Take them out of their family or neighbourhood, and they stand still; the mind finding no employment...'[43] Lacking 'business, extensive plans, or... excursive flights of ambition' to stimulate her mind and broaden her horizons, a housewife becomes a mere 'patient drudge... like a blind horse in a mill' whose husband, bored, drifts away of an evening to search out more 'piquant society'.[44] Poorer women, who must earn money to help support their families, are spared this fate, since gainful employment always bestows self-respect and dignity; but a middle-class woman wholly supported by her husband is in a truly deplorable state, becoming either a frivolous parasite or, if more attentive to domestic duties, a 'square-elbowed family drudge'.[45]

Family life narrows women's horizons, constricts their affections, curtails their sense of public responsibility: hardly what is wanted in a virtuous, vigorous citizenry. Wollstonecraft doesn't mean to take her argument this far, but the implication is certainly there. Anti-family sentiment, while by no means common in jacobin circles, had some influential radical exponents. Godwin and Thomas Holcroft both argued strongly against private attachments as antagonistic to the general good (Godwin, much criticised for this, later modified his position)[46] while Catharine Macaulay, replying to Burke's *Reflections*, scolded him for placing allegiance to family at the apex of human loyalties:

I hope we shall not...confound those *narrow affections* which bind small bodies together by the mutual ties of personal interest, to that *liberal benevolence*,
which, disdaining the consideration of every selfish good, chearfully [sic] sacrifices
a *personal interest* to the *welfare* of the community.[47]

Echoes of the argument are audible throughout Wollstonecraft's writings.
Its appeal to her must have been partly personal. After all, here was a woman
whose life was devoted to thinking, writing, arguing: a philosophic woman
who didn't like to cook, who employed a maid to assist with her child,[48]
and who deliberately stayed away from her husband during working hours
so that they could both concentrate on their writing. ('I wish you, from
my soul, to be rivetted in my heart; but I do not desire to have you always
at my elbow' she wrote to Godwin fondly.[49]) Apart from some delighted
fussing over Godwin's linen when they first became lovers, as a home-maker
Wollstonecraft made a very good writer (coming to visit her, Talleyrand
was startled to be served his wine in cracked teacups).[50] Small wonder
then that her panegyrics to family duties have a rather formulaic ring.
'My die is cast –' she wrote to Everina in 1790, from the home of a very
domesticated couple, the Gabells, whose constricted lifestyle left her feeling
alien and bored: 'I could not now resign intellectual pursuits for domestic
comforts.'[51] And, anyway, why should she? Francis Bacon – who ought to
know – had claimed that only men unfettered by family ties were capable
of pursuing great enterprises; and, Wollstonecraft boldly insists, 'I say the
same of women.'[52] Why should women of talent be expected to drown
their 'heroic virtues' in family cares?

though I consider that women in the common walks of life are called to fulfil the
duties of wives and mothers...I cannot help lamenting that women of a superiour
[sic] cast have not a road open by which they can pursue more extensive plans of
usefulness and independence.[53]

This exceptionalist argument was the closest Wollstonecraft came to
explicitly rejecting a primarily domestic role for women. And since 'the
welfare of society is not built on extraordinary exertions', her recommen-
dation for the generality of women is, it would seem, orthodox: 'When I
treat of the peculiar duties of women, as I should treat of the peculiar duties
of a citizen or father, it will be found that I do not mean to insinuate that
they should be taken out of their families, speaking of the majority.'[54] The
assurance, however, is immediately followed by a sharp indictment of all
those male writers (Rousseau, Fordyce *et al.*) who have 'earnestly laboured
to domesticate women' by 'prevailing on them to make the discharge of

such important duties the main business of life, though reason were insulted'.[55] Whatever their familial obligations, women have a *prior* duty 'to find themselves as rational creatures':

Connected with man as daughters, wives, and mothers, [women's] moral character may be estimated by their manner of fulfilling those simple duties; but the end, the grand end of their exertions should be to unfold their own faculties...[56]

Women's rights entail not only obligations specific to them as a sex, but the duty, common to all humanity, to fulfil individual potential – and it is here that Wollstonecraft, a lover of paradoxes, plunged straight into the paradox that was to characterise all subsequent feminisms: the simultaneous affirmation and denial of the 'peculiarity', the feminine specificity, of women's destiny.

* * *

As creatures of God, women's primary responsibility is to attain virtue, for which freedom is the prerequisite. Individuals who are prevented by others from freely pursuing virtue are not citizens but slaves: 'convenient slaves', as Wollstonecraft labels women, 'stripped of the virtues that should clothe humanity':

Liberty is the mother of virtue, and if women be, by their very constitution, slaves, and not allowed to breathe the sharp invigorating air of freedom, they must ever languish like exotics...[57]

Describing women's subordination as an enslavement, a commonplace of pro-woman writings since at least the mid seventeenth century, had its roots in the classical citizen/slave opposition. Wollstonecraft's use of the trope, however, while undoubtedly displaying traces of this classical influence (and the more recent impact of black colonial slavery, discussed in greater detail in chapter 9) had its immediate antecedents in the radical attack on government-sponsored religious intolerance mounted by Price and other Dissenting reformers, for whom civic liberty was above all a condition of ethical self-governance. A state or individual that, by imposing its 'arbitrary will' on others, inhibits moral self-rule, is always an enslaver, no matter how gently power is exerted. 'Individuals in private life, while held under the power of masters, cannot be denominated free,' Price wrote, 'however equitably and kindly they may be treated.'[58] '[T]o subjugate a rational being to the mere will of another...' as Wollstonecraft wrote, 'is a most cruel and undue stretch of power; and...injurious to morality.'[59] The chapter in the *Rights of Woman* where the argument is hammered home is, characteristically, the one dedicated to criticising parental rule, particularly as it pertains to girl children, who 'taught slavishly to submit to their parents...are prepared for the slavery of marriage'.[60] It is the 'irregular exercise of parental authority' to which 'girls are more subject than boys', Wollstonecraft writes, that does the initial damage to the female character:

> The will of those who never allow their will to be disputed, unless they happen to be in a good humour...is almost always unreasonable. To elude this arbitrary authority girls very early learn the lessons which they afterwards practice on their husbands...[61]

Young women (*pace* Sophie) are educated in servility. Marrying, they transfer this childish compliance and manipulative cunning from parents to husbands, so becoming locked in lifelong subservience to men. Having gained no self-respect to offset this, they respond by acquiring a slave mentality:

> the submissive demeanour of dependence, the support of weakness that loves, because it wants protection; and is forbearing, because it must silently endure injuries; smiling under the lash at which it dare not snarl. Abject as this picture appears, it is the portrait of an accomplished woman, according to the received opinion of female excellence, separated by specious reasoners from human excellence.[62]

The conclusion to be drawn is obvious: 'It is vain to expect virtue from women till they are in some degree independent of men...[for] [w]hilst they are absolutely dependent on their husbands they will be cunning, mean, and selfish...'[63] Only a liberated woman can become a good citizen.

* * *

Wollstonecraft's enthusiasm for independence, 'the grand blessing of life, the basis of every virtue', once widely regarded as symptomatic of her middle-class individualism, is now regarded by some scholars as evidence of her republicanism.[64] This is a more plausible reading, given republicanism's emphasis on material independence as a leading qualification for citizenship. But again, the definitional label obscures more than it illuminates – in this case, concealing the fact that the independence eulogised by Wollstonecraft and other British radicals was not the narrow landowning ideal of republicanism but a far more egalitarian concept, owing as much to radical Protestantism and natural-rights theory as to classical political thinking. To British jacobins, independence was an expression not of a few men's property but of every man's natural liberty, of a god-given entitlement to freedom from arbitrary political power, patrician patronage, and all other relations of clientage and subordination.[65] 'Man', however, was the critical term here since, even in this democratised version, independence remained a firmly masculine attribute, tied to a male citizen who was seen not as a freefloating individual but as a household head, the ruler of his own little kingdom: 'the natural guardian and virtual Representative...of his family and servants,' as one leading parliamentary reformer described him.[66] Like his classical forerunner, the independent citizen of 1790s radicalism remained a petty sovereign, with automatic sovereignty over his wife and children.[67] Even in Wollstonecraft's circle this idea was only rarely challenged; in the wider world of reform politics it was simply taken for granted. Dismissing the idea of female enfranchisement, Fox gave as his rationale that since 'by the law of nations, and perhaps also by the law of nature' women were men's subordinate dependents, 'their voices would be governed by the relation in which they stand in society'.[68]

The independent female citizen of the *Rights of Woman* emerged in direct response to this political situation. As an ideal, however, she remained partial and blurred. 'The laws respecting woman, which I mean to discuss in a future part, make an absurd unit of a man and his wife,' Wollstonecraft wrote; but the promised second volume never appeared, leaving readers with a scatter of half-formulated, often contradictory ideas, tantalising in their suggestiveness.[69] This is not incidental. Inserting feminist content into concepts derived from male-centred political discourses was a major challenge. Independence, with its robust manly connotations (and its shadowing by a counter-vocabulary of effeminacy, foppery, and other feminised varieties of social parasitism) demanded particular imaginative effort, and the strain was often evident, not least in Wollstonecraft's repeated exhortations to women to become 'more masculine and respectable'.[70] The negative position occupied by women in radical political discourse made it difficult to recruit them to citizenhood without either repudiating their womanhood or – as Rousseau had done – turning it into a sex-specific civic category. Wollstonecraft wishes to do neither: '[w]omen, I allow, may have different duties to fulfil; but they are *human* duties', requiring the same rights, education and 'independence of character' as are required from male citizens.[71] Sexual distinctions have no place in political life, Wollstonecraft repeatedly insists. But if this is true, what becomes of womanliness, once the figure of Woman disappears into the independent citizen?

Struggling with this question, Wollstonecraft answers it by outlining two models of female independence. The first, loosely conforming to standard radical thinking, is founded on an idealised version of the marital family. The second, most fully developed in *Maria*, is a vision of liberated womanhood based on self-sufficiency and an end to male conjugal power. Neither model does what Wollstonecraft wants, which is to give women satisfying lives as wives and mothers while simultaneously allowing them to function as free, economically independent agents. Two centuries later this aspiration, central to most varieties of western feminism, is still far from met. Confronting the dynamics of female subjection, then, Wollstonecraft's real achievement was not to provide clear-cut solutions but rather – for the first time – fully to expose the nature and extent of the problem.

* * *

The ideal citizen of 1790s radicalism is often represented by historians as a heroic individualist, an autonomous agent untrammelled by communal ties. In fact, as we have seen, the good citizen of British jacobinism was inveterately social, bound to his/her fellows by common interests and social affections. In the *Rights of Man*, Paine described society as a 'great chain of connexion' based on the 'mutual dependence and reciprocal interest which man has upon man'.[72] Applying this model of man-to-man reciprocity to male/female relations, Wollstonecraft evokes an image of the independent woman not as a free-floating individual but as an equal working partner in a common family enterprise. 'The being who discharges the duties of its station is independent,' she argues, going on to paint an extravagantly sentimentalised portrait of a humble rural abode inhabited by an exemplary homemaker and her diligent craftsman husband – 'a couple . . . equally necessary and independent of each other, because each fulfilled the respective duties of their station'.[73] Like the small farms and artisanal workshops Wollstonecraft admired so much (or indeed, like her own business partnership with Joseph Johnson) the properly ordered marriage was a fellowship of mutually reliant equals.

Interpreted in this way, female independence is not merely compatible with women's domestic obligations, but defined by them. It is only fashionable ladies refusing to perform home duties, Wollstonecraft insists, who should be condemned as 'mere dolls'.[74] The argument, a clear echo of the long-established companionate marital ideal, was one with which even anti-feminists could concur.[75] Having carefully laid out this scenario, however, Wollstonecraft edges past it. For it is not only a life conducted on equal terms, as a self-respecting helpmeet, that defines female independence, but the ability to pay for it. For women as for men, it is the power 'to earn their own subsistence', she insists, that is the 'true definition of independence'.[76] The 'really virtuous and useful' woman 'must not be dependent on her husband's bounty for her subsistence during his life, or support after his death' – for 'how can a being be generous who has nothing of its own? or virtuous, who is not free?'[77] Women's economic dependence underpins men's arbitrary rule; even more damagingly, it disallows those unfettered encounters with experiences, ideas, and, above all, God through which true virtue is acquired. Thus women can never become good, nor both sexes happily united, until women are economically self-reliant:

> If marriage be the cement of society, mankind should all be educated after the same model, or the intercourse of the sexes will never deserve the name of fellowship, nor will women ever fulfil the peculiar duties of their sex, till they become enlightened citizens, till they become free by being enabled to earn their own subsistence, independent of men; in the same manner, I mean, to prevent misconstruction, as one man is independent of another. Nay, marriage will never be sacred till women . . . are prepared to be [men's] companions rather than their mistresses . . .[78]

The argument is ostensibly in support of marital partnerships. But if women – let us look again at her wording – should be 'independent of men; in the same manner . . . as one man is independent of another . . .',[79] how would such manly independence square with their family role? Men, after all, have never been defined by their family position: does that mean that women should not be either?

Wollstonecraft's handling of these knotty issues is simultaneously pragmatic and revolutionary. At a practical level, why should women from modest backgrounds not have opportunities to support themselves if they wish to remain single; or, if married, to supplement family earnings? Glancing back to a time before middle-class women aspired to leisured ladyhood, Wollstonecraft urges all women, single and wed, not to 'waste life away the prey of discontent' when they 'might have practised as physicians, regulated a farm, managed a shop' or studied to become doctors, nurses and midwives. 'Businesses of various kinds, they might likewise pursue, if they were educated in a more orderly manner . . .'[80] The proposal is not especially innovative, since previous generations of middling women had often engaged in such remunerative activities. But in Wollstonecraft's writings it is harnessed to a much more subversive aim: to eradicate male familial power over women. No financially independent woman would ever 'marry for a support', she claims, thereby selling herself into 'legal prostitution'.[81] Her own subsistence (and that of her children) ensured, she would no longer be at the mercy of a feckless, cruel or merely careless husband. She would become a truly free agent, able to shape her own destiny. The argument, a foretaste of feminist claims not fully articulated until the twentieth century, is hinted at in the *Rights of Woman* and then made explicit in *Maria*, where the optimistic images of companionate sexual unions promoted in Wollstonecraft's earlier writings give way to an unrelievedly bleak account of marriage as juridical and practical chatteldom. 'She toiled from morning till night'; is the description of one of the many miserable wives depicted in

Wollstonecraft's final novel, 'yet her husband would rob the till, and take away the money reserved for paying bills; and, returning home drunk, he would beat her if she chanced to offend him, though she had a child at the breast... no slave in the West Indies had [a master] more despotic'.[82]

* * *

If *Maria*, as seems possible, was meant to replace the proposed second volume of the *Rights of Woman*, then events in the five years separating the two works produced a sequel that was probably very different from the one originally intended. In the interval, Wollstonecraft had logged up a lot more personal experience of the 'wrongs of women', including the humiliating breakdown of her romance with Fuseli and the birth of her illegitimate baby by Imlay, followed by Imlay's sexual betrayals and his eventual desertion of her and the child. The blows had been heavy, and no lighter because of Wollstonecraft's partial responsibility for them. Not that the younger Wollstonecraft had been any novice in female oppression. '[O]n many accounts I am averse to any matrimonial tie,' she had told her friend Jane Arden in 1780, after witnessing her parents' miseries; 'struggle with any obstacles rather than go into a state of dependence: – I speak feelingly. – I have felt the weight, and would have you by all means avoid it.'[83] Having then gone on to exploit every acceptable means of self-support, Wollstonecraft was absolutely determined to continue in this fashion, even when left with a tiny daughter to care for. 'Your continually asserting, that you will do all in your power to contribute to my comfort (when you only allude to pecuniary assistance), appears to me a flagrant breach of delicacy,' she wrote to Imlay in the winter of 1795 (shortly after her second suicide attempt), 'I want not such vulgar comfort, nor will accept it.'[84] She was 'still able to support my child,' she told him.[85] Slightly less than a year later, finding herself in a happier relationship, she wrote to her new lover of her continuing resolution to earn 'the money I want' with her pen 'or go to sleep forever'. She could never 'endure a life of dependence' she warned Godwin (who had shown no inclination to offer her one).[86]

Women who expect men to act as their natural 'protectors', Wollstonecraft wrote in 1792, are self-deluding, since most husbands are merely 'overgrown children' or selfishly tyrannical.[87] And even in the unlikely event of a husband proving kind and reliable, such a man is as prone to death or incapacity as anyone else: and then what happens to the unprotected wife and mother? '[E]ncumbered with children, how is she to obtain another protector – a husband to supply the place of reason?'[88]

Maria, which Wollstonecraft started writing during the final stages of her relationship with Imlay, dramatises this issue. Earlier we saw how in her last novel Wollstonecraft used romance as a vehicle to explore the ambiguous role of fantasy in feminine experience. Maria, gripped by erotic imaginings, concocts Henry Darnford as her personal St Preux, the perfect lover. In the conclusions Wollstonecraft drafted, this idealisation begins to give way to more realistic images: Darnford, like his prototype, stands revealed as a 'volatile' wayward man. The exposure, however, does not prevent him from serving as a useful foil to Maria's truly ghastly husband, George Venables, who despite his many crimes against his wife – adultery, exortion, kidnapping, and attempts to prostitute her to a friend – in the eyes of the law remains her guardian and protector. '[T]his was the man I was bound to respect and esteem,' Maria recalls, ensconsed in the lunatic asylum to which Venables has finally consigned her:

a wife being as much a man's property as his horse, or his ass, she has nothing she can call her own. He may use any means to get at what the law considers as his . . . and the laws of her country – if women have a country – afford her no protection or redress from the oppressor . . .'[89]

Marriage, Maria sums up, 'had bastilled me for life', and it is this institutionalised bondage that the novel probes in detail, showing how under the law of coverture all that a wife possesses, even what 'she earns by her own exertions', automatically belongs to her husband.[90] A married woman has no economic entitlements, nor any effective redress if abused, betrayed or deserted. A man who abandons his wife, Wollstonecraft writes scorchingly, is thought to have 'shaken of [f] a clog'; and if he continues to provide her with minimal financial support, is judged to have done his duty: 'Such is the respect paid to the master-key of property! A woman, on the contrary, resigning what is termed her natural protector (though he never was so, but in name) is despised and shunned, for asserting the independence of mind distinctive of a rational being, and spurning at slavery.'[91]

Maria is an heiress whose wealth, far from advantageous to her, merely encourages male avarice. Her husband ruthlessly enforces his rights: extorting large sums, gambling away her assets, hunting her down when she flees him, seizing his child, and, when she continues to defy him, incarcerating her. The narrative is breathlessly melodramatic, but the ordeals it describes, while extreme, were in fact experienced by many women at the time. Over the course of the eighteenth century, for reasons beyond the scope of this study, the economic status of married women, particularly middle-class women, had significantly deteriorated, leaving them more vulnerable to men than in previous centuries. According to Amy Erickson's authoritative research, female dependence on men had increased over the period to the point where the wife/slave equation, while clearly exaggerated, was by no means absurd.[92] We have seen how several of Wollstonecraft's friends suffered at the hands of financially irresponsible or exploitative husbands who, like Imlay, then found themselves raked with fire in the women's writings. 'The laws are made by man; and self-preservation is, *by them*, deemed the primary law of nature,' Mary Robinson wrote from bitter experience, 'Hence, woman is destined . . . to depend for support upon a being who is perpetually authorised to deceive her.'[93]

Maria is a work dedicated to exploring how sexual injustice variously afflicts women from different classes. Thus, having depicted the marital enslavement of a rich woman, Wollstonecraft goes on to examine the lot of women of humbler station. In contrast to the rosy picture of plebeian marriage drawn in the *Rights of Woman*, the novel draws mini-portraits of a number of lower-class women – including a sailor's wife, a small shopkeeper, and a lodginghouse landlady – whose conjugal victimisation or widowhood plunge them all into desperate poverty. '[H]e signed an execution on my very goods, bought with the money I worked so hard to get,' the landlady tells Maria, 'and they came and took my bed from under me, before I heard a word of the matter.'[94] Women 'must be submissive', this woman (one of the 'true Russian breed of wives') insists:

Indeed what could most women do? Who had they to maintain them, but their husbands? Every woman, and especially a lady, could not go through rough and smooth, as she had done, to earn a little bread.[95]

Such is the reality of male protectorship; yet even knowing this, Wollstonecraft shows, women are loathe to give up on male support, particularly when they have dependent children. Even Maria, whose history should surely teach her otherwise, looks to Darnford for the protection her husband has so singularly failed to provide. When Venables has Darnford charged with adultery, Maria defends him: 'Mr Darnford found me a forlorn and oppressed woman, and promised the protection women in the present state of society want.'[96] Nearly all the outline conclusions of the novel, however, indicate Darnford's failure to live up to his promise. Why is Maria so credulous? The answer lies partly in her romantic view of her lover, but also in the terrible vulnerability of mothers who, left to the mercies of men like Venables, are legally impotent, unable to '*lawfully* snatch from the gripe [sic] of the gambling spendthift, or beastly drunkard' the money needed for their babes.[97] Several of the women Maria encounters in her adventures describe to her their agony over the impoverishment of their children: deprivation which they are helpless to prevent. 'I exclaim,' Maria tells the trial judge, 'against the laws which...force women, when they claim protectorship as mothers, to sign a contract, which renders them dependent on the caprice of the tyrant...appointed to reign over them.'[98] How can a mother defend the interests of her children, when she has no legal right to defend her own?

Wollstonecraft's reflections on motherhood were not particularly original. On parenting in general her views were liberal, emphasising a light disciplinary hand and the need for mutual respect between parents and children.[99] On mothering in particular, however, her prescriptions were for the most part typical of eighteenth-century advice literature, except that her criticisms of prevailing maternal practices tended to be harsher than most. 'Woman...a slave in every situation to prejudice, seldom exerts enlightened maternal affection; for she either neglects her children, or spoils them by improper indulgence.'[100] The problem is particularly acute when it comes to female children who, as her children's stories demonstrated, needed rational upbringings to prevent them from becoming frivolous and silly. A feminist stance, of sorts; but where Wollstonecraft's feminism really came to life around mothering was not on childrearing issues but with the question of rights: a mother's rights over her children, and the juridical and political rights women need to meet their maternal obligations. 'Considering the care and anxiety a woman must have about a child before it comes into the world, it seems to me, by a *natural right*, to belong to her,' Wollstonecraft wrote to Imlay during her pregnancy:

When men get immersed in the world, they seem to lose all sensations, excepting those necessary to continue or produce life! – Are these the privileges of reason? Amongst the feathered race, whilst the hen keeps the young warm, her mate stays by to cheer her; but it is sufficient for a man to condescend to get a child, in order to claim it. – A man is a tyrant![101]

The point is serious, but the tone is light. Eighteen months later, however, she is describing Fanny as her 'poor lamb' and demanding of Imlay 'how can I expect that she will be shielded, when my naked bosom has had to brave continually the pitiless storm?'[102] Six months more and she is writing searingly, in reponse to some self-exculpatory remarks from Imlay about the moral superiority of an unconstrained sexuality, that with such views '[y]ou would render mothers unnatural – and there would be no such things as a father!' If this 'theory of morals is the most "exalted"', she told him, it was also 'certainly the most easy –...to please ourselves for the moment, let others suffer what they will!'[103]

'Meek wives are, in general, foolish mothers.'[104] Conversely, good mothers, uncompromising in their dedication to their children's wellbeing, are unlikely to make servile wives. '[W]hatever tends to incapacitate the maternal character, takes women out of their sphere', Wollstonecraft writes, which sounds conventional enough until she lists all the disabilities – poor education, lack of rights, economic dependence – that must be eliminated to ensure effective mothering.[105] And by the time a woman is sufficiently enlightened and independent to play her maternal role properly she has also, it seems, become a feminist:

The being who can think justly in one track, will soon extend its intellectual empire; and she who has sufficient judgement to manage her children, will not submit, right or wrong, to her husband, or patiently to the social laws which make a nonentity of a wife.[106]

A good wife/mother will not tolerate social injustice. She is, in other words, civic-spirited in the jacobin sense, that is, infused with egalitarian ideals and determined to 'regulate her conduct...by her own sense of right'.[107] Fettered by laws she has 'had no voice in framing', she is 'privileged to act above [their] dictates', particularly when they violate the higher laws of personal conscience.[108] Maria is no adulterer, she tells the judge at Darnford's trial, because having repudiated Venables she is no longer, 'in the eyes of heaven', his wife. If British law will not permit abused women to divorce their husbands, women must self-divorce. 'I wish my country to approve of my conduct,' she goes on,

but, if laws exist, made by the strong to oppress the weak, I appeal to my own sense of justice, and declare that I will not live with the individual, who has violated every moral obligation which binds man to man.[109]

Pushed beyond moral endurance, Maria revolts. Out of self-respect and for the sake of her infant daughter, she must 'break through all restraint',[110] even if it means becoming a social outlaw like her wardress and ally, the proletarian Jemima. To a modern reader the boldness of her stance is somewhat obviated by her reliance on the fickle Darnford, but to late eighteenth-century readers her resolution must have seemed breathtakingly audacious. Nor should we underestimate its subversive significance even now. 'French principles' is how the judge at Darnford's trial describes Maria's democratic-feminist sentiments, and by pushing these principles into the arena of conjugal relations Wollstonecraft's final novel made explosively plain what the *Rights of Woman* had only partially intimated: that women's entitlements – as citizens, mothers, and sexual beings – are incompatible with a patriarchal marriage system. 'How had I panted for liberty...!' Maria recalls of her marital years, such that the 'sarcasms of society, and the condemnation of a mistaken world' became as 'nothing to her, compared with acting contrary to those feelings which were the foundation of her principles'.[111]

For over a century political theorists had worked hard to keep these ideas at bay. From the moment the rights-bearing citizen strode onto the political stage, progressive thinkers had striven to contain her subversive impact on women's familial status. Maria's husband, Wollstonecraft tells us, 'pretended to be an advocate for liberty' while keeping his wife brutally subjugated.[112] The Venables' conjugal home is a mini old-regime autocracy. '[E]very family,' the *Rights of Woman* noted, 'might also be called a state' and, like most states, governed by 'arts that disgrace the character of man'.[113] But now that absolute monarchy was an acknowledged evil, what possible right of rule could any domestic despot claim?[114] Seen in the clear light of revolutionary reason, all masculine power over women revealed itself as a tawdry imposition, a 'brazen' tyranny as fraudulent as any other archaic despotism. 'Consider,' Wollstonecraft orders Talleyrand, 'whether, when men contend for their freedom...it be not inconsistent and unjust to subjugate women...? Who made man the exclusive judge, if woman partake with him the gift of reason?'[115]

This was not how the leaders of 1790s radicalism, either in France or in Britain, wished to have *egalité* and *liberté* interpreted – but the pressure was certainly there. Finding a language in which to voice those claims was, however, very difficult. The anti-feminine vocabulary of popular radicalism was an obstacle, but so too were the realities of women's lives. A necessary first move – acknowledging the existence of female needs and aspirations separate from those of husbands and children – was rendered especially problematic by the barriers erected against extra-familial roles for women. What was a woman, if she was not a wife/mother? The position of single women was often so bleak that it hardly seemed an attractive alternative. Yet when Wollstonecraft came to write her most militantly feminist text, *Maria*, it was two single women – one separated from her husband; the other outside the pale of sexual respectability – who were made to carry the political message. Maria and Jemima, but particularly Jemima, are maverick figures, 'outlaws' as the book labels them, whose feminist ideals arise at the extremes of female experience. Like all protagonists of jacobin novels, the two women are polemical constructs, designed, as Wollstonecraft wrote, to 'exhibi[t] the misery and oppression, peculiar to women, that arise out of the partial laws and customs of society'.[116] Joint victims of masculine cruelty, Maria and Jemima demonstrate the communality of feminine suffering.

As products of divergent class backgrounds, however, they also serve to illustrate the heterogeneity of female subjection. Wealthy Maria is a lady; working-class Jemima a 'female', in the gender class terminology of the period. Most eighteenth-century writings on women tended to merge all women into a single sex-based category, undifferentiated by nation, race or class. Wollstonecraft too, as we have seen, was prone to imagining Woman in this way, yet in her final writings this unitary feminine condition began to give way to 'the wrongs of different classes of women' which, while 'equally oppressive', were 'from the difference of education, necessarily various'.[117] The myth of a monolithic womanhood, such a huge stumbling-block to feminist social criticism, finally began to disintegrate under the pressure of divergent female realities.

9

Jemima and the beginnings of modern feminism

Still what should induce me to be the champion for suffering humanity? – Who ever risked any thing for me? – Who ever acknowledged
me to be a fellow-creature?

(Wollstonecraft, *Maria*)[1]

Although she always regarded herself as a rebel, Wollstonecraft never saw
herself as part of a collective female revolt. Far from calling on women to
mobilise for their rights, the *Rights of Woman* denounces women's com-
plicity in their oppression and turns instead to men – who, if they would
but forgo female subservience would, Wollstonecraft assures them, acquire
better wives and wiser mothers, 'in a word, better citizens'.[2] The fictive
Maria is certainly a feminist dissident, but hers is very much an individual
struggle. Like her author, Maria doesn't think much of the generality of her
sex, who by 'the evils they are subject to endure' have been 'degrade[d] . . .
so far below their oppressors, as almost to justify their tyranny'.[3] Whether
Wollstonecraft treated other women as contemptuously as she often wrote
about them is hard to judge, but it seems unlikely. She could be hyper-
critical and competitive, and sometimes fiercely envious, but no doubt so
could some of the other women with whom she sustained close relationships, including those – like Mary Hays and Mary Robinson – who shared
her women's rights philosophy.[4] Yet the idea of a feminist alliance among
women seems never to have occurred to her, or to any other British woman
radical of the period.

However, the last year of Wollstonecraft's life found her exploring the
'wrongs of women' from new directions. How do class differences inflect
the female experience? What impact do man-made laws and customs have
on women from varying backgrounds? *Maria*, where Wollstonecraft begins
to probe these questions, is in some respects a premonitory text. As the novel
takes its eponymous heroine through her agonising ordeals, an increasingly
audible note of female solidarity sounds between Maria and the women

she encounters, including her husband's deserted mistress; a fellow asylum inmate whom Maria – grieving for her stolen baby daughter – hears wailing with post-partum depression;[5] and, most importantly, the asylum wardress, Jemima, whose life-history is the novel's secondary narrative. Jemima, who enters Maria's life as part of the machinery of her subjugation, over the course of the story becomes her ally, her co-conspirator and finally, as Darnford begins to show his true colours, her best friend and protector. ' "Save me!" ' Maria cries, throwing herself into Jemima's arms as the two women flee the asylum, with Venables, Darnford and a diabolic madman dogging their footsteps.

As a representative of working-class womanhood, Jemima is a highly ambiguous figure. At no stage does the novel present her as Maria's equal, or endow her with any of Maria's romantic self-pride. Even when the two women, thanks to the wardress' courageous efforts, are living together in London, Jemima voluntarily retains a service role, insisting – quite properly, Wollstonecraft implies – 'on being considered as [Maria's] housekeeper, and to receive the customary stipend. On no other other terms would she remain with her friend'.[6] This unassuming attitude is in contrast to other working-class women in the novel, such as Maria's father's mistress, an 'artful kind of upper servant' who having installed herself as 'the vulgar despot' of his home 'could never forgive the contempt' with which Maria greets her efforts to appear well bred.[7] Yet it is the lower-class women Maria meets who, having suffered much themselves, empathise most powerfully with her afflictions. 'I know so well,' one sighs, after the two women have swapped tales of their legal victimisation at the hands of men, 'that women always have the worst of it, when law is to decide.'[8]

Women united; women divided: Wollstonecraft, who seems to have had no model for feminine fellowship except the gossipy world of fashionable ladies decried in the *Rights of Woman*, evokes these female affinities and disaffinities without any clear sense of their political import. Uneasy with 'distinctions' of any kind, she still displays plenty of conventional prejudices. Reflecting on Venables's depravity, Maria compares him to the urban poor, those 'squalid inhabitants of . . . the lanes and back streets of the metropolis' whom she is 'mortified . . . to consider . . . as my fellow creatures, as if an ape had claimed kindred with me'.[9] The 'ape' is Venables, who has just urged her to regard theirs as an open marriage in the elite mode, but also the bestial lower orders, in an unhappy echo of Burke's swinish multitude. The disgust at transgressed boundaries – animal/human; respectable/squalid; well-bred/low-bred – is irrepressible; yet, with Jemima, Wollstonecraft presses hard at these divisions, determined to test them further. 'I was the filching cat, the ravenous dog, the dumb brute,' Jemima says of herself, 'I had not even the chance of being considered as a fellow-creature...'[10]

References to slavery, including one to colonial slavery, also appear in the novel, as they did throughout Wollstonecraft's writings. Describing women as slaves, I noted earlier, was an ancient trope, rooted in the classical citizen/slave antinomy. Comparing a brutal husband to a West Indian slaveowner, however, as *Maria* does, carried new ideological baggage.[11] At a time when abolitionist opinion was rapidly gathering strength, the appeal to anti-slavery sentiments was a significant polemical move. Although not an active abolitionist, Wollstonecraft, like all radicals, lent the cause her firm support, writing with unforced indignation about the sufferings of entrapped Africans and favourably reviewing the autobiography of the ex-slave, Equiano, whose intellectual powers were on par, she judged, with the average European of 'subordinate station'.[12] The unselfconscious racism – common in abolitionist circles – is obnoxious. Yet it did not prevent her from siding with those arguing, in monogeneticist mode, for the existence of a single human race of 'like passions' and 'similarity of minds'; or from defending the natural humanity of the American Indians against imputations of bloodthirsty savagery[13]; or from suggesting, in an account of the Hottentots, that it was the planters who exploited these 'well meaning, affectionate' people who were the real savages, rather than the African natives themselves. 'Indeed, every account on record of the conduct of the invaders of newly discovered countries proves, how unfit half civilized men are to be entrusted with unlimited power. They apparently consider the inhabitants as making a part of the brute creation...'[14]

Nowhere, however, did Wollstonecraft tie this nascent critique of racial oppression to her analysis of sexual inequality, nor do black female slaves appear as a separate category in any of her writings. The absence is unsurprising. Yet in *Maria*, the repeated use of the woman/slave analogy, combined with representations of women from disparate class backgrounds, has a striking cumulative effect. Gradually a host of wronged, disfranchised women – some visible, some still in shadow – gather around Maria, encircling this well-to-do woman with a prefigurative outline of feminist constituencies to come: a fractured, diverse sorority whose half-glimpsed presence transforms the novel from a clumsily written gothic romance into what Wollstonecraft described in her preface as a 'history of woman' in general, the story of Everywoman as she is, has been, can become. The vision is embryonic yet prophetic, offering a preview of the tensions and divisions – as well as the solidarities – that would typify later feminist movements. In particular, Maria's relationship with Jemima displays something of the class fissures and prejudices that have marked organised feminist politics from their inception. Not an ideal image, then, but one that in its biases and inequalities as well as in its courageous complicities presages much about the future that Wollstonecraft helped to inaugurate.

* * *

Jemima is Wollstonecraft's angriest literary creation: a scream of feminist rage directed at cruel men, self-deluding women, hypocritical social reformers, and – above all – conventional ideals of feminine propriety, that 'false morality... which makes all the virtue of woman consist in chastity, submission, and the forgiveness of injuries'.[15] The illegitimate child of a servant-girl, Jemima has been a thief, a beggar, a whore. With an 'understanding above the common standard', she is tough, self-possessed, and almost wholly impenitent, seeing herself not as a criminal but as 'a slave, a bastard, a common property' who has been 'dragged through the very kennels of society'.[16] Preying 'on the society by which she had been oppressed' she has acquired a 'selfish independence' that she cherishes, knowing it to be her only bulwark against complete calamity.[17] She is, as she says, a 'social outcast', a pariah whose disreputable presence, like that of all pariahs, highlights unacknowledged features of the reputable norm. Jemima's afflictions are the wrongs of woman writ large. As one of the '*out-laws* of the world',[18] her condition serves to reveal the brutal sanctions underpinning patriarchal law in general, just as her alienated mentality is used by Wollstonecraft to convey a repudiatory rage – an absolute refusal of feminine servility – with which any wronged woman could identify, but no conventionally genteel heroine, like Maria, ever convincingly expresses.

Maria recognises her affinity with this victimised renegade. As Jemima tells her story, Maria is not repelled but filled with 'melancholy reflections' on the general condition of her sex:

Thinking of Jemima's peculiar fate and her own, she was led to consider the oppressed state of woman, and to lament that she had given birth to a daughter. Sleep fled from her eyelids, while she dwelt on the wretchedness of unprotected infancy, till sympathy with Jemima turned to agony, when it seemed probable that her own babe might even now be in the very state she so forcibly described.[19]

Like Jemima, whose abandoned mother died shortly after her birth, Maria's infant daughter has been made motherless by a father's brutality. Tracing her road to ruin, Jemima tells Maria it was this lack of maternal care that was the key factor. 'I had no one to love me... I was an egg dropped on the sand; a pauper by nature, hunted from family to family, who belonged to nobody – and nobody cared for me.'[20] The vulnerability had its predictable result. Working in an east London slop-shop, she was raped and impregnated by its owner. Thrown out by his wife, she had terminated her pregnancy and then become a prostitute, first on the streets and then in a brothel. The story, as Vivien Jones has pointed out, was in many ways typical of the sentimental prostitution narratives purveyed by late eighteenth-century humanitarian reformers.[21] Like the magdalens of the reform imagination, Jemima has been more sinned against than sinning; like them too, her redemption has been effected through contact with sympathetic social superiors. But whereas standard reform narratives maintained a sharp boundary between the pitiable whore and women of virtue, in Wollstonecraft's novel no such line is drawn. For like Jemima, Maria too has been married, defiled, and bartered for money. In a man's world, all women are prostituted.

The same message had already been conveyed in less vivid form in the *Rights of Woman*, where Wollstonecraft, having evoked the humanitarian image of the prostitute ('innocent girls... *ruined* before they know the difference between virtue and vice'[22]), went on to insist that male licentiousness debauches *all* women, including those technically chaste women who, while condemning the sexual depravity of the prostitute, 'assume, in some degree, the same character themselves'.[23] A respectable woman who 'studiously adorns her person only to be seen by men', and who looks to a man for financial support while considering her body 'as the proper return for his exertions', has 'a taint of the same folly' as the outcast women she proscribes, Wollstonecraft claims.[24] As usual in the *Rights of Woman*, the argument is directed as much against women as the men they entice. A few such seductresses appear in *Maria* too, but overall women there are no longer seen as sexually culpable in the way that they are in the *Rights of Woman*. Nor, however, are they angelicised in the fashion of most sentimental fallen-women narratives. Jemima is neither devil nor saint. Composed from a complex mix of class and gender imagery, she is sufficiently nuanced and idiosyncratic to stand well outside the conventional idealisation/denigration antinomy.

Working-class women featured throughout Wollstonecraft's writings, but in guises that altered significantly over the years. Her earliest writings presented them mostly as servants (to be handled firmly, but not unkindly) or as objects of middle-class philanthropy; occasionally as paragons of humble industriousness.[25] It is in this last character that they appear in the *Rights of Woman*, where the 'good sense which I have met with, among... poor women' is held up by Wollstonecraft as a counter-example to the follies of idle ladies.

Many poor women maintain their children by the sweat of their brow, and keep together families that the vices of the fathers would have scattered abroad; but gentlewomen are too indolent to be actively virtuous...[26]

Hard work always earned Wollstonecraft's highest kudos. In the next breath, however, the poor are described as morally corrupted by their indigence: the standpoint from which the Versailles marchers are condemned. Both viewpoints, positive and negative, reappear in *Maria*, but complicated by Jemima's lively presence. Thus while listening to Jemima's story, Maria and Darnford discuss with her the impact of poverty on emotional life and intellectual habits. The conclusions reached – the poor are pig-ignorant, unreflecting, emotionally impoverished – would seem belied by Jemima's own intellectually vigorous, passionate character, until we learn that she has been mentally uplifted by her time as mistress to a Hampstead intellectual, and that her responsive manner is largely due to Maria's beneficent influence. Native wit and warmth would not in themselves suffice, Wollstonecraft implies, given the debilitating ordeals Jemima has suffered. The argument is clearly intended as radical critique (only a grossly unjust world would maltreat the poor in this fashion), but comes across instead as bourgeois condescension. 'You merit a better fate,' Maria tells Jemima, 'and I will procure it for you'.[27] But in fact it is Jemima who engineers Maria's escape from the asylum, installs them both in a new life, and, in one draft conclusion, even finds Maria's daughter for her – all while Maria continues to look to the wayward Darnford for love and succour.

However, it is not just Jemima who has been deformed by adverse circumstances. Maria too has been subjectively misshaped by female oppression, although less and differently. An over-romantic imagination, as we have seen, is Maria's typically feminine defect, imprisoning her in idealising delusions. Against this overheated fancifulness Wollstonecraft sets Maria's maternal feelings, here represented (for the first and only time in Wollstonecraft's writings) as the mark of an authentic, uncorrupted femininity. Maria, who possesses a 'mother's tenderness, a mother's self-denial', would, she tells her lost baby (in a letter offering a feminist variation on the 'scandalous memoir' genre) do literally anything for her:

The tenderness of a father . . . might be great; but could it equal that of a mother – of a mother, labouring under a portion of the misery, which the constitution of society seems to have entailed on all her kind? It is, my child, my dearest daughter, only such a mother, who will . . . voluntarily brave censure herself, to ward off sorrow from your bosom.[28]

Gripped by this maternal ardour, Maria begs Jemima to help her, and it is when Jemima hears how Maria's child 'only four months old, had been torn from her' that a bond of female solidarity begins to form: 'the woman awoke in a bosom long estranged from feminine emotions, and Jemima determined to alleviate . . . the sufferings of a wretched mother . . .'[29] Her womanliness thus aroused, Jemima extends her hand to the frantic prisoner before her. 'In the name of God,' Maria pleads, 'assist me to snatch her from destruction! . . . and I will teach her to consider you as her second mother'.[30] Maria and her child are now both in Jemima's power, relying on her to save them, while Jemima, for her part, looks to Maria to keep her promise and assist her to a better future: 'on you it depends to reconcile me with the human race'.[31] A partnership has been created which, if not equal, is certainly reciprocal, rooted in mutual sympathy and congruent interests. Sisters in suffering, Jemima and Maria form a strategic pact which, unlike Maria's relationship with Darnford, is both effective and heroic, yet remains strongly marked by the two women's divergent class positions and expectations. Together yet apart, the women escape their prison for an uncertain future. Hardly a utopian vision then, but a prescient one: a century further on, and it was alliances like these – fragile, bias-ridden, courageous – that were to become the driving force of a mass feminist politics.

* * *

Sketching out the woman-to-woman compact between Maria and Jemima, Wollstonecraft made no real attempt to connect it to the wider world of radical politics. The years when she was writing *Maria* were gloomy ones for reformers, which may partly account for this. But the novel suggests other reasons as well. Venables, we may recall, spouts about liberty and freedom while mercilessly exploiting his wife. Jemima's Hampstead lover (a Rousseauist libertine) surrounds himself with progressive-minded literary friends. When he dies, leaving her destitute, Jemima writes to one of these friends – 'an advocate for unequivocal sincerity . . . [who] had often, in my presence, descanted on the evils which arise in society from the despotism of rank and riches' – asking for advice. He replies with a sanctimonious note urging her to 'look into herself, and exert her powers'. Misery, he assures her, is a consequence of indolence; anyone with Jemima's energy 'could never be in want of resources'. This may be true of men, Jemima reflects bitterly, but 'with respect to women, I am sure of its fallacy . . . A man with half my industry, and, I may say, abilities, could have procured a decent livelihood . . . whilst I . . . was cast aside as the filth of society.'[32] A woman, whatever her class, is differently positioned from a man, and it is precisely this difference that most reformers preferred to overlook. Championing universal justice, radical men, with some honourable exceptions, disregarded or denied the specific injustices women endured, and so, like the French revolutionists, kept them 'from participation in the natural rights of mankind'.[33] The radicalism of the 1790s may have been bold in its imaginings and brave in its battle with Old Corruption, but when it came to righting women's wrongs it hadn't even begun to do the job.

Epilogue: The fantasy of Mary Wollstonecraft

Take someone like Mary Wollstonecraft – if there ever was anyone else like Mary Wollstonecraft...

(Ellen Moers, *Literary Women*)[1]

Those who are bold enough to advance before the age they live in, and to throw off, by the force of their own minds, the prejudices which the maturing reason of the world will in time disavow, must learn to brave censure. We ought not to be too anxious respecting the opinion of others. – I am not fond of vindications. – Those who know me will suppose that I acted from principle. – Nay, as we in general give others credit for worth, in proportion as we possess it – I am easy with regard to the opinions of the best part of mankind – I *rest* on my own.

(Mary Wollstonecraft, letter to Mary Hays, 1797)[2]

Wollstonecraft was writing *Maria* when she died. She had worked very hard on the book, drafting and redrafting, asking Godwin and her friend George Dyson to comment on preliminary versions and then defending her formulations against their criticisms. She was afraid the story would be read biographically, as 'the strong delineations of a wounded heart'.[3] It was, but not in her lifetime. Published posthumously by Godwin with his 1798 *Memoirs*, in which the Fuseli and Imlay *affaires* were recounted in unblushing detail, the novel was inevitably seen as an exercise in sexual self-exoneration – a 'direct vindication of adultery' as Hannah More characteristically put it.[4] Sympathisers were taken aback; political enemies gloated.[5] In an atmosphere sour with political reaction, Wollstonecraft came to personify that Burkean nightmare of radical licence which, if enacted, 'must overturn the basis of every civilised state'.[6] Her piety and moral stringency (which were to surprise George Eliot a half-century later) were ignored in favour of a caricature of godless female lubricity.[7] 'A woman who has broken through all religious restraints,' Richard Polwhele sneered, in his anti-Wollstonecraft squib the 'Unsex'd Females', 'will commonly be found ripe for every species of licentious indecorum'.[8] Even public voices

previously raised in defence of her ideas now felt obliged to declare themselves 'shocked, and even disgusted' by her sexual behaviour.[9] By the end
of the century the chorus of condemnation was so loud that it reverber-
ated through her intellectual reputation as well as her personal character,
transforming her radical-feminist philosophy into libertine propaganda – a
'scripture... for propagating w—s', in the squalid prose of the *Anti-Jacobin
Review*.[10]

For other women writers, the message from these calumnies was unmis-
takeable. Conservative women, untroubled by the underlying misogyny
of the abuse, simply joined in, declaring themselves 'relieved to report'
that 'the champions of female equality, who were as inimical to the happiness and interest of the sex, as those who preached up the doctrine of
liberty and equality to the men, are no longer regarded as sincere and
politic friends...'[11] But for radical *literatae*, the position was more delicate
and troubling. 'I should... think it no discredit to be called one of Mrs
Wollstonecraft's female philosophers,' Mary Hays had one of her fictive
heroines declare in 1796, but by 1803 Hays had been so intimidated by
the fate of her erstwhile mentor that she silently excluded her from her
five-volume *Female Biography*.[12] Charlotte Smith and Mary Robinson continued to defend Wollstonecraft in print, but other former friends stayed
silent or, in one case at least, launched critical fusillades of their own.[13]
In 1804 Amelia Opie published *Adeline Mowbray*, a novel satirising the
Wollstonecraft/Godwin marriage as an absurd philosophical experiment.
Adeline, the daughter of a *soi-disant* learned lady, falls in love with a radical
theorist named Glenmurray who has previously won notoriety by publicly
denouncing marriage. To Glenmurray's dismay, Adeline takes his ideas so
seriously that she refuses his offer of marriage, insisting instead that they
form a free union. The result, when she becomes pregnant, is misery, humiliation, and finally death – an appropriate outcome, Opie implies, for
female moral delinquency. Four years earlier she had spelled the principle
out with stark brutality: a 'woman who has once transgressed the salutary
laws of chastity', she explained in her novel *Father and Daughter*, must suffer
penalties of 'unrelenting vigour', including social ostracism, since nothing
short of this will encourage her to acquire the 'virtues of self-denial, patience, fortitude and industry'.[14] Hard to imagine that this pitiless voice
belonged to the woman to whom Wollstonecraft had turned when other
female friends, shocked to discover that she had not been married to Imlay,
had snubbed her.[15]

In the decade following Wollstonecraft's death, other women writers,
including Maria Edgeworth and Elizabeth Hamilton, produced novels of

ostensibly anti-Wollstonecraftian intent, featuring feminist characters with battle-axe manners and extremist views.[16] The message of these works, however, was more ambiguous than appeared on the surface, since their storylines implicitly promoted many of Wollstonecraft's ideas while holding explicit rights-of-women advocacy up to ridicule. Fear of their own reputations being tarnished by charges of jacobin excess was presumably the motive here: an anxiety which, according to Flora Tristan, was still alive and well among 'so-called "progressive" women' some decades later. Visiting in London in 1842, Tristan was appalled by the dismayed reaction she got from women, including some radical women, to the mere mention of Wollstonecraft or her most famous book: 'oh, but that is an *evil* book!' they apparently told her.[17]

Tristan's account, however, paints too bleak a picture. Throughout the first half of the nineteenth century new generations of radical thinkers – leftwing Unitarians, Owenite socialists, equal-rights Chartists – continued to honour Wollstonecraft and her ideas.[18] Owenism, with its schemes for a New Moral World of class and sexual equality, contained the largest number of these admirers, including Robert Owen himself, a disciple of Godwin, who may have met Wollstonecraft not long before her death. '[Mr Owen],' Wollstonecraft's first daughter, Fanny, wrote to her younger sister in 1816, 'told me the other day that he wished our Mother were living, as he had never met before with a person who thought so exactly as he did, or who would have entered so warmly and zealously into his plans'.[19] Between 1820 and 1845 Owenite tracts and newspapers regularly reprinted passages from the *Rights of Woman* with eulogistic commentary. Verses from Shelley's Wollstonecraft-influenced poems, *Queen Mab* and *The Revolt of Islam*, dotted Owenite feminist works. Introducing one of the most important of these works, his 1825 *Appeal of One-Half the Human Race*, the leading socialist William Thompson declared that his aim in writing the book had been to

rais[e] from the dust that neglected banner which [Wollstonecraft's] hand nearly thirty years ago unfolded boldly, in face of the prejudices of thousands of years, and for which a woman's heart bled, and her life was all but the sacrifice...[20]

Thompson, like most Owenites, supported women's enfranchisement, as did some later campaigners for the People's Charter who, seeking to persuade their fellow Chartists to include the female vote among their demands, invoked Wollstonecraft's views in support of their position.[21] Extracts from the *Rights of Woman* were published in some Chartist newspapers.[22]

But if utopian socialists and ultra-democrats often remained keen Wollstonecraftians, within the emergent women's movement itself attitudes were much less enthusiastic. Mid century feminists, busy with practical schemes for female advancement and eager to win respectability for their cause, balked at claiming a free-living revolutionary as their political ancestor. A few, like the pioneering campaigner, Barbara Bodichon (a bohemian woman who at one point contemplated cohabiting with her lover) were admiring.[23] But most were nervously repelled by what the *English Woman's Journal* described as Wollstonecraft's 'wildness'.[24] Some, like the formidable Harriet Martineau, were bluntly hostile. 'I could never reconcile myself to Mary Wollstonecraft's writings, or to whatever I heard of her,' Martineau wrote in 1855:

Women who would improve the condition...of their sex must, I am certain, be not only affectionate and devoted, but rational and dispassionate...But Mary Wollstonecraft was, with all her powers, a poor victim of passion, with no control over her own peace, and no calmness or content except when the needs of her individual nature were satisfied. I felt...in regard to her, just what I feel now in regard to some of the most conspicuous denouncers of the wrongs of women at this day; – that their advocacy of Woman's cause becomes mere detriment, precisely in proportion to their personal reasons for unhappiness, unless they have fortitude enough...to get their own troubles under their feet, and leave them wholly out of the account in stating the state of their sex.[25]

The dilemmas of the female sex, Martineau concluded, could only be addressed politically by those untroubled women who realise that 'women, like men, can obtain, whatever they show themselves fit for' and that whatever a woman can do, 'society will be thankful to see her do, – just as if she were a man'. To Martineau and many of the activists of the Victorian women's movement, Mary Wollstonecraft had lived and spoken too much of the 'wrongs of women'.

In the same year that Martineau censured her, however, George Eliot offered a much friendlier account of Wollstonecraft, describing her as a woman of 'brave bearing', 'strong and truthful nature' and 'a loving... heart' (the last, however, in best Victorian fashion, having taught her 'not to undervalue the smallest offices of domestic care...').[26] A new edition of the *Rights of Woman* had appeared in 1844, without any outcry; four decades later the leftwing feminist Olive Schreiner was commissioned to write an introduction for yet another edition.[27] At about this time the (male) organiser of a progressive London club to which Schreiner belonged proposed that the Club be named after Wollstonecraft – a suggestion, however, vetoed by a majority of the Clubwomen.[28] Attitudes veered back and forth, particularly in the women's suffrage movement which by the end of the 1880s had achieved unprecedented size and strength. In 1891 the suffragist leader, Millicent Garrett Fawcett, was persuaded to write an introduction to the anniversary edition of the *Rights of Woman*. That Fawcett should bestow her *imprimatur* in this way was very important to Wollstonecraft's rehabilitation; the introduction, however, was a clean-up job, playing down what Fawcett described as the sickening irregularities of Wollstonecraft's personal history in favour of a sanitised image of her as a 'womanly woman' dedicated to home values and the stern promotion of Female Duty.[29] Wollstonecraft's 1898 biographer, Emma Rauscenbusch-Clough similarly strove to make her private life palatable to straitlaced readers. 'Not even the severest of [Wollstonecraft's] critics,' Rauscenbusch-Clough piously pointed out, 'has been able to bring forward a charge against her, that she neglected her parents, her brothers and sisters...'[30]

By the early decades of the twentieth century, however, the need for such exculpatory gestures had begun to wane. Seasoned suffrage fighters – increasingly confident of their place in the political sun, and eager to construct a historic genealogy for themselves – seized on Wollstonecraft: the first histories of English feminism, published at the height of the campaign, all opened with panegyrics to her as the movement's trail-blazer, the 'real forerunner of the Suffragettes', as one activist put it.[31] Meanwhile the warmer sexual climate of the times encouraged a new tolerance – sometimes even approbation – of her erotic history. In 1879, in a deliberate attempt to recuperate her moral reputation, the publisher Charles Kegan Paul put out an edition of her correspondence with Imlay, with an accompanying commentary praising her as 'a pure, high-minded and refined woman' who entered into the liaison 'not wantonly or lightly, but with forethought, in order to carry out a moral theory gravely and religiously adopted...'[32] Wollstonecraft's sexual heterodoxy, in other words, had been as principled as her political radicalism, both having been dictated by a refusal of despotic convention. The interpretation – bold at the time – soon found support among some *fin-de-siècle* feminists. To Olive Schreiner, whose own erotic career was very stormy, it was Wollstonecraft's advocacy of a 'mighty sexual change' that had been her most impressive achievement. 'We have had enough women sacrificed to...sentimental prating about purity,' the American feminist Elizabeth Cady Stanton insisted, 'We have crucified the Mary Wollstonecrafts...'[33] Other women emphasised the deeply feminine needs and hopes Wollstonecraft had brought to her lovers: a womanliness, it was implied, inherently radical in its excess, breaking the boundaries of patriarchal sexual convention. The suffragist Elizabeth Wolstenholme

Elmy who, modelling her life on Wollstonecraft's, lived in a free union
with her lover until her fellow suffragists finally persuaded her to marry,
was only one of numerous women who found in Wollstonecraft a suitable
heroine – a prototype New Woman – for feminism's heroic age.

By the time my generation of Women's Liberation activists entered the
ring then, a host of Mary Wollstonecrafts had traversed the feminist imagination, from the wild woman who so unnerved mid-Victorian activists, to
the domestic paragon of Millicent Garrett Fawcett's creation, to the bravely
iconoclastic figure of pre-World War I feminist radicalism. In the late 1880s
Eleanor Marx and Edward Aveling claimed Wollstonecraft for Marxism
(arguing that she had been the first to recognise that 'women's social condition is a question of economics, not of religion or of sentiment. The woman
is to the man as the producing class is to the possessing. Her "inferiority" in
its actuality and in its assumed existence is the outcome of the holding of
economic power by man to her exclusion'[34]), and three decades further on
she took on one of her most unlikely incarnations, as a Freudian theorist, in
Mary Stocks's 1929 introduction to a new edition of the *Rights of Woman*.
In the same year that Stocks's introduction was published, Virginia Woolf,
in what still remains Wollstonecraft's most eloquent testimonial, conjured
up a woman of 'high-handed and hot-blooded' vitality whose dauntless
optimism, while inspirational, was also in some respects touchingly childlike: 'Every day she made theories by which life should be lived; and every
day she came smack against the rock of other people's prejudices.'[35] This
Wollstonecraft, 'no cold-blooded theorist' but a woman 'sensual and...
intelligent, and beautiful into the bargain', was a new sort of heroine, one
in whom characteristics previously regarded as undesirable or irreconcilable in women – political rage, intellectual hubris, emotional vulnerability,
eroticism, maternal devotion – came together in a poignant union of reason and passion. It was an image of dissident Woman in which feminism
itself became a mark of personal integrity: an anti-womanhood that was
womanhood's most authentic expression. Here indeed was a woman, as the
young Ruth Benedict told herself in 1913, peering into the painted eyes of
the John Opie portrait, who had 'saved her soul alive'.[36]

Idealisations like these, supplying such rich materials for a feminist subjectivity, abounded among early twentieth-century feminists. But icons are
never allowed to rest easy. With the new wave of feminist militancy that
swept Britain and America in the late 1960s, yet another Wollstonecraft
rolled into view – one far less inspirational than many of her predecessors.
In a sharp reversal of Victorian attitudes, the most culpable feature of this
Wollstonecraft was not her erotic history, but her middle-class respectability.

She was, a host of critics complained, too bourgeois in her social attitudes, too narrowly reformist in her politics, too prim (and hypocritical?) in her sexual prescriptions, too wedded to domestic values and 'angel in the house' morality. To a generation of young women in revolt against the rigidities of 1950s sexual culture, she seemed in fact – rhetorically at least – hardly a feminist at all, more like a grundyish schoolmistress, full of priggish injunctions and dusty pieties.

This image, most common in the heady early phase of Women's Liberation, was soon competing with others. Between the late 1970s and the two-hundredth anniversary of the publication of the *Rights of Woman*, international feminist scholarship exploded – and Wollstonecraft's importance with it. Books and articles on her life and works poured out at such a rate that a computer search in the early 1990s produced a printout so long that I could hardly carry it. Sitting in some of the dozens of commemorative seminars and conferences held in 1992, I listened to papers criticising her class and racial prejudices,[37] her implication in bourgeois Enlightenment ideology, her repressive views on sex and romance; but also others praising her educational theories, her aesthetic sensibilities, her prophetic views on commercial society, even her immersion in a semiotic *chora* (*pace* the school of *écriture feminine*[38]). Above all, I encountered her as the canon-busting Woman Writer, the textual subversive who by the 1990s had become the subject of innumerable university courses with titles like 'Women and Literature' and 'Romanticism and Gender'. This was a Mary Wollstonecraft who, more ink-stained and consciously literary than in the past, was well adapted to scholarly feminist endeavour, but still with plenty of political energy left to stir up passions and controversies among new generations of readers.

* * *

Let people but watch their own hearts, and act rightly, as far as they can judge, and they may patiently wait till the opinion of the world comes round.[39]

What would Mary Wollstonecraft think of the woman she has become? Esteemed by fellow progressives in her lifetime, Wollstonecraft was nonetheless never keen on heroines. Why celebrate those few women who, 'emancipat[ing] themselves from the galling yoke of sovereign man', had managed to 'boldly claim respect on account of their great abilities or daring virtues', when the vast majority of the sex were still so disabled by oppression that even ordinarily right-minded behaviour was beyond them? 'I wish to see women neither heroines nor brutes; but reasonable creatures...'[40]

Nor did Wollstonecraft regard herself as particularly heroic. But she liked to be well thought of, and took criticism badly. Even more, she wanted her ideas to have consequences, to 'increase the sum of human happiness': ambitions that her experience of French politics had taught her were mostly a matter of good timing. Freedom's victory was inevitable, but could not be forced. The times must be ready for change.

Wollstonecraft died before her ideals felt the full blast of counter-revolution, and many decades before the rise of a British feminist movement. But in the summer of 1796, shortly after becoming Godwin's lover, she wrote him a short fable about a sycamore tree that, yearning for spring-time, burst into leaf on a fine February day. 'The morrow a hoar frost covered the trees and shrivelled up [the] unfolding leaves', so that the poor sycamore 'drooped, abashed' while a neighbour tree teased her, telling her that she must learn to distinguish winter from spring. 'Whether the buds recovered, and expanded, when the spring actually arrived – The Fable sayeth not –'[41] The sentimental tale was clearly meant to evoke her re-covery from Imlay and her wary hopes for her personal future, but it can also be read as a political fable: a metaphor for aspirations unmet, awaiting more auspicious conditions. (Tom Paine concluded his *Rights of Man* with an almost identical story.[42])

Women's lot in western society has changed a great deal since Woll-stonecraft's day, yet 'sexual distinctions' still play as large – and, arguably, as invidious – a role in our lives as in hers. It would be good to be able to bury Mary Wollstonecraft at last; to consign her and her ideas to his-tory. But history itself gives us little opportunity for this. It is not just the feminist academy that keeps Wollstonecraft intellectually alive when many of her contemporaries – some much more influential at the time – have become moribund. Looked at globally, twenty first century women can be seen to still suffer sex-based discrimination and hardship on a scale that makes notions like 'post-feminism' merely fatuous, and it is this reality that continues to breathe life into Wollstonecraft and her work. Constantly re-moulded in feminism's changing image, Wollstonecraft retains one en-during role: to represent women's hopes of a society free from misogyny and sexual injustice. However distant her ideas and imaginings may be from feminist thinking of the present – very distant indeed in some cases, as this book has shown – as a symbol of what remains to be achieved, Mary Wollstonecraft remains as vital and necessary a presence today as she was in the 1790s.

Notes

INTRODUCTION: MARY WOLLSTONECRAFT AND THE
PARADOXES OF FEMINISM

1. Wollstonecraft, *VRW*, *Works*, vol. 5, p. 126.
2. Thomas Beddoes, *Alexander's Expedition* (London, 1792), p. vi. Beddoes, a medical man and scientist with strong feminist views, was a friend of Wollstonecraft's: for his life see Dorothy A. Stansfield, *Thomas Beddoes, MD, 1760–1808* (Dordrecht: D. Reidel Publishing Co., 1984).
3. Jacqueline Rose, *States of Fantasy* (Oxford: Clarendon Press, 1998), p. 15.
4. Wollstonecraft, *VRW*, *Works*, vol. 5, p. 105.
5. Mary Wollstonecraft, letter to Everina Wollstonecraft, 3 March 1787, in Ralph Wardle (ed.), *Collected Letters of Mary Wollstonecraft* (London: Cornell University Press, 1979), p. 139.
6. Mary Wollstonecraft, letter to Joseph Johnson, 14 April 1787, in Wardle (ed.), *Letters*, p. 148.
7. Mary Wollstonecraft, letter to Everina Wollstonecraft, 24 March 1787, in Wardle (ed.), *Letters*, p. 144.
8. Mary Wollstonecraft, letter to the Revd Henry Dyson Gabell, 17 April 1787, in Wardle (ed.), *Letters*, p. 150.
9. *Ibid.*, p. 150.
10. *Ibid.*, p. 149.
11. Wollstonecraft, *Maria*, *Works*, vol. 1, p. 104.
12. Mary Wollstonecraft, letter to Gilbert Imlay, 22 September 1794, in Wardle (ed.), *Letters*, p. 263.
13. Quoted in John Barrell, *Imagining the King's Death: Figurative Treason, Fantasies of Regicide, 1793–96* (Oxford University Press, 2000), p. 23.
14. Edmund Burke, *Reflections on the Revolution in France* (Indianapolis: Hackett, 1987 [1790]), pp. 57, 56.
15. Wollstonecraft, *French Revolution*, *Works*, vol. 6, p. 22.
16. Thomas Hearn, *A Short View of the Rise and Progress of Freedom in Modern Europe* (London, 1793), quoted in Barrell, *Imagining the King's Death*, p. 23.
17. Barbara Taylor, *Eve and the New Jerusalem: Socialism and Feminism in the Nineteenth Century* (London: Virago Press, 1983), pp. 5–6.

18. Most of Wollstonecraft's biographers mention her piety, but none discuss it in any detail. Several recent articles exploring aspects of her theology are cited in chapter 3.

19. E. P. Thompson, 'Solitary Walker' (review of Claire Tomalin, *The Life and Death of Mary Wollstonecraft* (London: Weidenfeld and Nicholson, 1974)), *New Society*, 19 September 1974, p. 749.

20. See, for example, Susan Gubar, 'Feminist Misogyny: Mary Wollstonecraft and the Paradox of "It Takes One to Know One"', *Feminist Studies*, 20:3 (1994); Steven Blakemore, *Intertextual War: Edmund Burke and the French Revolution in the Writings of Mary Wollstonecraft, Thomas Paine and James Mackintosh* (London: Associated University Presses, 1997), pp. 37, 50; Roy Porter, *Enlightenment: Britain and the Creation of the Modern World* (London: Allen Lane, Penguin Press, 2000), p. xxiii.

21. William Godwin, *Memoirs of the Author of a Vindication of the Rights of Woman*, 1798 (Harmondsworth: Penguin, 1987), p. 206.

22. Mary Wollstonecraft, *Maria*, 1798, *Works*, vol. 1, p. 124.

23. *Ibid.*, p. 124.

24. Mary Wollstonecraft, letter to Eliza Bishop, 27 June 1787, in Wardle (ed.), *Collected Letters*, 1979, p. 155.

25. Godwin, *Memoirs*, p. 229.

26. *Ibid.*, p. 210.

27. Mary Wollstonecraft, letter to Gilbert Imlay, 10 October 1795, in Wardle (ed.), *Letters*, p. 316.

28. Ralph Wardle, *Mary Wollstonecraft: a Critical Biography* 1951 (Lincoln: University of Nebraska Press, 1966), p. 307.

29. Estimated sales of English editions of the *Rights of Woman* were 1500 to 3000 in its first five years in print (Janet Todd, *Mary Wollstonecraft: a Revolutionary Life* (London: Weidenfeld and Nicholson, 2000) p. 185). Given its popularity among circulating library members, and the widespread practices of reading aloud and lending of books, its actual audience would have been very much bigger than this. The Philadelphia printer Mathew Carey published a second American edition of 1792 in 1500 copies even after the London and a Boston edition were available (Susan Branson, *'Those Fiery Frenchified Dames': Women and Political Culture in Early National Philadelphia* (Philadelphia: University of Pennsylvania Press, 2001), p. 38).

30. Marilyn Butler and Janet Todd (eds.), *The Works of Mary Wollstonecraft* (London: Pickering and Chatto, 1989), 7 volumes. Surprisingly, however, the excellent 1979 edition of her collected correspondence, edited by Ralph Wardle (Cornell University Press), is no longer in print.

31. Janet M. Todd, *Mary Wollstonecraft: an Annotated Bibliography* (London: Garland Publishing Inc., 1976).

32. See for example, Porter, *Enlightenment*; Dorinda Outram, *The Enlightenment* (Cambridge University Press, 1995), pp. 81–9.

33. Emma Goldman, 'Mary Wollstonecraft' (1911), edited and with an afterword by Alice Wexler, *Feminist Studies*, 7:1, 1981, p. 121. For Eleanor Marx's admiration

for Wollstonecraft, see Edward Aveling and Eleanor Marx Aveling, *Shelley and Socialism*, 1888 (London: Journeyman Press, 1975), p. 13.

34. For a discussion of this, see below, pp. 165–8.

35. Margaret Tims, *Mary Wollstonecraft: a Social Pioneer* (London: Millington, 1976), p. 356.

36. There is even a book with this as its title: Ella Mazel (ed.), *Ahead of Her Time: A Sampler of the Life and Thought of Mary Wollstonecraft* (New York: Brunner/Mazel Trade, 1996).

37. Elaine Showalter, *Inventing Herself: Claiming a Feminist Intellectual Heritage* (London: Picador, 2001), p. 16. Showalter is here quoting approvingly some remarks by Ruth Benedict (see below, p. 19, for Benedict on Wollstonecraft).

38. See *The London Review of Books* (30 November, 14 December 2001; 4 January 2002) for a recent example of this. From Godwin's *Memoirs* onward, new Wollstonecraft biographies have often occasioned angry exchanges; for a particularly heated one, see the venomous attack on Wollstonecraft mounted by Richard Cobb in his review of Claire Tomalin's *The Life and Death of Mary Wollstonecraft* in *The Times Literary Supplement*, which elicited a series of indignant rebuttals, including one from Michael Foot writing from the House of Commons (*TLS*, 6, 13, 20 September 1974). Janet Todd later published a thoughtful rejoinder to Cobb in *Studies in Burke and His Time* (16:3, 1975). For an excellent discussion of recent biographical writing on Wollstonecraft, see Christine Stansell, 'Wild Wishes', *The New Republic*, 17.9.01, pp. 49–54.

39. *The Athenaeum*, 11 July 1885, p. 42.

40. Thompson, 'Solitary Walker', p. 749.

41. The most influential at this time was Mary Poovey's *The Proper Lady and the Woman Writer: Ideology as Style in the Works of Mary Wollstonecraft, Mary Shelley, and Jane Austen* (University of Chicago Press, 1984).

42. Mary Wollstonecraft, letter, probably to Mary Hays, *c.* summer 1797, in Wardle (ed.) *Letters*, p. 413.

43. Wollstonecraft, *French Revolution, Works*, vol. 6, pp. 6–7.

44. Anon [Mrs E Hayley], *Female Rights Vindicated; or the Equality of the Sexes Proved* (1758). Detailed research into this literature is still at a fairly early stage. For a good general discussion of it, see Alice Browne, *The Eighteenth Century Feminist Mind* (Brighton: Harvester Press, 1987); for the most recent research, see Sarah Knott and Barbara Taylor (eds.), *Women and Enlightenment* (London: Palgrave, 2004).

45. *Critical Review*, 4 (1792), p. 390.

46. Wollstonecraft, *VRW*, *Works*, vol. 5, p. 66.

47. This point was illuminated for me by Phyllis Mack's thoughtful discussion of attitudes toward freedom and personal agency among Quaker feminists ('Feminism and the Problem of Agency: Religious Dissenters in Enlightenment England', forthcoming in Knott and Taylor (eds.), *Women and Enlightenment*).

48. Wollstonecraft, *VRW*, *Works*, vol. 5, p. 266.

49. *Ibid.*, p. 76.

50. *Ibid.*, p. 169, 193.
51. *Ibid.*, p. 119.
52. *Ibid.*, p. 125.
53. *Ibid.*, p. 68.
54. *Ibid.*, p. 245.
55. *Ibid.*, p. 131.
56. *Ibid.*, p. 173.
57. *Ibid.*, p. 74.
58. For a discussion of these and other Scottish Enlightenment writings on women, see John Dwyer, *Virtuous Discourse: Sensibility and Community in late Eighteenth century Scotland* (Edinburgh University Press, 1987); Jane Rendall, *The Origins of Modern Feminism* (Basingstoke: Macmillans, 1985), chapter 1; Mary Catherine Moran, 'Between the Savage and the Civil: Dr John Gregory's Natural History of Femininity', forthcoming in Knott and Taylor (eds.), *Women and Enlightenment*.
59. Wollstonecraft, *Rights of Woman*, *Works*, vol. 5, p. 164.
60. See chapter 5 for an extended discussion of this.
61. For these negative images of women in political discourse, see chapter 7.
62. Wollstonecraft, *VRW*, *Works*, vol. 5, p. 73.
63. Catherine Macaulay, *Letters on Education* (1790).
64. Mary Hays, *Appeal to the Men of Great Britain on Behalf of Women* (London, 1798), pp. 82–3.
65. Wollstonecraft, *VRW*, *Works*, vol. 5, p. 75.
66. *Ibid.*, p. 144.
67. For illuminating discussions of these changes, see Harriet Guest, 'The Dream of a Common Language: Hannah More and Mary Wollstonecraft', *Textual Practice*, vol. 9, no. 2 (1995); Elizabeth Kowaleski-Wallace, *Consuming Subjects: Women, Shopping and Business in the Eighteenth Century* (New York: Columbia University Press, 1997); Amanda Vickery, *The Gentleman's Daughter: Women's Lives in Georgian England* (London: Yale University Press, 1998); John Brewer, *The Pleasures of the Imagination: English Culture in the Eighteenth Century* (London: HarperCollins, 1997).
68. [Mary Wollstonecraft], 'Review of *Juliet: or, The Cottager*', *AR*, vol. 5, December 1789, *Works*, vol. 7, p. 92.
69. Wollstonecraft, *VRW*, *Works*, vol. 5, p. 103.
70. *Ibid.*, pp. 145–6.
71. Wollstonecraft, letter to Joseph Johnson, *c.* late 1792, in Wardle (ed.), *Letters*, p. 221.
72. Mary Wollstonecraft, letter to Gilbert Imlay, 28 December 1794, in Wardle (ed.), *Letters*, p. 270.
73. Gubar, 'Feminist Misogyny', p. 460.
74. Wollstonecraft to Gilbert Imlay, 9 January 1795, in Wardle (ed.), *Letters*, p. 274.
75. Wollstonecraft, letter to Joseph Johnson, *c.* late 1792, in Wardle (ed.), *Letters*, p. 221.
76. Todd, *Wollstonecraft*, p. 383; Godwin, *Memoirs*, p. 218.

77. Godwin, *Memoirs*, p. 207.
78. Describing her childhood self to Godwin, Wollstonecraft told him how she had needed punishment from her mother as a way of 'reconciling her to herself' when she felt in the wrong (Godwin, *Memoirs*, p. 206): some indication perhaps of the source of her later self-punitiveness.
79. Wollstonecraft, *Short Residence*, *Works*, vol. 6, p. 325.
80. Rose, *States*, pp. 4–7.
81. Sally Alexander, *Becoming a Woman, and Other Essays in Nineteenth and Twentieth Century Feminist History* (London: Virago, 1994), p. 104.
82. Lorna Sage, 'The Death of the Author', *Granta*, 41 (1992), p. 238.
83. Ruth Benedict, 'Mary Wollstonecraft', in Margaret Mead (ed.) *An Anthropologist at Work: Writings of Ruth Benedict* (Boston: Houghton Mifflin, 1959), p. 519.
84. Quoted in Showalter, *Inventing Herself*, p. 71.
85. Ann Snitow, 'A Gender Diary', in M. Hirsch and E. Fox Keller (eds.), *Conflicts in Feminism* (London: Routledge, 1990), pp. 9, 33.
86. Snitow's article (see above) has a very good discussion of this.
87. Jacqueline Rose, *Sexuality in the Field of Vision* (London: Verso Books, 1986), p. 15.
88. Mary Hays, 'Memoirs of Mary Wollstonecraft', *Annual Necrology* 1797–8 (London, 1800, p. 416).
89. In general, historians are reluctant to employ psychoanalytic concepts, either because they find the concepts unpersuasive or because they think them inapplicable to past states of mind. Yet most historians routinely invoke unconscious motivations as causal factors. Even self-proclaimed opponents of psychoanalysis regularly ascribe unconscious feelings and purposes to the men and women they study. Desire and fantasy are everywhere represented as important historical forces. Without some notion of unconscious mental process, in other words, history becomes unintelligible. One of the main charges levelled against 'psycho-history' – that it is anachronistic, analysing past ideas and behaviours in terms of present-day psychological concepts – seems rather flimsy: why is using modern psychological theories to interpret past mental life any more anachronistic than applying present-day medical knowledge to past epidemics, or using modern categories of economic analysis to interpret pre-modern economic phenomena? Inasmuch as the functioning of the human mind remains constant over time, analysing its mechanisms with concepts like repression, identification, sublimation, seems entirely legitimate. However, another criticism of psychoanalytic-historical interpretations – that they ignore the historicity of mental *contents*, the transformations that beliefs, feelings and fantasies undergo over time (changes that are now receiving much attention from historians) – is more difficult to rebut, and in fact led me to make only limited use of psychoanalytic concepts here. The imagination, to return to this book's leitmotif, may operate in the same way in the twenty-first century as it did in the late eighteenth, but the visions it generates are in many respects radically different. How can we retain a sense of the historicity of psychic life

while at the same time exploring its deeper, continuous features? The question, far from resolved here, seems to me one of the most compelling confronting modern historians.

The majority of academic studies of Wollstonecraft have been by literary scholars, many of whom use psychoanalysis as a tool of textual analysis. Paradoxically, however, a fetishisation of the text in literary studies often makes for a low level of interest in the writer's personal psychology. This is of course not universal, and, as my footnotes make plain, I have learned much from feminist literary theorists. For a good summary discussion of psychoanalytic literary criticism, see Maud Ellman, *Psychoanalytic Literary Criticism*, Introduction (London: Longman, 1994), pp. 1–35.

90. Wollstonecraft, *VRW*, *Works*, vol. 5, p. 104.
91. Wollstonecraft, *Short Residence*, *Works*, vol. 6, p. 289.

I THE FEMALE PHILOSOPHER

1. Mary Wollstonecraft, *VRW*, *Works*, vol. 5, p. 168.
2. Mary Wollstonecraft, letter to William Roscoe, 3 January 1792, in Wardle (ed.), *Letters*, p. 205.
3. The complaint, from Mrs Anne MacVicar Grant, is quoted in Wardle, *Wollstonecraft*, p. 158.
4. Wardle, *Wollstonecraft*, pp. 158–9.
5. Wardle, *Wollstonecraft*, p. 159.
6. *AR*, vol. 12, March 1792, p. 248; Wardle, *Wollstonecraft*, p. 159.
7. Wollstonecraft, *VRW*, 103. The work has also been described as a conduct-book, meaning a contribution to the vast literature offering advice to women on manners and morals. In fact such prescriptive works, as well as those dedicated to educational issues, often came into the category of the philosophical (I am indebted to Mary Catherine Moran for this point: 'Between the Savage and the Civil'.
8. *The Monthly Review*, vol. 8, June, 1792, p. 206; *AR*, appendix to vol. 13, 1792, p. 489.
9. *The Monthly Review*, vol. 8, June 1792, p. 198.
10. Regina M. Janes, 'On the Reception of Mary Wollstonecraft's *A Vindication of the Rights of Woman*', *Journal of the History of Ideas*, 39, 1975.
11. The description is Wollstonecraft's: Mary Wollstonecraft, letter to Joseph Johnson, 1788, in Wardle (ed.), *Letters*, p. 179.
12. [Thomas J. Mathias], *The Pursuits of Literature: a Satirical Poem; in Four Dialogues*, 7th edn (London: 1798), pp. 221–2; xvi.
13. [Richard Polwhele], *The Unsex'd Females: a poem addressed to the author of the Pursuits of Literature* (London, 1798), p. 6.
14. *European Magazine and London Review*, vol. 33, April 1798, p. 246.
15. See below, pp. 247–8.
16. Sophia (A Person of Quality), *Woman Not Inferior to Man*, 1739 (London: Brentham Press, 1975), p. 24.

17. *Ibid.*, p. 43.
18. Quoted in Roy Porter, 'The Enlightenment in England', in R. Porter and M. Teich (eds.), *The Enlightenment in National Context* (Cambridge University Press, 1981), p. 5.
19. For a seminal discussion of Wollstonecraft's place in eighteenth-century English philosophy, to which my account is heavily indebted, see Carol Kay, 'Canon, Ideology and Gender: Mary Wollstonecraft's Critique of Adam Smith', *New Political Science*, 15 (1986).
20. Smith described philosophy as a 'trade' in an early draft of *The Wealth Of Nations*: see John Barrell, *The Birth of Pandora and the Division of Knowledge* (London: Macmillan, 1992), p. 91. Dugald Stewart, *Elements of the Philosophy of the Human Mind*, 1792 (London, 1811), p. 27.
21. For an insightful discussion of these issues, see David Simpson, *Romanticism, Nationalism and the Revolt Against Theory* (University of Chicago Press, 1993), especially chapter 5 which analyses Wollstonecraft's philosophic career in terms of the vicissitudes of eighteenth-century critical reason.
22. Maria Edgeworth, *Letters for Literary Ladies*, 1795 (London: J. M. Dent, 1993), p. 20.
23. *Ibid.*, p. 20; Brita Rang, 'A "learned wave": Women of Letters and Science from the Renaissance to the Enlightenment', in T. Akkerman and S. Stuurman (eds.), *Perspectives on Feminist Political Thought in European History From the Middle Ages to the Present* (London: Routledge, 1998), p. 50.
24. For the prestige enjoyed by mid eighteenth-century Englishwomen of letters, see Norma Clarke, *Dr Johnson's Women* (London: Hambledon, 2000).
25. Quoted in Hilda Smith, *Reason's Disciples: Seventeenth century English Feminists* (London: University of Illinois Press, 1982), p. 206.
26. Samuel Johnson, *The Adventurer*, 115, Dec 1753, *Works* (Yale University Press, 1958), vol. 2, p. 458.
27. Wollstonecraft, letter to Everina Wollstonecraft, 7 November 1787, in Wardle, *Letters*, p. 165.
28. *Ibid.*, p. 164.
29. Margaret Walters, 'The Rights and Wrongs of Women', in J. Mitchell and A. Oakley (eds.), *The Rights and Wrongs of Women* (Harmondsworth: Penguin, 1976), p. 323.
30. *Ibid.*, p. 313.
31. Mary Wollstonecraft, *Thoughts on the Education of Daughters*, 1787, *Works*, vol. 4, p. 5; *Ibid.*, p. 7.
32. *Ibid.*, p. 38.
33. John Knowles, *The Life and Writings of Henry Fuseli* (London, 1831), vol. 1, p. 164. Knowles is meant to be quoting from a letter Wollstonecraft wrote to Fuseli, but since none of these letters has been found (Fuseli claimed he destroyed them), there is no way of checking this.
34. *Ibid.*, vol. 1, p. 164.
35. Mary Wollstonecraft, *Mary, A Fiction* (1788), *Works*, vol. 1, p. 5.
36. *Ibid.*, vol. 1, p. 5.

37. Mary Wollstonecraft, letter to William Godwin, 4 September 1796, in Wardle, *Letters*, p. 345.

38. Wollstonecraft, *Mary, Works*, vol. 1, p. 5. The valuing of creative originality over imitative literary modes was a commonplace of the age: for a classic statement of the position see, E. Young, *Conjectures on Original Composition* (1759); for its importance to writers as a new source of cultural authority see K. Pask, *The Emergence of the English Author* (Cambridge University Press, 1996), pp. 146–61.

39. Wollstonecraft, *VRW*, *Works*, vol. 5, p. 168; Wollstonecraft, *ibid.*, p. 165.

40. Godwin, *Memoirs*, pp. 226–7.

41. Mary Wollstonecraft, *The Female Reader*, 1789, *Works*, vol. 4, p. 56.

42. Godwin, *Memoirs*, p. 226.

43. *The Female Reader* was published under the authorship of 'Mr Cresswick, Teacher of Elocution', but in his *Memoirs* (p. 226) Godwin makes clear that it was written by Wollstonecraft.

44. Mitzi Myers, 'Impeccable Governesses, Rational Dames, and Moral Mothers: Mary Wollstonecraft and the Female Tradition in Georgian Children's Books', *Children's Literature*, 14 (1986); Norma Clarke, 'The Cursed Barbauld Crew: Women Writers and Writing for Children in the late eighteenth Century', in M. Hilton, M. Styles and V. Watson (eds.), *Opening the Nursery Door: Reading, Writing and Childhood, 1600–1900* (London: Routledge, 1997).

45. Wollstonecraft, *Thoughts, Works*, vol. 4, pp. 32–3.

46. See Clarke, 'Cursed Barbauld Crew', for a very good discussion of this.

47. *Ibid.*, pp. 96–7.

48. Mary Wollstonecraft, letter to Joseph Johnson, 1787/8, in Wardle, *Letters*, p. 167.

49. Mary Wollstonecraft, *Fragment of Letters on the Management of Infants* (1798), *Works*, vol. 4, p. 459.

50. Godwin, *Memoirs*, p. 218.

51. Mary Hays, *Appeal to the Men of Great Britain on Behalf of Women* (London, 1798), p. 97.

52. Wollstonecraft, *Mary, Works*, vol. 1, p. 5.

53. *Ibid.*, p. 10.

54. *Ibid.*, p. 10.

55. *Ibid.*, p. 21.

56. *Ibid.*, p. 25.

57. The fictive Ann is a condescending portrait of Wollstonecraft's close friend, Fanny Blood. As the novel progresses, Ann, whom Mary initially idolises, increasingly disappoints her friend, who nonetheless stands by her until her premature death. The emotional letdown was very similar to Wollstonecraft's feelings for Fanny Blood, of which Godwin wrote that 'observation upon her own [Wollstonecraft's] mind and that of her friend, could not pass, without her perceiving that there were some essential characteristics of genius, which she possessed ... in which her friend was deficient' (*Memoirs*, pp. 216–17).

58. Wollstonecraft, *Mary*, *Works*, vol. 1, pp. 28, 33.

59. Mary Wollstonecraft, letter to Everina Wollstonecraft, 22 March 1797, in Wardle (ed.), *Letters*, p. 385. The full sentence runs: 'As for my Mary, I consider it as a crude production, and do not very willingly put in the way of people whose good opinion, as a writer, I wish for; but you may have it to make up the sum of laughter.'

60. Sylvia Harcstack Myers, *The Bluestocking Circle* (Oxford: Clarendon Press, 1990), p. 145.

61. [Mary Wollstonecraft], 'Review of *The Fair Hibernian*', *AR*, vol. 5, December 1789, *Works*, vol. 7, p. 191; [Mary Wollstonecraft, 'Review of *The Child of Woe*', *AR*, vol. 5, December 1789, *Works*, vol. 7, p. 82.

62. [Mary Wollstonecraft], 'Review of *Juliet: or, The Cottager*', *AR*, vol. 5, December 1789, *Works*, vol. 7, p. 92.

63. *Ibid*., p. 92; [Wollstonecraft], 'Review of *The Child of Woe*', *AR*, vol. 5, December 1789, *Works*, vol. 7, p. 82.

64. [Mary Wollstonecraft], 'Review of *Almeria Belmore*', *AR*, vol. 5, December 1789, *Works*, vol. 7, p. 192.

65. [Mary Wollstonecraft], 'Review of *The Fair Hibernian*', *AR*, vol. 5, December 1789, *Works*, vol. 7, p. 191.

66. For this see Clarke, *Dr Johnson's Women*, and Myers, *Bluestocking Circle*.

67. quoted in I. B. O'Malley, *Women in Subjection: a Study of the Lives of English-women before 1832* (London: Duckworth, 1933), p. 209.

68. Johnson, *Adventurer*, 11 December 1753, *Works*, vol. 2, p. 457.

69. Quoted in Ian Watt, *The Rise of the Novel*, 1957 (Harmondsworth: Penguin, 1977), p. 59.

70. James Boswell, *The Life of Samuel Johnson*, 1791 (Oxford University Press, 1989), p. 979.

71. The words are those of the bookseller, James Lackington, quoted in George Barker Benfield, *The Culture of Sensibility: Sex and Society in eighteenth Century Britain* (London: University of Chicago Press, 1992), p. 165.

72. Watt, *Rise of Novel*, p. 47.

73. *Monthly Review*, 1773, quoted in J. M. S. Tompkins, *The Popular Novel in England, 1770–1800* (Lincoln: University of Nebraska Press, 1961), p. 120. For a good summary discussion of the position of the woman writer in eighteenth-century Britain, see Stuart Curran, 'Women Readers, Women Writers', in S. Curran (ed.) *The Cambridge Companion to Romanticism* (Cambridge University Press, 1993).

74. Priscilla Wakefield, *Reflections on the Present Condition of the Female Sex* (London, 1798), chapter 8.

75. Elizabeth Boyd, quoted in Cheryl Turner, *Living By the Pen: Women Writers in the Eighteenth Century* (London: Routledge, 1992), p. 82.

76. For these activities, see Edward Copeland, *Women Writing About Money: Women's Fictions in England, 1790–1820* (Cambridge University Press, 1995).

77. Mary Wollstonecraft, letter to Mary Hays, 12 November 1792; in Wardle (ed.), *Letters*, p. 219.

78. *Ibid.*, p. 220.
79. Wollstonecraft, *Rights of Woman, Works*, vol. 5, p. 65.
80. Turner, *Living By the Pen*, p. 105; Frances Burney, *Evelina*, 1778 (Oxford University Press, 1970), p. 3.
81. Mary Wollstonecraft, letter to Everina Wollstonecraft, 7 November 1787, in Wardle (ed.), *Letters*, p. 164.
82. *Ibid.*, p. 164.
83. Quoted in Gerald P. Tyson, *Joseph Johnson: a Liberal Publisher* (Iowa City: University of Iowa Press, 1979), p. 118.
84. Mary Wollstonecraft, letter to Everina Wollstonecraft, *c.* 15 November 1787, in Wardle (ed.), *Letters*, p. 166.
85. See Wardle, ed., *Letters*, pp. 178, 198.
86. Mary Wollstonecraft, letter to William Roscoe, 12 November 1792, in Wardle (ed.), *Letters*, p. 218; Claire Tomalin, *The Life and Death of Mary Wollstonecraft* (London: Penguin, 1992 (1974)), p. 93.
87. Mary Wollstonecraft, letter to Joseph Johnson, late 1789 / early 1790, in Wardle (ed.) *Letters*, p. 186.
88. His support for literary women was celebrated in verse by the husband of one of them: see John Duncombe, *The Feminiad: a Poem* (London, 1754).
89. Turner, *Living By the Pen*, p. 107.
90. See Clarke, *Dr Johnson's Women*, pp. 30–3.
91. Wardle (ed.), *Letters*, pp. 177, 190, 201, 228, 384–5, 386–7. For Johnson's attitude toward his financial dealings with Wollstonecraft, see Claire Tomalin, 'Publisher in Prison: Joseph Johnson and the Book Trade', *Times Literary Supplement*, 2 December 1994, p. 16.
92. Mary Wollstonecraft, letter to Joseph Johnson, mid 1788, in Wardle (ed.) *Letters*, p. 177.
93. Mary Wollstonecraft, letter to Joseph Johnson, mid 1788, in Wardle (ed.) *Letters*, p. 177.
94. Mary Wollstonecraft, letter to Joseph Johnson, 13 September 1787, in Wardle (ed.) *Letters*, p. 159.
95. Mary Wollstonecraft, letter to Joseph Johnson, *c.* July 1788, in Wardle (ed.) *Letters*, p. 179.
96. Mary Wollstonecraft, letter to Joseph Johnson, *c.* mid 1788, in Wardle (ed.) *Letters*, p. 178.
97. Mary Wollstonecraft, letter to William Godwin, 4 September 1796, in Wardle (ed.) *Letters*, p. 345.
98. Mary Wollstonecraft, letter to George Blood, 16 May 1788, in Wardle (ed.) *Letters*, p. 174.
99. Tomalin, 'Publisher in Prison,' p. 16.
100. Hays, 'Wollstonecraft', p. 459.
101. Mary Wollstonecraft, letter to Jane Arden, 20 May – 3 June 1773, in Wardle (ed.) *Letters*, p. 56. Even after years of professional writing, and despite some coaching from Fanny Blood, Wollstonecraft remained uncertain in her grammar. Godwin, who was a stickler for such things, persuaded her to let him teach her (Todd, *Wollstonecraft*, pp. 395–6).

102. Knowles, *Fuseli*, p. 164.
103. Wollstonecraft's two *Vindications* are crammed with borrowings from enlightened philosophers, including Bacon, Locke, Adam Smith, Voltaire, Leibniz, Buffon, Hume, Monboddo, Hutcheson, Kant, Joseph Priestley, Richard Price, and of course Rousseau.
104. For her French, see Wardle (ed.), *Letters*, pp. 108, 112, 173.
105. Mary Wollstonecraft, letter to Joseph Johnson, late 1789 / early 1790, in Wardle (ed.), *Letters*, p. 186.
106. Wollstonecraft, *VRW*, *Works*, p. 92.
107. Quoted in Browne, *Feminist Mind*, p. 116.
108. Vicesimus Knox, *Essays Moral and Literary* (London, 1779), vol. 2, p. 334.
109. *Ibid.*, vol. 2, p. 330.
110. *Ibid.*, vol. 2, p. 329. 'As to the learned languages,' Hester Chapone warned women in her influential *Letters on the Improvement of the Mind*, '...I would by no means advise you...to engage in such studies. The labour and time which they require are generally incompatible with our natures, and proper employments'; and the same objections 'are perhaps still stronger with regard to the abstruse sciences...' (Hester Chapone, *Letters on the Improvement of the Mind, Addressed to a Young Lady*, 1773 (London, 1827), p. 83.
111. Hannah More, *Strictures on the Modern System of Female Education* (London, 1799), vol. 2, pp. 1–3.
112. *Ibid.*, vol. 2, pp. 3–4.
113. Knox, *Essays*, vol. 2, p. 333.
114. See Browne, *Feminist Mind*, chapter 5 for this, and for a very good general discussion of eighteenth-century attitudes toward female education.
115. *Critical Review*, 13, 1762; reprinted in Vivien Jones (ed.), *Women in the Eighteenth Century: Constructions of Femininity* (London: Routledge, 1990), p. 175.
116. Stuart Curran has argued that there was very little male resistance to the female presence in the book trade prior to the 1790s, and that expressions of hostility to 'scribbling ladies' were merely conventional (Curran, 'Women Readers', pp. 184–5). This seems to me an over-rosy view, particularly when one considers the amount of male ink expended attempting to distinguish genres appropriate to women from those that should remain the exclusive province of men. But since there is as yet no detailed study of the attitudes of male writers to female writers in eighteenth-century Britain, the disagreement is at present unresolvable.
117. James Fordyce, *The Character and Conduct of the Female Sex* (London, 1776), p. 83.
118. Chapone, *Letters on Improvement*, p. 83.
119. Anna Barbauld, *Works* (London, 1825), vol. 1, p. xviii.
120. Wollstonecraft, *Thoughts*, *Works*, vol. 4, p. 21.
121. Wollstonecraft, *VRW*, *Works*, vol. 5, p. 73.
122. *Ibid.*, p. 245.
123. *Ibid.*, p. 241.

124. *Ibid.*, pp. 240–1, 250.
125. *Ibid.*, pp. 161, 122.
126. *Ibid.*, p. 137.
127. *Ibid.*, pp. 145–6. For a beautifully annotated bibliography of collective female biographies, see Sybil Oldfield, *Collective Biography of Women in Britain, 1550–1900* (London: Mansell Publishing, 1999).
128. Wollstonecraft, *VRW, Works*, vol. 5, p. 174.
129. Bridget Hill, *The Republican Virago: the Life and Times of Catharine Macaulay* (Oxford: Clarendon Press, 1992), chapter 9. My account of Macaulay's career is heavily indebted to Hill's pioneering study.
130. *Ibid.*, p. 225.
131. *Ibid.*, p. 173.
132. [Mary Wollstonecraft], 'Review of Catharine Macaulay Graham, Letters on Education', *AR*, vol. 5, December 1789, *Works*, vol. 7, p. 314.
133. Mary Wollstonecraft, letter to Catharine Macaulay, December 1790; reprinted in Bridget Hill, 'The Links between Mary Wollstonecraft and Catharine Macaulay: new evidence', *Women's History Review*, 4:2, 1995, p. 177.
134. Catharine Macaulay, letter to Mary Wollstonecraft, 30 December 1790, reprinted in Hill, 'Links', p. 178.
135. Wollstonecraft, *VRW, Works*, vol. 5, pp. 175, 174.
136. Hill, *Republican Virago*, p. 134.
137. Macaulay, *Letters on Education*, p. 204.
138. Wollstonecraft, 'Review of Macaulay', *AR*, November 1790, p. 309.
139. Quoted in Janet Todd, *Wollstonecraft*, p. 256.
140. Hill, *Republican Virago*, p. 138.
141. Review of *A Vindication of the Rights of Men*, *English Review*, 17, 1791, p. 61.
142. Mary Wollstonecraft, *VRM, Works*, vol. 5, p. 8. For Wollstonecraft as a ciceronian rhetorician, see Gary Kelly, 'Mary Wollstonecraft as *Vir Bonus*', *English Studies in Canada*, 5, 1979.
143. Wollstonecraft, *VRM, Works*, vol. 5, p. 7.
144. *Ibid.*, p. 16.
145. Burke, *Reflections*, pp. 10, 39, 55–6.
146. Wollstonecraft, *VRW, Works*, vol. 5, p. 175.
147. *Ibid.*, pp. 169, 115, 234. For some interesting critical ruminations on the structure of the *Rights of Woman* see Elissa Guralnick, 'Rhetorical Strategy in Mary Wollstonecraft's *A Vindication of the Rights of Woman*', *Humanities Association Review*, 30, 1979.
148. Wollstonecraft, letter to William Roscoe, 3 January 1792, in Wardle (ed.), *Letters*, pp. 205–6.
149. *Ibid.*, p. 205.
150. Wollstonecraft, *VRW, Works*, vol. 5, p. 123.
151. *Ibid.*, p. 81.
152. *Ibid.*, p. 81.
153. *Ibid.*, pp. 81–2.

154. *Ibid.*, p. 65.
155. Wollstonecraft, *Short Residence, Works*, vol. 6, p. 325.
156. The summary description is Carol Kay's, 'Canon, Ideology and Gender', p. 67.
157. Wollstonecraft, *VRW, Works*, vol. 5, pp. 75–6.
158. Mary Wollstonecraft, letter to Mary Hays, 12 November 1792, in Wardle (ed.) *Letters*, p. 219.
159. Poovey, *Proper Lady*, pp. 67–8; Guralnick, 'Rhetorical Strategy', pp. 174–7; James T. Boulton, *The Language of Politics in the Age of Wilkes and Burke* (London: Routledge and Kegan Paul, 1963), pp. 167–76.
160. Compare, for example, her account of Versailles (*An Historical and Moral View of the Origin and Progress of the French Revolution*, 1794, *Works*, vol. 6, pp. 84–5) to that of Burke (*Reflections*, pp. 66–7).
161. Wollstonecraft, *VRW, Works*, vol. 5, pp. 181–2.
162. *Ibid.*, p. 175.
163. Thomas Paine, *Rights of Man*, 1791–2 (Harmondsworth: Penguin, 1977), p. 115.
164. Wollstonecraft, *French Revolution, Works*, vol. 6, p. 22.
165. The description is Mary Hays's, quoted in William St Clair, *The Godwins and the Shelleys: the Biography of a Family* (London: Faber and Faber, 1989), p. 146.
166. Quoted in St Clair, *Godwins and Shelleys*, p. 53.
167. *The Gentleman's Magazine*, February 1791, p. 151.
168. The 'assertrix' tag was Fuseli's: Wardle, *Wollstonecraft*, p. 289.
169. Wollstonecraft, *VRW, Works*, vol. 5, p. 65.
170. Mary Wollstonecraft, *The Wrongs of Woman, or Maria*, 1798, *Works*, vol. 1, p. 167.
171. Wollstonecraft, *VRW, Works*, vol. 5, p. 73.
172. *Ibid.*, p. 75.
173. *Ibid.*, p. 74.
174. Wollstonecraft, *Maria, Works*, vol. 1, p. 167.
175. Jean-Jacques Rousseau, *Politics and Arts: Letter to M D'Alembert on the Theatre*, 1758 (Ithaca: Cornell University Press, 1991), p. 87.

2 THE CHIMERA OF WOMANHOOD

1. Wollstonecraft, *VRW, Works*, vol. 5, p. 81. In describing Wollstonecraft as a rationalist, I am using the term in its loose sense and not to refer to epistemological rationalism with which Wollstonecraft had a complex philosophical relationship, combining as her own thought did Lockean empiricism with a Platonic approach to moral truth.
2. Mary Wollstonecraft, letter to Gilbert Imlay, 22 September 1794, in Wardle (ed.), *Letters*, p. 263. For an examination of the importance of the imagination to Wollstonecraft, see John Whale, *Imagination Under Pressure, 1789–1832* (Cambridge University Press, 2000).

3. See John Barrell's splendid *Imagining the King's Death,* which appeared after I had finished this chapter, for a discussion of eighteenth-century ideas about the imagination.

4. William Shakespeare, *A Midsummer Night's Dream*, Act v, Sc.i. line 15.

5. Elizabeth Carter, letter to Catharine Talbot, 1765, quoted in E. L. Tuveson, *The Imagination as a Means of Grace* (Berkeley: University of California Press, 1960), p. 162.

6. *Ibid*. My discussion of the imagination relies heavily on Tuveson's pioneering study; and see also James Engell, *The Creative Imagination* (Harvard University Press, 1981).

7. David Hume, *A Treatise of Human Nature*, 1739 (London: Penguin, 1987), p. 71.

8. Wollstonecraft, *VRW, Works*, vol. 5, p. 185. 'Individuality is ever conspicuous in those enthusiastic flights of fancy, in which reason is left behind, without being lost sight of.' (Mary Wollstonecraft, 'Hints'. [Chiefly designed to have been incorporated into the Second Part of the *Vindication of the Rights of Woman*], *Works*, vol. 5, p. 275.)

9. See Tuveson, *Imagination*, chapter 1, for the impact of the Lockean revolution on the concept of the imagination.

10. Joseph Addison, *Essays on Taste, and the Pleasures of the Imagination, from the Spectator* (London, 1834), p. 24.

11. *Ibid.*, p. 23.

12. *Ibid.*, p. 22.

13. Tuveson, *Imagination*, p. 148.

14. Samuel Johnson, *Rasselas, Works* (London, 1792), vol. 3, pp. 419–20.

15. Edmund Burke, *A Philosophical Enquiry into the Origin of Our Ideas of the Sublime and Beautiful*, 1757 (Oxford University Press, 1990), p. 24.

16. Tuveson, *Imagination*, pp. 33–4.

17. Wollstonecraft, *VRW, Works*, vol. 5, pp. 185–6.

18. William Duff, *Letters on the Intellectual and Moral Character of Women* (1807), pp. 29–30, quoted in Christine Battersby, *Gender and Genius: Towards a Feminist Aesthetics* (London: Women's Press, 1989), p. 78. Battersby's discussion of women and eighteenth-century ideas about genius is very helpful in relation to Wollstonecraft.

19. Fordyce, *Character and Conduct of Female Sex*, pp. 81, 86. Battersby, *Gender*, p. 85.

20. Duff, *Letters*, pp. 29–30, quoted in Battersby, *Gender*, pp. 78–9.

21. Battersby, *Gender*, chapters 4 and 5.

22. *Ibid.*, p. 33.

23. For ploughmen possessing natural genius, see Young, *Conjectures*, p. 35.

24. Rousseau, *Politics and Arts*, p. 103.

25. Burke, *Philosophical Enquiry*, p. 103.

26. *Ibid.*, pp. 60–1.

27. *Ibid.*, p. 60.

28. Mary Wollstonecraft, 'Extract of a Cave of Fancy', *Works*, vol. 1, p. 196.

29. *Ibid.*, p. 205.
30. Wollstonecraft, *VRM*, *Works*, vol. 5, p. 9.
31. See Barrell, *Imagining King's Death*, pp. 8–29, for radical criticisms of the Burkean imagination. Wollstonecraft appears in this discussion, *en passant*, as another of Burke's critics on this score, which makes her appear more unambiguously hostile to the imagination than she was.
32. Wollstonecraft, *VRM*, *Works*, vol. 5, p. 55.
33. *Ibid.*, p. 9.
34. Burke, *Reflections*, p. 67.
35. *Ibid.*, p. 66.
36. *Ibid.*, p. 67.
37. Wollstonecraft, *VRM*, *Works*, vol. 5, p. 15.
38. *Ibid.*, p. 25.
39. *Ibid.*, p. 15.
40. *Ibid.*, p. 48. The sneering emphasis on Burke's depravity that runs through these passages of the *Vindication of the Rights of Men* may also have been prompted by slanders about his sexuality. In 1780 a homosexual coachman died after being exposed in the London pillory. Burke bravely condemned this in Parliament, for which he was accused by a newspaper of being unduly sympathetic to homosexuals. He sued for libel and won. Four years later he was again forced to sue when another newspaper made the same accusation (Louis Crompton, *Byron and Greek Love: Homophobia in 19th Century England* (Berkeley: University of California Press, 1985), pp. 31–3). Wollstonecraft was almost certainly aware of these slanders and, like most eighteenth-century political polemicists, she was certainly willing to employ homophobic rhetoric when it suited her argument (see *VRW*, *Works*, vol. 5, p. 208.) For the likelihood that Burke *was* homosexual, or at least had strong homosexual leanings, see Isaac Kramnick, *The Rage of Edmund Burke* (New York: Basic Books, 1977).
41. Wollstonecraft, *VRM*, *Works*, vol. 5, p. 53.
42. Marilyn Butler, *Jane Austen and the War of Ideas*, 1975 (Oxford: Clarendon Press, 1987), p. 39.
43. See Claudia Johnson, *Equivocal Beings: Politics, Gender and Sentimentality in the 1790s* (University of Chicago, 1995), chapter 1, for Wollstonecraft's efforts to claim moral virility for women, in the face of Burkean sentimental effeminacy.
44. Wollstonecraft, *VRM*, *Works*, vol. 5, p. 33.
45. *Ibid.*, pp. 18, 20.
46. *Ibid.*, p. 32.
47. *Ibid.*, pp. 54, 31.
48. *Ibid.*, p. 28. Wollstonecraft is here discussing the psychotic illness suffered by King George III.
49. *Ibid.*, pp. 29, 54.
50. Mary Wollstonecraft, 'Hints', *Works*, vol. 5, p. 275.
51. Wollstonecraft, *VRM*, *Works*, vol. 5, p. 29.
52. *Ibid.*, p. 45.
53. *Critical Review*, 70 (1790), p. 694.
54. *VRM*, *Works*, vol. 5, p. 45.

55. *Ibid.*, p. 45.
56. *Ibid.*, pp. 45–6.
57. *Ibid.*, p. 46.
58. *Ibid.*, p. 45.
59. Wollstonecraft, *Mary*, *Works*, vol. 1, p. 9.
60. Wollstonecraft, *VRW*, *Works*, vol. 5, p. 255.
61. C. A. Patrides (ed.) *The Cambridge Platonists* (London: Edward Arnold, 1969), p. 24.
62. Frances Burney, *Camilla* (1796), quoted in Patricia Meyer Spacks, 'Ev'ry Woman is at Heart a Rake', *Eighteenth Century Studies*, 8:1, 1974, p. 40.
63. Spacks, 'Ev'ry Woman', p. 40.
64. [Mary Wollstonecraft], 'Review of Elizabeth Inchbald, *A Simple Story*', *AR*, vol. 10, 1791, p. 370.
65. Cora Kaplan, 'The Thorn Birds: Fiction, Fantasy, Femininity', in *Sea Changes: Essays on Culture and Feminism* (London: Verso, 1986), pp. 121–2.
66. *Ibid.*, p. 122.
67. Mary Wollstonecraft, letter to Gilbert Imlay, 12 June 1795, in Wardle (ed.), *Letters*, p. 291.
68. Wollstonecraft, *VRW*, *Works*, vol. 5, p. 143.
69. *Ibid.*, p. 143.
70. *Ibid.*, p. 143.
71. Mary Wollstonecraft, letter to Everina Wollstonecraft, 24 March 1787, in Wardle (ed.), *Letters*, p. 145.
72. Mary Wollstonecraft, letter to the Revd Henry Dyson Gabell, 13 September 1787, in Wardle (ed.), *Letters*, p. 162.
73. Wollstonecraft, *VRW*, *Works*, vol. 5, p. 90.
74. Mary Wollstonecraft, letter to Gilbert Imlay, 22 September 1794, in Wardle (ed.), *Letters*, p. 263.
75. Mary Wollstonecraft, letter to Everina Wollstonecraft, 24 March 1787, in Wardle (ed.), *Letters*, p. 145.
76. The 'Solitary Walker', a reference to Rousseau's *Reveries of the Solitary Walker* (1782), appeared in a letter to Godwin (7 August 1796) where, following a sudden loss of confidence in Godwin's feelings for her, Wollstonecraft told him she would once again become a 'Solitary Walker' (Wardle (ed.), *Letters*, p. 337); Wollstonecraft, *Mary*, p. 5.
77. [Mary Wollstonecraft], 'Review of M. Guigne, *Letters on the Confessions of J. J. Rousseau*', *AR*, vol. 11, 1791, p. 409.
78. Wollstonecraft, *VRW*, *Works*, vol. 5, p. 161.
79. Mary Wollstonecraft, letter to William Godwin, 17 August 1796, in Wardle (ed.), *Letters*, p. 337.
80. Mary Wollstonecraft, letter to Everina Wollstonecraft, 24 March 1787, in Wardle (ed.), *Letters*, p. 145. The literature on Rousseau's gender philosophy, and Wollstonecraft's critique of it, is extensive. Works I have found particularly useful are: Marshall Berman, *The Politics of Authenticity* (London: George Allen and Unwin, 1971); S. M. Okin, *Women in Western Political Thought* (Princeton University Press, 1979); M. S. Trouille, *Sexual Politics in the Enlightenment*

(Albany: State University of New York Press, 1997); J. B. Landes, *Women and the Public Sphere in the Age of the French Revolution* (Ithaca: Cornell University Press, 1988); Carole Pateman, *The Disorder of Women* (University of Chicago, 1980); Genevieve Lloyd, *The Man of Reason* (London: Methuen, 1984); Jacques Derrida, *Of Grammatology*, 1967 (Baltimore: John Hopkins Press, 1976); Joel Schwartz, *The Sexual Politics of Jean-Jacques Rousseau* (University of Chicago, 1984); Alan Bloom, *Love and Friendship* (New York: Simon and Schuster, 1993); and Jean Starobinski, *Jean-Jacques Rousseau: Transparency and Obstruction*, 1971 (University of Chicago, 1988).

81. [Mary Wollstonecraft], 'Review of J. J. Rousseau, Seconde Partie des Confessions', *AR*, vol. 6, 1790, pp. 232–3.

82. Wollstonecraft, *VRW*, *Works*, vol. 5, p. 160.

83. *Ibid.*, p. 161.

84. *Ibid.*, p. 160.

85. Jean-Jacques Rousseau, *The Confessions*, 1781 (London: Penguin, 1953), pp. 27–8.

86. Wollstonecraft, *Maria*, *Works*, vol. 1, p. 95. Jean-Jacques Rousseau, *La Nouvelle Héloïse* (1761); translated as *Eloisa, or a Series of Original Letters*, London, 1767 [1761], vol. 4, p. 157. Hereafter referred to as *NH*. I have, following advice given by Jenny Mander ('Rousseau à l'anglais', *History Workshop Journal*, 48, 1999), chosen to use the first English translation, by William Kenrick, in preference to the recent translation by Philip Stewart and Jean Vaché (*Julie or the New Heloise* (London: Hanover, 1997)).

87. Rousseau, *Emile*, p. 391.

88. For Rousseau's platonism, see below, pp. 110–11.

89. Rousseau, *Emile*, p. 329.

90. *Ibid.*, p. 329.

91. Wollstonecraft, *VRW*, *Works*, vol. 5, p. 186.

92. *Ibid.*, pp. 168, 244–5.

93. Schwarz, *Sexual Politics*, p. 163, n. 31.

94. There exist two brief unpublished essays by Rousseau on women – *Sur les Femmes* (1735) and *Essai Sur Les Événements Important Dont Les Femmes Ont Été La Cause Secrète* (1745) – that rehearse the types of egalitarian arguments common in early modern France. Of these, the second may have been written after his service for Mme Dupin (Schwarz, *Sexual Politics*, pp. 56–8; 163, n. 31).

95. The unfinished work, *Emile et Sophie ou les Solitaires*, is summarised in Shklar, *Men and Citizens*, pp. 234–5.

96. Alan Bloom, Introduction to *Emile*, p. 7.

97. Jean-Jacques Rousseau, *Discourse on the Origin and the Foundations of Inequality Among Men* (hereafter *Second Discourse*), 1755 (Cambridge University Press, 1997), pp. 150–4.

98. See for example, *Second Discourse*, p. 152.

99. *Ibid.*, pp. 155–6.

100. *Ibid.*, p. 155.

101. Rousseau, *Emile*, p. 211.

102. *Ibid.*, p. 219.
103. *Ibid.*, p. 333.
104. Rousseau, *Second Discourse*, pp. 154–6; 165.
105. *Ibid.*, p. 165.
106. Rousseau, *Emile*, p. 81.
107. *Ibid.*, p. 334.
108. *Ibid.*, p. 329.
109. *Ibid.*, p. 358.
110. Wollstonecraft, *VRW*, *Works*, vol. 5, p. 148.
111. Rousseau, *Emile*, p. 402.
112. *Ibid.*, p. 403.
113. For the influence of Francois de Fénelon's *Telemachus* (1699) on Rousseau, see Shklar, *Men and Citizens*, pp. 4–5. Like *Emile*, *Telemachus* recounts the education of a young man – in this case a prince (Fénelon was tutor to Louis XIV's grandson, the duc de Bourgogne) – into republican virtue. While *Emile* was clearly much more than just a reworking of Fénelon's famous text, there are strong similarities between the two works. Like Emile, Telemachus is guided by an omniscient Mentor which in his case is eventually revealed to be a female in disguise: Minerva, the goddess of Wisdom. In *Emile*, on the other hand, wisdom is linguistically assigned to Sophie, but the Mentor remains firmly masculine.
114. Rousseau, *Emile*, p. 405.
115. *Ibid.*, pp. 404, 405.
116. *Ibid.*, p. 405. For a different but very interesting treatment of this episode in *Emile*, see Berman, *Politics of Authenticity*, pp. 290–8.
117. *Ibid.*, p. 393.
118. *Ibid.*, p. 357.
119. *Ibid.*, p. 358.
120. *Ibid.*, p. 358.
121. *Ibid.*, p. 358. Rousseau sharply distinguished, however, between men's erotic audacity, which he regarded as natural and necessary, and brute sexual coercion of any kind, of which he strongly disapproved (see *Politics and Arts*, p. 85).
122. *Ibid.*, pp. 377, 359–60, 358.
123. *Ibid.*, p. 358.
124. Montesquieu, *The Spirit of the Laws*, quoted in Jane Rendall, *The Origins of Modern Feminism* (Basingstoke: Macmillans, 1985), p. 22.
125. Wollstonecraft, *VRW*, *Works*, vol. 5, p. 159.
126. *Ibid.*, pp. 158–9.
127. Rousseau, *Emile*, p. 358.
128. *Ibid.*, p. 359.
129. Rousseau, *Politics and Arts*, p. 47.
130. *Ibid.*, p. 82.
131. *Ibid.*, p. 100.
132. *Ibid.*, p. 87.

133. *Ibid.*, p. 87.
134. *Ibid.*, p. 109.
135. Rousseau, *Emile*, p. 361.
136. *Ibid.*, p. 369.
137. Rousseau, *NH*, vol. 1, p. 238.
138. Rousseau, *Emile*, pp. 358–9.
139. Rousseau, *Politics and Arts*, p. 82. For Rousseau's identification with women, see Carol Blum, *Rousseau and the Republic of Virtue* (Ithaca: Cornell University Press, 1986), pp. 120, 129.
140. Jean-Jacques Rousseau, *The Confessions*, 1781 (London: Penguin Books, 1978), p. 85. For this quotation I have, however, used Berman's translation (*Politics*, p. 102) in preference to that of the Penguin translator, J. M. Cohen.
141. Rousseau, *NH*, quoted in Berman, *Politics*, p. 142.
142. Rousseau, *Emile*, p. 386.
143. Rousseau, *NH*, vol. 1, p. 238.
144. *Rousseau, Emile*, p. 382; Rousseau, *NH*, vol. 1, p. 214n.
145. Rousseau, *NH*, Author's Preface, p. xxxiv. Rousseau, *Emile*, p. 369.
146. Wollstonecraft, *VRW*, *Works*, vol. 5, p. 152.
147. *Ibid.*, p. 175.
148. *Ibid.*, p. 161.
149. *Ibid.*, p. 148.
150. *Ibid.*, p. 148.
151. *Ibid.*, p. 74.
152. *Ibid.*, p. 112.
153. *Ibid.*, p. 186.
154. *Ibid.*, p. 151. The reference here is to French girls, but Wollstonecraft clearly thought it applied equally well to English girls.
155. *Ibid.*, pp. 186–7. Associationist psychology – as adumbrated by Locke and, even more influentially, David Hartley (*Observations on Man* [1749]) – was immensely popular among British progressives, for obvious reasons: if vicious or stupid behaviour resulted not from innate dispositions but from bad mental habits which were themselves a consequence of prejudicial circumstances, then any improvement in human circumstances, reverberating along the entire causal chain, must eventually result in greater virtue and happiness. Intervening in individuals' circumstances and education to 'break associations that do violence to reason' thus became a recipe for moral perfection. (Wollstonecraft, *VRW*, *Works*, vol. 5, pp. 185–90. See also some rather ambiguous remarks about free will versus psychological necessitarianism, in her review of Catherine Macaulay's *Letters on Education*: *AR*, vol. 8: 1790, *Works*, vol. 7, pp. 320–1.)
156. *Ibid.*, p. 113.
157. *Ibid.*, pp. 244–5.
158. *Ibid.*, p. 93.
159. *Ibid.*, p. 152.
160. Rousseau, *Emile*, pp. 39–40.

161. Rousseau, *Second Discourse*, p. 187.
162. *Ibid.*, p. 187.
163. Rousseau, *Emile*, p. 365.
164. Terry Eagleton, *The Ideology of the Aesthetic* (Oxford: Basil Blackwell, 1990), p. 24.
165. Rousseau, *NH*, vol. 2, p. 132.
166. Rousseau, *Emile*, p. 381.
167. *Ibid.*, pp. 381, 377.
168. *Ibid.*, p. 478.
169. Rousseau, *Second Discourse*, p. 121.
170. *Ibid.*, p. 122.
171. Mme Blandin-Demoulin, quoted in Trouille, *Sexual Politics*, p. 72.
172. Quoted in Schwartz, *Sexual Politics*, p. 125.
173. Rousseau, *Politics and Arts*, p. 87.
174. Wollstonecraft, *VRW*, *Works*, vol. 5, p. 125.
175. *Ibid.*, pp. 124–5.
176. *Ibid.*, p. 239.
177. Macaulay, *Letters on Education*, p. 214.
178. *Ibid.*, p. 213.
179. *Ibid.*, p. 215.
180. *Ibid.*, p. 222.
181. *Ibid.*, pp. 221, 206.
182. Wollstonecraft, *VRW*, *Works*, vol. 5, p. 136.
183. *Ibid.*, p. 136.
184. Snitow, 'A Gender Diary', p. 529.
185. Wollstonecraft, *VRW*, *Works*, vol. 5, p. 90.
186. *Ibid.*, p. 105.
187. *Ibid.*, p. 105.

3 FOR THE LOVE OF GOD

1. Wollstonecraft, *Short Residence*, *Works*, vol. 6, p. 271.
2. Godwin, *Memoirs*, p. 215.
3. Wollstonecraft, *Thoughts*, *Works*, vol. 4, p. 33.
4. Wollstonecraft, *Short Residence*, vol. 6, p. 276. Wollstonecraft is here describing the freethinking mentality of the Norwegians, 'the least oppressed people of Europe' (see below, pp. 169–70).
5. Godwin, *Memoirs*, p. 215. Godwin's account of Wollstonecraft's piety did not register with many of his readers, including one who claimed that his book gave 'a striking view of a Woman of fine talents...sinking a victim to the strength of her Passions & feelings because destitute of the support of Religious principles' (James Woodrow, quoted in Gary Kelly, *Women, Writing and Revolution, 1790–1827* (Oxford: Clarendon Press, 1993), p. 27).
6. Godwin, *Memoirs*, p. 236.

7. Mary Wollstonecraft, letter to William Godwin, 4 July 1797; in Wardle (ed.), *Letters*, p. 404.
8. Godwin, *Memoirs*, p. 215.
9. As Emma Rauschenbusch-Clough put it, Godwin was 'inclined to substitute his own philosophical views' for Wollstonecraft's religious beliefs (*Study of Wollstonecraft*, p. 48).
10. Hays, *Memoirs of Wollstonecraft*, p. 416.
11. *Ibid.*, p. 416.
12. Godwin, *Memoirs*, pp. 272–3.
13. Wollstonecraft, *VRW*, *Works*, vol. 5, p. 184.
14. Godwin, *Memoirs*, pp. 276–7.
15. Syndy M. Conger, *Mary Wollstonecraft and the Language of Sensibility* (London: Associated University Presses, 1994); George Barker-Benfield, *The Culture of Sensibility: Sex and Society in Eighteenth Century Britain* (University of Chicago Press, 1992); Mitzi Myers, 'Sensibility and the "Walk of Reason": Mary Wollstonecraft's Literary Reviews as Cultural Critique', in S. M. Conger (ed.), *Sensibility in Transformation* (Rutherford, NJ: Fairleigh Dickenson University Press, 1990), pp. 122–140.
16. Wollstonecraft, *Mary*, *Works*, vol. 1, p. 11.
17. *Ibid.*, p. 16
18. *Ibid.*, p. 17.
19. *Ibid.*, p. 73.
20. *Ibid.*, p. 63.
21. *Ibid.*, p. 64.
22. Quoted in Genevieve Lloyd, *The Man of Reason: 'Male' and 'Female' in Western Philosophy* (London: Methuen, 1984), pp. 30–1.
23. Wollstonecraft, *VRW*, *Works*, vol. 5, p. 103. Equality of souls was a mainstream Christian teaching. Spiritually, Eve was Adam's equal, the Church fathers explained; it was only in her mortal nature that woman was man's inferior. Those, like Wollstonecraft, who took the egalitarian case much further by insisting on the earthly equality of the sexes, had no choice but to tackle this orthodoxy. Many earlier feminists had done so, offering counter-interpretations of *Genesis* in which Eve featured not as Adam's culpable subordinate but rather as his companion, equal, and helpmate. Revisionist readings of the Bible dismissed literal interpretations of the Creation and Fall, arguing that these were Hebrew myths or allegories. It is this latter line that Wollstonecraft takes, describing *Genesis* as a 'poetical story' which 'proves that man, from the remotest antiquity, found it convenient to exert his strength to subjugate his companion, and his invention to shew that she ought to have her neck bent under the yoke, because the whole creation was only created for his convenience or pleasure.' (*VRW*, *Works*, vol. 5, p. 95).
24. Simone de Beauvoir, *The Second Sex*, 1949 (Harmondsworth: Penguin, 1972), p. 633. De Beauvoir's discussion of the egalitarian implications of Christianity for women is in many respects very reminiscent of Wollstonecraft, although in her case the perspective is psychological: 'A sincere faith is a great help to the

little girl in avoiding an inferiority complex: she is neither male nor female, but God's creature' (p. 633).

25. Mary Astell, *Some Reflections Upon Marriage*, 1700; 1706 edition in Bridget Hill, *The First English Feminist* (Aldershot: Gower Publishing, 1986), p. 84.

26. A Methodist woman preacher quoted in L. F. Church, *More About the Early Methodist People* (London, 1949), p. 168.

27. More, *Strictures on Female Education*, vol. 1, p. 25.

28. John Brown, *On the Female Character and Education* (London, 1765), pp. 10, 12.

29. *Ibid.*, p. 13.

30. *Ibid.*, p. 15.

31. Wollstonecraft, *Mary*, Works, vol. 1, p. 59.

32. *Ibid.*, p. 43.

33. Wollstonecraft, *VRW*, *Works*, vol. 5, p. 118.

34. John Gregory, *A Father's Legacy to His Daughters*, 1774 (London, 1823), pp. 159–60.

35. James Fordyce, *Sermons to Young Women*, 1765 (London, 1766), vol. 2, p. 163.

36. Wollstonecraft, *VRW*, *Works*, vol. 5, p. 164.

37. Wollstonecraft, *Original Stories*, *Works*, vol. 4, pp. 423, 431.

38. Wollstonecraft, *VRW*, *Works*, vol. 5, p. 101.

39. Wollstonecraft, letter to Everina Wollstonecraft, January 1784, in Wardle (ed.), *Letters*, p. 87.

40. Wollstonecraft, *Mary*, *Works*, vol. 1, p. 29.

41. Wollstonecraft, letter to George Blood, 17 January 1788, p. 170, in Wardle (ed.), *Letters*, p. 170.

42. Wollstonecraft, *VRM*, *Works*, vol. 5, p. 18.

43. Wollstonecraft, *VRW*, *Works*, vol. 5, p. 85.

44. Wollstonecraft, *French Revolution*, *Works*, vol. 6, pp. 21–2. In the *Rights of Woman* Wollstonecraft directly attacked the dogma of original sin: 'though the cry of irreligion, or even atheism, be raised against me, I will simply declare, that were an angel from heaven to tell me that . . . the account of the fall of man, were literally true, I could not believe what my reason told me was derogatory to the character of the Supreme Being . . .' (*Works*, vol. 5, p. 148).

45. Wollstonecraft, *VRW*, *Works*, vol. 5, pp. 265–6.

46. Wollstonecraft, *VRM*, *Works*, vol. 5, p. 34.

47. *Ibid.*, p. 51.

48. Basil Willey, *The Eighteenth Century Background* (London: Chatto and Windus, 1946), p. 7.

49. Rousseau, *Emile*, p. 286.

50. Wollstonecraft, *Mary*, *Works*, vol. 1, p. 27.

51. Richard Price, *A Review of the Principal Questions and Difficulties in Morals*, 1758 (Oxford: Clarendon Press, 1974), p. 180.

52. *Ibid.*, p. 181.

53. Wollstonecraft, *VRW*, *Works*, vol. 5, p. 105.

54. *Ibid.*, p. 89.
55. *Ibid.*, pp. 170–1.
56. *Ibid.*, p. 102.
57. *Ibid.*, p. 120.
58. *Ibid.*, p. 114. In an interesting side-swipe at enlightened ethical relativism, in 1795 Wollstonecraft condemned those 'semi-philosophers' who, using examples from 'nations just emerging from barbarism', had attempted to show 'that the vices of one country are not the vices of another; as if this would prove that morality has no solid foundation' (*French Revolution, Works*, vol. 6, p. 110).
59. *Ibid.*, p. 120.
60. Price, *Review*, p. 113.
61. Wollstonecraft, *VRW*, *Works*, vol. 5, p. 115.
62. Wollstonecraft, *VRM*, *Works*, vol. 5, p. 34.
63. Wollstonecraft, *VRW*, *Works*, vol. 5, p. 115.
64. For the Unitarian contribution to early British feminism, see Kathryn Gleadle, *The Early Feminists: Radical Unitarians and the Emergence of the Women's Rights Movement, 1831–51* (Basingstoke: Macmillan, 1995).
65. Wollstonecraft, *Short Residence*, *Works*, vol. 6, p. 307; *VRW*, *Works*, vol. 5, p. 266.
66. Hays, 'Wollstonecraft', p. 416.
67. Wollstonecraft, *VRM*, *Works*, vol. 5, p. 46. Sarah Hutton discusses Wollstonecraft's platonism in her unpublished paper, 'The Ethical Background of the Rights of Women: Damaris Cudworth, Catherine Macaulay and Mary Wollstonecraft', which I am grateful to her for allowing me to read.
68. James G. Turner, *One Flesh: Paradisical Marriage and Sexual Relations in the Age of Milton* (Oxford: Clarendon Press, 1987), p. 32. While Turner's book does not deal with eighteenth-century writers like Wollstonecraft, it gives an excellent account of the tensions within Christian attitudes towards erotic love that are evident in Wollstonecraft's writings.
69. Quoted in Turner, *One Flesh*, p. 32. For an influential discussion of the relationship between divine and earthly love in Christian theology, see Anders Nygren, *Agape and Eros* (London: SPCK, 1982).
70. Wollstonecraft, *VRW*, *Works*, vol. 5, p. 143.
71. Patrides, *Cambridge Platonists*, pp. 37, 28. See also Ernst Cassirer, *The Platonic Renaissance in England* (London: Thomas Nelson and Sons, 1953), pp. 94–128, and for the significance of Christian Platonism in the formation of eighteenth-century British moral philosophy, John K. Sheriff, *The Good-Natured Man: the Evolution of a Moral Ideal, 1660–1880* (Tuuscaloosa: University of Alabama Press, 1982).
72. Mary Astell and John Norris, *Letters Concerning the Love of God* (1695), pp. 134, 101; quoted in Ruth Perry, *The Celebrated Mary Astell* (University of Chicago Press, 1986), p. 77.
73. Mary Astell, *A Serious Proposal to the Ladies* (1694), p. 97; quoted in Perry, *Astell*, p. 113.

74. Robert Schofield, 'Joseph Priestley, Eighteenth-Century British Neoplatonism, and S. T. Coleridge', in E. Mendelsohn, *Transformation and Tradition in the Sciences* (Cambridge University Press, 1984), pp. 216–8.

75. For Price's Platonism, particularly his debt to the leading Cambridge Platonist Ralph Cudworth, see Henri Labouchiex, *Richard Price as Moral Philosopher and Political Theorist* (Voltaire Foundation, Oxford, 1982), pp. 68–72. See also Martha K. Zebrowski, 'Richard Price: British Platonist of the Eighteenth Century', *Journal of the History of Ideas*, 55:1, 1994, pp. 17–35. For Anna Barbauld's Platonism, see p. 186.

76. David Hartley, *Observations on Man, his Frame, his Duty, and his Expectations* (1749), vol. 2, pp. 283, 311–12. For a discussion of Hartley's 'theopathy' (a term he invented), see Richard Allen, *David Hartley on Human Nature* (SUNY Press, 1999), pp. 331–55; for his influence on Rational Dissent, see Schofield, 'Priestley', pp. 244–6.

77. John Milton, *Paradise Lost*, Bk 8: 586–94, in *Poetical Works* (Oxford University Press, 1992), p. 368.

78. Dustin Griffin, *Regaining Paradise: Milton and the Eighteenth Century* (Cambridge University Press, 1986), pp. 124–33; see also Jean Hagstrum, *Sex and Sensibility: Ideal and Erotic Love from Milton to Mozart* (University of Chicago Press, 1980), and John T. Shawcross, *John Milton and Influence* (Pittsburgh: Duquesne University Press, 1991). The influence of *Paradise Lost* on Wollstonecraft is apparent from the many allusions to the poem in her novels and correspondence, as well as in the *Rights of Woman*; see the excellent index to her *Works* (vol. 7, p. 524) for a full list of these.

   Another possible source of Wollstonecraft's platonism is Thomas Taylor ('the Platonist') with whom her family shared lodgings for a time in Walworth in 1778. But if Taylor preached platonism at his young neighbour, he didn't like what she later did with these ideas, since in 1792 he satirised the *Rights of Woman* in a pamphlet titled *A Vindication of the Rights of Brutes*.

79. Rousseau, *NH*, vol. 2, p. 14n.

80. Rousseau, *Emile*, p. 391; Rousseau, *NH*, vol. 2, p. 34. For the theme of transcendent love in *NH*, see Starobinski, *Transparency*, pp. 114, 117, 351; R. J. Howells, *Rousseau: La Nouvelle Heloïse* (London, Grant and Cutler Ltd, 1986), pp. 11–20; John Charvet, 'The idea of love in *La Nouvelle Heloïse*', in R. A. Leigh (ed.), *Rousseau after Two Hundred Years* (Cambridge University Press, 1982).

81. Rousseau, *NH*, vol. 2, p. 14.

82. *Ibid.*, vol. 4, p. 157.

83. *Ibid.*, vol. 4, p. 228.

84. Wollstonecraft, *Cave of Fancy*, *Works*, vol. 1, p. 204.

85. *Ibid.*, p. 201.

86. *Ibid.*, p. 206.

87. Wollstonecraft, *VRW*, *Works*, vol. 5, p. 180.

88. 'Hints', *Works*, vol. 5, p. 274.

89. Wollstonecraft, *VRW*, *Works*, vol. 5, pp. 103, 188–9.

90. Wollstonecraft, *Mary*, *Works*, vol. 1, p. 72.
91. *Ibid.*, p. 73.
92. *Ibid.*, p. 42.
93. *Ibid.*, pp. 40–1, 46.
94. Edward Young, *The Complaint, or Night Thoughts on Life, Death and Immortality* (1742), 1, 100. Young's famous poem made a deep impression on Wollstonecraft.
95. Wollstonecraft, *Mary*, *Works*, vol. 1, p. 46.
96. *Ibid.*, p. 47.
97. *Ibid.*, p. 47.
98. *Ibid.*, p. 47.
99. Wollstonecraft, *VRW*, *Works*, vol. 5, p. 255.
100. *Ibid.*, pp. 129, 208.
101. *Ibid.*, p. 207.
102. *Ibid.*, p. 208.
103. *Ibid.*, p. 208.
104. *Ibid.*, p. 99.
105. *Ibid.*, pp. 99, 141, 117–8.
106. *Ibid.*, p. 119.
107. Kaplan, *Sea Changes*, p. 41.
108. Poovey, *Proper Lady*, pp. 3–113.
109. Wollstonecraft, *VRW*, *Works*, vol. 5, p. 136.
110. Spacks, 'Ev'ry Woman', p. 27. Other studies of eighteenth century attitudes to female sexuality which I have found helpful are: Rita Goldberg, *Sex and Enlightenment* (Cambridge University Press, 1984); Barker Benfield, *Culture of Sensibility*; Vivien Jones, ' "The Tyranny of the Passions": Feminism and Heterosexuality in the Fiction of Wollstonecraft and Hays', in S. Ledger (ed.), *Political Gender: Texts and Contexts* (London: Harvester Wheatsheaf, 1994).
111. Quoted in Poovey, *Proper Lady*, p. 3.
112. Rousseau, *Emile*, p. 358.
113. Poovey, *Proper Lady*, chapter 1.
114. For some examples of the companionate marital ideal in practice, see Vickery, *The Gentleman's Daughter*.
115. Wollstonecraft, *VRW*, *Works*, vol. 5, p. 169.
116. *Ibid.*, p. 264.
117. *Ibid.*, p. 119. Wollstonecraft's view of friendship as 'the most sublime of all affections, because ... founded on principle, and cemented by time' (*ibid.*, p. 142) may, as some commentators have suggested, have classical echoes, but the companionate marriage ideal promoted by Christian moralists is probably its chief source.
118. *Ibid.*, p. 157.
119. *Ibid.*, p. 192.
120. *Ibid.*, p. 199.
121. *Ibid.*, p. 194.

122. Macaulay, *Letters on Education*, p. 212.

123. [Wollstonecraft], 'Review of Macaulay's *Letters*', p. 314.

124. Wollstonecraft, *VRW*, *Works*, vol. 5, p. 207; Macaulay, *Letters on Education*, p. 220.

125. Wollstonecraft, *VRW*, *Works*, vol. 5, p. 144.

126. *Ibid.*, p. 130.

127. Wollstonecraft, *Mary*, *Works*, vol. 1, p. 8.

128. *Ibid.*, p. 31.

129. *Ibid.*, p. 68.

130. Mary Wollstonecraft, letter to Gilbert Imlay, 27 November 1795, in Wardle (ed.), *Letters*, p. 321.

131. Wollstonecraft, *VRW*, *Works*, vol. 5, p. 65.

132. Mary Wollstonecraft, letter to Gilbert Imlay, *c.* August 1793, in Wardle (ed.) *Letters*, p. 235.

133. Mary Wollstonecraft, letters to Gilbert Imlay, 8 January 1794; 28 December 1794; 29 December 1794; in Wardle (ed.), *Letters*, pp. 245, 270, 272.

134. Mary Wollstonecraft, letter to Gilbert Imlay, 30 December 1794, in Wardle (ed.), *Letters*, p. 273.

135. Mary Wollstonecraft, letter to Gilbert Imlay, 12 June 1795, in Wardle (ed.) *Letters*, p. 291.

136. *Ibid.*, p. 291.

137. Mary Wollstonecraft, letter to Gilbert Imlay, 13 June 1795, in Wardle (ed.) *Letters*, pp. 292–3.

138. Mary Wollstonecraft, letters to Gilbert Imlay, 19 February, 27 September 1795, in Wardle (ed.) *Letters*, pp. 280, 313.

139. Mary Wollstonecraft, letter to Gilbert Imlay, 22 May 1795, in Wardle (ed.) *Letters*, p. 288.

140. *Ibid.*, p. 289.

141. Godwin, *Memoirs*, pp. 250–1.

142. Mary Wollstonecraft, letter to Gilbert Imlay, *c.* March 1796, in Wardle (ed.) *Letters*, pp. 329–30.

143. Wollstonecraft, *VRW*, *Works*, vol. 5, p. 188.

144. Ellen Moers, *Literary Women* (London: Women Press, 1978), p. 149.

145. Wollstonecraft, *VRW*, *Works*, vol. 5, p. 190.

146. Mary Wollstonecraft, letter to Gilbert Imlay, 8 December 1795, in Wardle (ed.) *Letters*, p. 323.

147. Mary Wollstonecraft, letter to Gilbert Imlay, 5 August 1795, in Wardle (ed.) *Letters*, p. 308.

148. Mary Wollstonecraft, letter to Gilbert Imlay, 3 July 1795, in Wardle (ed.) *Letters*, p. 302.

149. Mary Wollstonecraft, letter to Gilbert Imlay, 4 July 1795, in Wardle (ed.) *Letters*, p. 304.

150. Mary Wollstonecraft, letter to Gilbert Imlay, 9 February 1795, in Wardle (ed.) *Letters*, p. 277.

151. Tomalin, *Wollstonecraft*, p. 169. It would have been at about this time that she reportedly told Archibald Hamilton Rowan that 'no motive upon earth ought to make a man and wife live together a moment after mutual love and regard were gone' (Clark Durant, *Supplement*, 254).

152. Mary Wollstonecraft, letter to William Godwin, 11 August 1796, in Wardle (ed.), *Letters*, p. 336.

153. Mary Wollstonecraft, letter to William Godwin, 27 August 1796, in Wardle (ed.), *Letters*, p. 342.

154. Mary Wollstonecraft, letter to William Godwin, 13 November 1796, in Wardle (ed.), *Letters*, p. 360.

155. Mary Wollstonecraft, letter to William Godwin, 17 August 1796, in Wardle (ed.), *Letters*, p. 337.

156. Wollstonecraft, *Mary*, *Works*, vol. 1, p. 46.

157. Mary Wollstonecraft, letter to Gilbert Imlay, 17 June 1795, in Wardle (ed.), *Letters*, p. 296.

158. Wollstonecraft, *Short Residence*, *Works*, vol. 6, p. 267.

159. *Ibid.*, pp. 279–80.

160. *Ibid.*, p. 280.

161. Admiring references to her book can be found in the writings of Southey, Wordsworth, and Hazlitt; the Shelleys took a copy with them to France in 1814. For Southey's general admiration for Wollstonecraft, see Harriet Jump, ' "No Equal Mind": Mary Wollstonecraft and the Young Romantics', *The Charles Lamb Bulletin*, new series 79, July 1992. For the possibility that Coleridge's poem 'Kubla Khan' was influenced by Wollstonecraft's book, see Richard Holmes's introduction to the 1987 Penguin edition of the *Short Residence*, pp. 38–41; for Wollstonecraft's influence on Coleridge (despite his stated view that she had no 'talent for book-making'), see Anya Taylor, 'Coleridge, Wollstonecraft and the Rights of Woman', T. Fulford and M. D. Paley (eds.), *Coleridge's Visionary Languages* (Cambridge: D. S. Brewer, 1993). Sometime in 1796 (before reading the *Short Residence* or after?) Coleridge planned to write to Wollstonecraft 'urging her to Religion', but the letter seems never to have been written (Jump, ' "No Equal Mind" ', p. 227).

162. *The Monthly Magazine and American Review*, 1, no. 1 (1799), p. 331, quoted in Poovey, *Proper Lady*, p. 256 n. 8.

163. Wollstonecraft, *Short Residence*, *Works*, vol. 6, p. 281.

164. *Ibid.*, p. 311.

165. Godwin, *Memoirs*, p. 270.

166. *Ibid.*, p. 270. As Godwin implies, it is likely that Wollstonecraft felt no need of prayer since, like Julie in *La Nouvelle Héloïse,* she had no fear of hellfire and was confident that a virtuous life would be rewarded.

167. According to Godwin, these were her mother's dying words, 'repeatedly referred to by Mary in the course of her writings' (Godwin, *Memoirs*, p. 213). For Wollstonecraft's death, see Vivien Jones, 'The Death of Mary Wollstonecraft', *British Journal for Eighteenth Century Studies*, 20:2 (1997).

168. William James, *The Varieties of Religious Experience*, first published 1902 (London: Penguin, 1985), p. 259.

169. Mary Wollstonecraft, letter to Gilbert Imlay, 3 July 1795, in Wardle (ed.), *Letters*, p. 302.

170. Poovey, *Proper Lady*, p. 65.

171. Wollstonecraft, *VRM*, *Works*, vol. 5, pp. 39–40.

172. Mary Wollstonecraft, letter to Joseph Johnson, *c.* late 1795, in Wardle (ed.), *Letters*, p. 325.

173. Mary Wollstonecraft, letter to Everina Wollstonecraft, January 1784, in Wardle (ed.) *Letters*, p. 87.

174. Wollstonecraft, *VRM*, *Works*, vol. 5, p. 39.

175. Wollstonecraft, *VRW*, *Works*, vol. 5, p. 205. See also page 201: ' "Women," says some author, I cannot recollect who, "mind not what only heaven sees." Why, indeed, should they? it is the eye of man that they have been taught to dread...'

176. Mary Wollstonecraft, letter to Joseph Johnson, spring 1790, in Wardle (ed.), *Letters*, p. 189.

177. *Ibid.*, p. 189.

178. Wollstonecraft, *Mary*, *Works*, vol. 1, p. 11.

179. Wollstonecraft, *Maria*, *Works*, vol. 1, pp. 124, 126.

180. *Ibid.*, p. 83.

181. *Ibid.*, p. 83.

182. Mary Hays, *Memoirs of Emma Courtney*, 1796 (London: Pandora Press, 1987), p. xviii.

183. Wollstonecraft, *Maria*, *Works*, vol. 1, p. 83.

184. *Ibid.*, p. 88.

185. *Ibid.*, p. 104.

186. *Ibid.*, pp. 143–4.

187. *Ibid.*, p. 104.

188. *Ibid.*, p. 93.

189. *Ibid.*, p. 94.

190. *Ibid.*, pp. 92–3.

191. *Ibid.*, pp. 95–6, 104–6, 173.

192. *Ibid.*, p. 105.

193. *Ibid.*, p. 183.

194. *Ibid.*, pp. 144–5.

195. *Ibid.*, pp. 146–7.

196. *Ibid.*, p. 180.

197. *Ibid.*, p. 181.

198. *Ibid.*, p. 176.

199. *Ibid.*, p. 124.

200. *Ibid.*, p. 126.

201. *Ibid.*, p. 176.

202. *Ibid.*, p. 177.

203. *Ibid.*, p. 104.

204. Wollstonecraft, *Short Residence, Works*, vol. 6, p. 294.
205. *Ibid.*, p. 286.
206. Mary Wollstonecraft, 'On Poetry', *Works*, vol. 7, pp. 7, p. 9.
207. *Ibid.*, p. 8.
208. Meena Alexander, *Women in Romanticism: Mary Wollstonecraft, Dorothy Wordsworth and Mary Shelley* (London: Macmillan, 1989), p. 45; see also Anne K. Mellor, *Romanticism and Gender* (London: Routledge, 1993). Not much is to be gained, in my view, from classifying Wollstonecraft as a romantic or pre-romantic writer. Her debt to earlier eighteenth-century sources for her 'romantic' themes is readily traced (Edward Young and Hugh Blair are two obvious influences), and treating her ideas as anticipations of later romantic motifs is less illuminating to my mind than understanding them in their own terms.
209. Burke, *Reflections*, p. 30.
210. Surveying the Wollstonecraft/Godwin circle with a respectful but sceptical eye, Hazlitt observed that the 'whole' of their philosophy was 'nothing more than a literal, rigid, unaccommodating, and systematic interpretation of the text,... "Thou shalt love thy neighbour as thyself", without making any allowances for the weaknesses of mankind, or the degree to which this rule was practicable...' (William Hazlitt, *Memoirs of Thomas Holcroft* (London, 1816), p. 178). For the central part played by universal benevolence in 1790s radicalism, see Evan Radcliffe, 'Revolutionary Writing, Moral Philosophy, and Universal Benevolence in the Eighteenth Century', *Journal of the History of Ideas*, 54:2, 1993.
211. Richard Price, *A Discourse on the Love of Our Country*, 1789, in *Political Writings* (D. O. Thomas, ed., Cambridge University Press, 1991), p. 180.
212. Wollstonecraft, *Mary, Works*, vol. 1, pp. 15–16; pp. 56–7.
213. Wollstonecraft, *VRM, Works*, vol. 5, p. 52. In 1795 the radical Norwich magazine, *The Cabinet*, published an article 'On Public Charities', which looked forward to the day when 'the great work of reform' would have eliminated the need for all charitable assistance: 'particular *charities* shall subsist no longer, but all be absorbed in one grand... scheme of universal equity and benevolence...' Reprinting this article in the *Times Literary Supplement* (21.3.97), Penelope Corfield has suggested that its author might have been Wollstonecraft. The views expressed in the piece are certainly very like Wollstonecraft's, but the evidence, as Corfield says, is inconclusive.
214. *Ibid.*, p. 53.
215. *Ibid.*, p. 34.
216. Hazlitt, *Holcroft*, p. 179.

4 WOLLSTONECRAFT AND BRITISH RADICALISM

1. Wollstonecraft, *VRM, Works*, vol. 5, p. 33.
2. Virginia Woolf, 'Mary Wollstonecraft' (1929), Michèle Barrett (ed.), *Women and Writing* (London: Women's Press, 1979), p. 98.

3. Mary Wollstonecraft, 'Review of Richard Price, *A Discourse on the Love of Our Country*', *AR*, December 1789, *Works*, vol. 7, pp. 185–7.

4. Price, *Discourse*, *Political Writings*, pp. 195 6.

5. A. Cobban, *The Debate on the French Revolution* (London: Black, 1950), p. 31. The figure for the number of published contributions to the debate has been calculated by Gayle T. Pendleton ('Towards a Bibliography of the *Reflections* and *Rights of Man* Controversy', *Bulletin of Research in the Humanities*, 85:1 (1982), pp. 65–103). There was also a huge amount of ephemera generated by the controversy: Mark Philp has found over 600 ballads inspired by it between 1789 and 1815 (personal communication).

6. Mark Philp, 'English Republicanism in the 1790s', *Journal of Political Philosophy*, 6 (1998), p. 244.

7. Wollstonecraft, *VRW*, *Works*, vol. 5, p. 217.

8. E. P. Thompson, *The Making of the English Working Class* (London: Victor Gollancz, 1963). For working-class women's radical activism, see Dorothy Thompson, 'Women and Nineteenth-Century Radical Politics: a Lost Dimension', in Mitchell and Oakley (eds.), *Rights and Wrongs of Women*; Anna Clark, *The Struggle for the Breeches: Gender and the Making of the British Working Class* (London: Rivers Oram, 1995), ch. 8.

9. C. B. Cone, *The English Jacobins* (New York: Charles Scribner's Sons, 1968), p. 114; John Keane, *Tom Paine, a Political Life*, 1995 (London: Bloomsbury, 1996), p. 334.

10. Thompson, *Making of English Working Class*; Albert Goodwin, *The Friends of Liberty* (London: Hutchison, 1979); H. T. Dickinson, *Liberty and Property*, 1977 (London: Methuen and Co., 1979) and *The Politics of the People in 18th Century Britain* (Basingstoke: Macmillan, 1995); G. A. Williams, *Artisans and Sans Culottes* (London: Arnold, 1968).

11. Keane, *Paine*, p. 336.

12. However, according to Wollstonecraft's sister Eliza there was talk of burning Wollstonecraft in effigy at Upton Castle in January 1793 (Charles Kegan Paul, *William Godwin: His Friends and Contemporaries* [London, 1876], vol. 1, p. 211).

13. Quoted in Brian Simon, *The Two Nations and the Educational Structure, 1780–1870*, 1960 (London: Lawrence and Wishart, 1974), p. 79.

14. Goodwin, *Friends*, p. 390; Mary Wollstonecraft, letter to Gilbert Imlay, 1 October 1794, in Wardle (ed.), *Letters*, p. 267.

15. Mary Wollstonecraft, letter to Ruth Barlow, 1–15 February 1794, in Wardle (ed.), *Letters*, p. 230.

16. Mary Wollstonecraft, letter to Everina Wollstonecraft, 10 March 1794, in Wardle (ed.), *Letters*, p. 250.

17. *Ibid.*, p. 251.

18. *Ibid.*, p. 251.

19. Mary Wollstonecraft, letter to Joseph Johnson, 26 December 1792, in Wardle (ed.) *Letters*, p. 227. The sight of Louis going past, 'with more dignity than I expected', so upset Wollstonecraft that, 'lifting my eyes from the paper,

I have seen eyes glare through a glass-door opposite my chair, and bloody hands shook at me... I am going to bed – and, for the first time in my life, I cannot put out the candle.'

20. This incident is described in Richard Holmes, *Footsteps: Adventures of a Romantic Biographer*, 1985 (London: Penguin, 1986), pp. 112–13.
21. Todd, *Wollstonecraft*, p. 241.
22. Mary Wollstonecraft, letter to the Revd Henry Dyson Gabell, 16 April 1787, in Wardle (ed.), *Letters*, p. 150.
23. Wollstonecraft, *Short Residence*, *Works*, vol. 6, p. 302.
24. Quoted in Wardle, *Wollstonecraft*, p. 159.
25. Marilyn Butler, *Burke, Paine, Godwin and the Revolution Controversy* (Cambridge University Press, 1984), p. 2.
26. Quoted in Tomalin, *Wollstonecraft*, p. 123.
27. Anna Barbauld, *An Address to the Opposers of the Repeal of the Test and Corporation Acts*, 1790, reprinted in Cobban, *French Revolution*, p. 49.
28. The description is John Thelwall's: see Cone, *English Jacobins*, p. iv.
29. *Ibid.*, pp. iv–v.
30. Dickinson, *Liberty*, p. 195.
31. Philp, 'English Republicanism', pp. 255–6.
32. Mary Wollstonecraft, 'Review of Anon., *A Letter to the Right Honourable William Pitt, on the Subject of a Tax for Raising Six Millions Sterling...*', AR, May 1792, *Works*, vol. 7, p. 441.
33. Hazlitt, *Holcroft*, p. 178.
34. *Ibid.*, p. 206.
35. Catharine Macaulay, *Observations on the Reflections of the Right Hon Edmund Burke on the Revolution in France* (London, 1791), pp. 20–1.
36. Price, 'The Evidence for a Future Period of Improvement in the State of Mankind', 1787, *Political Writings*, p. 162. For Price and Priestley's millennialist views, see Jack Fruchtman, Jr, *The Apocalyptic Politics of Richard Price and Joseph Priestley: a Study in Late 18th century English Republican Millennialism* (Philadelphia: American Philosophical Society, 1983); Clarke Garrett, *Respectable Folly: Millenarians and the French Revolution in France and England* (Baltimore: Johns Hopkins University Press, 1975), ch. 6.
37. Wollstonecraft, *Mary*, *Works*, vol. 1, p. 51.
38. Wollstonecraft, *French Revolution*, *Works*, vol. 6, p. 22.
39. *Ibid.*, pp. 166, 154.
40. *Ibid.*, p. 45.
41. *Ibid.*, p. 154.
42. Wollstonecraft, *Short Residence, Appendix*, *Works*, vol. 6, p. 346.
43. Wollstonecraft, *French Revolution*, *Works*, vol. 6, p. 183.
44. Wollstonecraft, *French Revolution*, *Works*, vol. 6, p. 167. According to one of Wollstonecraft's Paris associates, even at the height of the Terror, when 'the hideous state of the then political horizon hurt her exceedingly', she 'always thought... it [the revolution] would finally succeed' (Todd, *Wollstonecraft*, p. 210).

5 PERFECTING CIVILISATION

1. Wollstonecraft, *French Revolution*, *Works*, vol. 6, p. 20.
2. David Spadafora, *The Idea of Progress in Eighteenth Century Britain* (London: Yale University Press, 1990), introduction.
3. Wollstonecraft, *French Revolution*, *Works*, vol. 6, pp. 6–7. For an excellent discussion of Wollstonecraft as philosophical historian see Jane Rendall, ' "The grand causes which combine to carry mankind forward": Wollstonecraft, history and revolution', *Women's Writing*, 4:2, 1997. Wollstonecraft's history of the Revolution relied heavily on other published accounts, particularly those carried in the *New Annual Register*.
4. Wollstonecraft, *French Revolution*, *Works*, vol. 6, p. 220.
5. The title of Godwin's best-known novel is *Things as They are; or the Adventures of Caleb Williams* (1794).
6. Wollstonecraft, *VRW*, *Works*, vol. 5, p. 73.
7. *Ibid.*, p. 82.
8. Wollstonecraft, *French Revolution*, *Works*, vol. 6, p. 235.
9. Wollstonecraft, *VRW*, *Works*, vol. 5, p. 129.
10. *Ibid.*, p. 66.
11. *Ibid.*, pp. 82, 129–30.
12. Karen O'Brien, *Feminist Debate in Eighteenth Century Britain* (forthcoming, Cambridge University Press): quoted with author's permission. I am grateful to the author for allowing me to see her book in manuscript.
13. For the gender dimension of Enlightenment histories of civilisation see Rendall, ' "The grand causes" '; Sylvana Tomaselli, 'The Enlightenment Debate on Women', *History Workshop Journal*, 20 (1985); Sylvana Tomaselli, 'Reflections on the History of the Science of Woman', in M. Benjamin (ed.), *A Question of Identity: Women, Science and Literature* (Rutgers: Rutgers University Press, 1993).
14. Thomas Gisborne, DD, *An Enquiry into the Duties of the Female Sex* (London, 1797), p. 17.
15. David Hume, *Of the Rise and Progress of the Arts and Sciences*, 1777, in *Essays: Moral, Political and Literary* (Indianapolis: Liberty Fund, 1985), p. 134.
16. Fordyce, *Sermons to Young Women*, vol. 1, p. 23.
17. Hume, *Arts and Sciences*, p. 130.
18. See, for example, A Clergyman of the Church of England [John Bennett], *Strictures on Female Education* (London, 1787), p. 77.
19. Adam Smith, *The Theory of Moral Sentiments*, 1759 (Indianapolis, Liberty Fund, 1982) p. 209; John Brown, *An Estimate of the Manners and Principles of the Times* (1757), p. 125. Chapter 11 of Harriet Guest, *Small Change: Women, Learning and Patriotism, 1750–1810* (University of Chicago Press, 2000) contains a very illuminating discussion of Woman as the amoral side of commercial society, and Wollstonecraft's place within this discursive paradigm.
20. Philip Carter, 'An "Effeminate" or "Efficient" Nation? Masculinity and Eighteenth-Century Social Commentary', *Textual Practice*, 11:3 (1997);

Kathleen Wilson, *The Sense of the People: Politics, Culture and Imperialism in England, 1715–1785*, 1995 (Cambridge University Press, 1998), pp. 185–205. For the cultural significance of effeminacy see also Barker Benfield, *Culture of Sensibility*, chapter 3.

21. Brown, *Estimate*, p. 117.
22. Carter, ' "Effeminate" . . . nation?', pp. 429–30.
23. James Burgh, *Britain's Remembrancer* (London, 1746), pp. 12–13, 18.
24. John Sekora, *Luxury: the Concept in Western Thought, Eden to Smollett* (Baltimore: Johns Hopkins University Press, 1977).
25. Wollstonecraft, *French Revolution*, *Works*, vol. 6, p. 121.
26. Mary Wollstonecraft, *Letter Introductory to a Series of Letters on the Present Character of the French Nation*, 1798, *Works*, vol. 6, pp. 443–4. This letter, which is dated 15 February 1793, was published by Godwin in his collection of Wollstonecraft's *Posthumous Works*.
27. Wollstonecraft, *French Revolution*, *Works*, vol. 6, p. 121.
28. Wollstonecraft, *Letter on French Nation*, *Works*, vol. 6, p. 444.
29. Wollstonecraft, *Short Residence*, *Works*, vol. 6, p. 266.
30. Wollstonecraft, *VRW*, *Works*, vol. 5, p. 146.
31. *Ibid.*, p. 125.
32. Wollstonecraft, *French Revolution*, *Works*, vol. 6, p. 123.
33. *Ibid.*, p. 121.
34. Wollstonecraft, *VRM*, *Works*, vol. 5, p. 10.
35. Wollstonecraft, *VRW*, *Works*, vol. 5, pp. 86, 92–3.
36. *Ibid.*, p. 92.
37. *Ibid.*, p. 120.
38. *Ibid.*, p. 126–7.
39. *Ibid.*, p. 127.
40. *Ibid.*, pp. 67–8.
41. *Ibid.*, pp. 113–14.
42. *Ibid.*, p. 114.
43. *Ibid.*, pp. 90–1.
44. *Ibid.*, p. 82.
45. Wollstonecraft, *French Revolution*, *Works*, vol. 6, p. 146.
46. Wollstonecraft, *Short Residence*, *Works*, vol. 6, p. 274.
47. Wollstonecraft, *French Revolution*, *Works*, vol. 6, p. 109.
48. Wollstonecraft, *VRW*, *Works*, vol. 5, p. 84.
49. Wollstonecraft, *VRW*, *Works*, vol. 5, p. 83; *Short Residence*, *Works*, vol. 6, p. 288.
50. Wollstonecraft, *VRW*, *Works*, vol. 5, pp. 84–5.
51. Wollstonecraft, *French Revolution*, *Works*, vol. 6, p. 235.
52. Wollstonecraft, *VRW*, *Works*, vol. 5, p. 87.
53. Wollstonecraft, *VRM*, *Works*, vol. 5, p. 13.
54. Godwin, *Memoirs*, p. 229.
55. Wollstonecraft, *French Revolution*, *Works*, vol. 6, p. 18.

56. Wollstonecraft, *VRM*, *Works*, vol. 5, p. 10.

57. Wollstonecraft, *French Revolution*, *Works*, vol. 6, p. 45.

58. O'Brien, *Feminist Thought*; Rendall, ' "Grand causes" ', pp. 158–62.

59. Wollstonecraft, *VRW*, *Works*, vol. 5, p. 110.

60. *Ibid.*, pp. 104, 106; see also *French Revolution*, *Works*, vol. 6, p. 45.

61. Wollstonecraft, *French Revolution*, *Works*, vol. 6, p. 167.

62. Wollstonecraft, *VRM*, *Works*, vol. 5, pp. 43, 21.

63. *Ibid.*, p. 21.

64. *Ibid.*, p. 56.

65. *General Magazine and Impartial Review*, 4 (1791), p. 26.

66. Wollstonecraft, *French Revolution*, *Works*, vol. 6, p. 61. Nor was it only Wollstonecraft on whom Rousseau had this effect: 'It was Rousseau,' William Hazlitt declared, 'who brought the feeling of irreconcilable enmity to rank and privileges, *above humanity*, home to the bosom of every man, – identified it with all the pride of intellect, and with the deepest yearnings of the human heart.' *Collected Works* (London, 1902) volume 4, p. 89n.

67. Wollstonecraft, *VRW*, *Works*, vol. 5, p. 85.

68. Wollstonecraft, *VRM*, *Works*, vol. 5, p. 39.

69. Gregory Claeys, 'Utopianism, Property and the French Revolution Debate' in K. Kumar and S. Bann, *Utopias and the Millennium* (London: Reaktion Books, 1993), pp. 54–5.

70. For charges of levelling directed at Wollstonecraft, see *Critical Review*, 5, 1792, pp. 138–9. According to the *Gentleman's Magazine*, reviewing Wollstonecraft's *Rights of Men*, her aim was to 'restore mankind to the level of the golden age . . . the object is, that there should be no property at all, rather than that one man should enjoy more than another.' (61:1, 1791).

71. Timothy J. Reiss, 'Revolution in Bounds: Wollstonecraft, Women and Reason', in L. Kauffman (ed.), *Gender and Theory* (Oxford: Basil Blackwell, 1989), p. 21. A host of writers make this case, arguing that Wollstonecraft applied the 'demands of the bourgeois revolution . . . to women on the same basis that they were extended to men' (Zillah Eisenstein, *The Radical Future of Liberal Feminism* [New York: Longman, 1981]), p. 91. See, for example, Donna Landry, *The Muses of Resistance: Labouring-Class Women's Poetry in Britain, 1739–96* (Cambridge University Press, 1990), pp. 260, 269.

72. E. P. Thompson, *Witness Against the Beast: William Blake and the Moral Law* (Cambridge University Press, 1993), pp. 109–112; *Raymond Williams, Problems in Materialism and Culture* (London: Verso, 1980), p. 157. See also Isaac Kramnick, *Republican and Bourgeois Radicalism* (London: Cornell University Press, 1990) for a good discussion of the class background of radicalism with whose conclusions, however, I disagree.

73. Wollstonecraft, *Short Residence*, *Works*, vol. 6, p. 296.

74. Edmund Burke, *Letters on a Regicide Peace*, 1795 (London, 1893), p. 65.

75. Mary Wollstonecraft, letter to William Godwin, 21 May 1797, in Wardle (ed.), *Letters*, p. 394.

76. Williams, *Materialism*, p. 157.
77. For attitudes toward the middle class in eighteenth-century Britain, see Paul Langford, *Public Life and the Propertied Gentleman, 1689–1798* (Oxford: Clarendon Press, 1991), and Dror Wahrman, *Imagining the Middle Class: the Political Representation of Class in Britain, c. 1780–1840* (Cambridge University Press, 1995).
78. Quoted in Langford, *Public Life*, p. 478; Price, 'Observations on the Importance of the American Revolution', 1785, *Political Writings*, pp. 144–5.
79. Wollstonecraft, *VRW*, *Works*, vol. 5, p. 126.
80. *Ibid.*, p. 129.
81. Wollstonecraft, *French Revolution*, *Works*, vol. 6, p. 70.
82. Wollstonecraft, *VRW*, *Works*, vol. 5, p. 220.
83. *Ibid.*, p. 68.
84. Wollstonecraft, *VRM*, *Works*, vol. 5, p. 33.
85. Wollstonecraft, *French Revolution*, *Works*, vol. 6, p. 229; Wollstonecraft, *VRM*, *Works*, vol. 5, p. 57.
86. Wollstonecraft, *French Revolution*, *Works*, vol. 6, p. 20.
87. Wollstonecraft, *Short Residence*, *Works*, vol. 6, p. 273.
88. *Ibid.*, p. 308.
89. *Ibid.*, p. 276.
90. *Ibid.*, p. 270.
91. *Ibid.*, p. 276.
92. *Ibid.*, p. 283.
93. *Ibid.*, p. 283.
94. *Ibid.*, p. 289.
95. *Ibid.*, p. 273.
96. *Ibid.*, p. 273.
97. *Ibid.*, p. 273. Norway, as it happens, was the first state in northern Europe to enfranchise women, in 1907.
98. *Ibid.*, p. 302.
99. Wollstonecraft, *French Revolution*, *Works*, vol. 6, p. 20.
100. Price, 'American Revolution', *Political Writings*, p. 145.
101. Mary Wollstonecraft, letters to Gilbert Imlay, 28 December, 30 December 1794, in Wardle (ed.) *Letters*, pp. 270, 274.
102. Mary Wollstonecraft, letter to Gilbert Imlay, 29 December 1794, in Wardle (ed.) *Letters*, p. 271.
103. Wollstonecraft, *Short Residence*, *Works*, vol. 6, pp. 325, 309.
104. Wollstonecraft, *Letter on French Nation*, *Works*, vol. 6, p. 444.
105. *Ibid.*, p. 445; Wollstonecraft, *French Revolution*, *Works*, vol. 6, p. 233.
106. Wollstonecraft, *French Revolution*, *Works*, vol. 6, p. 234.
107. *Ibid.*, p. 234.
108. *Ibid.*, pp. 226, 17–18.
109. Wollstonecraft, *VRM*, *Works*, vol. 5, p. 24. 'Property ... should be fluctuating, which would be the case if it were more equally divided amongst all the children of a family' (*VRM*, *Works*, vol. 5, p. 24).

110. Mary Wollstonecraft, letter to William Godwin, 10 June 1797, in Wardle (ed.), *Letters*, p. 397. The comment was prompted by observing the effect of an inheritance on a mutual friend.
111. Wollstonecraft, *Short Residence, Works*, vol. 6, p. 287.
112. *Ibid.*, p. 344.
113. Mary Wollstonecraft, review of Friend to the Poor, 'A Letter to the Right Reverend the Lord Bishop of Chester, on the Removal of poor Children ... to the Cotton and other Manufactories at Manchester', *AR*, vol. 8, May 1792, p. 442.
114. Robert Southey, letter to Samuel Coleridge, 16 January 1800: K. Curry, ed., *New Letters of Robert Southey* (New York: Columbia University Press, 1965), vol. 1, 215. Later Southey wrote again about Wollstonecraft's admiration for Babeuf, reporting her saying that 'she had never seen any person who possessed greater abilities, or equal strength of character' (*Quarterly Review*, 45, 1831; quoted in Todd, *Wollstonecraft*, p. 477n22).
115. Wollstonecraft, *French Revolution, Works*, vol. 6, pp. 17, 18.
116. Wollstonecraft, *Maria, Works*, vol. 1, p. 101.
117. *Ibid.*, p. 102.
118. Wollstonecraft, *Short Residence, Works*, vol. 6, p. 325.

6 GALLIC PHILOSOPHESSES

1. Hays, 'Wollstonecraft', p. 411.
2. [Mathias], *Pursuits of Literature*, p. 238.
3. Simpson, *Revolt Against Theory*, p. 105.
4. St Clair, *Godwins and Shelleys*, p. 105.
5. Donna T. Andrew, *London Debating Societies, 1776–1799* (London: London Record Society, 1994), p. 357.
6. John Gale Jones, *Sketches of a Political Tour* (London, 1796), p. 91.
7. George Dyer, *Poems* (London, 1792), p. 36. Dyer's observation appears as a footnote to his ode 'On Liberty', in which Liberty is addressed thus (p. 36):

> Or dost thou, sweet enthusiast, choose to warm
> With more than manly fire the female breast?
> And urge thy Wollstonecraft to break the charm,
> Where beauty lies in durance vile opprest?

8. The London Corresponding Society ran an advertisement for the *Rights of Woman* at the back of the 'Account of the Proceedings of a Meeting of the London Corresponding Society, Held in a Field near Copenhagen House, Monday, Oct. 26, 1795; Including the Substance of the Speeches of Citizens BINNS, THELWALL, JONES, HODGSON, & c., with the ADDRESS TO THE NATION, and the REMONSTRANCE TO THE KING. And the Resolutions passed by upwards of Two Hundred Thousand Citizens, then and there assembled' (London: Citizen Lee, 1795). The advertisement, on p. 16, reads:

'Shortly will be published, a New Edition of the RIGHTS OF WOMEN, by Mrs. Wollstonecroft [sic] – Price 6 d.' Thanks to Arianne Chernock for this reference.

9. Tomalin, *Wollstonecraft*, pp. 143–4.

10. 'To Mary Wollstonecraft', *Poems* (London, 1797).

11. Of the radical men who addressed women's issues, possibly the most interesting was Alexander Jardine, a friend of Godwin's, who in 1787 published a strongly feminist work, *Letters from Barbary, France, Spain... etc.* where he argued for women's innate equality with men, attacked gallantry, praised societies where women feel free to be as 'learned as they please', and suggested that men who vilified women intellectuals as 'masculine' were generally those who were not particularly 'manly or learned' themselves. Wollstonecraft reviewed Jardine's book for the *Analytical Review*: her review, while condescending and sarcastic in tone, is basically favourable, but makes only very brief mention of his 'singular' views on women (*AR*, 4, 1789, pp. 107–9, 154–6). Mary Hays, on the other hand, cited Jardine's book as a key feminist text whose appearance had almost convinced her to abandon her own projected work as superfluous (Hays, *Appeal*, 'Advertisement to the Reader').

12. Godwin, *Memoirs*, p. 256.

13. Janet Todd, 'Elizabeth Inchbald', Janet Todd (ed.) *Dictionary of British Women Writers*, 1989 (London: Routledge, 1991), pp. 344–7; S. R. Littlewood, *Elizabeth Inchbald and Her Circle* (London: Daniel O'Connor, 1921); Janet Todd, *The Sign of Angellica: Women, Writing and Fiction, 1660–1800* (London: Virago, 1989), ch. 12.

14. A. F. Wedd (ed.), *The Fate of the Fenwicks* (London: Methuen and Co, 1927); Janet Todd, 'Eliza Fenwick' in Todd, *British Women Writers*, pp. 241–2.

15. Turner, *Living by the Pen*, p. 98. Martin Fitzpatrick, 'Charlotte Smith', in Todd, *British Women Writers*, pp. 622–6.

16. Reprinted the following year as Anne Frances Randall [Mary Robinson], *A Letter to the Women of England, on the Injustice of Mental Subordination* (London, 1799).

17. Perdita [Mary Robinson], *Memoirs of the late Mrs Robinson, written by herself*, 1801 (London: Peter Owen, 1994), pp. 46, 62. Margaret Maison, 'Mary Robinson', Todd, *British Women Writers*, pp. 575–8.

18. Todd, *Sign of Angellica*, p. 218.

19. Hays, *Memoirs of Emma Courtney*, p. 35.

20. Todd, *Sign of Angellica*, chs. 12 and 13. For the likelihood that the 'doctor's daughter' who addressed a radical gathering in Norwich in 1794 was Amelia Alderson, see Browne, *Feminist Mind*, p. 120.

21. Laetitia Matilda Hawkins, *Letters on the Female Mind* (London, 1793), pp. 21, 23.

22. Polwhele, *Un-Sex'd Females*, p. 9.

23. Charlotte Smith, *Desmond, a Novel* (London, 1792), vol. 1, pp. iii–iv.

24. Elizabeth Inchbald, *Everyone Has His Fault* (London, 1793), quoted in Tomalin, *Wollstonecraft*, p. 328.

25. Randall [Robinson], *Letter to Women of England*, p. 72.

26. *Ibid.*, p. 79.
27. Wardle, *Wollstonecraft*, p. 159. Elizabeth Carter, according to her nephew, viewed Wollstonecraft's feminist ideas as 'wild', although he added that his aunt thought 'men exercised too arbitrary a power over [women], and considered them as too inferior to themselves. Hence she had a decided bias in favour of female writers...' (quoted in M. L. Williamson, 'Who's Afraid of Mrs Barbauld? The Bluestockings and Feminism', *International Journal of Women's Studies*, 3:1 (1980), p. 97).
28. Chapone found in it 'some strong sense' marred by 'absurdities, improprieties, and obvious indelicacies' (Hester Chapone, *Works* [London, 1807], vol. 2, p. 202.) For Seward see above, pp. 25–6.
29. Quoted in Tomalin, *Wollstonecraft*, p. 328.
30. The novel was *Adeline Mowbray* (1804): see below (p. 247).
31. Anna Laetitia Barbauld, *Works* (London, 1825), p. xix. G. A. Ellis, *A Memoir of Mrs Anna Laetitia Barbauld* (London, 1874); Betsy Rodgers, *Georgian Chronicle: Mrs Barbauld and Her Family* (London: Methuen and Co, 1958); A. L. Le Breton, *Memoir of Mrs Barbauld* (London, 1874).
32. Quoted in Le Breton, *Mrs Barbauld*, p. 87.
33. 'To a Lady with Some Painted Flowers', *Works*, pp. 100–1. Wollstonecraft reprinted this poem, with a disapproving note, in the *Rights of Woman* (*VRW*, *Works*, vol. 5, pp. 122–3).
34. Rodgers, *Georgian Chronicle*, p. 61.
35. *Ibid.*, pp. 108–10.
36. For a 1792 poem in celebration of the Revolution, see *Works*, p. 180.
37. A Volunteer [Anna Barbauld], *Sins of the Government, Sins of the Nation* (London, 1793).
38. Barbauld, *Works*, vol. 2, p. 194.
39. Williamson, 'Who's Afraid of Mrs Barbauld?', p. 91.
40. *Works*, vol. 2, p. 362.
41. O'Malley, *Women*, p. 209.
42. Barbauld, *Works*, vol. 1, p. 185. See n. 33, this page.
43. O'Malley, *Women*, p. 209.
44. Barbauld, *Works*, vol. 2, pp. 245–6.
45. 'Now if there be any persons,' Priestley wrote to her, 'who apply the language of 'profound adoration' to a human being, I consider it as a most abominable practice, as nothing less than a direct impiety... there is an infinite difference in the object of our attachment in these two cases...' (Joseph Priestley, *The Theological and Miscellaneous Works*, 25 vols. (London, 1817–31), vol. 1, pp. 280–1.
46. Gilbert Wakefield, *A General Reply to the Arguments Against the Enquiry into Public Worship* (London, 1792), p. 20.
47. Mr Cresswick, Teacher of Elocution [Mary Wollstonecraft], *The Female Reader, or Miscellaneous Pieces in Prose and Verse*, 1789, *Works*, vol. 4, p. 57.
48. Mary Hays to William Godwin, 8 March 1796, in A. F. Wedd (ed.), *The Love Letters of Mary Hays* (London: Methuen, 1925), p. 233. Jane Spencer, 'Mary Hays', Todd (ed.), *British Women Writers*, pp. 320–1; Kelly, *Women, Writing*

and Revolution, chs. 3 and 7; Marilyn L. Brooks, 'Mary Hays: Finding a "Voice" in Dissent,' *Enlightenment and Dissent*, 14, 1995, pp. 3–24.

49. William Godwin, letter to Mary Hays, 26 December 1797, in Wedd, *Love Letters*, p. 241.

50. Mary Wollstonecraft, letter to William Godwin, 10 September 1796, in Wardle (ed.), *Letters*, p. 347.

51. William Godwin, letter to Mary Hays, 10 April 1797, in Wedd (ed.), *Love Letters*, p. 241.

52. Kelly, *Women, Writing, and Revolution*, p. 84.

53. Spencer, 'Hays' p. 320.

54. Kelly, *Women, Writing, and Revolution*, p. 107.

55. *The Monthly Magazine and British Register*, 4, September 1797, pp. 232–3 and October 1797, p. 245; Hays, 'Memoirs of Wollstonecraft'; Mary Hays, *Female Biography* (London, 1803).

56. Mary Hays to William Godwin, 10 March 1796, in Wedd (ed.), *Love Letters*, pp. 235–6.

57. Elizabeth Hamilton, *Memoirs of Modern Philosophers: a Novel* (London, 1800).

58. Wedd (ed.), *Love Letters*, p. 11.

59. Mary Wollstonecraft, letter to Mary Hays, *c.* 1796, in Wardle (ed.), *Letters*, pp. 332–2.

60. Hays, *Emma Courtney*, pp. xvii, 21, 21, 20, 14.

61. Hays, *Emma Courtney*, pp. 25, 59. Like Rousseau's Emile, who falls in love with Sophie simply from hearing his Mentor's reports of her, Emma's love for Harley begins by seeing his portrait and hearing his mother's adoring accounts.

62. *Ibid.*, pp. 60, 86.

63. *Ibid.*, p. 125.

64. *Ibid.*, p. 149.

65. *Ibid.*, p. 126.

66. *Ibid.*, p. xviii.

67. *Ibid.*, p. 148; Wollstonecraft, *Short Residence, Works*, vol. 6, p. 280. Hays also used these words, this time acknowledging that they had been written by Wollstonecraft, to describe her feelings for William Frend (Todd, *Wollstonecraft*, pp. 375–8).

68. Hays, *Emma Courtney*, p. xvii.

69. *Ibid.*, p. 142. Much of the epistolary dialogue between Emma and her mentor was lifted directly from Hays's correspondence with Godwin.

70. *Ibid.*, p. 143.

71. *Ibid.*, p. 146.

72. *Ibid.*, p. 39.

73. *Ibid.*, p. 146.

74. *Ibid.*, p. 160.

75. Hazlitt described him as having acquired a 'sultry and unwholesome popularity' (Richard Holmes, introduction to Godwin, *Memoirs*, p. 11).

76. St Clair, *Godwins*, p. 151. Chapter 12 in St Clair's excellent book, 'Women', is delicately revealing.
77. George Dyer, letter to Mary Hays, n.d., in Wedd (ed.), *Love Letters*, p. 238.
78. Wollstonecraft, *VRW*, *Works*, pp. 167, 163.
79. Godwin, *Memoirs*, pp. 235–6.
80. Mark Philp, *Godwin's Political Justice* (London: Duckworth, 1986), pp. 122–9. See also St Clair, *Godwins*, pp. 29–178; Tomalin, *Wollstonecraft*, pp. 89–283.
81. Mary Wollstonecraft, letter to William Godwin, 25 June 1797, in Wardle (ed.), *Letters*, p. 399.
82. For her dislike of cooking see Wollstonecraft, *Short Residence*, *Works*, vol. 6, p. 315.
83. Mary Wollstonecraft, letter to Maria Reveley, 26 June 1797, in Wardle (ed.), *Letters*, p. 400.
84. *Sapere aude* ('Dare to know') was Kant's famous injunction to the would-be enlightened.
85. Thomas Holcroft, *Anna St Ives*, 1792 (Oxford University Press, 1970), p. 147.
86. *Ibid.*, p. 170.
87. *Ibid.*, p. 172.
88. Hays, *Emma Courtney*, p. 115.
89. Kegan Paul, *Godwin*, vol. 1, p. 71.
90. Godwin, *Memoirs*, p. 236.
91. William Hazlitt: 'He [Coleridge] asked me if I had ever seen Mary Wollstonecraft [sic], and I said, I had once for a few moments, and that she seemed to me to turn off Godwin's objections to something she advanced with quite a playful, easy air. He replied, that "this was only one instance of the ascendancy which people of imagination exercised over those of mere intellect". He did not rate Godwin very high ... but he had a great idea of Mrs Wolstonecraft's [sic] powers of conversation, none at all of her talent for book-making.' 'My First Acquaintance with Poets', *Selected Writings* (Harmondsworth: Penguin, 1985), p. 50.
92. *Critical Review*, April 1798.
93. Quoted in W. Clark Durant, *Supplement* to 1927 edition of Godwin, *Memoirs* (London: Constable and Co., 1927), p. 253.
94. Wollstonecraft, *Short Residence*, *Works*, vol. 6, p. 248.
95. Wollstonecraft, *VRW*, *Works*, vol. 5, p. 193n. Even more dangerously, in 1790, in her Introductory Address to Salzmann's *Elements of Morality*, Wollstonecraft argued that adults should 'speak to children of the organs of generation as freely as we speak of other parts of the body': a proposal that earned her much scurrilous criticism from political conservatives (*Works*, vol. 2, p. 9). For Wollstonecraft's views on sex education, see Vivien Jones, 'Advice and Enlightenment: the Case of Mary Wollstonecraft', forthcoming: I am grateful to her for letting me read this in manuscript.
96. Robert Bage, *Hermonsprong, or Man as He Is Not*, 1796 (London: Turnstile Press, 1951), p. 136.

97. Hays, 'Wollstonecraft', pp. 421, 423.
98. Quoted in Gary Kelly, *Revolutionary Feminism: The Mind and Career of Mary Wollstoncraft* (Basingstoke: Macmillan, 1992), p. 147.
99. Tomalin, *Wollstonecraft*, p. 164. In a typical elision of Jacobin radicalism with sexual libertarianism, the bluestocking Hester Thrale, hearing of Williams's liaison with Stone, described her as having sacrificed her personal reputation to her 'spirit of Politics' (Elizabeth Manor, *The Ladies of Llangollen* [Harmondsworth: Penguin Books, 1987], p. 79).
100. Mary Wollstonecraft, review of J. P. Brissot, *Nouveau Voyage Dans Les Etats Unis, Analytical Review*, September 1791, *Works*, vol. 7, p. 391.
101. Mary Wollstonecraft, letter to William Roscoe, 12 November 1792, in Wardle (ed.), *Letters*, p. 218.
102. Mary Wollstonecraft, letter to Gilbert Imlay, 1 January 1794, in Wardle (ed.), *Letters*, p. 242.
103. Mary Wollstonecraft, letter to Amelia Alderson, 11 April 1797, in Wardle (ed.) *Letters*, pp. 389–90.
104. Edmund Burke, *A Letter to a Member of the National Assembly* (London, 1791), p. 39.
105. Eudo C. Mason, *The Mind of Henry Fuseli* (London: Routledge and Kegan Paul, 1951); Tate Gallery Publications, *Henry Fuseli* (London: Tate Gallery, 1975); Tomalin, *Wollstonecraft*, ch. 7.
106. Mason, *Fuseli*, pp. 79, 134.
107. For Fuseli's 'fear and hatred' of women, and his fetishistic representations of them in his paintings, see Gert Schiff, 'Fuseli, Lucifer and the Medusa', Tate Gallery Publications, *Fuseli*, pp. 15–19.
108. Mason, *Fuseli*, p. 145.
109. *Ibid.*, p. 147.
110. Wollstonecraft, *VRW, Works*, vol. 5, pp. 142–3.
111. David Wootton, 'Pierre Bayle, Libertine?' in M. A. Stewart (ed.) *Studies in Seventeenth-Century European Philosophy* (Oxford University Press, 1997); Robert Darnton, *The Forbidden Best-Sellers of Pre-Revolutionary France* (London: HarperCollins, 1996); Taylor, *Eve and the New Jerusalem*; Lucy Bland, *Banishing the Beast: English Feminism and Sexual Morality, 1885–1914* (London: Penguin, 1995), ch. 7.
112. Wollstonecraft, *Maria, Works*, vol. 1, p. 172.
113. Holmes, *Footsteps*, p. 125.
114. Kelly, *Women, Writing, and Revolution*, p. 20.
115. Amanda Foreman, *Georgiana, Duchess of Devonshire* (London: HarperCollins, 1999), p. 174.
116. Modern admirers of Wollstonecraft, reading anti-jacobin propaganda describing her as a whore and a prostitute, have been properly angered. But it is worth checking our indignation for a moment to re-consider Wollstonecraft's sexual conduct in light of contemporary aristocratic codes. Was Wollstonecraft, consciously or otherwise, behaving in a ladylike, that is, elite-aspirational,

fashion when she bedded Imlay in Paris? The question, particularly given her relationship with Mary Robinson, at least deserves consideration.

117. Holcroft, *Anna St Ives*, p. 279.
118. *Ibid.*, p. 281.
119. William Godwin, *An Enquiry Concerning Political Justice* (London, 1793), p. 851.
120. Mary Wollstonecraft, letter to William Godwin, 4 October 1796, in Wardle (ed.), *Letters*, p. 356.
121. Mary Wollstonecraft, letter to William Godwin, 23 December 1796, in Wardle (ed.), *Letters*, p. 369.
122. Mary Wollstonecraft, letters to William Godwin, 10 November, 30 September 1796, in Wardle (ed.), *Letters*, pp. 360, 355; letter to Amelia Alderson, 11 April 1797, in Wardle (ed.), *Letters*, p. 389.
123. Godwin, *Memoirs*, p. 259.
124. Mary Wollstonecraft, letter to William Godwin, 21 May 1797, in Wardle (ed.), *Letters*, p. 394.
125. The poet Anna Seward, who had previously praised the *Rights of Woman*, was dismayed by the erotic anguish revealed in Wollstonecraft's letters from Scandinavia: 'If her system could not steel her own heart, as it seeks to fortify that of her sex in general, we should at least have expected her to conceal the weakness, whose disclosure evinced the incompetence of all her maxims' (quoted in Todd, *Wollstonecraft*, p. 369).
126. Wollstonecraft, *Short Residence*, *Works*, vol. 6, p. 337.

7 WOMEN VS THE POLITY

1. Mary Wollstonecraft, *Letter on the Present Character of the French Nation*, *Works*, vol. 6, pp. 444–5.
2. Wollstonecraft, *VRW*, *Works*, vol. 5, p. 83.
3. Wollstonecraft, *Letter*, *Works*, vol. 6, p. 445.
4. Wollstonecraft, *VRM*, *Works*, vol. 5, pp. 55, 52.
5. Quoted in Spadafora, *Idea of Progress*, p. 249.
6. Wollstonecraft, *VRW*, *Works*, vol. 5, p. 84.
7. Daniel Robinson, 'Theodicy versus Feminist Strategy in Mary Wollstonecraft's Fiction', *Eighteenth Century Fiction*, 9:2 (1997). Leibniz's case [*Theodicy* (1710)] that God's permission of evil was consistent with His benevolence was the most influential of the period. Discussing the ideal of female virtue represented by Richardson's Clarissa, who tells Lovelace that by raping her while she was unconscious he has robbed her of her honour, Wollstonecraft describes this as 'an excess of strictness', which she counters by quoting Leibniz: 'Errors are often useful; but it is commonly to remedy other errors' (VRW, *Works*, vol. 5, p. 141). Leibniz's optimism was reproduced in Pope's 'whatever is, is right' (*Essay on Man* [1733–4]) which in turn appeared in

Rousseau's *Emile* as 'Ce qui est, est bien.' Wollstonecraft quotes Rousseau's aphorism, following Pope, as 'Whatever is, is right', which she avers is a 'solemn truth with respect to God', but not so for mankind, who must seek to alter whatever is morally wrong, in fulfilment of God's longterm plan (*VRW*, *Works*, vol. 5, p. 154). For another thoughtful discussion of Wollstonecraft's theodicy, see Gordon Spence, 'Mary Wollstonecraft's Theodicy and Theory of Progress', *Enlightenment and Dissent*, 14, 1995.

Wollstonecraft's insistence that evil originates with God, in the early pages of the *Rights of Woman*, is in direct criticism of Rousseau's view of evil as positive: 'Everything is good as it leaves the hands of the Author of things; everything degenerates in the hands of man' (*Emile*, p. 37).

8. Wollstonecraft, *VRW*, *Works*, vol. 5, p. 154.
9. *Ibid.*, pp. 176–83.
10. Mary Wollstonecraft, letter to William Roscoe, 12 November 1792, in Wardle (ed.), *Letters*, p. 218.
11. Mary Wollstonecraft, letter to Ruth Barlow, 8 July 1794, in Wardle (ed.), *Letters*, p. 257.
12. Wollstonecraft, *French Revolution*, *Works*, vol. 6, p. 6.
13. *Ibid.*, p. 6.
14. Burke, *Reflections*, p. 9.
15. Wollstonecraft, *French Revolution*, *Works*, vol. 6, p. 6.
16. *Ibid.*, p. 230.
17. *Ibid.*, p. 123.
18. *Ibid.*, p. 123.
19. Wollstonecraft, *VRW*, *Works*, vol. 5, pp. 136, 261.
20. *Ibid.*, p. 259. In his *Theory of Moral Sentiments*, Adam Smith had argued that women feel only personal tenderness for others ('humanity') rather than that disinterested 'generosity' which is the essence of patriotic spirit. Wollstonecraft endorses Smith's argument (*Ibid.*, pp. 260–1), although, confusingly, in her terminology it is 'humanity' – here meaning Smithian generosity, i.e. public spirited benevolence – which women are deemed to lack.
21. *Ibid.*, p. 256.
22. *Ibid.*, p. 261.
23. Wollstonecraft, *French Revolution*, *Works*, vol. 6, pp. 213, 231.
24. *Ibid.*, p. 21.
25. Wollstonecraft, *VRW*, *Works*, vol. 5, p. 68.
26. Guest, *Small Change*, pp. 190, 81.
27. Wollstonecraft, *VRW*, *Works*, vol. 5, pp. 66–7.
28. *Ibid.*, p. 266.
29. *Ibid.*, p. 246.
30. Dorinda Outram, *The Body and the French Revolution* (London: Yale University Press, 1989), p. 125.
31. *Ibid.*, pp. 126, 125. See also Joan Wallach Scott, *Only Paradoxes to Offer: French Feminists and the Rights of Man* (Harvard University Press, 1996).
32. *Ibid.*, p. 126.

33. Karen Offen, *European Feminisms, 1700–1950* (Stanford University Press, 2000), p. 53.
34. *Ibid.*, p. 59.
35. Quoted in Mary Lyndon Shanley, 'Mary Wollstonecraft on sensibility, women's rights and patriarchal power', in Hilda Smith (ed.), *Women Writers and the Early Modern British Political Tradition* (Cambridge University Press, 1998), p. 151.
36. Joan W. Scott, 'The Imagination of Olympe de Gouges', in Yeo (ed.) *Wollstonecraft*, p. 43.
37. Offen, *European Feminisms*, p. 63.
38. *Ibid.*, p. 22.
39. *Ibid.*, p. 25.
40. Wilson, *Sense of the People*, pp. 219–27; Clark, *Struggle for the Breeches*, pp. 142–3.
41. Paine, *Rights of Man*, pp. 249, 102.
42. Wilson, *Sense of the People*, p. 220. For further discussion of this, see Johnson, *Equivocal Beings*, chapter 1.
43. Macaulay, *Letters on Education*, p. 213.
44. For this aspect of the republican tradition, see J. G. A. Pocock, 'Cambridge Paradigms and Scotch Philosophers: a study of the relations between the civic humanist and the civil jurisprudential interpretation of eighteenth-century social thought' in I. Hont and M. Ignatieff (eds.), *Wealth and Virtue: the Shaping of Political Economy in the Scottish Enlightenment* (Cambridge University Press, 1983), pp. 235–6, and his *Virtue, Commerce and History* (Cambridge University Press, 1985), pp. 98–100. See also A. C. Houston, *Algernon Sidney and the Republican Heritage in England and America* (Princeton University Press, 1991), pp. 163–4, and (for the republican influence on Wollstonecraft), Blakemore, *Intertextual War*, pp. 37–52.
45. Pocock, 'Cambridge Paradigms', p. 235; Ruth Bloch, 'The Gendered Meanings of Virtue in Revolutionary America', *Signs: Journal of Women in Culture and Society*, 13:1, 1987, pp. 39–47.
46. Philip Carter, *Men and the Emergence of Polite Society in Britain, 1660–1800* (Harlow: Pearson Education, 2001), chapters 2 and 3; Pocock, *Virtue, Commerce and History*, pp. 48–50, 234–6.
47. Mark Philp, 'English Republicanism in the 1790s', *The Journal of Political Philosophy*, 6:1, 1998.
48. J. G. A. Pocock, 'Catharine Macaulay: patriot historian', in Smith, *Women Writers*. Pocock's account of Macaulay, while characteristically engaging, ignores all aspects of her thought that do not tally with his portrait of her as a quintessentially republican thinker, including her theology, her natural-rights philosophy, and her feminism.
49. For the case that Wollstonecraft was a republican, see Judith A. Vega, 'Feminist Republicanism and the Political Perception of Gender', in Q. Skinner (ed.), *Republicanism: a Shared European Heritage*, vol. 3 (Cambridge University Press, 2000); G. J. Barker Benfield: 'Mary Wollstonecraft: Eighteenth Century

Commonwealthwoman', *Journal of the History of Ideas*, vol. 50, 1989; Anne Phillips, 'Feminism and Republicanism: Is This a Plausible Alliance?', *The Journal of Political Philosophy*, 8:2 (2000). Virginia Sapiro (*A Vindication of Political Virtue* [University of Chicago, 1992]) also refers to Wollstonecraft's republicanism but does not examine it at any length. Valuable points are made by all these writers, but their concern to push Wollstonecraft into the republican camp leads them to underplay or misinterpret key elements of her thought, including her natural-rights perspective and, above all, her religious commitments. The most sustained argument against the republican character-isation of late eighteenth-century Anglo-American radicalism has been made by Isaac Kramnick (*Republicanism and Bourgeois Radicalism*) who lands many telling blows against the 'republican synthesis', but whose counter-position, that radicalism was bourgeois in origin and orientation, I find unpersuasive.

50. Wollstonecraft, *VRW*, *Works*, vol. 5, p. 214.
51. *Ibid.*, p. 191.
52. Carter, *Men and Polite Society*, pp. 108–11. For the image of Washington as a gentle hero, see Sarah Knott, 'A Cultural History of Sensibility in the Era of the American Revolution' (D. Phil. thesis, Oxford University, 1999), pp. 229–37.
53. Scott, 'Olympe de Gouges', p. 43.
54. Langford, *Public Life*, p. 503.
55. Wollstonecraft, *VRM*, *Works*, vol. 5, p. 14.
56. Wollstonecraft, *VRW*, *Works*, vol. 5, p. 67.
57. *Ibid.*, p. 68.
58. Wollstonecraft, *VRM*, *Works*, vol. 5, p. 52.
59. See, for example, *French Revolution*, *Works*, vol. 6, p. 16.
60. Mark Philp, 'The Fragmented Ideology of Reform', in M. Philp (ed.), *The French Revolution and Popular Politics* (Cambridge University Press, 1991), p. 53.
61. Wilson, *Sense of the People*, p. 225.
62. James Burgh, *Political Disquisitions* (London: 1774/5), vol. 1, p. 37.
63. *Ibid.*, p. 37.
64. John Cartwright, in his *Legislative Rights of the Commonwealth Vindicated* (1776) raised the question of female enfranchisement only to dismiss it on the grounds that married women, who took precedence over single, were rightfully subject to their husbands. Similarly, in the 1780s Christopher Wyvill claimed the franchise for male householders on the grounds that such men, while hardly independent in the classical sense, as masters and fathers of families were entitled to act as political representatives for their servants, wives and children (Ian Hampshire-Monk, 'Civic Humanism and Parliamentary Reform: the Case of the Society of the Friends of the People', *Journal of British Studies*, 18:2 [1979], p. 87).
65. Dickinson, *Liberty and Property*, p. 253; Andrew, *London Debating Societies*, p. 378. As this book goes to press, Arianne Chernock's research on men's support for women's rights between 1780 and 1825 is revealing higher levels of male 'feminism' than has ever been suspected: I look forward to reading the results of this work.

66. Dickinson, *Liberty and Property*, p. 253.
67. Wollstonecraft, *VRW*, *Works*, vol. 5, p. 217. Exactly what sort of female political representation Wollstonecraft had in mind here is not clear: possibly the vote, but perhaps too the establishment of a female political chamber or the creation of a female group of MPs to be elected exclusively by women (ideas that found some support among feminists in the 1830s and forties).
68. Wollstonecraft, *VRM*, *Works*, vol. 5, p. 15.

8 THE FEMALE CITIZEN

1. Foreman, *Georgiana, Duchess of Devonshire*, p. 348. See also Elaine Chalus, ' "That Epidemical Madness": Women and Electoral Politics in the Late Eighteenth Century' in H. Barker and E. Chalus (eds.), *Gender in Eighteenth-Century England* (London: Addison Wesley Longman, 1997); Linda Colley, *Britons: Forging the Nation, 1707–1837* (London: Yale University Press, 1992), pp. 242–50.
2. Wollstonecraft, *VRM*, *Works*, vol. 5, p. 30.
3. Wollstonecraft, *French Revolution*, *Works*, vol. 6, pp. 196–207.
4. *Ibid.*, p. 207.
5. Wollstonecraft, *VRW*, *Works*, vol. 5, p. 153.
6. Wollstonecraft, *French Revolution*, *Works*, vol. 6, p. 207; Wollstonecraft, *VRW*, *Works*, vol. 5, p. 68.
7. Wollstonecraft, *VRW*, *Works*, vol. 5, p. 152.
8. *Ibid.*, p. 75.
9. *Ibid.*, p. 213.
10. *Ibid.*, pp. 217–19.
11. *Ibid.*, p. 213.
12. *Ibid.*, p. 66.
13. *Ibid.*, p. 227.
14. For the prevalence of this view within late eighteenth century radicalism, see Peter Miller, *Defining the Common Good: Empire, Religion and Philosophy in Eighteenth Century Britain* (Cambridge University Press, 1994), chapter 4.
15. Wollstonecraft, *VRM*, *Works*, vol. 5, p. 52.
16. Wollstonecraft, *VRW*, *Works*, vol. 5, p. 216.
17. [Sophia], *Woman Not Inferior*, p. 49.
18. Wollstonecraft, *VRW*, *Works*, vol. 5, p. 216.
19. Schwartz, *Sexual Politics of Rousseau*, p. 53.
20. Wollstonecraft, *VRW*, *Works*, vol. 5, pp. 84, 216.
21. *Ibid.*, p. 216.
22. *Ibid.*, p. 120.
23. Wollstonecraft, *VRM*, *Works*, vol. 5, p. 24.
24. Wollstonecraft, *VRW*, *Works*, vol. 5, p. 219.
25. *Ibid.*, pp. 216–17.
26. Knud Haakonssen, 'From Natural Law to the Rights of Man: a European Perspective on American Debates', in M. J. Lacey and K. Haakonssen, *A*

Culture of Rights: the Bill of Rights in Philosophy, Politics and Law (Cambridge University Press, 1991), p. 36.

27. Wollstonecraft, *VRW*, *Works*, vol. 5, p. 247.
28. See below (p. 250) for Fawcett's introduction to the 1891 edition of the *Rights of Woman*. Discussing Wollstonecraft's women's-rights position, Fawcett notes that it is grounded on the principle that 'a large measure of women's rights is essential to the highest possible conception and fulfilment of women's duties' (p. 23) – the same version of rights advocacy popular among suffrage activists.
29. Wollstonecraft, *VRW*, *Works*, vol. 5, p. 234.
30. Wollstonecraft, *VRM*, *Works*, vol. 5, p. 23.
31. Wollstonecraft, *VRW*, *Works*, vol. 5, p. 196.
32. *Ibid.*, pp. 194–5.
33. *Ibid.*, pp. 209–10.
34. For the notion that it *was* new, see, among others, Colley, *Britons*, pp. 273–4. The misconception seems to have arisen from an over-emphasis on the part played by classical-militarist ideals of public virtue in the formation of radical thought, at the expense of Protestant moral principles. The influence of J. G. A. Pocock's writings on the republican dimension of eighteenth-century political thought has no doubt been at least partly responsible for this, since Pocock tends to underplay the religious element in late eighteenth-century radicalism.
35. Pocock, *Virtue, Commerce and History*, chapter 2 and 6.
36. Wollstonecraft, *VRW*, *Works*, vol. 5, p. 114.
37. For the French case, see Landes, *Women and Public Sphere*, pp. 129–38; for the American, Rosemary Zagarri, 'Morals, Manners and the Republican Mother', *American Quarterly*, 44 (1992), pp. 193–215.
38. Landes, *Women and Public Sphere*, pp. 129–38, makes the most sustained case for Wollstonecraft as an advocate of republican motherhood; for a counterview, see Sapiro, *Vindication of Political Virtue*, pp. 269, 321.
39. Wollstonecraft, *French Revolution*, *Works*, vol. 6, p. 21.
40. Wollstonecraft, *VRM*, *Works*, vol. 5, p. 22.
41. *Ibid.*, p. 22.
42. Wollstonecraft, *VRW*, *Works*, vol. 5, p. 266.
43. *Ibid.*, pp. 67, 136, 135.
44. *Ibid.*, pp. 129, 136.
45. *Ibid.*, p. 136.
46. Radcliffe, 'Revolutionary Writing', pp. 226–33; Philp, Godwin, pp. 180–4.
47. Macaulay, *On Burke's Reflections*, pp. 38–9.
48. This was Marguerite, who had been acquired in Paris, and of whom nothing is known except from Wollstonecraft's letters, which refer to her 'arch, agreeable vanity' of a kind 'peculiar to the french', and a '[h]appy thoughtlessness' so alien to her employer's disposition that even when they were together Wollstonecraft felt mentally alone. Writing from Scandinavia, Wollstonecraft also refers several times to Marguerite's 'timidity', but since this description was

penned after days spent rolling about on violent seas (with Marguerite seasick while Wollstonecraft looked on condescendingly) or negotiating mountainous roads 'very rocky and troublesome', a compassionate reader begins to suspect that Marguerite's nervousness was entirely justified. To Wollstonecraft, however, who was a truly dauntless traveller, such anxieties were contemptible. Like her 'smooth hands', which showed that it was she and not Marguerite who was the 'lady', physical courage seems to have been regarded by Wollstonecraft as a mark of personal and class superiority. Marguerite remained with Wollstonecraft until her death, and then disappears from the record (probably having returned to France).

49. Mary Wollstonecraft, letter to William Godwin, 6 June 1797, in Wardle (ed.), *Letters*, p. 396.
50. Mary Wollstonecraft, letter to William Godwin, 10 November 1796, in Wardle (ed.), *Letters*, p. 360; Tomalin, *Wollstonecraft*, p. 147.
51. Mary Wollstonecraft, letter to Everina Wollstonecraft, 4 September 1790, in Wardle (ed.), *Letters*, p. 194.
52. Wollstonecraft, *VRW*, *Works*, vol. 5, pp. 132–3.
53. *Ibid.*, p. 217.
54. *Ibid.*, p. 132.
55. *Ibid.*, p. 133.
56. *Ibid.*, p. 95.
57. *Ibid.*, pp. 68, 105.
58. Price, 'Two Tracts on Civil Liberty, the War with America, and the Debts and Finances of the Kingdom', 1776–7, *Political Writings*, p. 77.
59. Wollstonecraft, *VRW*, *Works*, vol. 5, p. 224.
60. *Ibid.*, p. 226.
61. *Ibid.*, p. 227.
62. *Ibid.*, pp. 226, 102.
63. *Ibid.*, pp. 211–12.
64. The most developed case for this is made by Anne Phillips, 'Feminism and Republicanism', pp. 289–290.
65. Langford, *Public Life*, p. 484.
66. Wyvill, quoted in Hampshire-Monk, 'Civic Humanism', p. 87.
67. Clark, *Struggle for the Breeches*, pp. 142–57.
68. Dickinson, *Liberty and Property*, p. 253.
69. Wollstonecraft, *VRW*, *Works*, vol. 5, p. 215.
70. *Ibid.*, p. 76.
71. *Ibid.*, p. 120.
72. Paine, *Rights of Man*, p. 185.
73. Wollstonecraft, *VRW*, *Works*, vol. 5, p. 213.
74. *Ibid.*, p. 216."
75. It is this limited tradition of pro-woman thinking to which Anne Phillips refers when she argues that for Wollstonecraft an independent life was defined more by attitude and context than by its actual content:

what Wollstonecraft's arguments reveal is her deep conviction that it is the capacity to think and act for yourself that matters rather than one's place in the division of labour or one's level of income and wealth. You have to be free from the domination of others, you have to be serious not silly, you have to be governing yourself. But once these conditions are met, then a woman running her household and bringing up her children can be as free and worthy of respect as anyone running the country or earning vast monies in the more public world of work. ('Feminism and Republicanism', p. 289)

76. Wollstonecraft, *VRW*, *Works*, vol. 5, p. 155.

77. *Ibid.*, pp. 216–17.

78. *Ibid.*, p. 237.

79. *Ibid.*, p. 237.

80. *Ibid.*, p. 218.

81. *Ibid.*, p. 218.

82. Wollstonecraft, *Maria*, *Works*, vol. 1, pp. 158–9.

83. Mary Wollstonecraft, letter to Jane Arden, April–June 1780, in Wardle (ed.), *Letters*, p. 72.

84. Mary Wollstonecraft, letter to Gilbert Imlay, *c.* November 1795, in Wardle (ed.) *Letters*, p. 318.

85. Mary Wollstonecraft, letter to Gilbert Imlay, 8 December 1795, in Wardle (ed.) *Letters*, p. 323. This letter, however, also chastised Imlay for 'lavish[ing]' money away while refusing either to assist Wollstonecraft's family or to rid her of some 'trifling debts': an inconsistency that does not seem to have troubled her.

86. Mary Wollstonecraft, letter to William Godwin, 4 September 1796, in Wardle (ed.) *Letters*, p. 345.

87. Wollstonecraft, *VRW*, *Works*, vol. 5, p. 91.

88. *Ibid.*, p. 117.

89. Wollstonecraft, *Maria*, *Works*, vol. 1, p. 149.

90. *Ibid.*, pp. 146, 149.

91. *Ibid.*, p. 148.

92. Factors contributing to this included a lowering of the female age of first marriage; a decline in the value of female inheritance; increased stigmatisation of unwed women; and a diminishing role for women in family businesses. See Amy L. Erickson's *Women and Property in Early Modern England* (London: Routledge, 1995) for an illuminating account of these changes.

93. Randall [Robinson], *Letter to the Women of England*, p. 78.

94. Wollstonecraft, *Maria*, *Works*, vol. 1, p. 164.

95. *Ibid.*, p. 164.

96. *Ibid.*, p. 180.

97. *Ibid.*, p. 149.

98. *Ibid.*, p. 179.

99. Wollstonecraft, *VRW*, *Works*, vol. 5, pp. 224–8. The presiding influence in this chapter, 'Duty to Parents', is Locke, whose *Some Thoughts Concerning Education* (1693) Wollstonecraft cites in her discussion of discipline (p. 226).

100. *Ibid.*, p. 222.

101. Mary Wollstonecraft, letter to Gilbert Imlay, 1 January 1794, in Wardle (ed.), *Letters*, p. 242.
102. Mary Wollstonecraft, letter to Gilbert Imlay, 14 July 1795, in Wardle (ed.) *Letters*, p. 305.
103. Mary Wollstonecraft, letter to Gilbert Imlay, 27 November 1795, in Wardle (ed.) *Letters*, p. 321.
104. Wollstonecraft, *VRW*, *Works*, vol. 5, p. 223.
105. *Ibid.*, p. 248.
106. *Ibid.*, p. 249.
107. Wollstonecraft, *Maria*, *Works*, vol. 1, p. 180.
108. *Ibid.*, p. 172.
109. *Ibid.*, p. 180.
110. *Ibid.*, p. 123.
111. *Ibid.*, pp. 152, 178.
112. *Ibid.*, p. 151.
113. Wollstonecraft, *VRW*, *Works*, vol. 5, p. 249.
114. *Ibid.*, p. 110.
115. *Ibid.*, pp. 68, 67.
116. Wollstonecraft, *Maria*, *Works*, vol. 1, p. 83.
117. *Ibid.*, p. 84.

9 JEMIMA AND THE BEGINNINGS OF MODERN FEMINISM

1. Wollstonecraft, *Maria*, *Works*, vol. 1, p. 119.
2. Wollstonecraft, *VRW*, *Works*, vol. 5, p. 220.
3. Wollstonecraft, *Maria*, *Works*, vol. 1, p. 167.
4. Madeleine Schweitzer, a friend from Paris days, commented on Wollstonecraft's 'intolerant' attitude to her female peers (Clark Durant, *Supplement*, p. 247).
5. This unhappy woman is probably based on Wollstonecraft's sister, Eliza, whom Wollstonecraft removed from her husband's home after she suffered a severe post-partum psychosis.
6. Wollstonecraft, *Maria*, *Works*, vol. 1, p. 175. However, as Vivien Jones points out, Jemima's insistence on receiving wages from Maria might also be interpreted as evidence of her determination not to become her wealthy friend's economic dependent: Vivien Jones, 'Placing Jemima: Women Writers of the 1790s and the Eighteenth-Century Prostitution Narrative', *Women's Writing*, 4:2, 1997, pp. 215–16.
7. *Ibid.*, p. 133.
8. *Ibid.*, p. 165.
9. *Ibid.*, p. 157.
10. *Ibid.*, pp. 109–10.
11. *Ibid.*, p. 159.
12. Mary Wollstonecraft, review of O. Equiano, *The Interesting Narrative of the Life of Olaudah Equiano*, *AR*, vol. 4, May 1789, p. 100. For Wollstonecraft's attitude to slavery, see Moira Ferguson, 'Mary Wollstonecraft and the

Problematic of Slavery', in Yeo (ed.) *Wollstonecraft*, pp. 89–103 and D. L. Macdonald, 'Master, Slave and Mistress in Wollstonecraft's *Vindication*', *Enlightenment and Dissent*, 11 (1992), pp. 46–57.

13. C. G. Salzmann, *Elements of Morality... Translated from the German*, 1790, in Wollstonecraft, *Works*, vol. 2, pp. 6, 28. Wollstonecraft not only translated Salzmann's morality tales for children, but also added to and amended them; this story about kindly Indians is one of her additions.

14. Mary Wollstonecraft, review of M. Le Vaillant, *New Travels into the Interior Parts of Africa*, *AR*, vol. 15, May 1797, p. 481.

15. Wollstonecraft, *Maria*, *Works*, vol. 1, p. 180.

16. *Ibid.*, pp. 87, 112.

17. *Ibid.*, p. 91.

18. *Ibid.*, p. 146.

19. *Ibid.*, p. 120.

20. *Ibid.*, p. 110.

21. Vivien Jones, 'Scandalous Femininity: Prostitution and Eighteenth Century Narrative', in D. Castiglione and L. Sharpe (eds.), *Shifting the Boundaries: Transformation of the Languages of Public and Private in the eighteenth Century* (Exeter University Press, 1995), p. 66.

22. Wollstonecraft, *VRW*, *Works*, vol. 5, p. 140.

23. *Ibid.*, p. 208.

24. *Ibid.*, p. 209.

25. In her earliest writings, Wollstonecraft had some nasty things to say about servants, who 'are, in general, ignorant and cunning' (*Thoughts*, *Works*, vol. 4, pp. 38–9), and even her later writings, which urged that servants should be treated as family members, conformed to *bien pensant* opinion. Personally, she seems always to have been pleasant to servants: Godwin claimed that 'to her servants there was never a mistress more considerate or more kind' (*Memoirs*, p. 218), and the same was said of her by her otherwise rather critical friend, Madeleine Schweitzer, who wrote of Wollstonecraft that while she could be harsh with her peers 'to her servants, inferiors, and the wretched in general she was gentle as an angel' (Clark Durant, *Supplement*, p. 247).

26. Wollstonecraft, *VRW*, *Works*, vol. 5, p. 145.

27. Wollstonecraft, *Maria*, *Works*, vol. 1, p. 120.

28. *Ibid.*, p. 123.

29. *Ibid.*, p. 88.

30. *Ibid.*, p. 120.

31. *Ibid.*, p. 174.

32. *Ibid.*, pp. 115–17.

33. Wollstonecraft, *VRW*, *Works*, vol. 5, p. 69.

10 THE FANTASY OF MARY WOLLSTONECRAFT

1. Moers, *Literary Women*, p. 122.

2. Mary Wollstonecraft, letter, probably to Mary Hays, *c.* summer 1797, in Wardle (ed.) *Letters*, p. 413.

3. Wollstonecraft, *Maria*, *Works*, vol. 1, p. 83.
4. More, *Strictures on Female Education*, vol. 1, pp. 45–6.
5. For the reaction to the *Memoirs*, see Tomalin, *Wollstonecraft*, pp. 289–314; Wardle, Wollstonecraft, pp. 315–22; Nicola Trott, 'Sexing the Critic: Mary Wollstonecraft at the turn of the century', in R. Cronin (ed.), *1798: the Year of Lyrical Ballads* (London: Macmillan, 1998). I am grateful to Nicola Trott for allowing me to see her article prior to publication. Of course not all the verdicts of the *Memoirs*'s first readers were negative: Coleridge, for example, thought the book showed very clearly how Godwin was 'in heart and manner . . . all the better for having been the husband of Mary Wollstonecraft' (Wardle, *Wollstonecraft*, p. 315).
6. *The Monthly Visitor and Pocket Companion*, III (1798), p. 242.
7. George Eliot, 'Margaret Fuller and Mary Wollstonecraft', in T. Pinney (ed.), *Essays of George Eliot* (London: Routledge and Kegan Paul, 1963), p. 201.
8. Polwhele, *Unsex'd Females*, pp. 28–9.
9. St Clair, *Godwins*, pp. 184–5.
10. *Anti-Jacobin Review and Magazine*, 9 (1801), p. 518. In 1801 the *Anti-Jacobin Review* published an anonymous poem titled 'The Vision of Liberty' that contained the following verse:

> William hath penn'd a waggon-load of stuff,
> And Mary's life at last he needs must write,
> Thinking her whoredoms were not known enough,
> Till fairly printed off in black and white.
> With wondrous glee and pride, this simple wight
> Her brothel feats of wantonness sets down,
> Being her spouse, he tells, with huge delight,
> How oft she cuckolded the silly clown
> And lent, O lovely piece! herself to half the town
>
> (no. 9, 1801, p. 518)

11. *Ladies Monthly Museum*, 1 (September 1798), p. 186.
12. *The Enquirer* (*The Monthly Magazine*), April 1796.
13. In the preface to the 1798 edition of her *The Young Philosopher*, which has scenes set in an asylum, Charlotte Smith defended herself against possible charges of plagiarising Wollstonecraft's *Maria*. The asylum scenes were planned before she read Wollstonecraft's novel, she wrote, going on to praise Wollstonecraft as a writer 'whose talents I greatly honoured, and whose untimely death I deeply regret'.

    Mary Robinson's 1799 *Letter to the Women of England* opened with a panegyric to Wollstonecraft 'whose death has not been sufficiently lamented, but to whose genius posterity will render justice' (Randall [Robinson], *Letter to Women of England*, pp. 1–2). This was generous of Robinson, given that Wollstonecraft had published a very dismissive review of her novel, *Huber de Sevrac*, in the spring of 1797.
14. Amelia Opie, *The Father and Daughter*, 1800 (London, 1801), pp. 190–1.

15. See above, p. 196. It is possible that Opie, then Alderson, and Godwin may have been edging toward marriage shortly before Wollstonecraft and Godwin became lovers. It is also possible that John Opie may have hoped to marry Wollstonecraft before she married Godwin and he in his turn married Alderson.

16. Maria Edgeworth, *Belinda* (London, 1801); Hamilton, *Memoirs of Modern Philosophers*. In 1843 Anne Ellwood commented in her *Memoirs of Literary Ladies of England* (London, 1843), that it was the 'mode' rather than the 'matter' of Wollstonecraft's writings that had offended against 'the refinement of modern manners': 'many of her sentiments are certainly anything but feminine' (p. 145). Wollstonecraft, Ellwood went on, had been the most influential woman writer of the last fifty years, barring Mme de Staël, but the publication of Godwin's *Memoirs* had turned her from an 'idol' to an 'image of clay', and 'she became forgotten much sooner than she deserved to be' (p. 153).

17. Flora Tristan, *London Journal*, 1842 (London: Virago, 1982), p. 253.

18. For an interesting bit of evidence about the survival of her reputation among Unitarians, see Jenny Uglow, *Elizabeth Gaskell, A Habit of Stories* (London: Faber and Faber, 1993), p. 32, for an account of an early nineteenth-century Newcastle Unitarian minister writing to his daughter on the occasion of her marriage, telling her that he assumes that she has 'perused the strong and often coarse, though too often well-founded strictures of Mary Wollstonecraft'.

19. Quoted in Harold Silver, *The Concept of Popular Education* (London: MacGibbon and Kee, 1965), p. 90.

20. William Thompson, *Appeal of One-Half the Human Race, Women, Against the Pretensions of the Other Half, Men, to Retain Them in ... Slavery*, 1825 (London: Virago, 1983), xxiii.

21. Taylor, *Eve and the New Jerusalem*, p. 180, pp. 269–72.

22. See for example *The Chartist Circular*, vol. 1, no. 27, 1839.

23. Barbara Caine, 'Victorian Feminism and the Ghost of Mary Wollstonecraft', *Women's Writing*, 4:2, 1997, p. 268; Pam Hirsch, 'Mary Wollstonecraft, a Problematic Legacy', in C. Campbell Orr, *Wollstonecraft's Daughters: Womanhood in England and France, 1780–1920* (Manchester University Press, 1996), p. 54.

24. Caine, 'Victorian Feminism', p. 261.

25. Harriet Martineau, *Autobiography*, 1877 (London: Virago, 1983), vol. 1, p. 400.

26. Eliot, 'Fuller and Wollstonecraft', p. 201.

27. This edition was never published. For Schreiner's incomplete draft introduction, see 'Introduction to the Life of Mary Wollstonecraft and the Rights of Woman', with the accompanying essay by Carolyn Burdett, 'A Difficult Vindication: Olive Schreiner's Wollstonecraft introduction', *History Workshop Journal*, 37 (spring 1994), pp. 177–93.

28. Judith R. Walkowitz, *City of Dreadful Delight* (London: Virago Press, 1992), p. 140.

29. Millicent Garrett Fawcett, *Introduction* to *A Vindication of the Rights of Woman* (London, 1892).

30. Rauscenbusch-Clough, *Study of Wollstonecraft*, p. 23.

31. Margaret Clayton, *Mary Wollstonecraft and the Women's Movement of To-day* (London, nd – *c.* 1910?), p. 3. See Ethel Snowdon, *The Feminist Movement* (London: Nation's Library, 1911) p. 82, for a typical celebration of Wollstonecraft's pioneering role.

32. Charles Kegan Paul, *Mary Wollstonecraft: Letters to Gilbert Imlay* (London, 1879), p. ix.

33. Quoted by Miriam Brody in her introduction to the 1982 Penguin edition of the *Rights of Woman* (Harmondsworth, 1982), pp. 66–7. In February 1868 the American feminist journal, *The Revolution*, began serialising the *Rights of Woman*, prefacing it with an article that deplored the way Wollstonecraft's reputation had been 'blackened and calumniated', while at the same time apologising for her 'socialistic tendencies and shocking disregard for the marriage rites...'

34. Aveling and Aveling, *Shelley and Socialism*, p. 13.

35. Virginia Woolf, 'Wollstonecraft,' p. 99.

36. For another radical woman's admiration for Wollstonecraft, see Alice Wexler, 'Emma Goldman on Mary Wollstonecraft', *Feminist Studies*, no. 1 (1981), p. 132.

37. For criticism of Wollstonecraft's racial and imperial views, see Rajani Sudan, 'Mothering and National Identity in the Works of Mary Wollstonecraft', in A. Richardson and S. Hofkosh (eds.), *Romanticism, Race and Imperial Culture* (Bloomington: Indiana University Press, 1996); Himani Bannerji, 'Mary Wollstonecraft, Feminism and Humanism: a Spectrum of Reading', in Yeo (ed.) *Wollstonecraft*.

38. For a reading of Wollstonecraft via Julia Kristeva, see Laurie Langbauer, *Women and Romance: the Consolations of Gender in the English Novel* (Ithaca: Cornell University Press, 1990), ch. 3.

39. Wollstonecraft, *VRW*, *Works*, vol. 5, p. 174.

40. *Ibid.*, p. 103.

41. Mary Wollstonecraft, letter to William Godwin, 19 August 1796, in Wardle, *Letters*, p. 339.

42. Paine, *Rights of Man*, p. 295.

Bibliography

WORKS BY MARY WOLLSTONECRAFT

A complete edition of Wollstonecraft's works was published in 1989: Janet Todd and
Marilyn Butler (eds.), *The Works of Mary Wollstonecraft* (London: Pickering
and Chatto), 7 volumes (hereafter *Works*).

CHRONOLOGICAL LIST OF WORKS PUBLISHED DURING
AND AFTER WOLLSTONECRAFT'S LIFETIME

*Thoughts on the Education of Daughters: with Reflections on Female Conduct, in the
More Important Duties of Life* (1787). *Works*, vol. 4. Cited as *Thoughts*.

'The Cave of Fancy. A Tale' (written in 1787, published 1798). *Works*, vol. 1.

Mary, A Fiction (1788). *Works*, vol. 1. Cited as *Mary*.

*Original Stories From Real Life: with Conversations Calculated to Regulate the Affec-
tions and Form the Mind to Truth and Goodness* (1788). 1796 edition in *Works*,
vol. 4. Cited as *Original Stories*.

Of the Importance of Religious Opinions. Translation of work by Jacques Necker
(1788). *Works*, vol. 3.

Analytical Review. Wollstonecraft published reviews regularly in this magazine in
1788–92 and 1796–7. *Works*, vol. 7. Cited as *AR*.

The Female Reader: or Miscellaneous Pieces, in Prose and Verse [by Mr Cresswick,
teacher of elocution], (1789). *Works*, vol. 4. Cited as *Female Reader*.

*A Vindication of the Rights of Men, in a Letter to the Right Honourable Edmund
Burke* (1790). *Works*, vol. 5. Cited as *VRM*.

*Elements of Morality, for the Use of Children; with an introductory address to
parents*. Translation of work by Christian Gotthilf Salzmann (1790). *Works*,
vol. 2.

Young Grandison. A Series of Letters from Young Persons to Their Friends. Translation
of a work by Maria Geertruida van de Werken de Cambon (1790). *Works*,
vol. 2.

A Vindication of the Rights of Woman, with Strictures on Moral and Political Subjects
(1792). *Works*, vol. 5. Cited as *VRW*.

'Letter on the Present Character of the French Nation' (written in 1793, published
1798). *Works*, vol. 6.

An Historical and Moral View of the Origin and Progress of the French Revolution; and the Effect It Has produced in Europe (1794). *Works*, vol. 6. Cited as *French Revolution*.

Letters Written during a Short Residence in Sweden, Norway and Denmark (1796). *Works*, vol. 6. Cited as *Short Residence*.

'On Poetry, and Our Relish of the Beauties of Nature', *Monthly Magazine*, April 1797. *Works*, vol. 7.

The Wrongs of Woman, or Maria (1798). *Works*, vol. 1. Cited as *Maria*.

'Fragment of Letters on the Management of Infants' (1798). *Works*, vol. 4.

'Lessons' (fragment) (1798). *Works*, vol. 4.

'Hints' (1798). *Works*, vol. 5.

OTHER PRIMARY SOURCES

Addison, Joseph. *Essays on Taste, and the Pleasures of the Imagination, from the Spectator* (London, 1834).

Alexander, William. *The History of Women from the Earliest Antiquity, to the Present Time* (Dublin, 1779).

Anti-Jacobin Review and Magazine.

Astell, Mary. *A Serious Proposal to the Ladies* (1694).

    Some Reflections Upon Marriage, 1700; 1706 edition in Bridget Hill, *The First English Feminist* (Aldershot: Gower Publishing, 1986).

Bage, Robert. *Hermonsprong, or Man as He Is Not*, 1796 (London: Turnstile Press, 1951).

[Barbauld, Anna] A Volunteer. *Sins of the Government, Sins of the Nation* (London, 1793).

Barbauld, Anna. *An Address to the Opposers of the Repeal of the Test and Corporation Acts* (London, 1790).

    Works (London, 1825).

Beddoes, Thomas. *Alexander's Expedition*, 1792.

[Bennett, John] A Clergyman of the Church of England. *Strictures on Female Education* (London, 1787).

Blair, Hugh. *Lectures on Rhetoric and Belles Lettres* (London, 1783).

Brown, John. *An Estimate of the Manners and Principles of the Times* (London, 1757).

    On the Female Character and Education (London, 1765).

Burgh, James. *Britain's Remembrancer* (London, 1746).

    Political Disquisitions (London: 1774/5).

    The Dignity of Human Nature (London, 1754).

Burke, Edmund. *A Philosophical Enquiry into the Origin of Our Ideas of the Sublime and Beautiful*, 1757 (Oxford University Press, 1990).

    Letters on a Regicide Peace (London, 1795).

    Reflections on the Revolution in France, 1790 (Indianapolis: Hackett, 1987).

Chapone, Hester. *Letters on the Improvement of the Mind, Addressed to a Young Lady*, 1773 (London, 1827).

Critical Review, 1792.

Duff, William. *Letters on the Intellectual and Moral Character of Women* (1807).

Duncombe, John. *The Feminiad: a Poem* (London, 1754).

Dyer, George. *Poems* (London, 1792).

Edgeworth, Maria. *Belinda* (London, 1801).

    Letters for Literary Ladies, 1795 (London: J. M. Dent, 1993).

European Magazine and London Review, vol. 33, April 1798.

Fenwick, Eliza. *Secresy, or, the Ruin on the Rock* (London, 1796).

Fordyce, James. *Sermons to Young Women*, 1765 (London, 1766).

    The Character and Conduct of the Female Sex; and the Advantages to be Derived by Young Men from the Society of Virtuous Women (London, 1776).

Gisborne, Thomas. *An Enquiry into the Duties of the Female Sex* (London, 1797).

Godwin, William. *An Enquiry Concerning Political Justice* (London, 1793).

    Memoirs of the Author of A Vindication of the Rights of Woman, 1798 (Harmondsworth: Penguin, 1987).

    Things as They are; or the Adventures of Caleb Williams (London, 1794).

Gregory, John. *A Father's Legacy to His Daughters*, 1774 (London, 1823).

Hamilton, Elizabeth. *Memoirs of Modern Philosophers: a Novel* (London, 1800).

Hartley, David. *Observations on Man, his Frame, his Duty, and his Expectations* (London, 1749).

Hawkins, Laetitia Matilda. *Letters on the Female Mind* (London, 1793).

Hays, Mary. *Appeal to the Men of Great Britain on Behalf of Women* (1798).

    'Memoirs of Mary Wollstonecraft', *Annual Necrology*, 1797–8 (London, 1800).

    [Eusebia] *Cursory Remarks on an enquiry into the Expediency and Propriety of Public or Social Worship* (London, 1792).

    Female Biography (London, 1803).

    Memoirs of Emma Courtney, 1796 (London: Pandora Press, 1987).

Hazlitt, William (ed.). *Memoirs of Thomas Holcroft* (London, 1816).

    Selected Writings (Harmondsworth: Penguin, 1985).

Holcroft, Thomas. *Anna St Ives*, 1792 (Oxford University Press, 1970).

Hume, David. *A Treatise of Human Nature*, 1739 (London: Penguin, 1987).

    Of the Rise and Progress of the Arts and Sciences, 1777, in *Essays: Moral, Political and Literary* (Indianapolis: Liberty Fund, 1985).

Inchbald, Elizabeth. *A Simple Story* (London, 1791).

    Nature and Art (London, 1796).

Jardine, Alexander. *Letters from Barbary, France, Spain... etc.* (London, 1787).

Jones, John Gale. *Sketches of a Political Tour* (London, 1796).

Knowles, John. *The Life and Writings of Henry Fuseli* (London, 1831).

Knox, Vicesimus. *Essays Moral and Literary* (London, 1779).

Macaulay, Catharine. *Letters on Education, with Observations on Religious and Metaphysical Subjects* (London, 1790).

    Observations on the Reflections of the Right Hon Edmund Burke on the Revolution in France (London, 1791).

[Mathias, Thomas J.] *The Pursuits of Literature: a Satirical Poem; in Four Dialogues*, 7th edn (London: 1798).

Monthly Review, 1792.

More, Hannah. *Strictures on the Modern System of Female Education* (1799).

Opie, Amelia. *Adeline Mowbray* (London, 1804).

The Father and Daughter (London, 1800).

Paine, Thomas. *Rights of Man*, 1791–2 (Harmondsworth: Penguin, 1977).

Paley, William. *Principles of Moral and Political Philosophy* (London, 1785).

[Polwhele, Richard] *The Unsex'd Females: a poem addressed to the author of the Pursuits of Literature* (London, 1798).

Price, Richard. *A Review of the Principal Questions and Difficulties in Morals*, 1758 (Oxford: Clarendon Press, 1974).

Political Writings (D. O. Thomas, ed., Cambridge University Press, 1991).

[Robinson, Mary] Anne Frances Randall. *A Letter to the Women of England, on the Injustice of Mental Subordination* (London, 1799).

Memoirs of the late Mrs Robinson, written by herself, 1801 (London: Peter Owen, 1994).

Rousseau, Jean-Jacques. *Discourse on the Origin and the Foundations of Inequality Among Men*, 1755 (Cambridge University Press, 1997).

Emile, or On Education, 1762 (London: Penguin, 1991).

La Nouvelle Héloïse (1761); translated as *Eloisa, or a Series of Original Letters*, London, 1767.

Politics and Arts: Letter to M D'Alembert on the Theatre, 1758 (Ithaca: Cornell University Press, 1991).

The Confessions, 1781 (London: Penguin Books, 1978).

Smith, Adam. *The Theory of Moral Sentiments*, 1759 (Indianapolis: Liberty Fund, 1982).

Smith, Charlotte. *Desmond, a Novel* (London, 1792).

Sophia (A Person of Quality), *Woman Not Inferior to Man*, 1739 (London: Brentham Press, 1975).

Stewart, Dugald. *Elements of the Philosophy of the Human Mind*, 1792 (London, 1811).

Taylor, Thomas ('the Platonist'). *A Vindication of the Rights of Brutes* (London, 1792).

Wakefield, Gilbert. *A General Reply to the Arguments Against the Enquiry into Public Worship* (London, 1792).

Wakefield, Priscilla. *Reflections on the Present Condition of the Female Sex* (London, 1798).

Young, E. *Conjectures on Original Composition* (1759).

SECONDARY WORKS

BOOKS

Alexander, Meena. *Women in Romanticism: Mary Wollstonecraft, Dorothy Wordsworth and Mary Shelley* (London: Macmillan, 1989).

Alexander, Sally. *Becoming a Woman and Other Essays in 19th and 20th Century Feminist History* (London: Virago, 1994).

Andrew, Donna T. *London Debating Societies, 1776–1799* (London: London Record Society, 1994).

Barker-Benfield, George. *The Culture of Sensibility: Sex and Society in 18th Century Britain* (London: University of Chicago Press, 1992).

Barrell, John. *Imagining the King's Death: Figurative Treason, Fantasies of Regicide, 1793–96* (Oxford University Press, 2000).

The Birth of Pandora and the Division of Knowledge (London: Macmillan, 1992).

Battersby, Christine. *Gender and Genius: Towards a Feminist Aesthetics* (London: Women's Press, 1989).

Berman, Marshall. *The Politics of Authenticity* (London: George Allen and Unwin, 1971).

Blakemore, Steven. *Intertextual War: Edmund Burke and the French Revolution in the Writings of Mary Wollstonecraft, Thomas Paine and James Mackintosh* (London: Associated University Presses, 1997).

Bloom, Alan. *Love and Friendship* (New York: Simon and Schuster, 1993).

Blum, Carol. *Rousseau and the Republic of Virtue* (Ithaca: Cornell University Press, 1986).

Boswell, James. *The Life of Samuel Johnson*, 1791 (Oxford University Press, 1989).

Boulton, James T. *The Language of Politics in the Age of Wilkes and Burke* (London: Routledge and Kegan Paul, 1963).

Browne, Alice. *The Eighteenth Century Feminist Mind* (Brighton: Harvester Press, 1987).

Butler, Marilyn. *Burke, Paine, Godwin and the Revolution Controversy* (Cambridge University Press, 1984).

Jane Austen and the War of Ideas, 1975 (Oxford: Clarendon Press, 1987).

Cameron, Kenneth N. (ed.). *Shelley and His Circle*, vol. 1 (Cambridge University Press, 1961).

Carter, Philip. *Men and the Emergence of Polite Society in Britain, 1660–1800* (Harlow: Pearson Education, 2001).

Claeys, Gregory. *Thomas Paine* (London: Unwin Hyman, 1989).

Clark, Anna. *The Struggle for the Breeches: Gender and the Making of the British Working Class* (London: Rivers Oram, 1995).

Clarke, Norma. *Dr Johnson's Women* (London: Hambledon, 2000).

Clayton, Margaret. *Mary Wollstonecraft and the Women's Movement of Today* (London, nd – c. 1910?).

Cobban, A. *The Debate on the French Revolution* (London: Black, 1950).

Colley, Linda. *Britons: Forging the Nation, 1707–1837* (London: Yale University Press, 1992).

Cone, C. B. *The English Jacobins* (New York: Charles Scribner's Sons, 1968).

Conger, Syndy M. *Mary Wollstonecraft and the Language of Sensibility* (London: Associated University Presses, 1994).

Copeland, Edward. *Women Writing About Money: Women's Fictions in England, 1790–1820* (Cambridge University Press, 1995).

Crompton, Louis. *Byron and Greek Love: Homophobia in 19th Century England* (Berkeley: University of California Press, 1985).

Crossley, C. and Small, I. (eds.) *The French Revolution and British Culture* (Oxford University Press, 1989).

Curry, K. (ed.). *New Letters of Robert Southey* (New York: Columbia University Press, 1965).

De Beauvoir, Simone. *The Second Sex*, 1949 (Harmondsworth: Penguin, 1972).

Deane, S. (ed.), *The French Revolution and Enlightenment in England* (Cambridge, Mass: Harvard University Press, 1988).

Derrida, Jacques. *Of Grammatology*, 1967 (Baltimore: John Hopkins Press, 1976).

Dickinson, H. T. *Liberty and Property*, 1977 (London: Methuen and Co., 1979). *The Politics of the People in Eighteenth Century Britain* (Basingstoke: Macmillan, 1995).

Durant, W. Clark. *Supplement to William Godwin, Memoirs of the Author of 'A Vindication of the Rights of Woman'* (London: Constable and Co., 1927).

Dwyer, John. *Virtuous Discourse: Sensibility and Community in late Eighteenth century Scotland* (Edinburgh University Press, 1987).

Eagleton, Terry. *The Ideology of the Aesthetic* (Oxford: Basil Blackwell, 1990).

Eisenstein, Zillah. *The Radical Future of Liberal Feminism* [New York: Longman, 1981].

Ellis, G. A. *A Memoir of Mrs Anna Laetitia Barbauld* (London, 1874).

Ellwood, Anne. *Memoirs of Literary Ladies of England* (London, 1843).

Engell, James. *The Creative Imagination* (Harvard University Press, 1981).

Erickson, Amy L. *Women and Property in Early Modern England* (London: Routledge, 1995).

Ferguson, Moira (ed.). *First Feminists: British Women Writers, 1578–1799* (Bloomington: Indiana University Press, 1985).

Flexner, Eleanor. *Mary Wollstonecraft* (New York: Coward, McCann and Geoghegan, 1972).

Foreman, Amanda. *Georgiana, Duchess of Devonshire* (London: HarperCollins, 1999).

Fruchtman, Jack, Jr. *The Apocalyptic Politics of Richard Price and Joseph Priestley: a Study in Late 18th Century English Republican Millennialism* (Philadelphia: American Philosophical Society, 1983).

Garrett, Clarke. *Respectable Folly: Millenarians and the French Revolution in France and England* (Baltimore: Johns Hopkins University Press, 1975).

George, Margaret. *One Woman's 'Situation': a Study of Mary Wollstonecraft* (Urbana: Illinois University Press, 1970).

Gleadle, Kathryn. *The Early Feminists: Radical Unitarians and the Emergence of the Women's Rights Movement, 1831–51* (Basingstoke: Macmillan, 1995).

Goldberg, Rita. *Sex and Enlightenment* (Cambridge University Press, 1984).

Goodwin, Albert. *The Friends of Liberty* (London: Hutchison, 1979).

Griffin, Dustin. *Regaining Paradise: Milton and the Eighteenth Century* (Cambridge University Press, 1986).

Guest, Harriet. *Small Change: Women, Learning and Patriotism, 1750–1810* (University of Chicago Press, 2000).

Hagstrum, Jean. *Sex and Sensibility: Ideal and Erotic Love from Milton to Mozart* (University of Chicago Press, 1980).

Hill, Bridget. *The Republican Virago: the Life and Times of Catharine Macaulay* (Oxford: Clarendon Press, 1992).

Holmes, Richard. *Footsteps: Adventures of a Romantic Biographer*, 1985 (London: Penguin, 1986).

Houston, A. C. *Algernon Sidney and the Republican Heritage in England and America* (Princeton University Press, 1991).

Howells, R. J. *Rousseau: La Nouvelle Heloïse* (London, Grant and Cutler Ltd, 1986).

Jacobus, Mary. *First Things* (London: Routledge, 1995).

Johnson, Claudia. *Equivocal Beings: Politics, Gender and Sentimentality in the 1790s* (University of Chicago, 1995).

Jones, Vivien (ed.). *Women in the Eighteenth Century: Constructions of Femininity* (London: Routledge, 1990).

Kaplan, Cora. *Sea Changes: Essays on Culture and Feminism* (London: Verso, 1986).

Keane, John. *Tom Paine, a Political Life*, 1995 (London: Bloomsbury, 1996).

Kelly, Gary. *The English Jacobin Novel, 1780–1805* (Oxford: Clarendon Press, 1976).
Revolutionary Feminism: The Mind and Career of Mary Wollstonecraft (Basingstoke: Macmillan, 1992).
Women, Writing, and Revolution (Oxford: Clarendon Press, 1993).

Kramnick, Isaac. *Republicanism and Bourgeois Radicalism* (London: Cornell University Press, 1990).
The Rage of Edmund Burke (New York: Basic Books, 1977).

Landes, J. B. *Women and the Public Sphere in the Age of the French Revolution* (Ithaca: Cornell University Press, 1988).

Landry, Donna. *The Muses of Resistance: Labouring-Class Women's Poetry in Britain, 1739–96* (Cambridge University Press, 1990).

Langbauer, Laurie. *Women and Romance: the Consolations of Gender in the English Novel* (Ithaca: Cornell University Press, 1990).

Langford, Paul. *Public Life and the Propertied Gentleman, 1689–1798* (Oxford: Clarendon Press, 1991).

Laqueur, Tom. *Making Sex: Body and Gender from the Greeks to Freud* (London: Harvard University Press, 1990).

Le Breton, A. L. *Memoir of Mrs Barbauld* (London, 1874).

Littlewood, S. R. *Elizabeth Inchbald and Her Circle* (London: Daniel O'Connor, 1921).

Lloyd, Genevieve. *The Man of Reason: 'Male' and 'Female' in Western Philosophy* (London: Methuen, 1984).

Mason, Eudo C. *The Mind of Henry Fuseli* (London: Routledge and Kegan Paul, 1951).

Mellor, Anne K. *Romanticism and Gender* (London: Routledge, 1993).

Miller, Peter. *Defining the Common Good: Empire, Religion and Philosophy in Eighteenth Century Britain* (Cambridge University Press, 1994).

Moers, Ellen. *Literary Women* (London: Women Press, 1978).

Mullan, John. *Sentiment and Sociability: the Language of Feeling in the Eighteenth Century* (Oxford: Clarendon Press, 1988).

Myers, Sylvia Harcstack. *The Bluestocking Circle* (Oxford: Clarendon Press, 1990).

Nygren, Anders. *Agape and Eros* (London: SPCK, 1982).

O'Malley, I. B. *Women in Subjection: a Study of the Lives of Englishwomen before 1832* (London: Duckworth, 1933).

Offen, Karen. *European Feminisms, 1700–1950* (Stanford University Press, 2000).

Okin, S. M. *Women in Western Political Thought* (Princeton University Press, 1979).

Oldfield, Sybil. *Collective Biography of Women in Britain, 1550–1900* (London: Mansell Publishing, 1999).

Olwen, Hufton. *The Prospect Before Her: a History of Women in Western Europe* (London: HarperCollins, 1995).

Outram, Dorinda. *The Body and the French Revolution* (London: Yale University Press, 1989).

Pask, K. *The Emergence of the English Author* (Cambridge University Press, 1996).

Pateman, Carole. *The Disorder of Women* (University of Chicago, 1980).

Patrides, C. A. (ed.). *The Cambridge Platonists* (London: Edward Arnold, 1969).

Paul, Charles Kegan. *Letters to Imlay, with a Prefatory Memoir by CK Paul* (London, 1879).

William Godwin: His Friends and Contemporaries (London, 1876).

Paulson, Ronald. *Representations of Revolution, 1789–1820* (London: Yale University Press, 1983).

Perry, Ruth. *The Celebrated Mary Astell* (London: University of Chicago Press, 1986).

Philp, Mark. *Godwin's Political Justice* (London: Duckworth, 1986).

Pocock, J. G. A. *Virtue, Commerce and History* (Cambridge University Press, 1985).

Poovey, Mary. *The Proper Lady and the Woman Writer: Ideology as Style in the Works of Mary Wollstonecraft, Mary Shelley, and Jane Austen* (University of Chicago Press, 1984).

Porter, Roy. *Enlightenment: Britain and the Creation of the Modern World* (London: Allen Lane, Penguin Press, 2000).

Rendall, Jane. *The Origins of Modern Feminism* (Basingstoke: Macmillans, 1985).

Reynolds, Myra, *The Learned Lady in England, 1650–1760* (New York: Houghton Mifflin, 1920).

Riley, Denise. '*Am I That Name?' Feminism and the Category of 'Women' in History* (Basingstoke: Macmillan, 1988).

Robbins, Caroline. *The Eighteenth Century Commonwealthman* (Cambridge, Mass: Harvard University Press, 1959).

Rodgers, Betsy. *Georgian Chronicle: Mrs Barbauld and Her Family* (London: Methuen and Co., 1958).

Rose, Jacqueline. *Sexuality in the Field of Vision* (London: Verso Books, 1986).

Sapiro, Virginia. *A Vindication of Political Virtue* (University of Chicago, 1992).

Saunders, J. W. *The Profession of English Letters* (London: Routledge and Kegan Paul, 1964).

Schwartz, Joel. *The Sexual Politics of Jean-Jacques Rousseau* (University of Chicago, 1984).

Scott, Joan. *Only Paradoxes to Offer: French Feminists and the Rights of Man* (Cambridge, Mass: Harvard University Press, 1996).

Sekora, John. *Luxury: the Concept in Western Thought, Eden to Smollett* (Baltimore: Johns Hopkins University Press, 1977).

Shawcross, John T. *John Milton and Influence* (Pittsburgh: Duquesne University Press, 1991).

Sheriff, John K. *The Good-Natured Man: the Evolution of a Moral Ideal, 1660–1880* (Tuuscaloosa: University of Alabama Press, 1982).

Shklar, Judith. *Men and Citizens: a Study of Rousseau's Social Theory*, 1969 (Cambridge University Press, 1985).

Simpson, David. *Romanticism, Nationalism and the Revolt Against Theory* (University of Chicago Press, 1993).

Smith, Hilda. *Reason's Disciples: Seventeenth Century English Feminists* (London: University of Illinois Press, 1982).

Snowdon, Ethel. *The Feminist Movement* (London: Nation's Library, 1911).

Spadafora, David. *The Idea of Progress in 18th Century Britain* (London: Yale University Press, 1990).

St Clair, William. *The Godwins and the Shelleys: the Biography of a Family* (London: Faber and Faber, 1989).

Stansfield, Dorothy A. *Thomas Beddoes, MD, 1760–1808* (Dordrecht: D. Reidel Publishing Co., 1984).

Starobinski, Jean. *Jean-Jacques Rousseau: Transparency and Obstruction*, 1971 (University of Chicago, 1988).

Sunstein, Emily. *A Different Face: the Life of Mary Wollstonecraft* (New York: Harper and Row, 1974).

Tate Gallery Publications, *Henry Fuseli* (London: Tate Gallery, 1975).

Taylor, Barbara. *Eve and the New Jerusalem: Socialism and Feminism in the 19th Century* (London: Virago, 1983).

Taylor, Charles. *Sources of the Self: the Making of Modern Identity* (Cambridge, Mass: Harvard University Press, 1989).

Thomas, D. O. *The Honest Mind: the Thought and Work of Richard Price* (Oxford University Press, 1977).

Thompson, E. P. *The Making of the English Working Class* (London: Victor Gollancz, 1963).

Witness Against the Beast: William Blake and the Moral Law (Cambridge University Press, 1993).

Todd, Janet (ed.). *Dictionary of British Women Writers* 1989 (London: Routledge, 1991).

Mary Wollstonecraft, a Revolutionary Life (London: Weidenfeld and Nicholson, 2000).

Mary Wollstonecraft: an Annotated Bibliography (New York: Garland, 1976).

The Sign of Angellica: Women, Writing and Fiction, 1660–1800 (London: Virago, 1989).

Tomalin, Claire. *The Life and Death of Mary Wollstonecraft*, 1974 (London: Penguin, 1992).

Tompkins, J. M. S. *The Popular Novel in England, 1770–1800* (Lincoln: University of Nebraska Press, 1961).

Trouille, M. S. *Sexual Politics in the Enlightenment* (Albany: State University of New York Press, 1997).

Turner, Cheryl. *Living By the Pen: Women Writers in the Eighteenth Century* (London: Routledge, 1992).

Turner, James G. *One Flesh: Paradisical Marriage and Sexual Relations in the Age of Milton* (Oxford: Clarendon Press, 1987).

Tuveson, E. L. *The Imagination as a Means of Grace* (Berkeley: University of California Press, 1960).

Ty, Eleanor. *Unsex'd Revolutionaries: Five Women Novelists of the 1790s* (University of Toronto Press, 1993).

Tyson, Gerald P. *Joseph Johnson: a Liberal Publisher* (Iowa City: University of Iowa Press, 1979).

Vickery, Amanda. *The Gentleman's Daughter: Women's Lives in Georgian England* (London: Yale University Press, 1998).

Wahrman, Dror. *Imagining the Middle Class: the Political Representation of Class in Britain, c. 1780–1840* (Cambridge University Press, 1995).

Wardle, Ralph (ed.). *Collected Letters of Mary Wollstonecraft* (London: Cornell University Press, 1979).

Mary Wollstonecraft: a Critical Biography (Lincoln: University of Nebraska Press, 1951).

Watson, Nicola. *Revolution and the Form of the English Novel, 1790–1825* (Oxford: Clarendon Press, 1994).

Watt, Ian. *The Rise of the Novel*, 1957 (Harmondsworth: Penguin, 1977).

Wedd, A. F. (ed.). *The Fate of the Fenwicks* (London: Methuen and Co., 1927).

The Love Letters of Mary Hays (London: Methuen, 1925).

Whale, John. *Imagination Under Pressure, 1789–1832* (Cambridge University Press, 2000).

Whitney, Lois. *Primitivism and the Idea of Progress in English Popular Literature of the Eighteenth Century* (Baltimore: Johns Hopkins University Press, 1934).

Willey, Basil. *The Eighteenth-Century Background* (London: Chatto and Windus, 1946).

Williams, G. A. *Artisans and Sans Culottes* (London: Arnold, 1968).

Williams, Raymond. *Problems in Materialism and Culture* (London: Verso, 1980).

Wilson, Kathleen. *The Sense of the People: Politics, Culture and Imperialism in England, 1715–1785*, 1995 (Cambridge University Press, 1998).

Winch, Donald. *Riches and Poverty: an Intellectual History of Political Economy in Britain, 1750–1834* (Cambridge University Press, 1996).

Woolf, Virginia. *Women and Writing*, Michèle Barrett (ed.) (London: Women's Press, 1979).

Yaeger, Patricia. *Honey-Mad Women: Emancipatory Strategies in Women's Writing* (New York: Columbia University Press, 1988).

ARTICLES

Bannerji, Himani. 'Mary Wollstonecraft, Feminism and Humanism: a Spectrum of Reading', in Eileen Yeo (ed.) *Mary Wollstonecraft and 200 Years of Feminisms* (London: Rivers Oram, 1997).

Barker-Benfield, G. J. 'Mary Wollstonecraft: Eighteenth Century Commonwealth-woman', *Journal of the History of Ideas*, vol. 50, 1989.

'Mary Wollstonecraft's Depression and Diagnosis', *Psychohistory Review*, 13, 1985.

Benedict, Ruth. 'Mary Wollstonecraft', in Margaret Mead (ed.) *An Anthropologist at Work: Writings of Ruth Benedict* (Boston: Houghton Mifflin, 1959).

Binhammer, Katherine. 'The Sex Panic of the 1790s', *Journal of the History of Sexuality*, 6:3, 1996, pp. 409–34.

Bloch, Ruth. 'The Gendered Meanings of Virtue in Revolutionary America', *Signs: Journal of Women in Culture and Society*, 13:1, 1987.

Brody, Miriam. 'Mary Wollstonecraft, Sexuality and Women's Rights' in Dale Spender (ed.) *Feminist Theorists* (London: Women's Press, 1983).

Brooks, Marilyn L. 'Mary Hays: Finding a "Voice" in Dissent', *Enlightenment and Dissent*, 14, 1995, pp. 3–24.

Burdett, Carolyn. 'A Difficult Vindication: Olive Schreiner's Wollstonecraft intro-duction', *History Workshop Journal*, 37 (spring 1994).

Butler, Marilyn. *Introduction to Mary Wollstonecraft, Works*, vol. 1.

Caine, Barbara. 'Victorian Feminism and the Ghost of Mary Wollstonecraft', *Women's Writing*, 4:2, 1997.

Carpenter, Mary W. 'Sibylline Apocalyptics: Mary Wollstonecraft's *Vindication of the Rights of Woman* and Job's Mother's Womb', *Literature and History*, 12:2, 1986.

Carter, Philip. 'An "Effeminate" or "Efficient" Nation? Masculinity and Eighteenth Century Social Commentary', *Textual Practice*, 11:3 (1997).

Chalus, Elaine. ' "That Epidemical Madness": Women and Electoral Politics in the Late Eighteenth Century' in H. Barker and E. Chalus (eds.), *Gender in Eighteenth-Century England* (London: Addison Wesley Longman, 1997).

Charvet, John. 'The Idea of Love in *La Nouvelle Heloïse*', in R. A. Leigh (ed.), *Rousseau after Two Hundred Years* (Cambridge University Press, 1982).

Claeys, Gregory. 'The Origins of the Rights of Labor: Republicanism, Commerce and the Construction of Modern Social Theory in Britain, 1796–1805', *Journal of Modern History*, 66, 1994.

'Utopianism, Property and the French Revolution Debate' in K. Kumar and S. Bann, *Utopias and the Millennium* (London: Reaktion Books, 1993).

Clarke, Norma. 'The Cursed Barbauld Crew: Women Writers and Writing for Children in the late 18th Century', in M. Hilton, M. Styles and V. Watson (eds.), *Opening the Nursery Door: Reading, Writing and Childhood, 1600–1900* (London: Routledge, 1997).

Curran, Stuart. 'Women Readers, Women Writers', in Stuart Curran (ed.) *The Cambridge Companion to British Romanticism* (Cambridge University Press, 1993).

Donnelly, Lucy Martin. 'The Celebrated Mrs Macaulay', *William and Mary Quarterly*, 4 (1949).

Eliot, George. 'Margaret Fuller and Mary Wollstonecraft', in T. Pinney (ed.), *Essays of George Eliot* (London: Routledge and Kegan Paul, 1963).

Fawcett, Millicent Garrett. *Introduction to A Vindication of the Rights of Woman* (London, 1892).

Ferguson, Frances. 'Wollstonecraft Our Contemporary', in Linda Kauffman, ed., *Gender and Theory* (Oxford: Basil Blackwell, 1989).

Ferguson, Moira. 'Mary Wollstonecraft and the Problematic of Slavery', in Eileen Yeo (ed.) *Mary Wollstonecraft and 200 Years of Feminisms* (London: Rivers Oram, 1997).

Fitzpatrick, Martin. 'Charlotte Smith', in Janet Todd (ed.) *Dictionary of British Women Writers*, 1989 (London: Routledge, 1991).

Gubar, Susan. 'Feminist Misogyny: Mary Wollstonecraft and the Paradox of "It Takes One to Know One" ', *Feminist Studies*, 20:3 (1994).

Guralnick, Elissa S. 'Radical Politics in Mary Wollstonecraft's *A Vindication of the Rights of Women*', *Studies in Burke and His Time*, 18, 1977.

'Rhetorical Strategy in Mary Wollstonecraft's *A Vindication of the Rights of Woman*', *Humanities Association Review*, 30, 1979.

Haakonssen, Knud. 'From Natural Law to the Rights of Man: a European Perspective on American Debates', in M. J. Lacey and K. Haakonssen, *A Culture of Rights: the Bill of Rights in Philosophy, Politics and Law* (Cambridge University Press, 1991).

Hampshire-Monk, Ian. 'Civic Humanism and Parliamentary Reform: the Case of the Society of the Friends of the People', *Journal of British Studies*, 18:2 (1979).

Hill, Bridget. 'The Links between Mary Wollstonecraft and Catharine Macaulay: new evidence', *Women's History Review*, 4:2, 1995.

Hirsch, Pam. 'Mary Wollstonecraft, a Problematic Legacy', in C. Campbell Orr, *Wollstonecraft's Daughters: Womanhood in England and France, 1780–1920* (Manchester University Press, 1996).

Janes, Regina M. 'On the Reception of Mary Wollstonecraft's *A Vindication of the Rights of Woman*', *Journal of the History of Ideas*, 39, 1975.

Jones, Vivien. ' "The Tyranny of the Passions": Feminism and Heterosexuality in the Fiction of Wollstonecraft and Hays', in S. Ledger (ed.), *Political Gender: Texts and Contexts* (London: Harvester Wheatsheaf, 1994).

'Placing Jemima: Women Writers of the 1790s and the Eighteenth-Century Prostitution Narrative', *Women's Writing*, 4:2, 1997.

'Scandalous Femininity: Prostitution and 18th Century Narrative', in D. Castiglione and L. Sharpe (eds.), *Shifting the Boundaries: Transformation of the Languages of Public and Private in the 18th Century* (Exeter University Press, 1995).

'The Death of Mary Wollstonecraft', *British Journal for Eighteenth Century Studies*, 20:2 (1997).

Jump, Harriet. ' "No Equal Mind": Mary Wollstonecraft and the Young Romantics', *The Charles Lamb Bulletin*, new series 79, July 1992.

Kay, Carol. 'Canon, Ideology and Gender: Mary Wollstonecraft's Critique of Adam Smith', *New Political Science*, 15 (1986).

Kelly, Gary. 'Mary Wollstonecraft as *Vir Bonus*', *English Studies in Canada*, 5, 1979.

Macdonald, D. L. 'Master, Slave and Mistress in Wollstonecraft's *Vindication*', *Enlightenment and Dissent*, 11 (1992).

Maison, Margaret. 'Mary Robinson' in Janet Todd (ed.) *Dictionary of British Women Writers*, 1989 (London: Routledge, 1991).

Myers, Mitzi. 'Godwin's Memoirs of Wollstonecraft: the Shaping of Self and Subject', *Studies in Romanticism*, 20, 1981.

'Impeccable Governesses, Rational Dames, and Moral Mothers: Mary Wollstonecraft and the Female Tradition in Georgian Children's Books', *Children's Literature*, 14 (1986).

'Pedagogy as Self-Expression in Mary Wollstonecraft: Exorcising the Past, Finding a Voice', in Sheri Benstock (ed.), *The Private Self* (Chapel Hill: North Carolina University Press, 1988).

'Politics from the Outside: Mary Wollstonecraft's first *Vindication*', *Studies in Eighteenth-Century Culture*, 6, 1977.

'Reform or Ruin: "A Revolution in Female Manners".' *Studies in Eighteenth-Century Culture*, 11, 1982.

'Sensibility and the "Walk of Reason": Mary Wollstonecraft's Literary Reviews as Cultural Critique', in S. M. Conger (ed.), *Sensibility in Transformation* (Rutherford, NJ: Fairleigh Dickenson University Press, 1990).

Nicholson, Mervyn. 'The Eleventh Commandment: Sex and Spirit in Wollstonecraft and Malthus', *Journal of the History of Ideas*, 51:3, 1990.

Pendleton, Gayle T. 'Towards a Bibliography of the *Reflections* and *Rights of Man* Controversy', *Bulletin of Research in the Humanities*, 85:1 (1982).

Phillips, Anne. 'Feminism and Republicanism: Is This a Plausible Alliance?', *The Journal of Political Philosophy*, 8:2 (2000).

Philp, Mark. 'English Republicanism in the 1790s', *Journal of Political Philosophy*, 6:1 (1998).

'The Fragmented Ideology of Reform', in M. Philp (ed.), *The French Revolution and Popular Politics* (Cambridge University Press, 1991).

Pocock, J. G. A. 'Cambridge Paradigms and Scotch Philosophers: a study of the relations between the civic humanist and the civil jurisprudential interpretation of eighteenth-century social thought' in I. Hont and M. Ignatieff (eds.), *Wealth and Virtue: the Shaping of Political Economy in the Scottish Enlightenment* (Cambridge University Press, 1983).

'Catharine Macaulay: Patriot Historian', in Hilda Smith (ed.), *Women Writers and the Early Modern British Political Tradition* (Cambridge University Press, 1998).

Porter, Roy. 'The Enlightenment in England', in R. Porter and M. Teich (eds.), *The Enlightenment in National Context* (Cambridge University Press, 1981).

Price, John V. 'The Reading of Philosophical Literature', in I. Rivers (ed.), *Books and Their Readers in 18th Century England* (Leicester University Press, 1982).

Radcliffe, Evan. 'Revolutionary Writing, Moral Philosophy, and Universal Benevolence in the 18th Century', *Journal of the History of Ideas*, 54:2, 1993.

Rajan, Tilottama. 'Wollstonecraft and Godwin: Reading the Secrets of the Political Novel', *Studies in Romanticism* 27, 1988.

Rang, Brita. 'A "Learned Wave": Women of Letters and Science from the Renaissance to the Enlightenment', in T. Akkerman and S. Stuurman (eds.), *Perspectives on Feminist Political Thought in European History From the Middle Ages to the Present* (London: Routledge, 1998).

Reiss, Timothy J. 'Revolution in Bounds: Wollstonecraft, Women and Reason', in L. Kauffman (ed.), *Gender and Theory* (Oxford: Basil Blackwell, 1989).

Rendall, Jane. ' "The Grand Causes which Combine to carry Mankind Forward": Wollstonecraft, History and Revolution', *Women's Writing*, 4:2, 1997.

'Virtue and Commerce: Women in the Making of Adam Smith's Political Economy', in Ellen Kennedy and Susan Mendus (eds.), *Women in Western Political Philosophy* (Brighton: Wheatsheaf Books, 1987).

Richey, William. ' "A More Godlike Portion": Mary Wollstonecraft's Feminist Rereadings of the Fall', *English Language Notes*, 32:2, 1994.

Robinson, Daniel. 'Theodicy versus Feminist Strategy in Mary Wollstonecraft's Fiction', *Eighteenth Century Fiction*, 9:2 (1997).

Shanley, Mary Lyndon. 'Mary Wollstonecraft on sensibility, women's rights and patriarchal power', in Hilda Smith (ed.), *Women Writers and the Early Modern British Political Tradition* (Cambridge University Press, 1998).

Snitow, Ann. 'A Gender Diary', in M. Hirsch and E. Fox Keller (eds.), *Conflicts in Feminism* (London: Routledge, 1990).

Spacks, Patricia Meyer. 'Ev'ry Woman is at Heart a Rake', *Eighteenth Century Studies*, 8:1, 1974.

Spence, Gordon. 'Mary Wollstonecraft's Theodicy and Theory of Progress', *Enlightenment and Dissent*, 14, 1995.

Spencer, Jane. 'Mary Hays', in Janet Todd (ed.) *Dictionary of British Women Writers*, 1989 (London: Routledge, 1991).

Stewart, Sally. 'Mary Wollstonecraft's Contributions to the *Analytical Review*', *Essays in Literature*, 11:2, 1984.

Sudan, Rajani. 'Mothering and National Identity in the Works of Mary Wollstonecraft', in A. Richardson and S. Hofkosh (eds.), *Romanticism, Race and Imperial Culture* (Bloomington: Indiana University Press, 1996).

Taylor, Anya. 'Coleridge, Wollstonecraft and the Rights of Woman', T. Fulford and M. D. Paley (eds.), *Coleridge's Visionary Languages* (Cambridge: DS Brewer, 1993).

Taylor, Barbara. 'The Religious Foundations of Wollstonecraft's Feminism', in Claudia Johnson, ed., *Cambridge Companion to Mary Wollstonecraft* (Cambridge University Press, 2002).

'An Impossible Heroine? Mary Wollstonecraft and Female Heroism', *Soundings*, 3, 1996.

'Feminism and Misogyny: the Case of Mary Wollstonecraft', in C. Jones and D. Wahrman, *The Age of Cultural Revolutions: Britain and France, 1750–1830* (University of California Press, 2002).

'For the Love of God: Religion and the Erotic Imagination in Wollstonecraft's Feminism' in E. Yeo (ed.) *Mary Wollstonecraft and 200 Years of Feminisms* (London, Rivers Oram, 1997).

Introduction to Mary Wollstonecraft, A Vindication of the Rights of Woman (London, Everyman, 1992).

'Mary Wollstonecraft and the Wild Wish of Early Feminism', *History Workshop Journal*, no. 33, 1992.

Thompson, E. P. 'Solitary Walker' (review of Claire Tomalin, *The Life and Death of Mary Wollstonecraft* [London: Weidenfeld and Nicholson, 1974]), *New Society*, 19 September 1974.

Todd, Janet and Roberts, Marie Mulvey (eds.), *Women's Writing: Mary Wollstonecraft: a bicentennial* Special Number, 4:2, 1997.

Todd, Janet. 'Eliza Fenwick' in Janet Todd (ed.) *Dictionary of British Women Writers*, 1989 (London: Routledge, 1991).

Todd, Janet. 'Elizabeth Inchbald', Janet Todd (ed.) *Dictionary of British Women Writers*, 1989 (London: Routledge, 1991).

Tomalin, Claire. 'Publisher in Prison: Joseph Johnson and the Book Trade', *Times Literary Supplement*, 2 December 1994.

Tomaselli, Sylvana. 'Reflections on the History of the Science of Woman', in M. Benjamin (ed.), *A Question of Identity: Women, Science and Literature* (Rutgers University Press, 1993).

'The Death and Rebirth of Character in the Eighteenth Century', in Roy Porter (ed.), *Rewriting the Self* (London: Routledge, 1997).

'The Enlightenment Debate on Women', *History Workshop Journal*, 20 (1985).

Trott, Nicola. 'Sexing the Critic: Mary Wollstonecraft at the turn of the century', in R. Cronin (ed.), *1798: the Year of Lyrical Ballads* (London: Macmillan, 1998).

Vega, Judith A. 'Feminist Republicanism and the Political Perception of Gender, in Q. Skinner (ed.), *Republicanism: a Shared European Heritage*, vol. 3 (Cambridge University Press, 2000).

Wahrman, Dror. 'Percy's Prologue: from Gender Play to Gender Panic in 18th Century England', *Past and Present*, 159, May 1998, pp. 113–160.

Walters, Margaret. 'The Rights and Wrongs of Women', in J. Mitchell and A. Oakley (eds.), *The Rights and Wrongs of Women* (Harmondsworth: Penguin, 1976).

Wexler, Alice. 'Emma Goldman on Mary Wollstonecraft', *Feminist Studies*, no. 1 (1981).

Williamson, M. L. 'Who's Afraid of Mrs Barbauld? The Bluestockings and Feminism', *International Journal of Women's Studies*, 3:1 (1980).

Zagarri, Rosemary. 'Morals, Manners and the Republican Mother', *American Quarterly*, 44 (1992).

Index

Note: the abbreviations WG and MW are used to stand for William Godwin and Mary Wollstonecraft.
Page numbers *in italics* refer to illustrations.

Sweden 127
  see also Scandinavia; Wollstonecraft, Mary /
    WORKS / *A Short Residence in Sweden*
Swift, Jonathan 14

Talleyrand 40, 209–210, 213, 225, 236
Tarleton 180
Taylor, Thomas 277
Test Acts 103–104, 184–185
theatres 82–83, 84
Thelwall, John 176
  Rights of Nature 150
theopathy 110
Thompson, E P 4, 10–11
Thompson, William
  Appeal of One-Half the Human Race 248
Thrale, Hester 294
Times Literary Supplement
  1992 256
  1997 282
Todd, Janet 9, 256
Tomalin, Claire
  The Life and Death of Mary Wollstonecraft 10,
    256
Tooke, John Horne 146
Tristan, Flora 248
Trott, Nicola 305
Turner, James
  One Flesh 109, 276
Tuveson, Ernest 59–60

Unitarians *see* Rational Dissenters
universal benevolence 141–142, 145, 168, 282
utopianism and perfectibility 1–3, 4, 12, 19,
    77, 94, 151, 152, 155, 168–169, 170–171,
    173, 249
  sexual 198, 201

van Schurman, Anna Maria 30
virtue 12, 101, 107–108, 204, 205, 222–223, 226,
    227
'Vision of Liberty, The' 305
Voltaire 192

Wakefield, Gilbert 186, 187
Walpole, Horace 184
Walters, Margaret 31
Walworth 277
Washington, George 48, 212–213
wealth and the rich 16, 64, 160–161, 166, 171–172
  see also luxury
Westminster Forum 215
Wilkes, John 48, 150
Willey, Basil 104

Williams, Helen Maria 148, 176, 180–181, 182,
    195, 197, 199
  Letters Written From France 181
Williams, Raymond 167
wit 65
Wollstonecraft, Charles (brother of MW) 43
Wollstonecraft, Edward (father of MW) 5–6, 18,
    180
Wollstonecraft, Edward (Ned; brother of MW) 6
Wollstonecraft, Eliza (sister of MW) 303
  MW's letters to 6
Wollstonecraft, Elizabeth (mother of MW) 5–6,
    18, 128, 258, 282
  death 280
Wollstonecraft, Everina 42
  MW's letters to 1, 31, 40, 41, 73, 102, 129, 148,
    225, 262
Wollstonecraft, Mary 26
  birth 5
  family 5–6, 18, 43, 151
  childhood 5–6, 18, 43, 99, 124, 258
  education 43–44, 62, 263
  appearance 32
  conversational powers 194, 293
  personality 4–5, 17, 18, 148, 253
  self-image 11, 17, 31, 33, 130, 148, 253
  relationships 7–8, 17
  love affairs *see* Fuseli, Henry; Imlay, Gilbert
  early employment 6, 17, 31
  runs girls' school 6
  as governess 1, 17, 40
  first professional writing 35–40
  suicide attempts 8, 21, 123, 124, 128
  in France 148, 195–196, 197, 199, 283–284
  in Scandinavia 8, 123–124, 126, 127, 139, 162,
    169–170, 171, 175, 194, 300–301
  meets WG 8, 95–96, 187, 192
  MW/WG circle 148, 151, 177, 192–193, 200,
    225
  marriage to WG 8, 187, 196, 201–202
  death 8, 127–128
  funeral 8, 280
  biographies 9, 10–11, 31, 250, 256
  portrait 19, 251
  reputation 9–11, 247–252, 307
  WORKS 9
  as writer 31–33, 35–40, 52–53, 263
  earnings 42–43
  critical studies of 9, 10, 11, 252, 259
  'Cave of Fancy, The' 63–64, 111–112, 113
  Female Reader, A 7, 32, 33, 186
  pseudonym 33, 261
  *Fragment of Letters on the Management of
    Infants* 34

CAMBRIDGE STUDIES IN ROMANTICISM

GENERAL EDITORS
MARILYN BUTLER, *University of Oxford*
JAMES CHANDLER, *University of Chicago*